MAJOR BIBLE PROPHECIES

37 CRUCIAL PROPHECIES THAT AFFECT YOU TODAY

JOHN F. WALVOORD

ZondervanPublishingHouse
Grand Rapids, Michigan

A Division of HarperCollins*Publishers*

Major Bible Prophecies: 37 Crucial Prophecies that Affect You Today
Copyright © 1991 by John F. Walvoord

Requests for information should be addressed to:
Zondervan Publishing House
Grand Rapids, Michigan 49530

Library of Congress Cataloging-in-Publication Data

Walvoord, John F.
    Major Bible prophecies 37 crucial prophecies that affect you today /
John F. Walvoord.
        p.   cm.
    Includes indexes.
    ISBN 0-310-54128-X
    1. Bible–Prophecies.   2. Eschatology.   I. Title.
    BS647.2.W28   1991
    220.1'5–dc20   91-14505
                                                              CIP

Edited by John Vriend, L.G. Goss, and Laura Weller

Printed in the United States of America

98 99 00 01 02/DH/11 10 9 8 7 6 5

This edition is printed on acid-free paper and meets the American National
Standards Institute Z39.48 standard.

CONTENTS

Preface

The twentieth century has been an unprecedented period of change. At no time in history have more changes occurred in science and in the political structure of the world. More changes occur in science in a single year than formerly occurred in a century.

The events of the twentieth century have done much to change human life. Two world wars have torn our world. The advent of atomic weapons and missile warfare has shrunk its size and put it in jeopardy of another world war.

Events of the twentieth century have alerted Bible students to the tremendous potential for fulfilled prophecy. With Israel restored as a nation in 1948, the panorama of end-time prophecy came into a focus in which Israel will be a prominent player.

The introduction of the concept of a world government, made real by the United Nations, also paints a scenario that is in harmony with prophecy concerning a future world government.

Recent events in Europe have highlighted rapid political change and introduced the possibility of democracy becoming a major factor in the political scene. Though this is not a special subject of prophecy, it is entirely possible that people will

7

discover that democracy does not have the answer to our world's problems and may succumb to dictatorship, exactly as the Bible predicts for the end of the age.

In this whole context, the rapture of the church looms as an imminent event that will occur before many of these end-time events are fulfilled. Accordingly, the study of prophecy in its present fulfillment not only becomes important to theology as a whole in clarifying eschatology and Bible interpretation in its entirety; it also has a very practical relation to Christian hope and expectation. There has never been more reason than there is now for the church to expect the imminent return of Christ.

In light of these tremendous events and the clarification of so many details of eschatology in the twentieth century, a study of major Bible prophecies as they relate to human destiny holds great significance. I hope that this book will alert students of Scripture to the importance of prophetic study in the days in which we are living and to the hope of the Lord's imminent return.

I deeply appreciate the excellent stenographic services of Karen Grassmick, who has done much to present the material in this book in effective form.

The study of prophecy in this volume has been based on the New International Version unless otherwise specified.

John F. Walvoord

1

The Prophetic Chart of Human Destiny

The Questioning Mind

Children are full of questions. They want to know about everything that forms a part of their world. They ask questions about how a thing works or why it does what it does. Such activity is the secret of their rapidly expanding knowledge. As they grow older, they begin to ask more sophisticated questions about the meaning of life. Who is God? Why is a certain action wrong? Why do people die? What happens after a person dies? Humans have questioning minds.

Humans, created in the image and likeness of God, even though crippled by sin, have a natural tendency to seek an explanation of the world that lies about them. The early revelation given to Adam and Eve seems soon to have been lost by subsequent generations. Generally speaking, humankind seems to have assumed that there must be a God, One who is greater than humanity. But what kind of God is he? The concept of a God of love and grace who is infinitely good seems to have

9

escaped early humans, and worship often descended to a fearful search of means to appease gods who were superior to humans but just as wicked.

What is the meaning of life? Why do humans exist? What is really important in life? Is there a system of values? What is right and wrong? As history began to unfold, questions arose concerning life's meaning and the destiny of humanity. What does the future hold? Again, there seems to have been an almost uniform recognition of the afterlife. But what did this life consist of? Often the pursuit of answers to questions was hindered by the more immediate challenge of making a living, attaining success and power, and achieving human goals. Too often human sin intervened and rendered useless the search for truth.

The Search for Answers

Humankind continues to have questions that require answers. Since the advent of the potential for nuclear war, people have been jolted into considering ultimate questions of the future. What kind of a world are we living in? Does life have any meaning? What is really worthwhile in life?

For many, the blight of materialism has eliminated the search for ultimate answers, but the perennial questions still arise. What kind of God do we have? What is our future? What happens when we die? Is it possible that we may be nearing the end of life as we know it?

Prior to the writing of Scripture God revealed himself to certain individuals. Adam and Eve had an introductory revelation of who God is and of his purposes for humankind. Noah, through his experience in the Flood, had a graphic illustration of the sovereignty of God as he works in human affairs. God is able to create, and God is able to destroy. God is able to raise up, and God is able to put down. God is worthy of worship and obedience.

In Abraham's time God gave far-reaching prophecies concerning Abraham's personal role in the future and said that he would be the father of many nations. Through Abraham would come One who would bring blessing to the entire world. Also revealed to Abraham was the particular plan of God for the people of Israel who descended from him; much of the book of Genesis relates to Abraham and his descendants Isaac and Jacob. As these important revelations of God were later incorporated in Scripture, they constitute the background of the prophetic chart of human destiny.

The Old Testament Prophetic Chart of Human Destiny

The revelation of God to Adam and Eve. The Old Testament reveals a prophetic chart of the future of the human race. This began with the revelation that God gave Adam and Eve. In the Garden of Eden Adam and Eve were able to confer with God directly. They understood that he had created the world, that he was sovereign, and that they were responsible to him. They were given answers to some of life's most persistent questions.

When sin entered the human race through Adam and Eve, fellowship with God was partially broken. They were now sinners relating to a holy God. To Adam and Eve, nevertheless, God revealed his great purpose of salvation through One who would come from a woman (Gen. 3:15). This anticipated the virgin birth of Christ. Also apparently revealed to Adam and Eve was the principle of blood sacrifice as a means of atoning for sin. Adam and Eve knew God as a gracious and loving God but also as a God of righteousness and judgment. Unfortunately, the revelation given to Adam and Eve was not passed on to many who descended from them.

The revelation of God to Noah. By the time Noah and his family came on the scene, the human race had largely departed from God to the point where God himself said that Noah and his family were the only ones worthy of deliverance from judgment. When the Flood came as a tremendous demonstration of the sovereign power of God, Noah saw the world of his day wiped out and the task of beginning anew committed to him and his three sons. Noah had a clear revelation that God works in the world and is involved in history through his providence.

The revelation of God to Abraham. God made an important announcement about the future to Abraham. To him was made known the special purpose of God in calling out a people to be the express channel of his revelation. To Abraham, Isaac, and Jacob were committed the promises of the Abrahamic covenant, including the promise of a great nation and the promise that through them would come One who would be a blessing to the whole world. This obviously—from the Christian perspective— referred to Jesus Christ. From Genesis to Revelation the special purposes of God, such as his plan for the people of Israel and his plan for the Gentile world, follow their dual track. The ultimate fulfillment will not come until the end of the age.

The revelation of God to Moses. Moses, the first writer of Scripture, wrote the first five books of the Old Testament. Moses was sovereignly chosen by God to be the lawgiver. With the help of his thorough education in the palace and schools of Egypt and his discipline in forty years of shepherding in the wilderness, Moses was prepared by God to set forth the great truths of the first five books of the Old Testament. To him was given the commission of gathering the history of the race from Adam to his time. In Genesis, Exodus, Leviticus, Numbers, and Deuteronomy, Moses passed on to the children of Israel the revelation of God concerning the Law for Israel in its many details, its promises of mercy, and its threats of judgment. The entire Bible to some extent rests on the principles God gave Moses, even though their primary application was to the people of Israel.

The revelation of God to David. To David, king of Israel, God gave a special revelation concerning the future of his kingdom. David's throne and political power were to go on forever, though interrupted for long periods of time. The ultimate fulfillment of this, as in the case of the Abrahamic promise, was the coming of Jesus Christ. The revelation given to David, however, concerned Jesus' second coming rather than his first. The promises given to David were amplified extensively throughout the Old Testament in many chapters and pronouncements on the coming kingdom of God from heaven. Understanding these prophecies has become very important in helping us comprehend Christ's teachings and the significance of his second coming as well as answering questions about the future of Israel.

The revelation of God to Daniel. When Daniel lived as a prophet in Babylon from 605 B.C. to about 530 B.C., God gave him a series of prophecies that outline the future of the Gentile world as well as the future of Israel. Daniel was given the dual revelation of God's program for Israel, culminating in Christ's second coming, and God's program for the Gentile empires of the world, likewise culminating in Christ's second coming. This was a more far-reaching description of the future than that given by other prophets. Daniel came on the scene after two great empires, Egypt and Assyria, had come and gone. Through the prophet Daniel, God revealed that there would be four additional great empires—Babylon, Medo-Persia, Greece, and Rome. The scope of the prophecies reaches all the way to Christ's second coming. They give no details of the present age between Pentecost and the rapture. Rather they tell of the seven years preceding the Second Coming and describe the finale for Gentile power in world government. These prophecies are very important in understanding God's plans for the future.

The program Daniel was given for Israel paralleled God's program for the Gentiles, but, according to Daniel's revelation, it would begin with the time of Nehemiah when Jerusalem was to be rebuilt. Israel's program was to continue throughout the Old Testament to the time of the Messiah, Jesus Christ. Then the prophecy, like the prophecy for the Gentiles, skips the present age and resumes its revelation in the last seven years leading up to the Second Coming. In God's two-track program for the Gentiles and Israel, he revealed his sovereignty; his solemn purpose; his plan to use the Gentile empires to display his power and sovereignty; and his concern for Israel, which was manifested in his faithfulness, grace, and righteousness. Added to Daniel's revelation, the major and minor prophets join their voices in tracing God's plan and purpose for the Gentiles, including his ultimate judgment upon them and his plan and purpose for Israel, including her ultimate restoration at the Second Coming. To understand the program of God for the future, one must study Daniel. Only the Bible gives this information. No other religion provides such a significant schedule of prophecy to be fulfilled as well as prophecies already fulfilled. Anyone who wants to know the future of our world must study these prophecies.

The New Testament Prophetic Chart of Human Destiny

Revelation through Jesus Christ. The New Testament adds many additional prophecies to Old Testament revelation. In the New Testament Jesus Christ is introduced as the One who fulfilled many prophecies himself and also taught much about the future. John 1:17 succinctly states, "The law was given through Moses; grace and truth came through Jesus Christ." Christian faith begins with the truth of grace provided in salvation. The first coming of Christ was preeminently a revelation of the grace of God. Though salvation was clearly taught in the Old Testament, it is questionable whether Old

Testament believers understood that the Messiah, when he came, would die on a cross and be himself the Lamb of God who takes away the sin of the world. This is a revelation which the disciples were at first unwilling to accept, for it was contrary to their concept of Christ as the glorious King.

The grace of God was manifested in many ways in Jesus Christ's life on earth. Jesus' mercy, as revealed in the many miracles he performed, was a demonstration of the grace of God. His teaching of the necessity of forgiveness was in keeping with this revelation. The supreme revelation, of course, came when Christ died on the cross for our sins and rose again. Difficult as it was for the disciples to understand at the time, it was to be the cornerstone of their message as they went out preaching the Gospel. The world was to hear that there was a Savior. God himself, who had sent his only Son to die on behalf of sinful humans, manifested his love and grace by making salvation possible for those who did not deserve it.

The coming of Christ was also a revelation of divine truth. Jesus was the greatest of the prophets, and his teaching ministry is recorded in the four Gospels. It could well be cataloged as a systematic theology. He taught that Scripture was inspired by God. He revealed the various attributes of God, including his grace, love, mercy, goodness, omniscience, omnipotence, omnipresence, and the Trinity—God the Father, God the Son, and God the Holy Spirit. Jesus had much to say about angels and their power and limitations. He frequently spoke about the sin of the human race and its desperate need of God. Especially in the Gospel of John he unfolded the doctrine of salvation by faith in Christ. Though most of his message revolved around the kingdom he would bring in his second coming, he also introduced the subject of the church, and especially in John 13–17 he outlined the major prophecies that would be fulfilled in the present age in God's dealings with Jew and Gentile in Christ. In answering the disciples' questions concerning the end of the age, Jesus outlined the major events leading up to the Second Coming in Matthew 24–25. He described his glorious second coming from heaven to earth and the judgments that would follow. He anticipated also the millennial kingdom and assured his disciples that they would sit on thrones judging the twelve tribes of Israel. The revelation given through Jesus Christ, as extensive as it is detailed, affords a view of the present and the future that no other prophet could provide.

The Acts of the Apostles. In the book of Acts the experiences of the early church are recorded in detail. Most important to observe is the coming of the Holy Spirit on the Day of Pentecost, baptizing believers into one body and in this way forming the church, God's special purpose in the special age. Jew and Gentile were to be united and the partition between them broken down. The book of Acts also reveals that in the present age the primary power of God is going to be revealed through the Holy Spirit.

The theology of the New Testament. In addition to the truth revealed in the Gospels and Acts, the Epistles unfold the wonderful truths that are the heart of our Christian faith. The basic theology of the New Testament was the revelation given through Paul in his various epistles. The expansive nature of this revelation is seen in the fact that it touches almost every area of theology. Paul had much to say about the Bible itself, the doctrine of God, including the doctrine of the Trinity, especially focusing on the Person and work of Christ. He also referred to the nature of angels and humans. He provided the basis for understanding salvation by grace. He disclosed the distinctive character of the church and finally spoke of Christ's second coming. Other books of the New Testament not written by Paul likewise added their contribution in these various fields.

The climactic disclosure of the book of Revelation. The last book of the New Testament, Revelation, reaches its climax in its portrayal of Jesus Christ in glory, his second coming, his reign on earth, and the supremacy of the new heaven and new earth.

Also imparted in the book of Revelation is Christ's last word to seven churches in Asia, local churches chosen as representatives of churches throughout the church age. To each of them Christ directed a practical word of exhortation, praise, and revelation.

Most of the book of Revelation, however, concerns the detailed prophecy of the period leading up to the second coming of Christ—more specifically, the Great Tribulation. Here is the climax of ordinary human history—God's judgment upon Gentile power and upon sin, and God's fulfillment of his purpose in bringing Israel to her point of restoration following Christ's second coming. This period of great suffering will follow the rapture of the church.

The New Testament does not dwell on the doctrine of the Millennium, though one chapter is devoted to it (Rev. 20). The Millennium is the theme of so many Old Testament prophecies that this truth did not need to be repeated. The climactic chapters, Revelation 21–22, however, draw aside the veil of eternity and reveal the new heaven, new earth, and New Jerusalem, as the final chapter of the prophetic chart of human destiny.

Though philosophers and scientists in various fields have attempted to understand and chart the human race, no book ever written has been a prophetic chart of human destiny like the Bible. It explains the nature of God and his purposes, his working among the nations of the world, his special plan for Israel, and his special plan for the church as well as the Consummation. In these God demonstrates his sovereignty and his righteous judgment as well as his marvelous grace in the salvation of those who inherit the new earth and New Jerusalem. A study of this prophetic chart brings awe and wonder to believers as they contemplate the immensity and detail of God's plan and purpose in his sovereign outworking in the human race to the present hour and on to its consummation. The examination of this chart furthers the hope of believers in the future, as well as their confidence in the God of grace who can meet humans in their present situations. Though understanding all the details of prophecy may be difficult, the most important truths stand out. Jesus came the first time to save us from our sins by dying on the cross. He will come at the rapture to take his own to heaven. In his second coming he will bring justice and deliverance to the earth. Ultimately the wonderful truth of our eternal home in the New Jerusalem brings God's work of salvation to its completion. Prophecy, the fear of the wicked, is the bright hope of the children of God.

2

The First Prophecy:
Sin and Death

"And the LORD God commanded the man, 'You are free to eat from any tree in the garden; but you must not eat from the tree of the knowledge of good and evil, for when you eat of it you will surely die'" (Gen. 2:16–17). Though it is hard to realize today, the world, when created, was without sin.

Sin and death are faced by every individual as well as by every religion. Understanding God and salvation requires an understanding of what sin is. The Christian faith stands in contrast to other religions. Pagan religions have gods, but they are as sinful as humans. Accordingly, pagans fear their gods because they are wicked and vengeful. The question of holiness is never considered. Pagans, accordingly, try to devise ways to appease their angry deities and often resort to human sacrifice.

What a contrast is found in the God of the Bible! He is holy, loving, gracious, and just. God judges sin, but he also provides a gracious escape from judgment in salvation in Christ. Though death comes as a result of sin, resurrection is promised, and the future of those who trust in Jesus Christ is glorious.

17

Accordingly, when one studies what the Bible reveals about sin and death, what is revealed should be contrasted to the beliefs of the pagan world and their deities.

The Primeval World (Gen. 1:1–2:25)

The created world without sin. As created by God, the world of Adam and Eve was free from the laws of sin and death. In every respect the environment was flawless, illustrating the perfection of God's handiwork. There was nothing in the environment to create a problem for either Adam or Eve.

As created by God, Adam and Eve had no sin nature. They were created "in the image of God" (Gen. 1:27). It was natural that they would desire food and drink and that they would have a sense of beauty and a sense of self-worth as persons created by God. But there was no inclination toward evil and no temptation within or without.

Satan, the source of evil. The only problem in the newly created world was the existence of Satan, who appeared to Eve in the form of a serpent (Gen. 3:1). The Scripture here presents no explanation of the origin of an evil created being. Later scriptural revelation would account for Satan as one originally created as a holy angel who fell from his holy estate into sin long before the events of the created world as described in Genesis. Prophecies directed at Babylon and the King of Tyre go far beyond their sins to that of Satan in the prehistoric world (Isa. 14:12–14; Ezek. 28:12–19). These passages have been so interpreted since the early church fathers. The world as created by God had no evil; the serpent possessed by Satan was the only source of evil. The resulting record of the temptation and fall into sin of Adam and Eve account for the whole philosophic and theological problem of sin and evil in a world that God had created good.

God originally planted two unusual trees in the Garden of Eden, "the tree of life" and "the tree of the knowledge of good and evil" (Gen. 2:9). No explanation is given of the special character of these two trees, but the clear implication is that partaking of the fruit of the Tree of the Knowledge of Good and Evil would permit the one partaking of it to know good and evil while the one partaking of the Tree of Life would partake of eternal life.

God had issued a sweeping warning to Adam and Eve that

partaking of the Tree of the Knowledge of Good and Evil would result in their certain death (Gen. 2:17). Significantly, nothing is said about their partaking of the Tree of Life. The implication is that if they had obeyed God in regard to the forbidden fruit, they might have eaten of the Tree of Life and lived forever. As subsequent events unfolded, however, this was not to be realized by Adam and Eve.

Satan's Method: Questioning the Word of God

The question of how sin entered the human race is explained in these early chapters of Genesis. Satan tempted Adam and Eve to sin by partaking of the Tree of the Knowledge of Good and Evil. Basically, Satan's method in all temptation is to question the Word of God.

Satan's first question. Satan asked, "Did God really say, 'You must not eat from any tree in the garden'?" (Gen. 3:1). This age-long question of Satan concerning whether God has given clear revelation is the cornerstone of his entire method. Ignoring the rich provision of God in creation for Adam and Eve, Satan selected only the fact that they were not to eat of the Tree of the Knowledge of Good and Evil.

Misquotation of the Word of God. Satan's misquoting what God had said characteristically stresses the negatives but not the positives of obedience to God. Adam and Eve were free to eat of any tree in the garden except the Tree of the Knowledge of Good and Evil (Gen. 2:16). No mention is made of the fact that God had said, "You will surely die" (v. 17). Satan's partial quotation of what God had said was a deliberate misrepresentation of the total revelation of God. All temptation begins by questioning a clear revelation of Scripture.

The Woman's Flawed Comprehension of What God Had Said

Misunderstanding the extent of God's blessings. Satan realized that Eve only partially understood what God had said, for she disparaged the wonderful freedom she and Adam had of partaking of the entire garden except for the Tree of the Knowledge of Good and Evil. In so doing, she overemphasized the prohibition and underemphasized the privileges.

Adding severity to God's command. In repeating the prohibition Eve added to the severity of the prohibition statement, "You must not touch it" (Gen. 3:3). Though it probably was best not to touch the fruit, God had not included this in his prohibition. The tendency is to make God's prohibition unreasonable and more severe than it really is.

Questioning the certainty of punishment. Eve also questioned whether the prophesied punishment was certain. In quoting the punishment, she stated that God had said, "You will die" (Gen. 3:3), but she left out the word "surely." The certainty and extent of the punishment is not comprehended. The three elements in the woman's flawed comprehension of what God had said illustrate the human process in justifying one's response to temptation. Eve had not realized the extent of her freedom, had felt that God was too severe, and had questioned the certainty of the punishment.

In contrast to the woman's failure to respond appropriately to the serpent, the New Testament records that Christ replied to the temptation of Satan by quoting the Word of God accurately and decisively (Matt. 4:4, 7, 10).

Satan's Contradiction of the Word of God

Questioning the Word of God leads to contradiction and unbelief. Though at first Satan only questioned the Word of God, his method led to ultimate contradiction. He proceeded to deny the Word of God.

Satan's denial of the Word of God. Having discovered Eve's flawed comprehension of God's commands, including her obvious questioning as to whether the results of sin would be as God declared, Satan openly denied the Word of God when he said, "You will not surely die" (Gen. 3:4). This is the lie the world today believes in contradiction of the revealed Word of God. If there is no certain punishment for sin, then there is no certain reason for not sinning.

Satan questions the character of God. Questioning God's Word leads to questioning God's character. Satan questioned the character of God by implying that God is not good and is not concerned with bestowing good upon humankind. He charged, "For God knows that when you eat of it your eyes will be opened, and you will be like God, knowing good and evil' " (Gen. 3:5). His implication was that God wanted to keep Adam and Eve from knowing good and evil lest they be like God. To be like God was, of course, Satan's desire. He did not warn Adam and Eve that they would come into the knowledge of what is good without the power to do good and would have the knowledge of evil without the power to avoid evil.

Satan questions the certainty of judgment. Satan suggested that, inasmuch as the punishment is uncertain, disobedience will be rewarded, not judged. Denial of the Word of God, impugning the character of God, and questioning the judgment of God are the three major premises for sin as embraced by the human race.

The Revealed Pattern of Temptation

First John 2:16 describes how temptation comes to us: "For everything in the world—the cravings of sinful man, the lust of his eyes and the boasting of what he has and does—comes not from the Father but from the world." As illustrated in the temptation of Eve, all temptation comes through one or more of the three major avenues of temptation.

The flesh. "The cravings of sinful man" (1 John 2:16) are the natural desires of the flesh, or the sin nature—"the fruit of the tree was good for food" (Gen. 3:6). It is only natural that humans as created would have an appetite for food, as this would be essential to their health and well-being. But like all other human inclinations, it must be controlled by the Word of God. In this case the natural human appetite in creation was to be controlled; humans were not allowed to eat of the Tree of the Knowledge of Good and Evil. In their fallen state humans have a sin nature often referred to in Scripture as "the flesh," and though not all natural human cravings are evil, those that are evil lead humans to sin. Temptation not only comes to them along these three major lines, but often one aspect of this temptation becomes prominent in the life of individuals. The natural cravings of humans are illustrated in David's sin with Bathsheba and the subsequent murder of her husband Uriah (2 Sam. 11:1–27).

The desire for beauty. "The lust of his eyes" (1 John 2:16) is seen in the fact that the fruit was "pleasing to the eye" (Gen. 3:6). The love of beautiful things, whether beauty of form, color, or movement, was implanted in the original creation of humans. However, like other impulses of human nature even in their innocent form, it must be conformed to the control of the Word of God. Love of beautiful things can lead to materialism, wealth, physical achievement, and the lure of beautiful women. All of this is illustrated in the life of Solomon, who loved beautiful things, beautiful women, and material benefits of life. Though Solomon is portrayed in Scripture as a man of unusual wisdom in many respects (1 Kings 4:29–34), he also was given to beautiful things (10:4–29). His love for beauty went beyond things that were within the will of God. The Scriptures simply say, "King Solomon, however, loved many foreign women" (11:1), and contrary to God's command, he had acquired many horses and chariots (10:26–29). What is pleasing to the eye of sinful humans is not necessarily pleasing to God.

Pride. "Boasting of what he has and does" (1 John 2:16)— pride corresponds to "desirable for gaining wisdom" (Gen. 3:6). Here again Satan misrepresented partaking of the Tree of the Knowledge of Good and Evil. Eating the forbidden fruit would give humankind knowledge but not wisdom—that is, the ability to use knowledge in the proper way. Humans in their pride— "boasting of what he has and does" (1 John 2:16)—demonstrates their sinfulness, inadequacy, and lack of knowledge of God. Like the sin of Satan, human sin is centered in what humans are and can do. A scriptural illustration of pride is found in the history of Saul, who began in humility but ended in pride (1 Sam. 18:6–9).

Regardless of its particular point of attack, sin always results from a failure to comprehend the need for the control of God's Word and from the false conclusion that sin provides benefits which would otherwise be lost.

The Fall: Result for Satan, Adam, and Eve (Gen. 3:7–21)

Judgment was immediate. When Adam and Eve partook of the fruit from the Tree of the Knowledge of Good and Evil, they gained from it an experience of such knowledge but without the power to do good and without the power to avoid evil. The result of their sin was to bring upon them immediate spiritual death and ultimately physical death (Gen. 5:5). Because of their sinful state and disobedience, they were alienated from God and afraid of his holy presence (3:8), as is humankind today apart from the grace of God.

The result of the sin of Adam and Eve was that they became sinners by nature and in action (Gen. 3:7–21). After partaking of the Tree of the Knowledge of Good and Evil, Adam and Eve for the first time became aware of their nakedness and sewed fig leaves to make a covering for themselves. This is typical of man's vain attempts to hide his sinfulness from God.

Because Adam and Eve were now afraid of God, when they heard the sound of God walking in the garden, they attempted to hide from God (Gen. 3:8). One of the tragic results of sin is that it breaks fellowship between humans and a holy God.

God's penetrating question was, "Where are you?" In his omniscience, of course, God knew where Adam and Eve were. His question was intended to evoke a response from them. The intended answer, however, was not locale but was related to the fact that Adam and Eve were now in sin.

When Adam told God he was afraid because he was naked, God replied, "Who told you that you were naked? Have you eaten from the tree that I commanded you not to eat from?" (Gen. 3:11).

Adam gave the lame excuse, "The woman you put here with me—she gave me some fruit from the tree, and I ate it" (Gen. 3:12). Here, as always, humans attempt to blame others for their sins. Adam implied that God was to blame because he gave Eve to him, and she led him into sin.

When God asked Eve, "What is this you have done?" she replied, "The serpent deceived me, and I ate" (Gen. 3:13), excusing herself on the basis that she was tempted by Satan. As this passage makes abundantly clear, though there may be excuses and reasons for temptation, the guilt of sin remains with the one who yields to the temptation.

The Judgment

The judgment: Death. The results of eating of the forbidden fruit were summarized in the judgment of death that affected Satan, Adam, and Eve. The serpent was condemned to crawl on his belly (Gen. 3:14), and Satan's ultimate defeat is captured in the sweeping prophecy, "And I will put enmity between you and the woman, and between your offspring and hers; he will crush your head, and you will strike his heel" (v. 15). The descendants of Adam and Eve will be in continual strife and contention with the offspring of Satan, the demon world as well as wicked humans. The ultimate struggle, however, will be that the serpent will have his head crushed, a deadly blow, though he will strike the heel of the offspring of the woman. This will be treated next in the study of prophecies that anticipate the downfall of Satan.

The curse. God pronounced upon Eve the curse of increased pain in childbearing (Gen. 3:16). In addition God declared, "Your desire will be for your husband, and he will rule over you" (Gen. 3:16). The phrase, "Your desire will be for your husband" refers to the woman's desire for man leading her by domination. Adam was declared to be her master, who would "rule over" her.

To Adam, God declared that the ground would be cursed and would bring forth fruit only as a result of painful toil. The ground he tilled would ultimately receive his dead body; he would return to the dust from which he was made (Gen. 3:17–19).

The divine provision of blood redemption. In the midst of this scene of judgment and death, blood redemption was introduced. The conclusion of the incident is provided in Genesis 3:21: "The LORD God made garments of skin for Adam and his wife and clothed them." Though not explained here, for the first time the principle of blood redemption was introduced. An animal had to be killed to provide the skin to cover Adam and Eve. Typically, it graciously represented God's salvation in grace in contrast to the fig leaves of humanity's own righteousness.

Summary

Prophecy true in details. The first prophecy, with its pronouncement of judgment upon the sin of disobedience, provides important guidelines for interpreting prophecy. Prophecy is not only fulfilled in general terms but specifically corresponds to the details of each prophetic pronouncement, as in this case.

Prophecy to be interpreted literally. Prophecy is not only to be interpreted in detail, but literally. Adam and Even literally died spiritually and ultimately died physically. Even their redemption, which God apparently provided, did not stop the process of physical death.

Revelation of the nature of temptation. In the details of the fall of Adam and Eve into sin, all the indications of what normally takes place in a temptation are mentioned: (1) denial of the truth and even of the content of prophecy; (2) the danger of inadequate comprehension that God means exactly what he says in describing prophetic events; and (3) Satan's method of casting doubt on or denying the Word of God, questioning the character of God, and the teaching that disobedience to God results in gain, not loss.

The initial account of human sin provides the elements that explain all subsequent acts of disobedience and sin from the time of Adam and Eve until the Consummation.

3

Salvation and Spiritual Warfare

Genesis 3:15 records the curse God placed on Satan: "I will put enmity between you and the woman, and between your offspring and hers; he will crush your head, and you will strike his heel" (Gen. 3:15).

One of the common experiences all Christians share is the conflict with temptation after they have been saved. Though salvation introduces the hope of eternal life, it does not eliminate the problems Christians have with their sin nature, the sinful world, or Satan.

Eden Replaced by a Sinful World

Paradise lost. The entrance of sin had changed the Garden of Paradise into a world of sin and death. The opening chapters of Genesis record the creation of Paradise for Adam and Eve (Gen. 2:8–17), but they also record how Paradise was lost (3:1–24). Instead of abundant life, now their lot is characterized by physical and spiritual death. The pleasant surroundings of the

26

garden are now replaced by a world of pain and suffering. Instead of abundance, they now will endure toil, sweat, and tears. From perfect fellowship with God as provided in creation, they now will face spiritual death, separation, and alienation from God.

As a result of the dramatic change brought about by the advent of sin into the human situation, God pronounced judgments related to life for Satan and for fallen men and women, conditions that would continue at least until the millennial kingdom of Christ.

The curse on Satan. The original sin of Satan in heaven, when as a holy angel he rebelled against God, now spread to the world of Adam and Eve. The result was that both Satan and the created world came under God's curse. Satan, who had spoken through the serpent, received first of all the pronouncement, "Cursed are you above all the livestock and all the wild animals! You will crawl on your belly and you will eat dust all the days of your life" (Gen. 3:14).

The curse upon creation. A curse was also pronounced upon the human race. The sin of Adam and Eve not only plunged them and the human race into sin, but apparently extended to the created world, to both the animate and the inanimate aspects of creation. The apostle Paul wrote, "We know that the whole creation has been groaning as in the pains of childbirth right up to the present time. Not only so, but we ourselves, who have the firstfruits of the Spirit, groan inwardly as we wait eagerly for our adoption as sons, the redemption of our bodies" (Rom. 8:22–23).

The question is often raised as to how a good God could create such a world of sin and death. The answer is that he did not; man's choosing the path of sin caused this. As illustrated in the curse pronounced on Adam and Eve, they would now labor in a difficult world of pain, suffering, sweat, toil, and death. Our present world with its sickness, catastrophe, earthquakes, sorrow, and death exemplifies the results of sin. A reminder of this is reflected in the curse upon the serpent: he was required by God to crawl on his belly and eat dust even though he was beautiful in design.

As Satan is the embodiment of satanic religion and the object of worship in some pagan religions, so he was put down by the greater power of God and labored under a curse of being anti-God, subject to divine judgment. The far-reaching effect of this curse upon Satan and creation is all too evident in the history of the world (Rom. 2) in the enmity between Satan and the woman. *Enmity between Satan and the woman.* God further declared, "And I will put enmity between you and the woman" (Gen. 3:15). As a result of the fall into sin, the world is engulfed in spiritual warfare between the descendants of the woman, pictured as opposing Satan, and Satan and those who are in allegiance to him, whether fallen angels or the human race. This warfare has an early illustration in Cain and Abel as Cain, representing evil, kills Abel, representing righteousness (4:8).

Spiritual warfare. Spiritual warfare continued not only in that which is visible between the righteous and the evil but also in the unseen contest between the demon world led by Satan and the holy angels led by Michael. Paul put it like this: "For our struggle is not against flesh and blood, but against the rulers, against the authorities, against the powers of this dark world and against the spiritual forces of evil in the heavenly realms" (Eph. 6:12). In this warfare the child of God is encouraged to put on the full armor of God (vv. 13–18). Christ had this in mind when he said, "In this world you will have trouble. But take heart! I have overcome the world" (John 16:33). The appalling sin, suffering, and death that characterizes our present world had its source in the original sin of Adam and Eve and God's resulting curse upon the created world.

Human suffering. The enmity of Satan is particularly against those who are identified as the people of God, the holy angels, and all who are saved. Accordingly, in the permission of God, Christians have been afflicted, have suffered, and have even been martyred in the continuous spiritual conflict. Here is the ultimate explanation of human suffering—a puzzle to human philosophy that attempts to solve these problems without divine revelation. The disordered world is a result of sin, and only the order Christ himself can bring into the human life or to the world as a whole, as in the millennial kingdom, will restore peace and victory.

The Promise of the Ultimately Victorious Redeemer

Victory over sin and death is promised. In his final pronouncement upon Satan, God said, "He will crush your head, and you will strike his heel" (Gen. 3:15). Though the preceding verse referred to individuals in the plural, the final victory will be caused by one who is declared here to be the seed of the woman, anticipating the Virgin Birth. "He," referring to Christ, "will crush your head"—that is, inflict a mortal wound on Satan that will be devastating and lead to his ultimate judgment. This first promise of the Redeemer and Savior begins the long line of prophecy through the Scriptures of the godly seed leading to Christ, including Abel, Seth, and Noah (Gen. 4:4, 25; 6:8–10); Shem (9:26–27); Abraham (12:1–4); Isaac (17:19–21); Jacob (28:10–14); Judah (49:10); David (2 Sam. 7:5–17); and Christ as Emmanuel (Isa. 9:6–7).

The final pronouncement on Satan was that he would strike the heel of the offspring of the woman, indicating the crucifixion of Christ as well as all the harm done to and through the human race. The ultimate result will be that Satan himself will be judged, and salvation will triumph.

The Curse Upon the Woman

Eve, representative of the women of the world, was cursed. Because of the sin of Adam and Eve the lot of women would be painful. There would first of all be increased childbearing, made necessary by death, and increased pain in childbearing (Gen. 3:16). Her relationship to her husband would be one of submission as he would rule her. The curse is made more severe by the fact that often in human relationships both the man and the woman are unsaved and not able to achieve the fellowship that is possible for believers in Christ who are married.

The Curse Upon Adam

Adam, representing the human race, was cursed because of sin. Because Adam had heeded his wife and had partaken of the fruit, disobeying God's expressed command, the ground was cursed because of him: "Cursed is the ground because of you; through painful toil you will eat of it all the days of your life. It will produce thorns and thistles for you, and you will eat the plants of the field. By the sweat of your brow you will eat your food" (Gen. 3:17–19). No longer would he experience the joy of partaking of fruit in the beautiful garden. Now the earth would be cursed and growing food would be difficult.

Even as Adam wrested food from the soil, the food he would eat in turn would ultimately be taken back by the soil from which he had been originally created. God said, "For dust you are and to dust you will return" (Gen. 3:19). The entrance of sin had changed God's beautiful creation into a world of conflict, sorrow, and death.

The woman, created equal to the man in many respects, though different, would have multiplied sorrow and trouble. The easy living in the garden would be replaced by toil. Joy would be replaced by sorrow, and life with its mortality would be the lot of man instead of immortality. The world as a whole would be caught up in the deceptive power of Satan. Christians, representing those redeemed by the blood of Christ, would be engaged in spiritual warfare beyond their strength or ability and would suffer conflict, pain, and ultimately death. Although victory in Christ would finally be achieved, the paradise provided for Adam and Eve was now lost.

The Promise of Salvation Symbolized by Garments of Skin for Adam and Eve

God promised salvation. To replace Adam and Eve's self-made garments of leaves, which were now inappropriate and inadequate, God provided for them garments of skin. This provision involved the slaying of an animal and the shedding of blood. In this way, salvation and redemption by blood was symbolized as being the only way by which human sin could be temporarily covered or the victory could ultimately be wrought.

Though Adam and Eve were given the provision of salvation in type, God drove them out of the garden and made it impossible for them to return and partake of the Tree of Life that would have given them physical immortality. Now that they had sinned, it would be far better for their bodies to die and to return to dust to be reclaimed in the beauty of resurrection in holiness and righteousness. Though a judgment from God, it was an act of mercy and grace as well (Gen. 3:22–24). In cameo form Genesis 2 and 3 reflect the whole of human history leading up to the consummation, when the present heaven and earth will be destroyed.

4

Prophecy and the Covenant With Noah

"So the LORD said, 'I will wipe mankind, whom I have created, from the face of the earth—men and animals, and creatures that move along the ground, and birds of the air—for I am grieved that I have made them'" (Gen. 6:7).

The Motif of Blessing and Cursing

Introductory character of Genesis 1–11. In the early chapters of Genesis a mixed motif of blessing and cursing was revealed. The record was not intended to be a complete history of the human race. Only eleven chapters were used to trace the entire history of the world from creation to Abraham. By contrast, Genesis 12–50, a far longer section, was devoted to the story of Abraham, Isaac, Jacob, and the twelve sons of Jacob, a few hundred years. Most conservative scholars agree that Moses was the author of Genesis and wrote it as a background to the history of Israel. Guided by the Spirit and providing general truths for all people, Moses justified God's selecting from the mass of

31

humanity a particular family, Abraham, Isaac, Jacob, and the twelve sons of Jacob, as the objects of his special care and revelation. The justification for this selective process is found in the sequence of blessing and cursing as it unfolds in the early chapters of Genesis. This process continues in our present world as some are saved and others lost.

The blessing of redemption from sin. There may have been an earlier judgment on the angels before man was created. In the statement "Now the earth was formless and empty, darkness was over the surface of the deep" (Gen. 1:2), one may perhaps read that the earth's devastation and incomplete character was due to the judgment of the fallen angels much earlier than the creation of humanity. Though this is not entirely clear in Scripture, it is possible that, in condemning the angels who sinned, God also judged and destroyed the earth, though it had been perfect previously. In the reconstruction of the earth in Genesis, God was setting the stage for humans to inhabit the earth. Creation therefore was presented as a step of blessing after failure on the part of the angels. In this preparation of the earth for human habitation, God would introduce redemption from sin after Adam and Eve failed. In contrast, the fallen angels have no way of salvation or redemption.

The movement to sin and cursing and then blessing. The changing scene from blessing to cursing is seen in the Garden of Eden. The perfection of the Garden of Eden and the innocent state of humans was suddenly terminated by the sin of Adam and Eve, resulting in God's curse upon Satan, the ground, and Adam and Eve.

The movement from blessing to cursing and then back to blessing was introduced in the garments of skin (Gen. 3:21), which signified the blessing of redemption through shed blood.

The grace extended by God to Adam and Eve, however, was followed by continual human failure, as indicated in the murder of Abel and the wickedness of subsequent generations. This failure set the stage for another step of divine judgment upon the world in the form of the Flood.

The Flood: A new beginning for Noah and his family. In the flood of Noah a new start was made (Gen. 6:1–8:22). Noah and his family were a righteous island in a sea of corruption. In this family the human race was continued. The scene changed from cursing to blessing, to be followed by another failure.

Movement back to sin and cursing. As the account of Noah

and subsequent generations unfolds, after the Flood there was again failure (Gen. 9:20–23). Noah's descendants attempted to build the Tower of Babel in defiance of the true God (11:1–9). This justified God's judgment on the Tower of Babel as well as his selection of Abraham for a new start and a new work of grace and blessing for those who are redeemed.

The call of Abraham. A new return to blessing followed the judgment on the Tower of Babel. Having demonstrated the evil of the human race generally, the narration of Genesis now turns to the particular family with which God would deal in special grace and through which God would bring redemption in Christ. Genesis 1–11, accordingly, is an introduction and an explanation of why God chose Abraham and his descendants for a special favor.

Noah's Commission to Build the Ark (Gen. 6:9–7:5)

God's purpose to destroy life and cleanse the earth (Gen. 6:4–7). Hundreds of years had passed since God created Adam and Eve. God had blessed Seth as a descendant of Adam to replace the murdered Abel (Gen. 4:25), but the race as a whole continued its mad course of disobedience to God. In the time of Noah the entire human race, with the exception of Noah and his family, had rebelled against God. Accordingly, Noah was commissioned to build an ark to save the race from extinction (6:5–7:5).

Noah and his family alone in favor with God (Gen. 6:8–9). Of the human race only Noah and his family, descendants of Seth, were still honoring the Lord. In his plan to destroy the earth, God determined to save Noah and his family and through them to make a new beginning of the human race.

Instructions for building the ark and saving the animals and birds in addition to Noah's own family (Gen. 6:13–22). The ark as described by God had the dimensions of a large seagoing vessel able to withstand the storms of the Flood and having ample accommodations for the animals as well as Noah and his family. The dimensions of the ark as recorded in Scripture stand in sharp contrast to the mythological accounts of the Flood, which in some cases picture an ark 3,000 feet long and 1,200 feet wide, which would be impossible to build and would not be seaworthy.

Noah was instructed to bring into the ark two pairs of birds and beasts but with a special provision in regard to clean animals. He was to bring seven pairs of these and also seven pairs of birds, for the purpose of keeping their various species alive (Gen. 7:2–3). In addition, Noah was instructed to take in food for his family as well as for the animals (6:21). In building the ark and providing provisions for the time of the Flood, Noah was completely obedient to God (7:5).

The Destruction of the Genesis Flood (Gen. 7:6–24)

The Flood begins. Once the ark was completed and the animals and Noah's family entered, the Flood began (Gen. 7:6–24). Noah and his family entered the ark on the tenth day of the second month, seven days before the Flood came (vv. 4, 10). This was in the six hundredth year of Noah's life. On the seventeenth day of the second month the floods began. "On that day all the springs of the great deep burst forth, and the floodgates of the heavens were opened. And rain fell on the earth forty days and forty nights" (vv. 11–12). In addition to the rain that fell, water was released from the ocean, possibly caused by great earthquakes which opened up subterranean water. However it may be explained, it apparently added to the Flood and caused the Flood to come on quickly.

The water recedes. After the rain stopped on the twenty-seventh day of the third month (Gen. 7:12), the water receded for another 110 days, making a total of 150 days in which the water prevailed on the earth. Finally the ark rested on Mount Ararat on the seventeenth day of the seventh month (7:24; 8:4).

The water continues to recede. For 150 days after the ark rested on Mount Ararat the water continued to recede. On the first day of the tenth month, the tops of the mountains became visible, 74 days after the ark rested on Mount Ararat (Gen. 8:5). Another 40 days followed. Then Noah sent out a raven and a dove to explore the situation. This occurred on the eleventh day of the eleventh month (vv. 6–9). The dove returned, having apparently found no place to rest.

After seven more days passed, the dove was sent out, but this time it returned with a leaf, indicating its discovery of vegetation. This occurred on the eighteenth day of the eleventh month (Gen. 8:10–11). Seven days later, the dove was sent out a third time and did not return (v. 12). Another 22 days later, or 150 days after the ark had rested on the mountain, the water continued to recede (v. 3, 13).

Dry land reappears. Dry land reappeared in the six hundred and first year, the first day of the first month (Gen. 8:13). Finally, on the twenty-seventh day of the second month, the land was completely dry (vv. 14–19), and Noah was able to leave the ark. The total number of days spent in the ark, including the seven days of waiting, were 377 days or one year and 17 days. In all of this, prophecy was being fulfilled. When the animals and birds left the ark, Noah and his family also returned to the earth.

The Covenant With Noah (Gen. 8:20–9:17)

Noah's sacrifice (Gen. 8:20). Upon leaving the ark, Noah built an altar to the Lord and offered a sacrifice of clean animals and clean birds (v. 20). In so doing, he expressed once again his devotion to God and his recognition of the need of blood sacrifice, sacrifice which had been impossible while on the ark. In reply, God gave Noah a new covenant that he would never again judge the earth with a flood (8:21–9:17).

In response to Noah's pleasing sacrifice, God declared, "Never again will I curse the ground because of man, even though every inclination of his heart is evil from childhood. And never again will I destroy all living creatures, as I have done. As long as the earth endures, seedtime and harvest, cold and heat, summer and winter, day and night will never cease" (Gen. 8:21–22). Though God might inflict other punishments upon humans because of their sin, there never would be another universal destruction by a flood. Other Scriptures reveal that the present earth will ultimately be destroyed by fire before the new heaven and new earth are created (2 Peter 3:10–13).

God's covenant with Noah included a number of promises. (1) Noah was instructed, "Be fruitful and increase in number and fill the earth" (Gen. 9:1). (2) God placed everything in creation under human authority, whether beasts or birds or fish (vv. 2–3). (3) For the first time God gave Noah the right not only to eat of the green plants but to eat meat from animals (vv. 3–6). Before this, the human race had been vegetarian. In eating meat, however, they were commanded not to leave the lifeblood in it (v. 4), and a new regulation was added recognizing the sanctity of human life. God said, "And from each man, too, I will demand an accounting for the life of his fellow man. Whoever sheds the blood of man, by man shall his blood be shed; for in the image of God has God made man" (vv. 5–6). (4) God promised that he would never again bring a flood on the earth like the flood of Noah. "I establish my covenant with you: Never again will all life be cut off by the waters of a flood; never again will there be a flood to destroy the earth" (v. 11).

The sign of the covenant (Gen. 9:12–16). As a sign of the promise never again to destroy the earth with a flood, God set a rainbow in the clouds. Rain seems to have fallen for the first time in connection with the Flood, and it is not likely, therefore, that there were rainbows prior to this time. Before this, a mist seems to have watered the earth (2:5–6). In any case, from this point on, the rainbow became a sign of the covenant with Noah regarding universal judgment on the earth. The sign was therefore established not only to signify the covenant with Noah but with all life on earth. God said, "This is the sign of the covenant I have established between me and all life on the earth" (9:17).

The prophecy involved in the covenant of Noah brought a new situation. Once again, in spite of sin and judgment, God brought blessing on the earth, repeating the cycle of blessing followed by cursing then followed by blessing.

Noah's Sin

Noah becomes drunk (Gen. 9:20–21). Even though the earth had been cleansed and Noah and his family rescued from the Flood, the narrative immediately confronts us with the fact that the Flood had not changed the character of humans. Noah, though a righteous man, having made wine from grapes from the vineyard he planted, became drunk and lay uncovered inside his tent (v. 21).

The sin of Ham. Ham, coming into his father's tent, saw him uncovered and apparently joked about this with this two brothers Shem and Japheth (Gen. 9:22). Shem and Japheth, however, recognizing the problem, walked backward and covered their father's nakedness so they would not see their father in his drunken state (v. 23).

Noah's prophecy. When Noah awoke and discovered what had happened, he pronounced a solemn curse upon Canaan, "Cursed be Canaan! The lowest of slaves will he be to his brothers" (Gen. 9:25).

Though a number of explanations have been given to the incident of Ham and his father, the best explanation seems to be that exposure of a father in the ancient world was considered a serious sin reflecting on the sanctity of the human family and on the dignity of fatherhood. The Canaanites, who were Ham's descendants, became a very wicked people and were perpetually enemies of Israel. They were particularly involved in sexual sin. Subsequent history recorded that the Canaanites occupied the place of slaves in relationship to Israel. This did not immediately stem from Noah's condemnation but rather as a judgment of God upon them for their licentious lives. In Genesis 14 the Canaanites were enslaved by kings from the East, and later the Gibeonites, who also were descendants of Ham, became water carriers and woodcutters for the congregation and altar of the Lord (Josh. 9:27).

The concept that this explains the slavery of blacks is not scriptural, therefore, as it is questionable whether the Canaanites were black. The prediction rather anticipated the sinfulness of those who came from the Canaanite line and prophesied that their sins would be judged by servitude. Eventually the Canaanites disappeared from the pages of history.

In contrast, Noah blessed Japheth, implying that his descendants would be a great people. Shem was blessed with Canaan as his slave: "Blessed be the LORD, the God of Shem! May Canaan be the slave of Shem. May God extend the territory of Japheth; may Japheth live in the tents of Shem, and may Canaan be his slave" (Gen. 9:26–27). The accounts of Noah's and Ham's sin after the Flood are part of the pattern of the early chapters of Genesis, showing that after blessing there often comes sin and cursing. For that reason God selected a particular family to bless and to use in the generations ahead.

The Epilogue: The Tower of Babel

Decision to build a tower (Gen. 11:1–4). The sinfulness of the human race was illustrated in the building of a tower. The descendants of Noah decided to build a great tower, or ziggurat, as a unifying symbol lest they be scattered over the earth (v. 4). Ziggurats were generally used in the worship of pagan gods.

God confused their language. In response to the people's sinful behavior, God confused their language, saying, "If as one people speaking the same language they have begun to do this, then nothing they plan to do will be impossible for them. Come, let us go down and confuse their language so they will not understand each other" (Gen. 11:6–7).

Confusion introduced in the earth (Gen. 11:8–9). By introducing languages the people could not understand, God brought into the earthan element that has hindered the unification of the human race in its common endeavors ever since. The tower was called "Babel," meaning "confused." This name led to the word "Babylon," an area that became significant in subsequent world events.

Conclusion of the cycle of blessing and cursing. The cycle of blessing and cursing in Genesis 1–11 ends with Abraham. Having traced the course of blessing and cursing from Genesis 1 through 11:9, the Bible now sets the stage for God's declaration of his special purpose, beginning with Abraham. In writing the history of the world extending over thousands of years in such brief compass, Moses was preparing the way for God's purpose through Abraham, Isaac, and Jacob, which would occupy not only the book of Genesis but the rest of the Bible. The prophecies made and fulfilled emphasized that redemption is selective. Not all will be saved, not all will be blessed, not all will be cursed, but God has a plan for the human race that includes the redemption and salvation of the elect as well as the damnation of the unrepentant. The early chapters of Genesis present in cameo the entire history of the human race.

The principles of fulfilled prophecy confirmed. The events of the Flood confirm the principles of interpreting prophecy and fulfillment. The Flood was literal. The judgment of the Flood destroying life on earth was literal. The events that followed the Flood were also literal. The Flood proved that prophecy is specific and that details are subject to literal fulfillment. This leads to the conclusion that the revelation given to Abraham is also subject to literal fulfillment.

5

The Prophetic Covenant
With Abraham

"The LORD had said to Abram, 'Leave your country, your people and your father's household and go to the land I will show you. I will make you into a great nation and I will bless you; I will make your name great, and you will be a blessing. I will bless those who bless you, and whoever curses you I will curse; and all peoples on earth will be blessed through you'" (Gen. 12:1–3).

A New Beginning

Abraham chosen. Beginning with Abraham, Scripture charts a new course for God's people. The choice of Abraham marked a new narrowing of the redemptive purpose of God. As we saw in the previous eleven chapters of Genesis, in beginning the human race God selected Abel to exemplify the righteous line. After Abel was killed, he was replaced by Seth (Gen. 4:25). The human race having been destroyed by the Flood, God began again with Noah, a descendant of Seth, and Noah's three sons

39

(5:32). God selected Shem as the ancestor of the godly line. After the judgment of the human race at the Tower of Babel, God chose Terah (11:26) and, through Terah, his son Abraham to be the progenitor of the godly line.

Genesis: History of Abraham, Isaac, and Jacob. The book of Genesis is largely occupied with the history of Abraham, Isaac, and Jacob. Humanity began in the Garden of Eden and moved to Egypt. Genesis was the book of beginnings only, however. The line of Abraham continued through Isaac (Gen. 21:12), Jacob (25:23; 28:13–15), Judah (49:10), David (2 Sam. 7:9–11, 16), Nathan (Luke 3:31), and Mary (Matt. 1:16) to Jesus Christ.

Redemption as a purpose of God. The importance of God's choosing a people becomes obvious as his plan for redemption unfolds. From Genesis 12 through the book of Revelation, Israel is shown to be one of the major purposes of God. God revealed himself through the prophets of Israel, through both his blessing and judging of Israel, through the twelve apostles and other writers of Scripture, and ultimately through Jesus Christ, Lord and Savior. In addition to God's purpose for Israel in the redemptive plan as revealed in the Old Testament, the New Testament imparts the special purpose of God in the present age of calling out his church composed of both Jews and Gentiles. The prophecies of Scripture provide the background and outline for the destiny of the human race and especially God's plan of eternal salvation for his elect, or chosen ones.

The Provisions of the Covenant

Abraham instructed to go to the Promised Land. Certain promises stand out in God's covenant with Abraham. As the introduction to the covenant states (Gen. 12:1), Abraham had been called to leave his home and relatives in Ur of the Chaldeans and go to a land that God would show him. As there is some indication that Abraham was in a comfortable and prosperous situation in Ur, the call of God to go to a strange land and live in a tent with his household was not an enticing one. The fact that Abraham and his father started out for the Promised Land is evidence that though they may have participated in the worship of pagan deities of the time, at this important juncture in their life they recognized the true God and henceforth obeyed and worshiped him. Their path of obedience, however, was not perfect.

Abraham had been told to leave not only his country but also his people and his father's household. Circumstances combined to make this a difficult command, because Abraham recognized the leadership of his father, and his father took the initiative to involve Abraham as well as his great-nephew Lot on the journey. Further, they settled in Haran (Gen. 11:31) and stayed there until Abraham's father died. It was only then that Abraham left for the final destination, and it was not until later that he separated from Lot (13:5–11).

The promise of a great nation. In addition to the important place of the land in God's covenant with Abraham, God promised that Abraham would father many descendants. The central promise of the prophetic covenant given to Abraham is contained in the statement, "I will make you into a great nation" (Gen. 12:2). Abraham was destined to be the progenitor of many nations, but most important, he was to be the progenitor of the line that would lead to Jesus Christ. The nation that came from Abraham would be great not only in number, as God frequently reminded Abraham, but also great in importance.

In attempting to understand the revelation God gave Abraham, the interpreter of the Abrahamic promise is faced with the decision as to whether this should be taken in its literal meaning, that is, physical descendants, as premillenarians believe, or whether it should be spiritualized to represent the spiritual company of the elect of Israel and even of Gentiles, as amillenarians believe. As the exposition of the covenant throughout the book of Genesis will demonstrate, the promise was literal, that is, Abraham understood the promise of a great nation to refer to his physical descendants, and this was also God's intent.

Because so many try to understand prophecy as nonliteral and sometimes in a vague sense, it is important to understand that the promise was literal. That Abraham would also have spiritual children (Gal. 3:6–9) does not change the literal promise. Even the spiritual children of Abraham were a literal fulfillment of prophecy. The lineage from Abraham to Christ is a literal lineage, and Christ was literally born. The fulfillment of the literal promise was essential to God's purpose not only for the physical seed of Abraham but also for the spiritual seed. Without the literal, the spiritual could not have been fulfilled. It is significant that Galatians 3:5 does not trace the promise to the covenant that made Abraham the progenitor of the great nation of Israel, but rather to the promise of blessings to all people (Gen. 12:3), which is literally being fulfilled by Christ as the Savior.

The promise of personal blessing. The promise of personal blessing to Abraham was a central feature of the Abrahamic covenant. God stated three aspects of this, "I will bless you; I will make your name great, and you will be a blessing" (Gen. 12:2). These personal blessings were also literally fulfilled.

Fulfillment of the covenant to Abraham. First, the covenant anticipated prophetically how God's hand of blessing would rest upon Abraham. This is illustrated throughout his life in that God made him a wealthy man, a powerful man, and a miraculous channel through which Isaac was to be born. Abraham was blessed above any other person in his generation, and this promise, like other promises in the covenant, was literally fulfilled.

Second, Abraham was promised that his name would be great—that is, he would be a major actor in God's redemptive program. He is mentioned as Abram or Abraham about three hundred times in the Bible. Unquestionably, he is one of the most important characters of the Old Testament and is mentioned many times in the New Testament as well. This prophecy has been literally fulfilled.

Third, God declared to Abraham, "You will be a blessing" (Gen. 12:2). Unquestionably, Abraham was a blessing to his own generation and to his own family, and through the centuries he has been an illustration of faith and obedience that has challenged all who follow the Lord. God's faithful dealings with Abraham, even when he fell short of perfect obedience, are a great encouragement to the people of God and help to fulfill this promise. The ultimate fulfillment, however, is found in the aspects of the covenant referring to blessings on the whole world.

Fulfillment of the covenant to nations dealing with Israel. The covenant included promises of blessing and cursing on the nations. In recognition of the greatness of Abraham and of the promises that God gave him, God declared, "I will bless those who bless you, and whoever curses you I will curse" (Gen. 12:3). This prophecy is intrinsic in the nature of the case as those who bless God will bless Abraham and those who curse God will curse Abraham. God, however, makes this a general principle that is observed throughout history. The nations that have been kind to Israel have in turn been blessed by God even though they were evil nations. Those who cursed Israel because of her wickedness and rebellion against God received God's righteous judgment. This has been illustrated in the great nations of the world. Egypt, the greatest nation of the ancient world, served Israel well for several generations but ended up enslaving Israel. This was the ultimate downfall of Egypt, and God's judgment on Egypt has been executed so faithfully throughout history that even today she is a minor nation.

The Assyrian Empire also comes under this pronouncement, for Assyria was the nation that led the ten tribes into captivity (722 B.C.). Though Assyria was an instrument of divine judgment, nevertheless, when Nineveh fell in 612 B.C., the nation was suddenly and completely destroyed. The story is not yet complete, for God, in fulfillment of prophecy, is dealing and will continue to deal with Syria in judgment. Babylon also, though the captor of the two tribes of Israel, faced judgment in history in the fall of Babylon in 539 B.C., and prophetic Scripture describes the ultimate fall of Babylon in its modern character (Rev. 17–18).

The Medes and the Persians, who followed the Babylonians, were relatively kind to Israel and permitted her return to the land. Medo-Persia continued for two hundred years without serious intervention by God.

In the Grecian Empire God dealt with each portion of the empire according to its dealings with Israel. He especially judged Antiochus Epiphanes.

The Roman Empire, the greatest of the empires of biblical times, was gradually destroyed. In later years Spain, Germany, Russia, and other countries that persecuted the Jews suffered God's judgment. By contrast, the United States, relatively kind to the Jews, has had unusual blessings in spite of her many shortcomings. The principle of blessing those who bless Abraham and his posterity and cursing those who curse Abraham and his posterity has been fulfilled to the present hour and will continue in the future.

Fulfillment of the covenant to all peoples. The greatest promise given to Abraham was that "all peoples on earth will be blessed through you" (Gen. 12:3). As has already been brought out, this is fulfilled in God's unfolding plan for Abraham and his posterity. Blessing has come to Israel and to the world as a whole through the prophets, through the writers of Scripture, through the apostles, and preeminently through Jesus Christ. Blessings which God has promised Abraham have been showered on the recipients through many centuries up to the present time and will continue until the end of human history.

In studying the Abrahamic promise, care must be taken to observe meticulously the difference in the promises. Some promises were addressed to Abraham himself—namely, that he would be the father of a great nation and would have a great name and would experience God's personal blessing. Some promises applied to his physical posterity, for more than one great nation descended from him. Some promises would be fulfilled by Israel. The promises have to be observed as they unfold, as some of the promises were given to a portion of Abraham's descendants but not to all. The greatest of all promises, of course, was the promise of blessing to all peoples of the earth, and it is here that the church of the New Testament comes in (Gal. 3:6–9). The interpretation that the church is blessed because it is the inheritor of Israel's promises is not what the Scriptures teach. It is rather that through Abraham, the man of faith, "all peoples" who trust in God as Abraham did will be blessed through Abraham and his posterity.

Important Aspects of the Fulfillment of the Abrahamic Covenant

The covenant with Abraham requires study along several lines.

Physical descendants of Abraham. First, the Abrahamic promises were fulfilled in those who descended physically from Abraham. The guiding hand of God and the tremendous extended revelation given to the sons of Abraham merit a study of this line of truth.

Promise of the land. Second, the promise of the land remained a central doctrine of the Abrahamic covenant and one that is most revealing in connection with the issue of whether the promises of Abraham are literal and unconditional.

Promise of kings. Third, the promise that through Abraham would come kings was fulfilled primarily through David, and is another area of prophecy traced through Scriptures into the prophetic future.

Promise of grace to Israel as well as to all believers. Fourth, the new covenant, providing God's grace for Israel as well as for all who trust in Christ, is another major outgrowth of the Abrahamic covenant. Although it stands as a separate covenant, obviously its roots come from the promise of God to bless all people of the earth through Abraham. The new covenant, continuing as it does in the New Testament, provides a major revelation of God's plan of grace for those who trust him.

These major fulfillments of the Abrahamic covenant are worthy of separate study and will be undertaken in succeeding chapters. These fulfillments are not only important for an understanding of prophecy, but they are the basis of our faith that God will fulfill his promises to everyone who believes in Jesus Christ. Israel is a great example of the fact that God keeps his Word. The very existence of Israel today, four thousand years after Abraham, is a reminder that God continues to keep his Word even through thousands of years. Christians can rest assured that in the years ahead, God, who does not change, will continue to keep his promises to them.

6

The Messianic Genealogy of Jesus Christ

The Promise of a Great Nation

The promise of the covenant (Gen. 12:1–3). In the original covenant given to Abraham, he was promised that he would be the forefather of a great nation. Abraham was already an old man when the promise was given, and he was childless. The delay occasioned by Abraham's stay in Haran resulted in Abraham being seventy-five years of age before he arrived in the land (v. 4). Obviously the covenant depended on Abraham having descendants, and it became increasingly evident that he might not have an heir. This was a trial of Abraham's faith and became a greater problem as the years rolled on. Though not clearly stated in the original promise, the fact that his posterity would be a blessing to all nations involved not only Abraham's being the forefather of a great nation, but also his serving as a forefather of the line leading to Jesus Christ.

Suggestion that Eliezer be an heir rejected. When another ten years had elapsed with no heir, Abraham suggested that Eliezer,

a favorite servant, be made his heir. But Abraham's offer of
Eliezer of Damascus as his heir was rejected by God. Abraham
said, "O Sovereign LORD, what can you give me since I remain
childless and the one who will inherit my estate is Eliezer of
Damascus?" (Gen. 15:2). He continued, "You have given me no
children; so a servant in my household will be my heir" (v. 3).
According to the customs of that day, a couple with no heir
would pass on their estate to a designated servant.

The Lord's answer was clear and emphatic; the promise of a
son was to be literally fulfilled: "Then the word of the LORD
came to him: 'This man will not be your heir, but a son coming
from your own body will be your heir'" (Gen. 15:4). God then
told Abraham, "'Look up at the heavens and count the stars—if
indeed you can count them.' Then he said to him, 'So shall your
offspring be'" (v. 5).

In support of the promise of God, Scripture records that God
made a covenant with Abraham concerning the promise of the
land to his descendants and gave the geographic description of it
(Gen. 15:18–21). Obviously a literal land with literal boundaries
was indicated.

Ishmael rejected (Gen. 16:1–16; 17:15–19). Sarah, recognizing the problem of not having a son and heir and feeling
somewhat responsible because she should have been a mother
of a child, suggested to Abraham that he have a child by Hagar,
the Egyptian maidservant that he had brought back from Egypt.
Ishmael was born, and when he had reached his early teens,
Abraham still had no other child.

The promise of a son reaffirmed. The birth of Ishmael was not
God's plan. When Abram was ninety-nine years of age (Gen.
17:1), God reaffirmed his covenant. Abram's name was changed
to Abraham, meaning "father of many." He was given the added
information:

> I will make you very fruitful; I will make nations of you, and
> kings will come from you. I will establish my covenant as an
> everlasting covenant between me and you and your de-
> scendants after you for the generations to come, to be your
> God and the God of your descendants after you. The whole
> land of Canaan, where you are now an alien, I will give as
> an everlasting possession to you and your descendants after
> you; and I will be their God. (vv. 6–8)

After instituting the rite of circumcision as a sign of the covenant, "God also said to Abraham, 'As for Sarai your wife, you are no longer to call her Sarai; her name will be Sarah. I will bless her and will surely give you a son by her. I will bless her so that she will be the mother of nations; kings of peoples will come from her'" (Gen. 17:15–16). The name Sarai, possibly meaning "contentious," is changed to Sarah, meaning "princess." This is partially in recognition of the fact that kings would come from her.

The pronouncement from God that Sarah would have a child moved Abraham to laughter. "Abraham fell facedown; he laughed and said to himself, 'Will a son be born to a man a hundred years old? Will Sarah bear a child at the age of ninety?' And Abraham said to God, 'If only Ishmael might live under your blessing!'" (Gen. 17:17–18). God however, reaffirmed his promise: "Yes, but your wife Sarah will bear you a son, and you will call him Isaac. I will establish my covenant with him as an everlasting covenant for his descendants after him" (v. 19). In recognition of the fact that Abraham had laughed to himself, God gave Abraham's promised son the name Isaac, meaning "he laughs." God subsequently revealed that Ishmael would also become a nation (v. 20).

In Genesis 18 we read, "The LORD appeared to Abraham near the great trees of Mamre while he was sitting at the entrance to his tent in the heat of the day" (v. 1). Abraham saw three men approaching him. In keeping with the rules of traditional courtesy, he invited them to remain, to wash their feet, and to rest and be refreshed. Abraham instructed Sarah to prepare bread while he ran to the herd and selected a young calf, which he prepared for their meal. The men asked, "Where is your wife Sarah?" Abraham replied, "There, in the tent" (v. 9).

Scripture continues, "Then the LORD said, 'I will surely return to you about this time next year, and Sarah your wife will have a son'" (Gen. 18:10). The change in the text from the three men speaking to that of the Lord himself would indicate that one of the three men was a theophany—that is, an appearance of Jesus Christ in the form of an angel—and the other two men who accompanied him were angels. Sarah, who was now ninety years of age, was listening at the door of the tent. Scripture explains, "Abraham and Sarah were already old and well advanced in years, and Sarah was past the age of childbearing" (v. 11). When Sarah heard the prophecy that she would have a son, she "laughed to herself as she thought, 'After I am worn out and my master is old, will I now have this pleasure?'" (v. 12).

"Then the LORD said to Abraham, 'Why did Sarah laugh and say, "Will I really have a child, now that I am old?" Is anything too hard for the LORD? I will return to you at the appointed time next year and Sarah will have a son'" (Gen. 18:13–14). The record then reveals, "Sarah was afraid, so she lied and said, 'I did not laugh,'" to which the Lord replied, "Yes, you did laugh" (v. 15).

At the conclusion of this interview the Lord told Abraham about the coming destruction of Sodom and Gomorrah. This introduces the account of Lot leaving Sodom and the city being destroyed.

The birth of Isaac fulfills the promise (Gen. 21:8). Twenty-five years after Abraham left Haran, as he waited for some evidence of the covenant being fulfilled, the promise of God, impossible as it seemed to Abraham and Sarah, was fulfilled, and Isaac was born. In recognition that Isaac was a covenant child, Abraham circumcised him on the eighth day (v. 4). When Isaac was finally weaned, Abraham held a great feast in honor of his son (v. 8).

The narrative of ten chapters of Scripture, from the time the covenant was given to the time Isaac was born, emphasizes the importance of this fulfilled prophecy. In keeping with many other scriptural instances, the prophecy was fulfilled literally, not figuratively or nonliterally. The answer came in spite of Abraham and Sarah's unbelief and their inability to contemplate the omnipotence of God in doing what is impossible to humans. The fulfillment of the promise illustrates again the unconditional and absolutely certain fulfillment required in the provisions and promises of the Abrahamic covenant.

The Birth of Jacob and Esau

Jacob and Esau born to Isaac. As in the case of Abraham, where a long delay occurred between the giving of the promise and its fulfillment, so it was in the birth of Jacob and Esau to Isaac. In the beautiful story of the servant of Abraham seeking a bride for Isaac (Gen. 24), Rebekah is selected and becomes the wife of Isaac. In due time Abraham died, leaving everything to Isaac (Gen. 25:5–11).

As the years passed, however, Isaac became concerned

because his wife, like Sarah, was barren. "Isaac prayed to the LORD on behalf of his wife, because she was barren. The LORD answered his prayer, and his wife Rebekah became pregnant" (Gen. 25:21). By this time Isaac was sixty years old (v. 26).

The older, Esau, to serve the younger, Jacob. When Rebekah became conscious that she was to bear twins, she inquired of the Lord as to what this meant: "The babies jostled each other within her, and she said, 'Why is this happening to me?' So she went to inquire of the LORD" (Gen. 25:22).

In reply, the Lord informed her that the elder would serve the younger, contrary to tradition:

> *Two nations are in your womb,*
> *and two peoples from within you will be separated;*
> *one people will be stronger than the other,*
> *and the older will serve the younger. (Gen. 25:23)*

The sale of the birthright. The fact that Jacob, the younger, was the Lord's chosen was soon confirmed. "The boys grew up, and Esau became a skillful hunter, a man of the open country, while Jacob was a quiet man, staying among the tents. Isaac, who had a taste for wild game, loved Esau, but Rebekah loved Jacob" (Gen. 25:27–28).

When, on one occasion, Esau came in unusually hungry, he asked Jacob for some stew he was cooking. "He said to Jacob, 'Quick, let me have some of that red stew! I'm famished!' (That is why he was also called Edom)" (Gen. 25:29–30). Edom means "red." "Jacob replied, 'First sell me your birthright' " (v. 31). Esau replied, "Look, I am about to die. What good is the birthright to me?" (v. 32). Esau sold his birthright and ate the lentil stew that Jacob supplied, thus despising his birthright (vv. 33–34).

Later Rebekah connived with Jacob to secure from Isaac the blessing that would normally go to the eldest son. To make the deception work, Rebekah had Jacob put on Esau's clothes and cover his hands and the smooth part of his neck with goatskins to simulate Esau's hairy skin (Gen. 27:15–17). Jacob went to see Isaac, succeeded in deceiving him, and thus received the blessing that Isaac intended for Esau: "May God give you of heaven's dew and of earth's richness—an abundance of grain and new wine. May nations serve you and peoples bow down to you. Be lord over your brothers, and may the sons of your mother bow down to you. May those who curse you be cursed and those who bless you be blessed" (vv. 28–29). The blessing pronounced upon Jacob was in keeping with the fact that he would be of the chosen line. Esau, the elder, would serve Jacob, the younger.

The Abrahamic Covenant Confirmed to Isaac

God forbids Isaac to go down to Egypt. Like Abraham, his father, Isaac wanted to go down to Egypt, which was outside the Promised Land. To have done so would have exposed him to the same temptations and problems that Abraham faced when he went to Egypt. Isaac had already gone to the land of the Philistines to escape the famine that was in the Promised Land. It was there that the Lord appeared to Isaac. The Lord said, "Do not go down to Egypt; live in the land where I tell you to live" (Gen. 26:2).

The blessing of Abraham given to Isaac. In support of his command to stay in the land, the Lord blessed Isaac:

> Stay in this land for a while, and I will be with you and will bless you. For to you and your descendants I will give all these lands and will confirm the oath I swore to your father Abraham. I will make your descendants as numerous as the stars in the sky and will give them all these lands, and through your offspring all nations on earth will be blessed, because Abraham obeyed me and kept my requirements, my commands, my decrees and my laws. (Gen. 26:3–5)

In making this covenant with Isaac and selecting him to be in the line of the Redeemer, God ignored Ishmael even though he was older than Isaac. The redemptive process, as subsequent Scripture illustrates, is selective. The promises originally given to Abraham are here reiterated, including the major elements of a great posterity, ultimate possession of the land, and bringing blessing to all nations of the earth.

The Covenant Confirmed to Jacob

Jacob's conflict with Esau. "Esau held a grudge against Jacob because of the blessing his father had given him. He said to himself, 'The days of mourning for my father are near; then I will kill my brother Jacob'" (Gen. 27:41).

Esau's antagonism toward Jacob made clear that he did not have confidence in God's promises. If God's blessing and prophecies concerning Jacob were to be fulfilled, Esau's plans to kill him would not be consummated. Rebekah, however, realized the problem and asked Isaac's permission for Jacob to return to her homeland so that he would avoid marrying a Canaanite woman (Gen. 27:46).

Isaac approved this plan and told Jacob to go to his mother's family to take a wife from the daughters of Laban, his mother's brother (Gen. 28:1–2). Isaac pronounced another blessing upon Jacob, "May God Almighty bless you and make you fruitful and increase your numbers until you become a community of peoples. May he give you and your descendants the blessing of Abraham, so that you may take possession of the land where you now live as an alien, the land God gave to Abraham" (vv. 3–4). Rebekah, possibly because she had joined Jacob in deceiving Isaac, never saw Jacob, her favorite, again.

Jacob receives confirmation of the covenant. Starting out on his journey, Jacob reached a certain place and stopped for the night (Gen. 28:11). While asleep he had a dream in which God said to him:

> I am the LORD, the God of your father Abraham and the God of Isaac. I will give you and your descendants the land on which you are lying. Your descendants will be like the dust of the earth, and you will spread out to the west and to the east, to the north and to the south. All peoples on earth will be blessed through you and your offspring. I am with you and will watch over you wherever you go, and I will bring you back to this land. I will not leave you until I have done what I have promised you. (vv. 13–15)

The main elements of the covenant with Abraham were here transferred to Jacob, including the fact that God would be the God of Jacob, giving him the land in which he was lying and promising a great posterity as well as bringing a blessing to the entire world. Jacob went to Haran, apparently with God's permission and blessing, for God promised to watch over him while he was gone and bring him back (Gen. 28:15). Haran was situated near the Euphrates, the boundary of the Promised Land to the north and east, and did not have the temptations found in Egypt. In response to the covenant, Jacob himself made a vow:

"If God will be with me and will watch over me on this journey I am taking and will give me food to eat and clothes to wear so that I return safely to my father's house, then the LORD will be my God. This stone that I have set up as a pillar will be God's house, and of all that you give me I will give you a tenth" (vv. 20–22).

Jacob's posterity multiplied. Two chapters (Gen. 29–30) are devoted to the account of how Jacob married four wives and had many children. Because God had greatly multiplied not only Jacob's children but his flocks, enmity grew between Jacob and Laban's sons, the accusation being that Jacob had robbed Laban of his property. As a result, Jacob left Laban, as recorded in Genesis 31.

Jacob renamed Israel. On the way back home, Jacob realized that he would encounter Esau and sent a message ahead requesting his favor. The messengers returned, however, reporting that Esau was coming with four hundred men (Gen. 32:1–6). Because of Jacob's fear of Esau, he engaged in a special prayer to God asking for his protection and care (vv. 9–12). Hoping to placate Esau, Jacob sent ahead to him gifts of goats, rams, camels, cows, bulls, and donkeys.

After sending his family across the ford of the Jabbok (Gen. 32:22), Jacob was left alone and wrestled with a man until daybreak. In the Hebrew there is a play on words as the word "Jabbok" is similar to Jacob and the word for wrestling is also similar to Jacob. Scripture does not reveal the character of this wrestling match between Jacob and his adversary, and it does not say that this is a theophany in angelic or human form. However, the wrestling is very real, and Jacob was not overcome until his assailant caused Jacob's hip to go out of joint (v. 25).

Jacob, however, was struggling because he needed a blessing from God. Jacob interpreted the encounter with the assailant as seeing God face to face (Gen. 32:30). God gave Jacob the name Israel (v. 28). Though the name Jacob had been given to him because he grasped Esau's heel at the time of birth, now he is called Israel, probably meaning, "He strives with God" (but see *ISBE*, 2:907).

After this important event in Jacob's life, he met Esau and was received in friendship (Gen. 33:4). Subsequent to his encounter with Esau, Jacob arrived at Shechem in Canaan, where he bought a small piece of ground. Jacob set up an altar there to worship God (v. 20). In the several chapters in Genesis dedicated to recounting the story of Jacob, there was early confirmation of the fulfillment of the prophecy of a large posterity in the birth of Jacob's sons. The healing of the rift between Jacob and Esau that took place when Jacob returned permitted Jacob once again to dwell in the Promised Land as God himself had promised to provide.

The rest of the book of Genesis, a total of sixteen chapters, is devoted to the story of Jacob, his twelve sons, and their going down to Egypt. It is obvious that in a book where only two chapters are devoted to Creation and so many chapters to Abraham, Isaac, and Jacob, God was emphasizing one of his central purposes—namely, to call and to bless Israel and through them to bring redemption and revelation of himself to the world.

The Prophecy Concerning Judah

Judah to be a prominent tribe. In Jacob's prophetic blessing upon his sons, the prophecy of Judah is far-reaching in its significance. The prophecy begins with a statement that Judah will triumph over his enemies and that even his father's sons will bow down to him: "Judah, your brothers will praise you; your hand will be on the neck of your enemies; your father's sons will bow down to you. You are a lion's cub, O Judah; you return from the prey, my son. Like a lion he crouches and lies down, like a lioness—who dares to rouse him?" (Gen. 49:8–9). The prophecy of Judah's numerous victories was fulfilled in the history of this predominant tribe. Judah along with Benjamin formed the kingdom of Judah in the divided kingdom.

The future King to come from Judah. Included in Jacob's prophecy was the prediction of a future King from Judah. This important prophecy about Judah concerns the scepter, the symbol of the kingdom: "The scepter will not depart from Judah, nor the ruler's staff from between his feet, until he comes to whom it belongs and the obedience of the nations is his" (Gen. 49:10). As later Scripture supports, the line of David descended from the tribe of Judah, from which Christ the Messiah would come. The various rulers who would serve as kings, however, would culminate in the one who "comes to whom it belongs" (v. 10). This verse is translated in the NASB, "Until Shiloh comes." Instead of the formal name, "Shiloh," it is better to translate the name "To whom it belongs," which refers to the Messiah as the ultimate One who has the right to rule. In other words, the scepter will remain with Judah until it is claimed by the final Ruler, who will be the Messiah, Jesus Christ, as King of Kings and Lord of Lords and the One who is entitled to sit on the throne of David. His reign will not be simply over the Davidic kingdom; the nations will also be obedient to him.

The Messiah to be blessed. The Messiah is described as reigning in a time of abundance: "He will tether his donkey to a vine, his colt to the choicest branch; he will wash his garments in wine, his robes in the blood of grapes. His eyes will be darker than wine, his teeth whiter than milk" (Gen. 49:11–12). What is described here is the abundance of the millennial kingdom where the vine will be so plentiful that a donkey will be tethered to it. Wine will be so abundant that it will affect the eyes, and the teeth will be affected by an abundance of milk. The poetic language speaks of the abundance that will be evident in the millennial kingdom (Isa. 61:6–7; 65:21–25; Zech. 3:10). The most important point in this prophecy is that the Messiah will come from the tribe of Judah.

Prophecy Concerning David

The Messiah to descend from David. The important point of the Davidic covenant is that the Messiah coming from Judah will descend through David. This is clearly revealed in the Davidic covenant (2 Sam. 7:5–17). This covenant will be treated in greater detail later. The fact that the messianic genealogy will come through David is declared to David by Nathan the prophet: "The LORD declares to you that the LORD himself will establish a house for you: When your days are over and you rest with your fathers, I will raise up your offspring to succeed you, who will come from your own body, and I will establish his kingdom" (vv. 11–12). The facts of David's sure place in the lineage is clearly stated: "Your house and your kingdom will endure forever before me; your throne will be established forever" (v. 16).

The throne of David to continue forever. As indicated in the promise, David's line and his throne will continue forever (2 Sam. 7:16). The importance of this prophecy will be considered later under the treatment of the Davidic covenant. The providence of God in selecting, maintaining, and fulfilling the line from Abraham to the Messiah becomes increasingly clear as the Old Testament unfolds. The Messiah would be a son of Abraham, of the house of Jacob, of the tribe of Judah, and of the family of David.

The Genealogies of Joseph and Mary Fulfilling Prophecy

The genealogical line of Solomon to Joseph. The genealogies listed in Matthew and Luke bring out the distinctive genealogy of Joseph as contrasted with the genealogy of Mary. In keeping with the Gospel of Matthew, the validity of Christ's claim to be the Son of David and the rightful King and Messiah is supported by the genealogy from David to Joseph that is provided. This genealogy comes from Abraham to David and then through Solomon to Joseph. The purpose of this genealogy is to determine the legitimacy and legality of Christ's claim to be the promised messianic King. The genealogy of Mary, descendant of Nathan, a son of David, provides the physical link with David.

Some unusual features characterize these genealogies. The Gospel of Matthew contains only fourteen generations from Abraham to David, fourteen generations from David to the Captivity, and fourteen generations from the Captivity to Christ. The genealogy is not intended to be complete, for there are notable omissions, such as that of Ahaziah, Joash, and Amaziah, and kings mentioned in 1 Chronicles 3:11–12. In Matthew 1:13–15, which records the genealogy from Zerubbabel to Joseph, names are mentioned that are not found in the Old Testament.

The two genealogies separate. When the genealogy of Matthew is compared with that of Luke, it is clear that the two genealogies are entirely separate. In Luke 3:23–38 the genealogy is traced to Adam. Many believe that there are some omissions, as was common in genealogies of this kind. For instance, in Genesis 11:12 Cainan was omitted; however his name is recorded in Luke 3:36. In the genealogies of the priesthood in Ezra 7:1–5, six generations were omitted. The point of the genealogies is not so much to trace every individual involved but to provide a genuine lineage from the past to the present. The careful examination of Luke's genealogy indicates that it is the genealogy of Mary rather than of Joseph. The important difference in the genealogy appears, however, between the genealogies of David to Joseph and to Mary. The preceding genealogies are the same. The genealogy of Mary in Luke traces the lineage of Christ through Nathan, the son of David, rather than through Solomon (Luke 3:31). A question naturally arises concerning this difference in genealogies.

The curse upon the line of Jehoiachin. In the history of the apostasy preceding the Babylonian captivity, a solemn curse was put upon Jehoiachin (also called Coniah): "Record this man as if childless, a man who will not prosper in his lifetime, for none of his offspring will prosper, none will sit on the throne of David or rule anymore in Judah" (Jer. 22:30). Actually, Jehoiachin had children, but they did not survive him on the throne.

In Jeremiah 36, which records the delivery of Jeremiah's scroll to Jehoiakim, a further prophecy was given condemning this line. Jehoiakim was actually the father of Jehoiachin, but the account of Jeremiah's scroll being presented to the king and destroyed appears later in Jeremiah 36. When the king ordered the scroll cut and burned, the pronouncement was made:

> Therefore, this is what the LORD says about Jehoiakim king of Judah: He will have no one to sit on the throne of David; his body will be thrown out and exposed to the heat by day and the frost by night. I will punish him and his children and his attendants for their wickedness; I will bring on them and those living in Jerusalem and the people of Judah every disaster I pronounced against them, because they have not listened. (vv. 30–31)

Actually Jehoiachin, his son, reigned on the throne for a brief period, but he did not have a permanent reign.

The important point of this prophecy is that no descendant of Jehoiakim or Jehoiachin would be able to fulfill the messianic promise of sitting on the throne of David.

Matthew's genealogy traces the line of David through Solomon and through Jehoiakim and Jehoiachin, and no actual descendant of this line could occupy the throne of David. Matthew recorded this genealogy to show the legitimacy of the throne passing through Joseph, the legal heir of David, but actually, Jesus Christ had to come from a different line in the flesh through another son of David, Nathan. This leads to Mary, the actual mother of Christ. Accordingly, while the legal title passed to Christ through Joseph, the physical claim of being a descendant of David comes through David and Nathan instead of David and Solomon.

This line of truth also tends to confirm the doctrine of the virgin birth of Christ, for if Christ were the son of Joseph, he would not be able to sit on the throne of David in view of the curse put on that line. When the full prophecy is brought into view concerning Mary and the line from Nathan, it brings out beautifully the fact that the details of prophecy were literally fulfilled, requiring the lineage of David through Nathan to Mary instead of the cursed line of David through Solomon to Joseph. The modern tendency to gloss over the details of prophecy and arrive only at general conclusions is unfortunate in the light of the detailed study of the prophetic Word. Prophecy is found to be literal and intended for literal fulfillment.

7

Prophecy of the Future of Israel As a Nation

For a Gentile believer of the twentieth century, prophecy concerning the future of Israel may seem unimportant. However, from a prophetic perspective, the future of Israel is very important. In fact, the prophecies about Israel form the background of understanding prophecy as a whole.

One of the main causes for current confusion in understanding prophecy is the failure to take Israel-related prophecies literally. Attempts to transfer the promises relating to Israel to the church have been a major obstacle to understanding God's prophetic purposes as a whole. Once prophecies about Israel are distinguished from prophecies concerning the church or the Gentiles, the main programs of God as outlined in prophecy begin to be clear.

We can see from the analysis of Old Testament prophecy in the preceding chapters that a pattern of literal fulfillment has been established. The promise to Adam and Eve of death for disobedience was literally fulfilled. The promise of salvation, first revealed to Adam and Eve, has also unfolded in history and had its climax in the death and resurrection of Christ. The predictions of the Flood and the covenant with Noah also came to dramatic and literal fulfillment. The Abrahamic covenant, in its broad provisions as originally outlined to Abraham, has, in general, already been completely fulfilled in that Abraham became a great man who had many descendants. The line of the Messiah leading to Mary has unfolded. In all of these predictions and their fulfillment, the principle of literal fulfillment of prophecy has been confirmed.

Though there is general recognition that many of the promises given to Abraham have had literal fulfillment, the question as to whether there is yet a future for Israel as a nation is a matter of dispute principally between the amillennial and the premillennial interpretation. The amillennial interpretation, which does not believe in a millennial reign after the second coming of Christ, tends to deny any future literal fulfillment, though the possibility of spiritual revival in Israel in the present age is sometimes recognized. In contrast, the premillennial interpretation pictures the second coming of Christ as bringing in a kingdom of glorious release and freedom for Israel, the seating of Christ on the throne of David, Israel's occupation of the Promised Land, and Israel as the object of God's special divine grace. Accordingly, the question as to whether Israel still has a future as a nation becomes an important aspect of the interpretation of the prophetic account.

The Promise of the Future of Israel as Fulfilled

Pattern of literal fulfillment. As brought out in previous studies, the prediction that from the line of Abraham would come One who would be a blessing to the entire world has already been fulfilled in Christ. Additional fulfillment is found in the prophets of the Old Testament and the apostles of the New Testament as they contributed to the spiritual blessing God has bestowed on his people. The inspiration of the written Word of God is another aspect of the fulfillment of the promise of blessing. All of these factors detailing fulfilled prophecy in a literal fashion should be taken into consideration in determining whether there is a future promise to be fulfilled.

The emergence of the nation Israel. Throughout history it has become obvious that the descendants of Abraham have emerged as a nation with millions of people. In Egypt the family of seventy may have became a people of two million or more at the time of the Exodus. Though for many generations they were persecuted and reduced in number, the people of Israel today are estimated to number from 15 to 25 million inhabitants in various parts of the world. The promise that Abraham would be a father of a great nation has been given factual support in Israel's current existence in the world.

The nation Israel recognized today. Though some extremists of one kind or another attempt to explain away any literal fulfillment of the existence of Israel today, the fact is that the world as a whole has recognized Israel as a political state and has assigned her certain territories in the Middle East. The people of Israel are very conscious of their lineage, their history, their religion, and their culture, and all of this combines to make the nation Israel what it is today. Up to the present time a literal fulfillment of the promises given to Abraham has been clearly confirmed by history.

Is a Future for the Nation Israel Certain?

The question of the future of Israel is important because it determines the interpretation of so many passages of the Bible. To some, the theological arguments may seem technical, but the question simply put is whether the prophecies about Israel should be taken in their plain and natural meaning as revealing Israel's future. The debate is between the amillennial view, which claims that there is no literal Millennium after the second coming of Christ, and the premillennial position, which believes Israel has a future Millennium after this event.

The objections of amillennialism. Even a casual examination of the evidence would indicate that inasmuch as the promises to Israel have been literally fulfilled up to the present time, a continuation of this progression of fulfillment in the future may be expected. However, the amillennial view of Scripture, which denies a future Millennium after the second coming of Christ, tends to interpret prophecy in a way which voids any literal fulfillment of a future for the nation Israel. Amillennial objections take many forms, but one of their main lines of argument is the statement that the Abrahamic covenant is conditional, that the conditions have not been met, and that therefore the Abrahamic covenant will not be fulfilled in the future.

It is true that Abraham was obedient to God when he left his homeland and went to a land that God would show him. It is also true that Abraham was obedient in a number of particulars in his walk with God. On the other hand, it is also true that he was out of the will of God when he went down into Egypt, when he suggested Eliezer as his heir, and when he wanted Ishmael as his heir. His partial unbelief in God's promises later turned to complete faith. The promises given to Abraham by their nature, however, could not be conditional in that God promised Abraham fulfillment *forever,* as is illustrated in the many promises and reiterations of the Abrahamic covenant.

It is true that partial fulfillment of the Abrahamic covenant to any one generation and God's blessing on that generation were contingent on their obedience. The history of Israel reveals that they were frequently disobedient. In fact, Israel went down to Egypt in the time of Jacob when it was questionable whether they should have taken that step. It is also clear that, after their return to their land, they departed from God, a fact that resulted in the Assyrian and Babylonian captivities. When Israel rejected Christ, they were scattered all over the world in fulfillment of God's warning concerning disobedience.

The fact is, however, that in the midst of Israel's apostasy and sin, God gave them additional revelation concerning their future restoration. The prophet Jeremiah recorded that Israel would come back to their home after seventy years of captivity in Babylon (29:10). This was literally fulfilled, though Israel at the time was in apostasy and was spiritually unprepared to fulfill God's purpose. It is also true that through Jeremiah, in the midst of Israel's apostasy, God gave promises of Israel's ultimate blessing (see 23:5–8, a passage we will consider more at length later). Also through Jeremiah the new covenant, with its promise of ultimate blessing upon Israel, was given (31:10–14; this covenant will be considered more at length later). In other words, it is clear from Scripture that the certainty of the ultimate fulfillment of the prophecy was such that even Israel's apostasy would not thwart God's ultimate purpose.

The fulfillment of the promise will be realized by those who are spiritually prepared to receive it—that is, by the godly remnant at the time of the second coming of Christ. The fact that there will be a godly remnant and that God will rescue them and place them in the millennial kingdom is a matter of specific prophecy, and the disobedience of Israel as a nation will not deter God from fulfilling this prophecy in the future. In spite of these obvious evidences that there is a future for Israel, a number of objections are brought up by the amillenarian interpretation.

Amillenarians point to the judgment on Nineveh, which was predicted by Jonah but not inflicted because of their repentance, as evidence that blessing follows obedience. The answer to this, of course, is that this was not a covenant arrangement, and it is true that their deliverance for 150 years resulted from their repentance.

The judgment on Eli the priest for his sin is cited as evidence of an implied condition of obedience in connection with God's appointment of his line as the priestly line (1 Sam. 2:30; cf. Ex. 29:9; Jer. 18:1–18; Ezek. 3:18–19). But Eli lived under the conditional Mosaic covenant.

In these illustrations it is clear that blessing followed obedience and punishment followed disobedience, but in neither of these cases is there an ultimate promise in question. In connection with God's dealings with the nations, he was free to pluck up and cast down. He was also free to discipline any one generation of Israelites, as is illustrated many times in the Old Testament, but the continuing promise was made in spite of their apostasy and sin. When God proposed that he put aside the children of Israel and start over with Moses, there was immediate reference to the fact that God had a covenant with Israel (Ex. 32:13–14), and God did not bring this judgment on Israel.

In the Old Testament the rite of circumcision is cited as a condition for blessing. This related to the individual—that is, an uncircumcised Israelite was cut off from the covenant promise— but did not alter the promise to the nation.

Amillenarians use Esau as an illustration because he was excluded from some of the promises of blessing. This again is based on a misunderstanding. God's covenant with Abraham did not promise blessing on all his descendants but only on some; and in the extension of the Abrahamic covenant, Esau and Ishmael were expressly excluded, whereas the line of blessing went from Abraham to Isaac to Jacob and on to the twelve sons of Jacob.

Sometimes amillenarians appeal to the obedience of Christ as the ultimate argument for their position. It clearly was necessary for Christ to go to the cross to provide grace in order to fulfill the promises given to Israel, but this very argument works against the amillennial contention because the final restoration of Israel does not rest on their obedience but on the grace of God. A nation that does not deserve God's blessings will receive them, much as Christians, who do not deserve God's blessings because of their imperfections, are showered with his blessings in both time and eternity.

Amillenarians offer other objections besides the conditional nature of the promises. Some amillenarians point to partial fulfillment of the promises as sufficient to answer the problem. The development of Israel into a large nation, of course, was a partial fulfillment of the promise, but this was not what the promise required, since God promised Israel blessings that would continue for eternity.

Some amillenarians hold that the promise of the land was fulfilled in the time of Solomon, but this does not explain the many references in the Major and Minor Prophets to the land as subject to yet future fulfillment. Even in Solomon's day the land was not completely possessed though much of it was put under tribute.

Accordingly, the amillennial arguments, though numerous, are based on the insupportable premise that all the promises of God are conditional or have already been fulfilled. If the promises are conditional, there would be no sure fulfillment of any prophecy, because there are always uncertainties and contingencies involved. The ultimate question is "What has God promised?" If he has predicted a future event, then there should be no question concerning its future fulfillment.

Support for the unconditional character of the Abrahamic covenant. In denial of the concept that God's covenant with Abraham is conditional, a number of reasons can be cited as support for the concept of absolute certainty of the fulfillment of God's covenants.

All agree that the Mosaic covenant was conditional—that is, its blessings were conditioned on obedience, and its judgments would follow disobedience. But the other covenants of Israel, such as the Abrahamic covenant, the Palestinian covenant, the Davidic covenant, and the new covenant, are unconditional as far as their ultimate fulfillment is concerned, even though the blessings of the covenant in any given generation may be sacrificed by disobedience. When the Abrahamic covenant is repeated in passages subsequent to its original revelation, it is declared to be eternal and, therefore, necessarily unconditional (Gen. 17:7, 13, 19; 1 Chron. 16:16–17; Ps. 105:9–10).

Likewise, the Palestinian covenant is everlasting in its character (Ezek. 16:60), as are the Davidic covenant (2 Sam. 7:13, 16, 19; 1 Chron. 17:12; 22:10; Isa. 55:3; Ezek. 37:25) and the new covenant, which relates to Israel's future (Isa. 61:8; Jer. 32:40; 50:5; Heb. 13:20). In the nature of an eternal promise, conditions would be irrelevant, because the promise could not be eternal if contingent on obedience.

The Abrahamic covenant was subject to repetition and enlargement in subsequent Scriptures, but in none of these were the promised blessings conditioned on obedience.

The Abrahamic covenant, particularly the promise of the land (to be treated later), was solemnly confirmed by the shedding of blood (Gen. 15:7–21; Jer. 34:18). The geographic boundaries of the land were stated in Genesis 15:18–21. These promises were given at a time when Abraham was approaching God in unbelief, and it was to sustain and support what faith Abraham had that the covenant was solemnly confirmed.

The fact that circumcision was required of individuals who wanted to claim blessing under the Abrahamic covenant does not change its unconditional character. It is clear that individuals who were not circumcised were excluded from the promise. But this did not alter the fact that the promise would be fulfilled to the nation as a whole. Circumcision was a physical sign that they belonged under the covenant blessing (Gen. 17:9–14).

It is important to realize that when the covenant of Abraham was repeated to Isaac and Jacob, no conditions were mentioned. In fact, God's covenant with Isaac came at a time when he was trying to leave the land and was used as a deterrent to keep him in the Promised Land (Gen. 26:2–5). Likewise, the covenant was confirmed with Jacob as he was running away from home because of Esau (27:41–43). He also received the covenant promise without conditions (28:13–15).

As previously pointed out, even in the apostasy of Jeremiah's day, the eternal promises were not conditioned, and Jeremiah, in the midst of the apostate generation in which he lived, was given the revelation of the certain future of Israel (cf. Jer. 23:5–8; 30:5–11).

One of the most determinative passages on the unconditional character of the Abrahamic covenant is found in Hebrews 6:13–18:

When God made his promise to Abraham, since there was no one greater for him to swear by, he swore by himself, saying, "I will surely bless you and give you many descendants." And so after waiting patiently, Abraham received what was promised. Men swear by someone greater than themselves, and the oath confirms what is said and puts an end to all argument. Because God wanted to make the unchanging nature of his purpose very clear to the heirs of what was promised, he confirmed it with an oath. God did this so that, by two unchangeable things in which it is impossible for God to lie, we who have fled to take hold of the hope offered to us may be greatly encouraged.

In this passage God's promise to Abraham is declared to be immutable and unchangeable. His purpose is declared to be "unchanging" (v. 17). This passage is especially significant in view of the fact that the religious leaders of Israel had rejected Christ and caused his crucifixion. In spite of this fact, the book of Hebrews points out that Israel has a certain and unchangeable promise of the fulfillment of the covenant. (See chapter 8.)

Many amillenarians, having abandoned the idea that the Abrahamic covenant is conditional, now favor interpreting it nonliterally. One approach is to regard Abraham's descendants, whether Israelites or other nations, as representing the church and thereby wiping out the necessity of a future for Israel.

The literal land, literal physical descendants, literal kings, and, ultimately, a literal Messiah combine to support a literal interpretation of the Abrahamic covenant. The Old Testament consistently supports a literal interpretation of the covenant, and the New Testament adds its confirming word, including the prophecy of a millennial kingdom following the Second Coming. The variety of solutions offered by the amillenarians themselves is evidence that none of their solutions really solve their problem of denying a future Millennium and a future for the nation Israel.

The Meaning of the Name Israel

The term Israel *as used in the Scriptures.* One way to avoid the conclusion that the Abrahamic covenant is subject to future literal fulfillment involving a future for the nation Israel is to redefine the term *Israel* so that it includes the church, thus considering the promises to Israel unliteral. Some amillenarians use this approach, claiming that Israel does not have a future because her future will be fulfilled by the church composed of Jews and Gentiles.

This raises a question as to how the term *Israel* is used in the Bible itself. The terms *Israel* and *Israelite* are found approximately 2300 times in the Old Testament, and in every case they refer to those racially descended from Jacob. In the New Testament Israel is mentioned approximately 75 times. Also, Israel is referred to as *the Jews* 80 times in the Old Testament and about 170 times in the New Testament. In all of these many references, only one or two passages leave any question concerning the reference to the twelve tribes of Israel. Obviously, the burden of proof would be on anyone who suggests that the term *Israel* includes Gentiles, though it has been characteristic of amillennialism to affirm dogmatically that Israel is a synonym for the church in the present age. In the last generation, even among amillenarians, there has been a trend away from this doctrine for a number of reasons.

One of the problems faced by those who want to make the church and Israel synonymous is that though there are many promises of blessing for Israel, there are also threats of cursing, and this complicates the identification of the two. Usually amillenarians, who hold that the church is Israel, claim only the blessings. Other problems arise because of the sheer weight of the hundreds of references to Israel that obviously do not include the church. Also in Scripture Israel is constantly contrasted with other entities.

Israel contrasted with the Gentiles. In the New Testament as in the Old there are numerous messages addressed to Israel, and this continues after the institution of the church in Acts 2 (cf. Acts 3:12; 4:8, 10; 5:21, 31, 35; 21:28; et al.). In these references it is obvious that only those who are racially Israelites are included. The same is true of Paul's prayer for Israel's salvation (Rom. 10:1), which he bases on the fact that he also is an Israelite.

The use of the term *Jew* beginning in the Old Testament in the book of Esther and continuing in the New Testament, clearly describes those who are Israelites and not Gentiles. This is made obvious in the distinction of 1 Corinthians 10:32, where the threefold division of the human race into (1) Gentiles, (2) Jews, and (3) the church of God makes clear that these three separate divisions continue in the present age.

In Paul's discussion of Israel's situation in his day, he points out that the Israelites have many particular privileges (Rom. 9:4–5), none of which pertain to the church. Paul's fervent prayer for Israel (vv. 2–3) is another instance of the term *Israel,* referring to twelve tribes and not to Gentiles.

The New Testament also points out that while the Jews had certain privileges, Gentiles were excluded from them, as in Paul's statement in Ephesians 2:12: "Remember that at that time you were separate from Christ, excluded from citizenship in Israel and foreigners to the covenants of the promise, without hope and without God in the world." This and other passages clearly distinguish Israel from the Gentiles.

The church contrasted with unsaved Israel. Amillenarians agree that Scripture distinguishes Israel from the church, because unsaved Israelites are obviously not part of the church. If natural Israel, including the unsaved, exists apart from the church, it is impossible to transfer promises given to the nation Israel to the church, which is composed of those who are saved in the present age.

In continuance of this contrast, the New Testament speaks of a future program for Israel as distinct from God's program for the church. In the classic passage in Romans 9–11, where the apostle is tracing Israel's relationship to what he has previously discussed in the book of Romans, he raises the specific question as to whether God has cast off the nation of Israel: "I ask then: Did God reject his people? By no means! I am an Israelite myself, a descendant of Abraham, from the tribe of Benjamin. God did not reject his people, whom he foreknew" (11:1–2). God has a program for Israel that goes beyond his program in the present age for Israel as a part of the church.

Paul recognized the present lost state of many in Israel. As a nation Israel has turned from God and is not operating under God's blessing. This is illustrated in the olive tree with the natural branches, referring to Israel, broken off, and Gentiles, represented by a wild olive shoot, grafted in (Rom. 11:17). Paul warns Gentiles as a group, however, that God has a future for Israel nationally and that "all Israel will be saved" (v. 26). By this he means, not that every individual will be saved spiritually, but that Israel as a nation will be delivered when the Deliverer comes from Zion, referring to the second coming of Christ (v. 26). These promises, developed so fully in Romans 11, will be treated later. Sufficient for the present study are the facts that the nation of Israel and the church are contrasted and that the nation of Israel has a future.

The Scriptures also contrast spiritual Israel with Gentile Christian believers. Here the question as to whether Gentile Christians are designated as Israelites is faced squarely. Some amillenarians teach that the church takes the place of Israel completely and that both Gentiles and Israelites fulfill the promises originally given to Israel.

Of the hundreds of passages referring to Israel and to the Jews, only two or three could possibly be interpreted as confusing the Gentiles and Israel.

According to Romans 9:6, "It is not as though God's word had failed. For not all who are descended from Israel are Israel." What is being contrasted here is the difference between those in Israel who are spiritual, or believers, and those who are only natural, that is, descendants of Jacob but not believers. In each generation Israelites who are believers inherit the promises. Gentile believers are not in view.

As has been pointed out, the promises given to Abraham concerning the nation Israel are narrowed to Isaac, not Ishmael, and to Jacob, not Esau, and to the twelve sons of Jacob. Only descendants of Jacob inherit the the broad promises of God relating to the nation. Among the descendants of Jacob, however, some are true believers and inherit the spiritual promises as well as the national promises. This is what Paul refers to as the election of grace (Rom. 11:5-10). In the present age Israelites who are saved become part of the church, but unbelieving Israelites are lost and are declared to be blinded.

In Romans 9:25 Paul quotes Hosea 2:23, "I will call them 'my people' who are not my people; and I will call her 'my loved one' who is not my loved one." This passage has been cited as an instance where Israel and the church are viewed together and Gentiles and Jews are considered as one people. The Hosea passage, however, is contrasting Israelites who are not the Lord's people, because of their lack of faith, with those who are true Israelites who believe in God. In the Hebrew of Hosea 2:23 there is a play on words where "Not my loved one" is a translation of the Hebrew *Lo-Ruhamah* and is contrasted with "Not my people," which is a translation of the Hebrew *Lo-Ammi*. This is quoted in Romans, not to merge the Gentiles and Israel, but to serve as an application. Just as God would bless some in Israel who, before they believed in Christ, were not of true Israel, so God would bless Gentiles who were not formerly saved. It is a matter of application rather than interpretation, and there is no reason here to confuse Gentiles with Israel. However, God does deal with them in a similar way in this passage. Both Israelites who believe and Israelites who do not believe are genuine descendants of Jacob, but only those who believe are saved. And the racial distinction between Jew and Gentile is observed.

Amillenarians also cite Galatians 6:15–16 as evidence that the church can be viewed as Israel: "Neither circumcision nor uncircumcision means anything; what counts is a new creation. Peace and mercy to all who follow this rule, even to the Israel of God." The NIV translation, however, is questionable, since the word *even* is a translation of the Greek *kai*, which normally means "and." A more accurate translation is, "and upon the Israel of God," as in the NASB, ASV, KJV, NKJV, and NRSV. What Paul is saying is that he wishes peace and mercy upon all who are believers but especially upon the Israel of God—that is, Israelites who are saved. Though the NIV translation may have pleased amillennial scholars, a grammatically correct translation would preserve the distinction between Israel and Gentiles, in keeping with dispensational and premillennial teaching.

If the passages in Romans 9 and Galatians 6 are considered in light of hundreds of passages where the word *Israel* is distinctly a reference to the descendants of Jacob, the overwhelming evidence is in favor of maintaining this distinction. Even if the amillennial interpretation is upheld, it still does not generate a broad principle that any promise given to Israel can be claimed by the church or that the promises given to Israel are canceled. Even amillenarians tend to avoid this conclusion in current literature.

Have the promises to the nation Israel been canceled? It should be clear from the historical evidence that, up to the present, God has faithfully kept his promises to Israel. Israel is still a great nation and is still blessed by God. Through Israel the Messiah has come, and many of the blessings promised have already been fulfilled. The question that remains is whether there is any scriptural evidence that Israel has been cast aside.

As pointed out briefly, the evidence of Romans 11 is to the contrary, where Paul promises a future for Israel as a nation. A few passages, however, should be considered as possibly teaching that Israel has been cast aside. In Matthew 21:43, referring to the rejection of Christ by his generation, Christ said, "Therefore I tell you that the kingdom of God will be taken away from you and given to a people who will produce its fruit." What is meant by the principal terms "kingdom of God" and "a people who will produce its fruit"? Matthew mainly uses the term "kingdom of heaven," but here is one of the few references to the "kingdom of God." In Matthew as well as other New Testament writings, the kingdom of God always refers to holy angels or people who are saved. The program of salvation, therefore, will be taken away from those who reject Christ as the Capstone.

But who are the people who are referred to as not producing fruit? Some are the scribes and Pharisees who would never be saved as long as they persisted in their unbelief. Since the early church was predominantly Jewish, this passage cannot be interpreted as taking the kingdom of God away from Israel. It is also clear that the kingdom of God did not refer to the millennial kingdom. Taking all factors into consideration, what Jesus is saying is that those who reject the King will have the kingdom of God taken away from them and given to any people who produce its fruit—both Jews and Gentiles. This is exactly what has happened in the church; both Jews and Gentiles who are saved become a part of the kingdom of God. In any case, it is clear that the Gentiles as a whole do not inherit the kingdom of God any more than unbelieving Israel does in the present age.

Another passage amillenarians use to try to justify the idea that Israel as a nation has been cast aside forever and its promises nullified is found in Romans 11:1–32, a passage already dealt with in part. However, as the opening verses of this chapter indicate, when Paul poses this question, "Did God reject his people?" his emphatic answer is, "By no means!" (Rom. 11:1). As the chapter unfolds, the answer is that God has not rejected his people because he has a present purpose for them—becoming members of the body of Christ through faith in Christ—and a future for them when the present age is over and deliverance, the second coming of Christ, occurs.

On the basis of the evidence, Scripture supports the conclusion that Israel has a great future as a nation. The details of this future will be considered in later chapters.

The return of millions of Jews to the land of Israel in the twentieth century has focused the attention of the world on this tiny land. Does the Jew have any hope of ever having peace and tranquillity in his ancient land? After all, does it belong to the Arab world or to Israel? Several wars and the extension of Israel to the west bank of Jordan have caused continual tension between Israel's claim on the land and Arab resistance to her expansion. From a theological point of view, the return of Jews to Israel has again raised the question of Israel's future. Many church scholars have held that Israel has no future as a nation, and for many years they predicted that Israel would never go back to her land.

The return of Jews to Israel has renewed the study of what the Bible promises Israel in regard to the future. Many have concluded that the Word of God promises Israel ultimate possession, and if she is already possessing a portion of her land, it raises the questions of whether the prophecies about the end of the present age are about to be fulfilled and whether the second coming of Christ may be near.

8

The Promised Land

One of the important aspects of the Abrahamic covenant was the promise of possession of the land. God had said to Abraham, "Leave your country, your people and your father's household and go to the land I will show you" (Gen. 12:1). Upon Abraham's arrival in the Promised Land, God repeated this promise: "To your offspring I will give this land" (v. 7).

Various Interpretations of the Promise

Simple as the promise is, the interpretation of this promise has been a watershed in biblical prophecy. Questions have been raised as to whether this promise of the land was unequivocal or unconditional and as to whether the fulfillment would be literal.

Amillennial and postmillennial interpretations. Because a literal fulfillment of the promise would require occupation of the land after the Second Coming, amillenarians and postmillenarians, in keeping with their general interpretation of prophecy, must find some way to avoid a literal interpretation of this promise. Two broad approaches have been adopted.

First, the most common amillennial and postmillennial approach today is to hold that the promise is not a promise of literal land but rather a promise of heaven. Because the Old Testament never has that form of interpretation, appeal is made to Hebrews 11:9–10, where it is said concerning Abraham: "By faith he made his home in the promised land like a stranger in a foreign country; he lived in tents, as did Isaac and Jacob, who were heirs with him of the same promise. For he was looking forward to the city with foundations, whose architect and builder is God." The reference to the city is commonly interpreted as meaning the New Jerusalem in eternity future. Undoubtedly, Abraham did have such an eternal hope though this is not stated in detail in Genesis. This does not, however, affect the promise of the land, which was to be fulfilled in time and not in eternity according to a literal interpretation. Abraham had hope both for the possession of the land in the Millennium and for residence in the New Jerusalem in eternity.

In searching for evidence in support of a nonliteral interpretation of the promise, one soon becomes aware that the Old Testament in its many repetitions of the promise always implies that it is a literal promise and offers hope of literal fulfillment. Accordingly, some amillenarians and postmillenarians have adopted a second point of view—namely, that the promise is literal; Israel was promised literal possession of the land, but it is a conditional promise that will never be fulfilled because of Israel's disobedience.

There is a measure of truth in this approach, because Moses and later prophets warned the children of Israel that if they did not obey God, they would be driven out of the land. This was fulfilled in the Assyrian and Babylonian captivities as well as in the worldwide dispersion of A.D. 70. Old Testament prophecy, however, goes on to explain that though Israelites were being dispersed and scattered, they would be regathered and brought into their Promised Land. This will become evident as we consider later repetitions of this promise in the Old Testament.

The basic error in this amillennial approach is a failure to comprehend that just as the church is saved by the grace of God, so Israel will be regathered and restored by the grace of God, and it does not depend upon human faithfulness. Israel does not deserve to be restored and given the land, but God's initial promise to Abraham was gracious and unconditional. Though the people of Israel were dispersed from the land, they were also promised that they would be regathered from all over the world.

The premillennial interpretation. Those who find evidence in Scripture for a kingdom on earth after the second coming of Christ, in keeping with premillennial interpretation, can take this promise literally. That is, Israel will actually be given her Promised Land in the period following the second coming of Christ when Christ will reign on earth. This interpretation is confirmed throughout the Old Testament.

The premillennial interpretation is also in keeping with Abraham's understanding. In God's original instruction, he told Abraham to leave Ur of the Chaldeans and go to the land that he would show Abraham. If the land were merely a type of heaven, Abraham could have remained in Ur of the Chaldeans and believed in his ultimate possession of a place in the New Jerusalem. However, the land became a very important factor in Abraham's understanding of the prophecy. Possession of the land was obviously linked to the question of whether Abraham would have an heir, and the fulfillment of the promise of his descendants is linked to the promise of the land.

Abraham was not only given the original promise but also had this promised confirmed repeatedly in later experiences in his life. In connection with Lot being separated from Abraham in Genesis 13, God told Abraham, "Lift up your eyes from where you are and look north and south, east and west. All the land that you see I will give to you and your offspring forever. I will make your offspring like the dust of the earth, so that if anyone could count the dust, then your offspring could be counted. Go, walk through the length and breadth of the land, for I am giving it to you" (vv. 14–17). It should be obvious that this promise to Abraham related to the physical land that he would actually see with his eyes, something that would never be true of the New Jerusalem in Abraham's lifetime. Further confirmation was given to Abraham when he began to question whether he would have literal offspring. In confirming the fact that he would have an heir, God said to Abraham, " 'Look up at the heavens and count the stars—if indeed you can count them.' Then he said to him, 'So shall your offspring be' " (15:5).

Later on the same day God confirmed his covenant with Abraham regarding the land in a solemn ceremony in which blood was shed and the boundaries of the land were given, as stated in Genesis 15:18, "On that day the LORD made a covenant with Abram and said, 'To your descendants I give this land, from the river of Egypt to the great river, the Euphrates.'" There follows a list of the heathen tribes that lived in that area at that time. Heaven is not described even allegorically as the area between the river of Egypt and the Euphrates. If a promise is interpreted nonliterally, there must be some correspondence between the promise and a nonliteral interpretation, and in this case the area was occupied by heathen tribes—certainly not typical of heaven.

Abraham had another confirmation of the promise at the time it was announced that Sarah would have a child. At that time God said, "The whole land of Canaan, where you are now an alien, I will give as an everlasting possession to you and your descendants after you; and I will be their God" (Gen. 17:8). The subsequent birth of Isaac (21:1–3) was no doubt considered by Abraham another confirmation not only of his promised descendants but also of the Promised Land. It is significant that those who uphold the amillennial and postmillennial point of view do not trace the promise through these various confirmations of the promise to Abraham because the emphasis is clearly on the literal fulfillment of the promise.

The Promise in Relation to Isaac and Jacob

The promise of the land given to Isaac. The birth of Isaac was a confirmation of God's purpose to give Abraham heirs. Isaac was also designated as the promised seed instead of Ishmael. Further confirmation is found in the fact that Isaac himself had the promise of the land repeated to him in Genesis 26 when God told him not to go down to Egypt:

> Stay in this land for a while, and I will be with you and will bless you. For to you and your descendants I will give all these lands and will confirm the oath I swore to your father Abraham. I will make your descendants as numerous as the stars in the sky and will give them all these lands, and through your offspring all nations on earth will be blessed, because Abraham obeyed me and kept my requirements, my commands, my decrees and my laws (vv. 3–5).

Throughout this promise there is repetition of reference to the land in which Isaac was living, the same land being promised to his descendants and his offspring. It is significant that the promise is related to Abraham's obedience, not to Isaac's, as the promise now becomes immutable and certain of fulfillment.

The promise in relation to Jacob. Just as Isaac was born in Abraham's old age, so Jacob and Esau were born when Isaac was sixty years old. Scripture is clear that Jacob, the younger of the twins, was selected to be the promised heir rather than Esau. Before their birth, Rebekah, questioning God about the presence of twins and was instructed by God:

> *Two nations are in your womb,*
> *   and two peoples from within you will be separated;*
> *one people will be stronger than the other,*
> *   and the older will serve the younger. (Gen. 25:23)*

Because of the antagonism between Jacob and Esau stemming from Jacob's purchase of Esau's birthright, Rebekah sent Jacob back to her homeland, Haran, with instructions to seek a wife from her relatives.

On the journey to Haran God revealed himself to Jacob in a dream as recorded in Genesis 28:12–15:

> He had a dream in which he saw a stairway resting on the earth, with its top reaching to heaven, and the angels of God were ascending and descending on it. There above it stood the LORD, and he said: 'I am the LORD, the God of your father Abraham and the God of Isaac. I will give you and your descendants the land on which you are lying. Your descendants will be like the dust of the earth, and you will spread out to the west and to the east, to the north and to the south. All peoples on earth will be blessed through you and your offspring. I am with you and will watch over you wherever you go, and I will bring you back to this land. I will not leave you until I have done what I have promised you.

God not only promised a posterity to Jacob, fulfilled in his twelve sons, but also that the rest of the covenant given to Abraham would be fulfilled in him—that is, he would have many descendants and would bring blessing to all peoples of the earth. In keeping with this, God repeated the promise of the land and pledged to bring Jacob back to it. A careful study of these passages makes clear that the promise of the land was intrinsic to the whole covenant given to Abraham. Inasmuch as Abraham became a great man, had a great posterity, and brought blessing to the whole world through Christ, it is reasonable to assume that the rest of the Abrahamic covenant will be fulfilled just as literally as these provisions. The nonliteral or conditional interpretation of these promises is not supported in Scripture.

The Promise of the Land

The departure of the children of Israel for Egypt. In anticipation of the fact that Israel would go down into Egypt and return, God had told Abraham, "Know for certain that your descendants will be strangers in a country not their own, and they will be enslaved and mistreated four hundred years. But I will punish the nation they serve as slaves, and afterward they will come out with great possessions" (Gen. 15:13–14). The departure from the land and settlement in Egypt were accomplished when Joseph invited his family to come and dwell in Egypt during the famine. As the subsequent history of Israel demonstrates, they grew from a family of about seventy to a nation of two to three million in the four hundred years they were in Egypt.

In considering the question as to whether the promise of the land was literal, one must realize that the promise of going down into Egypt was literal, not spiritual. Israel did not simply depart from God spiritually; they physically left the land and went to Egypt. It is also significant that the promise of their return was literal. The book of Exodus and subsequent Scriptures record their departure from Egypt and their arrival in the Promised Land.

The physical exodus of Israel from Egypt to the Promised Land is a subject of five major books of the Old Testament—Exodus, Leviticus, Numbers, Deuteronomy, and Joshua. All conservative interpreters of Scripture, whether amillennial, postmillennial, or premillennial, have to acknowledge that the prophecy of their departing from the Promised Land to a strange land and their literal return is a matter of history. It is also significant that Scripture devotes four books to this massive movement of more than two million individuals from one land to another. In the process, God miraculously worked on Israel's behalf and gave them the foundation for the Mosaic Law that was to govern their lives until the time of Christ.

The call of Moses. The early chapters of the book of Exodus record the birth of Moses and the background of Israel's slavery in Egypt. Moses' providential rescue and adoption by Pharaoh's daughter and his thorough education in the king's palace were to prepare him to be the leader of Israel as well as the writer of the Pentateuch. After fleeing Egypt, Moses resided in the desert for forty years, and while there he received the call at the burning bush to return to Israel. Though a reluctant leader, he was aided by his brother Aaron in his contest with Pharaoh.

The plagues of Egypt. The background of Israel's exodus from Egypt was a series of miraculous plagues which God inflicted upon the Egyptians before they were willing to let the children of Israel go. In the process, Moses' leadership and appointment by God were confirmed. After the tenth plague, Pharaoh allowed the children of Israel to leave.

The forty years in the wilderness. At the outset of their departure from Egypt, Israel experienced the miracle of deliverance through the Red Sea in which Pharaoh and his armies perished. Their faith was soon tested by the desert's lack of water and food, but God miraculously supplied them.

In the wilderness Israel received the Law of Moses which was to govern their lives for centuries. With it came the appointment of the priests, the construction of the tabernacle, and the system of sacrifices that characterized the Law. In spite of the many evidences of a supernatural God caring for them when they came to Kadesh-Barnea, Israel made the fatal mistake of doubting God's ability to give them the land that he had promised. Once again, this emphasizes the importance of the land in God's program for Israel. When they sent out the twelve spies, only two, Joshua and Caleb, were willing to take the stand that God would give the people of Israel their Promised Land. Because of their unbelief, Israel was condemned to forty years of wandering in the wilderness, enduring the hardships of desert life. But they were miraculously sustained by manna from heaven and water out of the rock. Scripture records Israel's series of failures to trust God's promise to care for them in fulfillment of his pledge that they would return to the land.

In the book of Deuteronomy, where the major elements of the Law were rehearsed by Moses late in his life, God solemnly warned Israel how important it was to obey the law. If Israel did obey the law, God would allow them to live in the land in the blessings which God would shower upon them, but if they did not, they would be driven out of the land.

The solemn words of Moses are the tragic prophecy of Israel's experience of dispersion from the land:

> Just as it pleased the LORD to make you prosper and increase in number, so it will please him to ruin and destroy you. You will be uprooted from the land you are entering to possess. Then the LORD will scatter you among all nations, from one end of the earth to the other. There you will worship other gods—gods of wood and stone, which neither you nor your fathers have known. Among those nations you will find no repose, no resting place for the sole of your foot. There the LORD will give you an anxious mind, eyes weary with longing, and a despairing heart. You will live in constant suspense, filled with dread both night and day, never sure of your life. In the morning you will say, "If only it were evening!" and in the evening, "If only it were morning!"— because of the terror that will fill your hearts and the sights that your eyes will see. (Deut. 28:63–67)

These verses were literally fulfilled as are many other promises in relation to the land. The point is made clearly in Scripture that though the ultimate possession of the land at the time of the second coming of Christ will certainly be fulfilled, the possession of the land by any one generation of Israel was dependent on the grace of God and the obedience of Israel to their law.

The possession of the land under Joshua. As the book of Joshua records, the children of Israel eventually crossed over the Jordan from the east bank and began the conquest of the Promised Land at Jericho. As God made plain to Joshua, he was operating on the basic Abrahamic promise of the land for Israel, but possession of it in his generation depended on his act of faith in possessing it.

God told Joshua, "Moses my servant is dead. Now then, you and all these people, get ready to cross the Jordan River into the land I am about to give to them—to the Israelites. I will give you every place where you set your foot, as I promised Moses. Your territory will extend from the desert to Lebanon, and from the great river, the Euphrates—all the Hittite country—to the Great Sea on the west. No one will be able to stand up against you all the days of your life. As I was with Moses, so I will be with you; I will never leave you nor forsake you" (Josh. 1:2–5). God's promise to Joshua was literally fulfilled in his lifetime. Every portion of the land that Israel possessed was theirs. However, as the book of Joshua makes plain, they did not conquer all the Promised Land. Joshua 21:43–45 says: "So the LORD gave Israel all the land he had sworn to give their forefathers, and they took possession of it and settled there. . . . Not one of all the LORD's good promises to the house of Israel failed; every one was fulfilled." Some have attempted to interpret this as complete fulfillment of what God had promised Abraham. However, this was not the case. The promise of possession was a promise of possession forever, which was not fulfilled in Joshua's case, since later the children of Israel once again were dispersed. The book of Judges makes plain that they still had to conquer much of the land. According to Judges 1:19, "The LORD was with the men of Judah. They took possession of the hill country, but they were unable to drive the people from the plains, because they had iron chariots." Judges 1:21 says, "The Benjamites, however, failed to dislodge the Jebusites, who were living in Jerusalem; to this day the Jebusites live there with the Benjamites."

According to Judges 1:27, "Manasseh did not drive out the people of Beth Shan or Taanach or Dor or Ibleam or Megiddo and their surrounding settlements, for the Canaanites were determined to live in that land." The passage goes on to say that they "never drove them out completely" (v. 28). Likewise, the Canaanites in Gezer and the Canaanites in Kitron or Nahalol and many others as listed in Judges 1:29–36 remained in possession of portions of the Promised Land. Those who were left in the land became thorns in the side of Israel, and their altars and false gods became a snare to Israel (Judg. 2:1–3).

Seven Centuries of Partial Possession of the Land

Israel's problems in the period of the Judges. As the book of Judges records, Israel went through a series of apostasies and restorations, each time sinking lower than before. In the process, the promise of the land was not fulfilled.

In response to Israel's spiritual need, God raised up the prophet Samuel, who became the last of the judges and the first of the order of prophets, and through him Israel was led back to some extent into the worship and service of God. At the close of Samuel's life, at God's instructions, Samuel anointed Saul and later David to be kings over Israel. Partially under Saul but extensively through David, more of the land was possessed than ever before, and David set up a glorious and wealthy kingdom.

Israel under Solomon. Under Solomon, the kingdom of Israel grew to an extent of wealth and recognition never achieved before or after. The extensive wealth and influence of Solomon is portrayed in Scripture (1 Kings 4:1–34; 2 Chron. 9:13–28). "He ruled over all the kings from the River to the land of the Philistines, as far as the border of Egypt" (2 Chron. 9:26). On the basis of this, some amillenarians hold that this fulfilled the promise of the land to Abraham—that is, that Solomon extended his kingdom over the entire area promised in Genesis 15:18–21. A careful reading of the text, however, makes clear that while Solomon put the entire area under his control in the sense that he demanded tribute from these countries, they were not actually incorporated into the state of Israel. This made their defection easy once Solomon died and the power of the kingdom began to decline. The extent to which the promises were fulfilled to Solomon also failed to fulfill the requirement that the land would be possessed forever, for Solomon's influence was limited to his reign. Further evidence is found for the fact that Solomon's reign did not fulfill the Abrahamic covenant in that many later prophecies picture a future fulfillment. In fact, the promise of the land in its ultimate fulfillment fails to find completion in the entire Old Testament. Hebrews 11 indicates concerning the men of faith, that they looked forward to fulfillment of God's plans and purposes but did not live to see their complete fulfillment.

Israel after Solomon. Following Solomon's reign, the kingdom of Israel was divided into the ten-tribe kingdom, Israel, and the two-tribe kingdom, Judah. Israel continued to depart from God. All of the kings of the ten-tribe kingdom were evil, and though there were occasional revivals in the two-tribe kingdom of Judah, the prophets had to repeat the warning that unless the people kept the law they would be driven out of the land.

The Second Dispersion of Israel

The warnings of the dispersion. Following the first dispersion of Israel, the journey of Jacob and his family to Egypt at the invitation of Joseph, the prophets warned of a possible second dispersion. Moses had laid down the principle that obedience to the law was necessary for any one generation to possess the land (Deut. 28). Now in the time of Israel's apostasy, the prophets foretold the Assyrian captivity. The prophet Isaiah, who lived approximately 740–680 B.C., predicted the Assyrian captivity which took place in 722–721 B.C. Isaiah recorded:

> The LORD spoke to me again: "Because this people has rejected the gently flowing waters of Shiloah and rejoices over Rezin and the son of Remaliah, therefore, the LORD is about to bring against them the mighty floodwaters of the River—the king of Assyria with all his pomp. It will overflow all its channels, run over all its banks and sweep on into Judah, swirling over it, passing through it, and reaching up to the neck. Its outspread wings will cover the breadth of your land, O Immanuel!" (8:6–8)

The Assyrian armies are pictured like the flood of the Euphrates overflowing its banks and sweeping through both the kingdoms of Israel and Judah. The warning was repeated in Isaiah 10:5–6: "Woe to the Assyrian, the rod of my anger, in whose hand is the club of my wrath! I send him against a godless nation, I dispatch him against a people who anger me, to seize loot and snatch plunder, and to trample them down like mud in the streets." In the midst of this prophecy of Israel's being conquered and led into captivity by the Assyrians, God gave a promise of their return (vv. 20–27). He declared, "A remnant will return, a remnant of Jacob will return to the Mighty God" (v. 21). Here again we have the familiar prophecies of leaving the land and coming back to the land, both of which were literally fulfilled in the Old Testament period.

The prophet Jeremiah, who lived in the seventh century B.C., prophesied that Babylon would conquer the two remaining tribes and carry them off into captivity. In a series of encounters, he clearly prophesied this in contradiction to the false prophets who told the king of Judah that Babylon would not conquer Israel. Jeremiah prophesied

> Now I will hand all your countries over to my servant Nebuchadnezzar king of Babylon; I will make even the wild animals subject to him. All nations will serve him and his son and his grandson until the time for his land comes; then

many nations and great kings will subjugate him. If, however, any nation or kingdom will not serve Nebuchadnezzar king of Babylon or bow its neck under his yoke, I will punish that nation with the sword, famine and plague, declares the LORD, until I destroy it by his hand. So do not listen to your prophets, your diviners, your interpreters of dreams, your mediums or your sorcerers who tell you, "You will not serve the king of Babylon." They prophesy lies to you that will only serve to remove you far from your lands; I will banish you and you will perish. But if any nation will bow its neck under the yoke of the king of Babylon and serve him, I will let that nation remain in its own land to till it and to live there, declares the LORD. (27:6–11)

Fulfillment of the prophecy of dispersion. Jeremiah not only prophesied the coming of Babylon but also recorded the historic fulfillment as stated in Jeremiah 39:1–2: "This is how Jerusalem was taken: In the ninth year of Zedekiah king of Judah, in the tenth month, Nebuchadnezzar king of Babylon marched against Jerusalem with his whole army and laid siege to it. And on the ninth day of the fourth month of Zedekiah's eleventh year, the city wall was broken through." The chapter records the tragic capture of Zedekiah, the killing of his sons before his eyes, and his being blinded and taken to Babylon (39:5–7). Jeremiah also recorded the destruction of Jerusalem and the burning of the palace (vv. 8–10). This occurred in 605 B.C.

Later a large contingent of Israelites was taken into captivity in 597 B.C., and ultimately the temple was destroyed in 586 B.C. (2 Chron. 36:14–21). The leaders of Israel for the most part were killed, the articles of the temple were carried off to Babylon, and the temple itself and the wall of Jerusalem were destroyed along with the palaces and everything of value. Second Chronicles closes by saying that the land would enjoy its sabbath rest denied to it by Israel for seventy years (36:21). It also records Cyrus's proclamation issued approximately 538 B.C., which allowed the children of Israel to return.

In the first year of Cyrus king of Persia, in order to fulfill the word of the LORD spoken by Jeremiah, the LORD moved the heart of Cyrus king of Persia to make a proclamation throughout his realm and to put it in writing:
"This is what Cyrus king of Persia says:

'The LORD, the God of heaven, has given me all
the kingdoms of the earth and he has appointed me
to build a temple for him at Jerusalem in Judah.
Anyone of his people among you—may the LORD
his God be with him, and let him go up' " (36:22–
23).

Once again we see the pattern of literal fulfillment. Just as
Israel went literally into Egypt and came back literally, so she
was carried off into the Assyrian and Babylonian captivities, but
the promise, as recorded in Scripture, was that she would be
brought back once again to her ancient land. Regardless of
eschatological viewpoint, all interpreters of the Bible have to
agree that these promises were literally and graphically fulfilled.

The Third and Final Dispersion of Israel

Predicted in the Old Testament. Just as both Israel's first
dispersion into Egypt and second dispersion into Assyria and
Babylon were fulfilled with Israel's literal return to the Promised Land, so the Old Testament predicted a third and worldwide dispersion, the extent of which was never realized in
Israel's earlier dispersions. As contained in the prophecy of
Moses previously mentioned, God declared, "Then the LORD
will scatter you among all nations, from one end of the earth to
the other" (Deut. 28:64). Prophecy goes on to describe the
anxiety, persecution, and trouble Israel would face as they were
scattered all over the world. This worldwide scattering was
never fulfilled in the Old Testament, however, as in the
Assyrian and Babylonian captivities the dispersion was limited
to these countries.

Predicted in the New Testament. Israel's ultimate dispersion
was anticipated by Christ when he prophesied the destruction
of the temple: "I tell you the truth, not one stone here will be
left on another; every one will be thrown down" (Matt. 24:2).
Jesus described the destruction of Jerusalem preceding the third
dispersion in graphic terms:

When you see Jerusalem being surrounded by armies, you
will know that its desolation is near. Then let those who are
in Judea flee to the mountains, let those in the city get out,
and let those in the country not enter the city. For this is the
time of punishment in fulfillment of all that has been

written. How dreadful it will be in those days for pregnant
women and nursing mothers! There will be great distress in
the land and wrath against this people. They will fall by the
sword and will be taken as prisoners to all the nations.
Jerusalem will be trampled on by the Gentiles until the
times of the Gentiles are fulfilled" (Luke 21:20–24).

Third dispersion fulfilled. These prophecies, like other prophecies, were literally fulfilled, and the destruction of Jerusalem
took place in A.D. 70 with terrible persecution and the killing of
tens of thousands of Israelites. Jesus prophesied that the
dispersion would be "to all the nations" (Luke 21:24). History
has recorded the sad fulfillment.

Following A.D. 70 and the destruction of Jerusalem, Israel was
driven out of the land, their cities destroyed, their orchards
ruined, their wells filled with stones. Every effort was made to
make the land unlivable, resulting in probably fewer than
fifteen thousand Jews remaining in the land. The rest were
scattered all over the world, a process that continued to the
twentieth century. Even this dispersion, however, anticipated
Israel's future regathering, for Jesus said, "Jerusalem will be
trampled on by the Gentiles until the times of the Gentiles are
fulfilled" (Luke 21:24). As in the other dispersions, this dispersion over the entire world would eventually be ended and Israel
would return to its land.

The Prophecy of the Final Regathering of Israel to the Promised Land

Amillennial objection to the future regathering of Israel. In
previous discussion, the amillennial contention that the promise
of the land was fulfilled in the time of Joshua, or later in the time
of Solomon, has been considered and found untenable. Later
prophecies anticipated a future fulfillment, so it is clear that the
partial fulfillments, plainly indicated as partial in Scripture, did
not fulfill the promise of the Abrahamic covenant.

One further reference is found in Nehemiah 1:8–9: "Remember the instruction you gave your servant Moses, saying, 'If you
are unfaithful, I will scatter you among the nations, but if you
return to me and obey my commands, then even if your exiled
people are at the farthest horizon, I will gather them from there
and bring them to the place I have chosen as a dwelling for my
Name.'" The foundational fact that the covenant of the land

stems from the Abrahamic promise was repeated. Furthermore, we are told that God kept his promise.

There is no evidence in this passage that the entire area from Egypt to the Euphrates River was possessed by Israel at this time. The facts indeed are quite to the contrary. The most extensive possessions of Israel occurred in the reign of Solomon, but even they did not incorporate the entire area into the land of Israel.

As pointed out previously, however, all these references in the Old Testament fall short of one important requirement—that the land was to be given to Israel forever, and they were not to be dispersed from it again (Amos 9:13–15).

Because these arguments do not satisfy the Abrahamic covenant, most amillenarians are content to spiritualize the promise of the land and make it equivalent to heaven or to the spiritual blessings believers in Christ enjoy. This conclusion, however, is likewise without scriptural confirmation, as the land is never mentioned as meaning this in the entire Old Testament. The New Testament also, though it extends the eternal hope of being in the New Jerusalem forever, does not include fulfillment of the promise of the land as given to Abraham. Instead, the promises of the regathering from the third dispersion, if taken literally, make clear that they are subject to future fulfillment.

Promises in Isaiah of a future regathering of Israel. The promises of a future regathering of Israel are imbedded in the promises of a future reign of the Messiah on earth. These promises are found in so many passages that it is amazing that efforts have been made to ignore or explain away these prophecies.

In the description of the messianic kingdom in Isaiah 11:1– 12, Isaiah declared:

> In that day the Lord will reach out his hand a second time to reclaim the remnant that is left of his people from Assyria, from Lower Egypt, from Upper Egypt, from Cush, from Elam, from Babylonia, from Hamath and from the islands of the sea. He will raise a banner for the nations and gather the exiles of Israel; he will assemble the scattered people of Judah from the four quarters of the earth. (vv. 11–12)

Inasmuch as the glorious kingdom described in this chapter is future, so the regathering of Israel is future.

Isaiah said further, "The LORD will have compassion on Jacob; once again he will choose Israel and will settle them in their own land" (14:1). Isaiah 27:13 records the prophecy that "those who were perishing in Assyria and those who were exiled in Egypt will come and worship the LORD on the holy mountain in Jerusalem."

In 43:5–7 Isaiah recorded this word from God: "Do not be afraid, for I am with you; I will bring your children from the east and gather you from the west. I will say to the north, 'Give them up!' and to the south, 'Do not hold them back.' Bring my sons from afar and my daughters from the ends of the earth— everyone who is called by my name, whom I created for my glory, whom I formed and made." Note that this implies worldwide regathering, which could only follow A.D. 70 when worldwide dispersion took place. Isaiah described in chapter 60 the glorious kingdom reign of Christ: "Then will all your people be righteous and they will possess the land forever" (v. 21). The missing ingredient in the regatherings from the first and second dispersions was Israel's possession of the land forever. This will be fulfilled in their third and final regathering. The regathering of Israel "from all the nations" is mentioned again in Isaiah 66:20.

Promise in Jeremiah of future regathering. The prophet Jeremiah, living a century later than Isaiah, during the apostasy of the kings of Judah frequently referred to the regathering of Israel. This emphasizes an important point in the doctrine that the people of Israel would return to their land—namely, that they would return to the land not because they deserved it but because they are the recipients of God's grace. Even in their apostasy God reminded them that they would be regathered:

> "However, the days are coming," declares the LORD, "when men will no longer say, 'As surely as the LORD lives, who brought the Israelites up out of Egypt,' but they will say, 'As surely as the LORD lives, who brought the Israelites up out of the land of the north and out of all the countries where he had banished them.' For I will restore them to the land I gave their forefathers. But now I will send for many fishermen," declares the LORD, "and they will catch them. After that I will send for many hunters, and they will hunt them down on every mountain and hill and from the crevices of the rocks" (16:14–16).

This passage brings out emphatically that the regathering will be from all countries and that it will be complete; every Israelite will be brought back to his ancient land. According to Ezekiel 20:33–38, the unbelievers will be purged out, but the godly remnant of Israel will be allowed to enter the Promised Land. This promise, obviously, has never been fulfilled to the present hour. In the first dispersion all of the children of Israel left Egypt, but it is questionable whether those who went to Assyria and Babylon in the second dispersion all came back. In the final regathering, however, every Israelite will be brought back to his ancient land.

One of the most comprehensive prophecies concerning Israel's regathering in connection with the future reign of Christ on earth is found in Jeremiah 23:5–8:

"The days are coming," declares the LORD,
    "when I will raise up to David a righteous Branch,
a King who will reign wisely
    and do what is just and right in the land.
In his days Judah will be saved
    and Israel will live in safety.
This is the name by which he will be called:
    The LORD Our Righteousness.

> "So then, the days are coming," declares the LORD, "when people will no longer say, 'As surely as the LORD lives, who brought the Israelites up out of Egypt,' but they will say, 'As surely as the LORD lives, who brought the descendants of Israel up out of the land of the north and out of all the countries where he had banished them.' Then they will live in their own land."

In this passage the final regathering of Israel is in connection with the reign of Christ on earth, a time when the kingdoms of Judah and Israel will be brought back together. The regathering of Israel is going to be in contrast to the regathering from Egypt and will be "out of all countries where [the LORD] had banished them" (Jer. 23:8). This, of course, has not yet been fulfilled and requires literal fulfillment in the future.

Another comprehensive statement of this regathering of Israel is found in Jeremiah 30:8–11, following a passage dealing with the Great Tribulation (vv. 5–7), from which time of trouble

Jacob will be saved. God promises to deliver Israel from their oppressors:

> "In that day," declares the LORD Almighty,
>   "I will break the yoke off their necks
> and will tear off their bonds;
>   no longer will foreigners enslave them.
> Instead, they will serve the LORD their God
>   and David their king,
>   whom I will raise up for them.
>
> "So do not fear, O Jacob my servant;
>   do not be dismayed, O Israel,"
>   declares the LORD.
> "I will surely save you out of a distant place,
>   your descendants from the land of their exile.
> Jacob will again have peace and security,
>   and no one will make him afraid.
> I am with you and will save you,"
>   declares the LORD.
> "Though I completely destroy all the nations
>   among which I scatter you,
>   I will not completely destroy you.
> I will discipline you but only with justice;
>   I will not let you go entirely unpunished."
>   (Jer. 30:8–11)

The regathering is in keeping with God's purpose not to destroy Israel but to preserve Israel forever. Jeremiah 31:10–14, another extended passage, speaks of bringing Israel back to her ancient land.

The time of Israel's regathering will involve the fulfillment of the new covenant for Israel (Jer. 31:31–37), which will be treated separately later in chapter 17.

The time of Israel's regathering will occur when Jerusalem will be rebuilt, according to Jeremiah 31:38–40:

> "The days are coming," declares the LORD, "when this city will be rebuilt for me from the Tower of Hananel to the Corner Gate. The measuring line will stretch from there straight to the hill of Gareb and then turn to Goah. The whole valley where dead bodies and ashes are thrown, and

all the terraces out to the Kidron Valley on the east as far as the corner of the Horse Gate, will be holy to the LORD. The city will never again be uprooted or demolished."

It is of great significance that the portion of the city described here throughout Israel's ancient history was a place for a garbage heap and dead bodies. Only in the twentieth century was this area of Jerusalem repossessed by Israel and transformed from a garbage heap into an area where beautiful apartments have been built. Accordingly, the fulfillment of this promise, inasmuch as it involves twentieth-century events, also points to a future regathering of Israel. Further, note the important statement, "The city will never again be uprooted or demolished" (Jer. 31:40). It is a remarkable promise that indicates that time is running out for the present age and that the future restoration of Israel is impending. In view of the many times that Jerusalem has been destroyed and rebuilt, this promise stands out.

Still another comprehensive prophecy of Israel's regathering is found in Jeremiah 32:37–44:

> "I will surely gather them from all the lands where I banish them in my furious anger and great wrath; I will bring them back to this place and let them live in safety. They will be my people, and I will be their God. I will give them singleness of heart and action, so that they will always fear me for their own good and the good of their children after them. I will make an everlasting covenant with them: I will never stop doing good to them, and I will inspire them to fear me, so that they will never turn away from me. I will rejoice in doing them good and will assuredly plant them in this land with all my heart and soul.
>
> "This is what the LORD says: As I have brought all this great calamity on this people, so I will give them all the prosperity I have promised them. Once more fields will be bought in this land of which you say, 'It is a desolate waste, without men or animals, for it has been handed over to the Babylonians.' Fields will be bought for silver, and deeds will be signed, sealed and witnessed in the territory of Benjamin, in the villages around Jerusalem, in the towns of Judah and in the towns of the hill country, of the western foothills and of the Negev, because I will restore their fortunes, declares the LORD."

Here are all the familiar promises that have preceded—namely, that they would be gathered "from all the lands where [God] banish[es] them" (v. 37). When they came back they would "live in safety" (v. 37). God's goodness and grace to them will never stop (v. 40). In the context of the other quotations from Jeremiah, it is clear that this refers to the final regathering.

Prophecies in Ezekiel of future regathering. Ezekiel added his confirming word concerning Israel's future. After describing the purging judgment on Israel in which rebels would be prohibited from entering the land (20:33–38), Ezekiel quoted the Lord, "Then you will know that I am the LORD, when I bring you into the land of Israel, the land I had sworn with uplifted hand to give to your fathers" (v. 42).

In 34:13 Ezekiel recorded this word from the Lord: "I will bring them out from the nations and gather them from the countries, and I will bring them into their own land. I will pasture them on the mountains of Israel, in the ravines and in all the settlements in the land."

In connection with Ezekiel's promise of the restoration of the nation of Israel in the valley of dry bones, another promise of the regathering of Israel was given: "This is what the Sovereign LORD says: I will take the Israelites out of the nations where they have gone. I will gather them from all around and bring them back into their own land. I will make them one nation in the land, on the mountains of Israel. There will be one king over all of them and they will never again be two nations or be divided into two kingdoms" (37:21–22).

In connection with this promise, the Lord declared: "My servant David will be king over them, and they will all have one shepherd. They will follow my laws and be careful to keep my decrees. They will live in the land I gave to my servant Jacob, the land where your fathers lived. They and their children and their children's children will live there forever, and David my servant will be their prince forever" (37:24–25).

The reference to David's reigning over Israel clearly points to a future restoration of Israel and a future kingdom that has not yet been fulfilled. Though some have tried to spiritualize this promise to get away from its literalness, the passage clearly teaches that David will share with Christ as a co-regent and rule over the children of Israel in the millennial kingdom. This is confirmed also in Ezekiel 34:23–24: "I will place over them one shepherd, my servant David, and he will tend them; he will tend them and be their shepherd. I the LORD will be their God, and my servant David will be prince among them. I the LORD have spoken." While Jesus Christ as King of Kings and Lord of Lords will be King over the entire world as well as ruling over the house of Israel, David apparently will share the throne as far as the kingdom of Israel is concerned. Inasmuch as David will be resurrected before the millennial kingdom, this is plausible and provides a sensible explanation of this passage.

In 39:25–29 Ezekiel gave another remarkable promise concerning the extent of Israel's regathering. First the Lord declared, "I will now bring Jacob back from captivity and will have compassion on all the people of Israel, and I will be zealous for my holy name" (v. 25). Then he stated further:

> "When I have brought them back from the nations and have gathered them from the countries of their enemies, I will show myself holy through them in the sight of many nations. Then they will know that I am the LORD their God, for though I sent them into exile among the nations, I will gather them to their own land, not leaving any behind. I will no longer hide my face from them, for I will pour out my Spirit on the house of Israel, declares the Sovereign LORD." (vv. 27–29)

The remarkable factor in this prophecy is not only that they will be gathered from all nations but that the Lord will "gather them to their own land, not leaving any behind" (v. 28). This same truth is brought out in Jeremiah 16:14–16. Because this was never fulfilled in any of the previous regatherings, it obviously refers to a third and future regathering in connection with the second coming of Christ.

It would seem redundant to deal with passage after passage referring to this future regathering if it were not for the fact that amillenarians deny a future regathering of Israel in spite of these many solid prophecies embedded in the context of the future kingdom on earth.

Promise in the Minor Prophets of future regathering. What was emphasized in Isaiah, Jeremiah, and Ezekiel is also found in the Minor Prophets. According to Hosea 3:4–5, "For the Israelites will live many days without king or prince, without sacrifice or sacred stones, without ephod or idol. Afterward the Israelites will return and seek the LORD their God and David their king. They will come trembling to the LORD and to his blessing in the last days." Hosea, acknowledging that the throne of Israel would be vacant for many years and that sacrifices would cease, nevertheless reaffirmed that Israel would come back to God and to David their king, obviously a reference to the prophetic statement that David will share the throne of Christ in his future millennial kingdom. Joel added his word of prophecy on this subject after graphically describing the preceding judgments of God: "Judah will be inhabited forever and Jerusalem through all generations. Their bloodguilt, which I have not pardoned, I will pardon'" (3:20–21). Amos, after a long recounting of the sins of Israel and God's judgment upon them, nevertheless promised a day of restoration for Israel (9:11–15). He referred to this as a restoration of "David's fallen tent" (v. 11). He pictured the abundant crops of Israel in that day and then concluded: "'I will bring back my exiled people Israel; they will rebuild the ruined cities and live in them. They will plant vineyards and drink their wine; they will make gardens and eat their fruit. I will plant Israel in their own land, never again to be uprooted from the land I have given them,' says the LORD your God" (vv. 14–15).

The promised restoration of Israel will include rebuilding their ancient cities, planting vineyards, and making gardens. Some of these prophecies have current fulfillment. The final verse states plainly that Israel will be restored to its land and never again be driven out of it. Inasmuch as the first and second dispersions are to be followed by a third, this regathering is the final one that is a part of the kingdom promises given to Israel in connection with the second coming of Christ. As such, it is clear that this promise has not yet been fulfilled in any literal way.

To these promises of the future restoration of Israel to her land can be added that of Obadiah 17–21 that Israel will possess the land. Micah also gave a picture of this future kingdom (4:1–8). In this passage Israel is described as secure in peace and safety and enjoying her vines and fig trees. Her future restoration is related to the Abrahamic covenant (Mic. 7:20). Zephaniah added his chapter to Israel's future regathering to her ancient land (chap. 3). In Zechariah, the people of Israel are pictured returning from countries of the east and west (Zech. 8:7–8). In confirmation of this as a future kingdom promise, Jerusalem is described as the capital of the earth (v. 22). Zechariah 14 describes the second coming of Christ and the millennial kingdom which follows. This would necessarily include the fulfillment of the promises of the land.

Important conclusions. Certain conclusions can be reached regarding the promises of the land to Israel as a whole. (1) It is obvious that Israel has not possessed the land permanently, having been dispersed after the two previous regatherings. (2) Based on clear promises from the prophets, Israel will be regathered from the third dispersion and be in her land during the millennial kingdom. (3) It is evident that the promises given to Israel will not be fulfilled by the church or by the Gentiles. (4) The promise must be fulfilled by the physical seed of Jacob, in keeping with the Abrahamic covenant. (5) Inasmuch as the promise of possession is an unending promise, it is obviously related to a future kingdom, since all the previous possessions have terminated in dispersions. If Israel is going to possess the land, the premillennial view of the Lord's return is correct.

9

The Davidic Covenant: The Future Davidic Kingdom

Along with many promises to Israel about the land are prophecies about the Davidic kingdom. Like the promises of the land, the promises of the kingdom have often been spiritualized or interpreted nonliterally, with attempts to find fulfillment in the present age. Once again the issue is whether prophecies should be interpreted literally. And this again raises the question of whether prophecies to Christians are to be fulfilled literally in the prophetic future.

Early Prophecies of the Future Kingdom

The kingdom promised to David is important because it explains the history of the past as well as prophesying the future. At stake is the question of whether there will be a future Davidic kingdom on earth following the second coming of Christ as taught by premillenarians.

Early prophecies relate the covenant of Abraham to the promise of future kings and kingdoms. In Genesis 17:6, in connection with the confirmation of the promise that Abraham would have many nations descending from him, God said, "I will make you very fruitful; I will make nations of you, and kings will come from you." The promise given to Abraham was repeated in connection with Sarah, "I will bless her and will surely give you a son by her. I will bless her so that she will be the mother of nations; kings of peoples will come from her" (v. 16).

These promises were subsequently passed on to Isaac (Gen. 26:2–5) and to Jacob (28:13–15). Later scope of the promise was narrowed to Judah, the son of Jacob: "The scepter will not depart from Judah, nor the ruler's staff from between his feet, until he comes to whom it belongs and the obedience of the nations is his" (49:10). This prophecy not only confines the fulfillment to Judah and his descendants but also anticipates the coming of Christ, to whom the power of king properly belongs. From these references it may be concluded that the concept of a future kingdom is an important aspect of the Abrahamic covenant.

The Promise of the Kingdom Revealed to David

The provisions of God's covenant with David concerning his future kingdom are recorded in 2 Samuel 7 and 1 Chronicles 17, with only minor differences in the two passages. The occasion for the covenant was David's desire to build a temple for God. He had constructed an elaborate palace for himself, but the ark was still in the tentlike structure that God had given instructions to construct in the wilderness. When David contacted Nathan, a young prophet, he immediately gave David permission to go ahead, but Nathan had failed to consult God. God had to instruct Nathan to go back to David with a different outline of God's purpose for him. The result was a larger revelation of God's plan for David, which included the provision that David's son, not yet born, would build the temple and that God would do something even greater for David. He would raise up for him a house, not of physical material, but a house in the sense of descendants whom God would bless. The Davidic covenant included a number of important pronouncements.

David is promised a son. As a preface to his divine revelation, God reviewed with David how he had taken him from shepherding sheep to shepherding God's people Israel. God reminded David that he had never told him to build a house or a temple for the Lord. David had been blessed. God had cut off his enemies and now was going to make David's name great (2 Sam. 7:9). God's purpose in David's victories was to provide a safe home for the people of Israel where they would not be oppressed by the wicked (v. 10).

God declared to David, "When your days are over and you rest with your fathers, I will raise up your offspring to succeed you, who will come from your own body, and I will establish his kingdom" (v. 12). This son was Solomon, and God promised that he would establish the kingdom of Solomon.

David's son would build the temple. In addition to establishing Solomon's kingdom, God would empower Solomon to build the temple: "He is the one who will build a house for my Name, and I will establish the throne of his kingdom forever" (2 Sam. 7:13). In contrast to Saul, who was deposed because he wandered from the Lord, Solomon was promised that even if he did wrong, God would not take away his love from him as he had from Saul: "I will be his father, and he will be my son. When he does wrong, I will punish him with the rod of men, with floggings inflicted by men. But my love will never be taken away from him, as I took it away from Saul, whom I removed from before you" (vv. 14–15).

David himself would have his throne and kingdom established forever. The covenant goes on, however, to state concerning David, "Your house and your kingdom will endure forever before me; your throne will be established forever" (2 Sam. 7:16).

There is a meticulous accuracy in this prophecy. As has been pointed out in an earlier chapter, Solomon's line was to end physically in Joseph, the husband of Mary, a fact that would give Jesus Christ, his legal son, the legal right to the throne. Mary, however, was to descend from David through another son, Nathan (not to be confused with Nathan the prophet), and therefore would have a different physical lineage. This is taken into consideration in the Davidic covenant. Solomon was promised that his throne would continue forever but not that his house would continue forever, in contrast to David, whose throne and house were promised to continue forever. This covenant, accordingly, introduces the descending line from David to Christ and points to the conclusion that Jesus Christ is the ultimate fulfillment of this promise to David.

David's understanding of the covenant. After the covenant was declared to David,

> King David went in and sat before the LORD, and he said: "Who am I, O Sovereign LORD, and what is my family, that you have brought me this far? And as if this were not enough in your sight, O Sovereign LORD, you have also spoken about the future of the house of your servant. Is this your usual way of dealing with man, O Sovereign LORD? What more can David say to you? For you know your servant, O Sovereign LORD. For the sake of your word and according to your will, you have done this great thing and made it known to your servant." (2 Sam. 7:18–21)

David expressed his understanding of the covenant: "You have established your people Israel as your very own forever, and you, O LORD, have become their God" (v. 24). It is clear from the verses that follow that David understood that this promise would go on forever (vv. 26, 29). And in verse 24 it is plain that David regarded the people of Israel as well as his own descendants as going on forever (v. 24).

It is important to note that David's understanding of the covenant was that it referred to the people of Israel, not to any other people, and that it referred to his physical descendants. David was overwhelmed that God would reveal such a far-reaching promise: "O Sovereign LORD, you have also spoken about the future of the house of your servant. Is this your usual way of dealing with man, O Sovereign LORD?" (2 Sam. 7:19). There was no confusion in David's mind between his own throne and his own physical descendants and the throne of God in heaven and the people of God as a whole. The familiar pattern of trying to make this promise refer to the heavenly throne and every believer instead of to the political throne of David and his physical descendants is the result of reading into the passage what it does not say and, in fact, contradicts. The throne of David is an earthly throne relating to the political direction of Israel, not a heavenly throne on which David himself never sat.

The Promises of the Kingdom Confirmed in the Old Testament

The amillennial view of the kingdom. Conservative amillenarians interpret the covenant with David to be a covenant with the people of God, that is, the church. In doing so, they equate the throne of David with the throne of God in heaven, and they equate the people of Israel who were ruled by David as the people of God in general, not Israel. In studying the confirmation of the covenant in the Old Testament, however, there is no hint anywhere that this was the correct understanding of the covenant. Rather, the Scriptures plainly say that the promise and its fulfillment relate to the line of physical descendants of David consummating in Christ and the people of Israel who are descendants of Jacob. The throne of David is a symbol of authority in a political kingdom, not a universal kingdom, and the subjects of the kingdom are Israelites who are descendants of Jacob. There is no scriptural authorization to interpret this in any other than its literal meaning. Confirmation of the Davidic covenant in the Old Testament confirms the Davidic character of the promise.

The promise of the kingdom is unconditional and is subject to literal fulfillment. One of the most important passages confirming the kingdom promise to David is found in Psalm 89. No other passage makes quite so clear that the kingdom refers to David and the people of Israel and that the covenant is unconditional and certain of fulfillment. God's description of David makes specific that God will fulfill his promise to David forever (vv. 20–29). The psalmist writes,

> You said, "I have made a covenant with my chosen one,
>   I have sworn to David my servant,
> 'I will establish your line forever
>   and make your throne firm through all generations.'"
>
> (vv. 3–4)

This same thought is repeated:

> "I will maintain my love to him forever,
>   and my covenant with him will never fail.
> I will establish his line forever,
>   his throne as long as the heavens endure."
>
> (vv. 28–29)

That the promise is unconditional is stated emphatically:

"If his sons forsake my law
    and do not follow my statutes,
if they violate my decrees
    and fail to keep my commands,
I will punish their sin with the rod,
    their iniquity with flogging;
but I will not take my love from him,
    nor will I ever betray my faithfulness.
I will not violate my covenant
    or alter what my lips have uttered.
Once for all, I have sworn by my holiness—
    and I will not lie to David—
that his line will continue forever
    and his throne endure before me like the sun;
it will be established forever like the moon,
    the faithful witness in the sky." (vv. 30–37)

In these promises God has made clear that the Davidic covenant is not subject to human conditions and that God has vowed on the basis of his own trustworthiness that he will fulfill the covenant. It is also clear that the promise was given to David, not to someone else, though it will be fulfilled by Christ as the descendant of David, and that the fulfillment relates to the people of God, in this context the people of Israel.

Isaiah frequently refers to the Davidic covenant and its fulfillment. In Isaiah 9:6–7 the specific prophecy is given concerning Christ, his birth, his government, his reign on the throne of David, and the fact that God himself will accomplish this.

For to us a child is born,
    to us a son is given,
    and the government will be on his shoulders.
And he will be called
    Wonderful Counselor, Mighty God,
    Everlasting Father, Prince of Peace.
Of the increase of his government and peace
    there will be no end.
He will reign on David's throne
    and over his kingdom,
establishing and upholding it
    with justice and righteousness

> *from that time on and forever.*
> *The zeal of the LORD Almighty*
> *will accomplish this.*

The son predicted is obviously Jesus Christ, for only he could be called "Mighty God." David's throne again is the reference to the political throne of David over the house of Israel. The fact that it will never end is asserted again,

> *establishing and upholding it*
> *with justice and righteousness*
> *from that time on and forever. (v. 7)*

The passage contains no justification for taking the prophecy in less than its literal and physical significance.

In Jeremiah 23:5–8 another clear reference to the throne of David is revealed:

> *"The days are coming," declares the LORD,*
> *"when I will raise up to David a righteous Branch,*
> *a King who will reign wisely*
> *and do what is just and right in the land." (vv. 5–6)*

As has been brought out in previous discussions, the person referred to is none other than Jesus Christ who is given the title "The LORD Our Righteousness" (v. 6). The kingdom promise of David will coincide with the restoration of the people of Israel who are gathered from all over the world back to their ancient land (v. 8).

According to Jeremiah 30:9, the people of Israel who serve with David their king will be resurrected at the beginning of the millennial reign of Christ:

> *"Instead, they will serve the LORD their God*
> *and David their king,*
> *whom I will raise up for them."*

Again, the reference is clearly to a Davidic rule, a kingdom on earth where foreigners will not be able to enslave them, and the period will follow her time of special trouble (v. 7). The fulfillment will coincide with the regathering of Israel (v. 10), which will be consummated immediately after the second coming of Christ.

A most specific promise is given in Jeremiah 33:14–17:

> "The days are coming," declares the LORD, "when I will fulfill the gracious promise I made to the house of Israel and to the house of Judah. In those days and at that time I will make a righteous Branch sprout from David's line; he will do what is just and right in the land. In those days Judah will be saved and Jerusalem will live in safety. This is the name by which it will be called: The LORD Our Righteousness." For this is what the LORD says: "David will never fail to have a man to sit on the throne of the house of Israel."

The promise and its fulfillment is related to "the land" (v. 15) and will be related to the earthly Jerusalem (v. 16). Again, there is no justification to interpret this in any other sense than to understand its fulfillment as being subsequent to the second coming of Christ in the kingdom on earth.

Ezekiel added his word of confirmation, and specifically related that the future kingdom of David is to take place when the regathering of Israel is complete:

> " 'This is what the Sovereign LORD says: I will take the Israelites out of the nations where they have gone. I will gather them from all around and bring them back into their own land. I will make them one nation in the land, on the mountains of Israel. There will be one king over all of them and they will never again be two nations or be divided into two kingdoms. They will no longer defile themselves with their idols and vile images or with any of their offenses, for I will save them from all their sinful backsliding, and I will cleanse them. They will be my people, and I will be their God.
> " 'My servant David will be king over them, and they will all have one shepherd. They will follow my laws and be careful to keep my decrees. They will live in the land I gave to my servant Jacob, the land where your fathers lived. They and their children and their children's children will live there forever, and David my servant will be their prince forever. I will make a covenant of peace with them; it will be an everlasting covenant. I will establish them and increase their numbers, and I will put my sanctuary among them forever. My dwelling place will be with them; I will

be their God, and they will be my people. Then the nations will know that I the LORD make Israel holy, when my sanctuary is among them forever.'" (Ezek. 37:21–28)

Ezekiel made plain that the fulfillment of the Davidic promise will be in connection with the regathering of Israel to their Promised Land. It will occur when David is resurrected from the dead at the second coming of Christ. Subsequent to this, Israel will live in the Promised Land (37:25) and David will continue his reign forever as a resurrected person (v. 25). The covenant will be everlasting (v. 26), and the world will know that the Lord has dealt with Israel in a special way (v. 28). The prophecy in its natural and literal meaning refers to the events relating to the second coming of Christ and his subsequent kingdom on earth.

Hosea 3:4–5 indicates that the throne of David will be unoccupied for long periods of time: "For the Israelites will live many days without king or prince, without sacrifice or sacred stones, without ephod or idol. Afterward the Israelites will return and seek the LORD their God and David their king. They will come trembling to the LORD and to his blessings in the last days." This is not contradicted by Jeremiah 33:17, which says, "David will never fail to have a man to sit on the throne of the house of Israel." The point is that throughout this period, right on down to Joseph, the husband of Mary, there will always be a legitimate heir to the throne. Though there will be interruptions in the reign of David on the throne of Israel, the ultimate fulfillment of the Davidic promise is related to Christ resurrected and David resurrected, which assures that the covenant will have continuous fulfillment in the future.

As previously pointed out, another prophecy was given concerning the restoration of "David's fallen tent" (Amos 9:11). This refers again to the restoration of the Davidic kingdom following the second coming of Christ. In Zechariah 14, which pictures Christ at his second coming, the prediction is made, "The LORD will be king over the whole earth. On that day there will be one LORD, and his name the only name" (v. 9). The Davidic throne will extend God's political authority as vested in Christ over the house of Israel, but Christ will also rule over the universal kingdom of God in the Millennium.

The Old Testament states and then confirms repeatedly that the promises given to David are valid promises that will be fulfilled in connection with Christ's second coming. There is no hint in any of these passages that the promise was intended to extend beyond the people of Israel or beyond the Davidic throne to God's heavenly throne.

The Promise of the Kingdom Confirmed in the New Testament

Amillennial interpretation of New Testament passages. Conservative amillenarians can see that the Old Testament, taken in its plain, ordinary language, predicts a political kingdom on earth in connection with the second coming of Christ. They assert, however, that the New Testament interprets the Old Testament in a nonliteral way and that, therefore, the intent of the prophecy was not to predict the restoration of the Davidic kingdom but rather the triumph of God and the church and that this is fulfilled in the present age. An examination of the New Testament, however, does not provide any confirmation of this. In fact, it adds its own word to the Old Testament concerning the Davidic kingdom. To be sure, the New Testament does not have long passages or detailed statements concerning the Davidic kingdom, but it allows the Old Testament predictions to stand as previously interpreted, and nowhere does Christ or do his disciples affirm any change in the expectation of Israel.

The confirmation of the Davidic covenant to Mary. When Gabriel announced to Mary that she was to be the mother of Christ, he said, "Do not be afraid, Mary, you have found favor with God. You will be with child and give birth to a son, and you are to give him the name Jesus. He will be great and will be called the Son of the Most High. The Lord God will give him the throne of his father David, and he will reign over the house of Jacob forever; his kingdom will never end" (Luke 1:30–33).

If there were any time when a correction of the prevailing expectation of Israel for the fulfillment of the Davidic covenant in a literal and political way would be required, it would be at the outset of the New Testament narrative, beginning with the birth of Christ. Mary, along with all other people of Israel at that time, was expecting the coming of One who would deliver Israel politically from Rome and, according to the prophets, would bring in a glorious kingdom. It would be natural for her to understand Gabriel's announcement in its most literal meaning. The throne of David was a political throne, the house of Jacob encompassed the literal descendants of Jacob, and the prediction that Jesus' kingdom would never end was a repetition of the perpetuity of the Davidic kingdom. Mary would understand the content of the announcement precisely as it was revealed in the Old Testament. The concept that the kingdom was a spiritual kingdom embracing all believers, including Gentiles, and that it was basically a kingdom from heaven rather than a kingdom on earth, was entirely foreign to her thinking.

The kingdom of David considered in its literal interpretation by the mother of Zebedee's sons. The Scriptures record that the mother of Zebedee's sons requested of Christ, "Grant that one of these two sons of mine may sit at your right and the other at your left in your kingdom" (Matt. 20:21). Christ denied her request but, in effect, approved the idea of such a throne, though asserting that these places would be filled at the choice of God the Father (v. 23). It is obvious that the woman's request as well as Jesus' reply coincided with the expectation of an earthly kingdom. Certainly the concept of sitting on the Father's throne in heaven was not in view here, but rather the fulfillment of the Old Testament fulfillment of an earthly kingdom.

The prediction of Christ that the disciples would sit on thrones and judge the twelve tribes of Israel. In connection with the revelation of the disciples' future reward, the Lord told his disciples, "And I confer on you a kingdom, just as my Father conferred one on me, so that you may eat and drink at my table in my kingdom and sit on thrones, judging the twelve tribes of Israel" (Luke 22:29–30).

The interpretation that this passage refers to the heavenly kingdom and the eternal state is not justified in the context. The statement requires an earthly kingdom and the necessity of there being judges over the twelve tribes of Israel in the earthly political kingdom of David. The promise, accordingly, coincides with the expectation of the disciples that Christ would bring in a kingdom on earth and deliver Israel from her oppressors.

The prediction of the time of restoration of the kingdom of Israel. At the time of Christ's ascension into heaven, the disciples asked, "Lord, are you at this time going to restore the kingdom to Israel?" (Acts 1:6). Christ replied, "It is not for you to know the times or the dates the Father has set by his own authority" (v. 7). Certainly, if the promise of the future kingdom were a spiritual promise to be inherited by all believers in Christ and fulfilled in the present age, this would have been an appropriate time for Christ to correct the prevailing belief that the kingdom of Israel would be literally restored. The fact that Christ did not deny this concept but merely told his disciples that it was not for them to know the time is, in effect, an affirmation of it.

Christ's reply also includes the declaration of what would happen in the present age: "But you will receive power when the Holy Spirit comes on you; and you will be my witnesses in Jerusalem, in all Judea and Samaria, and to the ends of the earth" (Acts 1:8). Rather than a fulfillment of the Davidic kingdom promise, there would be a ministry of the Holy Spirit in the present age, calling out the church and empowering it in its witness to the death and resurrection of Christ. This coincides with the rest of the New Testament. In this passage, as in others, the New Testament confirms rather than denies the expectation of Israel.

The conclusion of the Council at Jerusalem. The precise question as to whether the present age was designed to fulfill the promises to David was the crux of the discussion at the Council of Jerusalem. The question had arisen as to whether it was necessary for converts to Christianity to be circumcised as proselytes as required of Israel by the Mosaic Law. The conclusion of the Council was that they were not required to maintain the law. In this connection James brought the concluding word:

> When they finished, James spoke up: "Brothers, listen to me. Simon has described to us how God at first showed his concern by taking from the Gentiles a people for himself. The words of the prophets are in agreement with this, as it is written: 'After this I will return and rebuild David's fallen tent. Its ruins I will rebuild, and I will restore it, that the remnant of men may seek the Lord, and all the Gentiles who bear my name, says the Lord, who does these things' that have been known for ages." (Acts 15:13–18)

The order of fulfillment, according to James, is that God's program for the present age is to form the church among the Gentiles. James pointed out that this is in keeping with the revelation of the book of Amos, which largely details Gentile supremacy over Israel. After an extensive review of this, however, Amos concluded that after the Gentile period of supremacy, David's fallen tent would be restored. This is precisely what the Old Testament anticipated—that the restoration of Israel and the throne of Israel would come after the time of Gentile power ended at the second coming of Christ and would be fulfilled only when Christ himself returned and inaugurated his kingdom. In this passage, as in previous quotations from the New Testament, the Old Testament interpretation of the Davidic covenant is confirmed explicitly in the New Testament.

The Fulfillment of the Promise to David

Are the Davidic promises to be fulfilled literally? In consideration of the many prophecies concerning the perpetuity of the throne of David and his lineage, the question resolves itself into whether these prophecies are to be fulfilled literally. Among conservative interpreters there is no question that the promises will be fulfilled by Christ, but the issue is whether it will be fulfilled in the present age as contended by amillenarians or whether it will be fulfilled in the future in connection with the second coming of Christ.

As brought out in the many Scripture references cited, the fulfillment of the covenant promise is related to the resurrection of David and a kingdom on earth. It should be obvious that David has not been resurrected and will not be resurrected until the second coming of Christ. It is also clear that Christ is not reigning on the earth in any literal sense. Jerusalem is not his capital nor are the people of Israel responsive to his rule at the present time. To attempt to find fulfillment in the present age requires radical spiritualization and denial of the plain, factual statements related to the kingdom.

Is there evidence against literal interpretation of the Davidic covenant? Most conservative interpreters of the Bible agree that there is a spiritual kingdom in the world. The Scriptures speak of God's throne in heaven and Christ's being seated at the right hand of the Father. The confusion of the heavenly throne with the Davidic throne, however, overlooks the nature of the heavenly throne, which has always been in existence and related to the overall government of God in the world as a whole, not simply the Davidic kingdom over Israel.

In the present age Christ is seated on the throne of the Father in heaven. According to Psalm 110:1–2, "The LORD says to my

Lord: 'Sit at my right hand until I make your enemies a footstool for your feet.' The LORD will extend your mighty scepter from Zion; rule in the midst of your enemies." This passage pictures Christ seated on the throne with the Father but awaiting a future extension of his power when he will return to rule over the earth, including his rule over the Davidic kingdom. Jesus Christ is the designated King to sit on the Davidic throne, but he is not exercising this power now. Nowhere in Scripture is the heavenly throne declared to be the Davidic throne. David never sat on it, and at the present time no one is seated on the throne of David even though Christ is obviously qualified to do so. His reign will not begin until he comes back to reign over the earth. Like David who waited many years after being anointed king before assuming the throne, so Christ awaits that future enthronement. At the time of his return, he will rule with absolute authority (Rev. 19:5) from the throne of David (Jer. 23:5) and will judge the wicked and bring in his kingdom of righteousness and peace. These prophecies are not being fulfilled in the present age but await the second coming of Christ.

The relation of fulfillment to other prophecies. As intimated in previous discussion, prediction of the Davidic covenant and its fulfillment is part of the overall prophetic vision of the end of the age. This will include the Great Tribulation which precedes the Second Coming. It includes the Second Coming itself. It includes the regathering of Israel from all over the world. It involves judging the wicked who live on the earth and putting to death those who are not saved (Matt. 25:46). It involves the beginning of the kingdom on earth and the establishment of a throne on the earth, which is not the case at the present time (Matt. 25:31). The fulfillment of the Davidic covenant, accordingly, is in keeping with all these other predictions and their fulfillment, and they coincide to speak of the future triumph of Christ on earth. The promise of the Davidic kingdom is still valid and will find its fulfillment when Christ returns. If these prophecies are correctly interpreted, the fulfillment of the Davidic covenant is future and is not being fulfilled in the present age.

10

The Messianic Kingdom in the Old Testament

The teaching of a messianic kingdom is a major doctrine that threads its way through both the Old and New Testaments.

Many of the prophecies we have already considered have implied or specifically prophesied a future messianic kingdom on earth. In Genesis 3:15 it is anticipated that the coming Messiah would be victorious, crushing Satan and his efforts to control the world. The Abrahamic covenant contained a number of specific promises, including the prophecy that Abraham would be father of a great nation, the nation later called Israel, and that the blessings of the coming Messiah would extend to all peoples. Incorporated in the Abrahamic covenant was the promise that Israel would possess the land forever. The Davidic covenant gave specific promises to David concerning his future kingdom on earth and anticipated Christ's reigning on the throne of David. The genealogies of the Old Testament as confirmed in the New Testament describe the lineage of the Messiah who would reign. One of the most specific areas of prophecy relates to the Promised Land and combines the promises given to Abraham and to David. A literal fulfillment of these many promises assures that there will be a future messianic kingdom on earth.

The truth of the messianic kingdom involved in these prophecies is further confirmed by many other evidences in both the Old and the New Testament. Because the concept of the messianic kingdom has been disputed and a large portion of the church has rejected the idea that there will be an earthly kingdom over which Christ will reign, it becomes necessary to marshall the evidence in support of this truth, if it is indeed a scriptural doctrine.

Major Doctrinal Issues of the Messianic Kingdom

The promise of the land. The importance of the promise of the land soon becomes evident in determining the character of the messianic kingdom. The issue is whether this should be interpreted literally as referring to an actual geographic entity or whether it refers to a spiritual kingdom.

The promises to David. Coupled with the promise of the land are the promises of the Davidic covenant, which assured David that One would come who would sit upon his throne. Here the issue is whether the Davidic throne is a political throne on earth or, as in the promise of the land, whether it should be made into a spiritualized kingdom.

Israel's restoration. The future of Israel and her promised restoration becomes a major issue in this doctrine, and some have denied that Israel is subject to future restoration. A future messianic kingdom would allow literal fulfillment of the promises given to Israel.

The kingdom on earth. The final question is whether the many passages that describe a kingdom on earth should be taken in their literal sense. If so, a messianic kingdom is prophesied.

Unfortunately the church has been divided on this question since the third century, and most Christians have chosen to ignore the literal meaning of these prophecies and have adopted them only in a nonliteral sense. The result has been what has characterized postmillennial and amillennial interpretation in the history of the church.

Postmillennial Interpretation of the Messianic Kingdom

Definition. Postmillennialism is a doctrinal belief that Christ will come after (*post*) the Millennium and usher in the eternal state. It is in contrast to premillennialism, the belief that Christ's return will be before (*pre*) the Millennium and that his second coming will usher in the thousand-year reign of Christ. In its broadest definition, postmillennialism would include amillennialism, but in the history of the church the two can be contrasted.

History. Though amillennialism arose in the last ten years of the second century A.D. and eventually dominated the theological scene, postmillennialism in its distinctive character came on much later. In contrast to amillennialism, postmillennialism was the more optimistic theory that the Gospel would be triumphant and would eventually bring in a thousand years of golden victory for the Gospel and the Christianizing of the entire world.

One of postmillennialism's earliest representatives was Joachin of Floris. His viewpoint contemplated three dispensations: the first from Adam to John the Baptist, the second from John the Baptist to Saint Benedict (A.D. 480–543), who founded many monasteries. The third dispensation, however, was to have had its final triumph about 1260. By that time the Gospel would have triumphed, and the world would have been turned to Christ.

Modern postmillennialism, however, did not really come to the fore until 1700, with the rise of Daniel Whitby, though there are many others who could be so classified. Whitby held that Revelation 20 was a recapitulation of previous prophecies in the book of Revelation. He held further that the Millennium was still future but that any generation was capable of starting the thousand years of this golden age of righteousness and peace on earth.

Because of the prevailing optimism of the day, as the world seemed to be on the threshold of new scientific developments, postmillennialism became an influential system of theology and probably the majority view in the eighteenth and nineteenth centuries.

In the latter part of the nineteenth and the early part of the twentieth centuries, due to the influence of the theory of evolution, liberal theologians also took up the view of postmillennialism and viewed it as describing the progress of the human race by its scientific and natural means. Conservative postmillenarians, however, opposed this evolutionary influence.

Postmillennialism in the twentieth century. Postmillennialism continued to be a dominant view of theology until World War I. With the advent of the period when Germany, the cradle of the Protestant Reformation, became the enemy attacking other countries in Europe, the idea of postmillennialism had a serious setback; and with World War II, many considered that postmillennialism was dead. The eschatology of the church was largely divided between amillennialism, which gained the most converts, and premillennialism, which also began to be a strong influence in the church.

Postmillenarians had difficulty with the exposition of Revelation 20. Though they were quite sure that the premillennial interpretation was wrong, they were divided as to whether the souls described in Revelation 20:4–6 were martyrs who came out of the preceding period or whether they were a description of the intermediate state, that is, souls in heaven. In general, postmillenarians held that the kingdom of God was in the hearts of men, not proceeding from a throne on earth, and that the kingdom promised in the Old Testament was being fulfilled in the spiritual life of believers. More liberal postmillenarians tended to extend the period into a long era embracing the future of humankind to the foreseeable future. Conservative postmillenarians continued to view the events that precede the Second Advent as the worldwide proclamation of the Gospel, the conversion of the elect, the conversion of the Jews, and a final climax with the coming of the Antichrist. At the Second Advent, according to the postmillenarians, all the righteous would be raised, as well as those who were not righteous. There would be a general judgment, the world as we know it would end, and life would proceed to the new heaven and new earth for eternity.

Since World War II, postmillennialism has largely been a dead issue, though there is a small but vocal group of postmillenarians still affirming the ultimate triumph of the Gospel and the Christianizing of the entire world.

Decline of postmillennialism. Postmillennialism declined for a number of important reasons: (1) Its principle of spiritualizing Scripture did not lead to a unified interpretation of passages teaching a future Millennium. (2) Postmillennialism was subject to being adopted by liberals who liked the idea of not taking Scripture literally. (3) The postmillennial explanation did not fit the historical situation in the twentieth century with World War

I and World War II. (4) The resulting trend was toward amillennialism and, in some cases, to premillennialism.

The apparent demise of postmillennialism, though with a few modern adherents, led to renewed emphasis on amillennialism as a prevailing eschatology of the church.

Amillennial Interpretation of the Messianic Kingdom

Definition. Amillennialism, like postmillennialism, viewed the second coming of Christ as the consummation of history and the introduction of the eternal state. However, unlike postmillennialism, which had an optimistic and rosy view of the Millennium, amillennialism was content to adopt the idea of a dual development. Both the kingdom of God and the kingdom of Satan would unfold in the present age and be judged at the Second Coming following a brief but violent rejection of the Gospel.

History. Amillennialism has a much longer history than postmillennialism in its modern form and goes back to the year A.D. 190. It is difficult to find anyone who qualifies as an amillenarian before that date, though some early Fathers did not make clear their eschatological point of view. Many scholars concede that the first two centuries were premillennial in theology.

About A.D. 190 the school of theology at Alexandria, Egypt, began to have pervasive influence. Its theologians attempted to harmonize the Scriptures with the pure idealism of the Greek philosopher Plato. The result was that Christian theology was subverted and removed from its historic statement. In addition to perverting other doctrines, this school had a devastating effect on premillennialism, which was largely destroyed in Northern Africa.

The church as a whole continued to grapple with the problem, but it was not until Augustine (A.D. 354–430), the famous bishop of Hippo, that a solution was found. Augustine's point of view was that though the Alexandrian spiritualization of Scripture was wrong, it fit the eschatology of the church. Accordingly, he felt that while most of the Bible should be accepted in its historical, grammatical sense, eschatology was a special case. Like the school of Alexandria, he rejected the idea of a literal kingdom on earth following the second coming of Christ.

According to Augustine, the present age is a conflict between the city of God and the city of Satan; it could also be viewed as a conflict between the church and the world. He held that the dual line of development would continue right up to the Second Coming, when the church would triumph.

Augustine seems to have held that the binding of Satan (Luke 10:18) took place during the earthly life of Christ. He viewed the Millennium as well advanced in his day. Some suggest that he thought the Millennium would terminate about A.D. 650, but this is hard to prove.

Augustine rejected premillennialism for a superficial reason, giving little attention to the prophecies that support the premillennial interpretation. He held that premillennialism viewed the Millennium as a period of carnal enjoyment, whereas he himself felt that it was a time of spiritual victory. On the ground that the view of premillennialism was carnal and unscriptural, he rejected a literal interpretation of Revelation 20. Augustine seems to have agreed that the Millennium was a thousand years in duration and began several centuries before Christ. Under his teaching, however, there was no specific Millennium in the sense of a literal kingdom on earth but rather a spiritual reign of Christ in the heart of believers.

Though Augustine did much to restore some of the doctrines of Christian theology to their proper place, it is obvious that he did little to clarify the church's eschatological viewpoint. His view that Satan is bound in this present age is contradicted by numerous passages that picture Satan as extremely active (1 Cor. 5:5; 7:5; 2 Cor. 2:11; 11:14; 1 Tim. 1:20; 1 Peter 5:8). His explanation of Luke 10:18 as being the same event as Revelation 12:7–9 and 20:2–3 is obviously flawed. Augustine held that the first resurrection of Revelation 20:5 refers to the regeneration of Christians, a view which, of course, is contradicted by the context.

Augustine was impressed with the power of sin he encountered in his own life and so regarded the present age as one of conflict between evil and good even though, ultimately, the good would triumph.

Modern viewpoint. Though Augustinian amillennialism continues to be the main explanation in current theology, other views have been advanced, including the concept that the Millennium is the intermediate state—that is, the period between a believer's death and his resurrection—or a combination of the two, which would make the kingdom reign coexistent in the hearts and minds of believers on earth as well as in the intermediate state. Another contemporary explanation is that the millennial kingdom is synonymous with the new heaven and new earth of Revelation 21–22. It is notable that, in offering these positions, their advocates do not provide detailed exegesis of passages that relate to it, nor do they consider the problems that contradict this interpretation. This comes out more clearly when the premillennial interpretation is considered alongside these other contending views.

The Premillennial Interpretation of the Messianic Kingdom

Proof for the premillennial interpretation has already been considered in our treatment of the Abrahamic covenant, the Davidic covenant, and the promise of the land. The premillennial interpretation, because it is pervasive and determines the interpretation of major sections of the Bible, is found throughout the Old and the New Testament, and the amassing of the evidence provides an excellent background for recognizing the contradictions of the postmillennial and amillennial interpretation.

The evidence from history. The history of the Old Testament, accompanied by its prophetic revelation, provides a solid base for the premillennial interpretation. Even those who do not accept premillennialism admit that if the prophecies are interpreted literally, they lead to the premillennial point of view. It is obvious from the many prophecies of the Old Testament that the people of Israel expected their coming Messiah to deliver them from their enemies and bring in a glorious kingdom of righteousness and peace in which Israel would be prominent. This is presented not simply in a few texts but throughout the Old Testament.

Though admitting that the Old Testament teaches a future messianic kingdom on earth, amillenarians attempt to support their own view by advancing two major considerations. First, they admit that the Jews were looking for a messianic kingdom on earth but claim that the New Testament contradicts this expectation and the interpretation was therefore wrong. The other point of view, which many amillenarians adopt, is that the literal interpretation was correct but that the promises are conditional and are not fulfilled because of Israel's failures. We will examine the Old Testament prophecies to see if they allow for either one of these two explanations.

As has already been brought out in previous chapters, the promises of the future messianic kingdom were often delivered by prophets who lived in the midst of apostasy, such as Jeremiah. Nevertheless, Jeremiah boldly predicted the future blessing of Israel following Christ's return as in 23:5–8 and 30:4–11. Typical of this treatment is Jeremiah's statement:

> " 'I am with you and will save you,'
>   declares the LORD.
> 'Though I completely destroy all the nations
>   among which I scatter you,
>   I will not completely destroy you.
> I will discipline you but only with justice;
>   I will not let you go entirely unpunished.' "
>   (Jer. 30:11)

Likewise, the exiled prophet Ezekiel stated emphatically that God would bring the children of Israel back from all the countries in which they were exiled (39:25–29). And in Psalm 89 the Davidic covenant was declared to be absolutely sure even if David's descendants were to forsake the law:

> "I will establish his line forever,
>   his throne as long as the heavens endure.
>
> "If his sons forsake my law
>   and do not follow my statutes,
> if they violate my decrees
>   and fail to keep my commands,
> I will punish their sin with the rod,
>   their iniquity with flogging;
> but I will not take my love from him,
>   nor will I ever betray my faithfulness.
> I will not violate my covenant
>   or alter what my lips have uttered.
> Once for all, I have sworn by my holiness—
>   and I will not lie to David—
> that his line will continue forever
>   and his throne endure before me like the sun;

> *it will be established forever like the moon,*
> *the faithful witness in the sky."* *(vv. 29–37)*

The history of interpretation in the New Testament likewise gives credence to the fulfillment of the promise of the messianic kingdom. As brought out in connection with the Davidic covenant, Mary was assured that her child, Jesus, would sit on the throne of David and reign over the house of Jacob forever (Luke 1:32–33). Obviously, Mary shared the faith of other Jews that when the Messiah came he would set up his kingdom on earth. Gabriel's reaffirmation is evidence that this was God's interpretation of the Old Testament prophecies.

Jesus himself affirmed that the disciples would sit on thrones judging the twelve tribes of Israel in the future kingdom (Luke 22:29–30). When the disciples asked Jesus about the time of the restoration of the kingdom of Israel in Acts 1:6, he told them that God had not revealed the time (v. 7), but he did not say that they were in error.

Paul took up this same issue in Romans 9–11, emphatically replying to his own query of whether Israel had been cast off and had no hope for the future, by saying that God had not rejected his people or forsaken his promises (11:1–27). Paul, in fact, affirmed that after the period of Gentile blessing,

> *" 'The deliverer will come from Zion;*
> *he will turn godlessness away from Jacob.*
> *And this is my covenant with them*
> *when I take away their sins.' "* *(vv. 26–27)*

Further confirmation is given in the book of Revelation. The disputed passage, Revelation 20, when properly interpreted, clearly supports the concept of a thousand-year kingdom following the second coming of Christ.

The question has been raised as to what the early church believed. Research of the New Testament as well as of extrabiblical literature reveals no trace of amillennialism in the first century. In fact, several early church Fathers who lived in the period can be listed as supporters of premillennialism. Among them are Aristion and John the Presbyter. Papias lists the apostles Andrew, Peter, Philip, Thomas, James, John, and Matthew as holding the premillennial point of view. Others born in the first century were also premillennial, such as

Clement of Rome, Barnabas, Hermas, Ignatius, and Polycarp. Except for Barnabas, who is a disputed premillenarian, not a single amillenarian can be named in the first century. To be sure, some of the early church fathers did not speak on the subject, and their views cannot be classified, but each one who offers any observations in regard to the premillennial interpretation and a future messianic kingdom on earth can be cited as evidence that there was a prevailing view of premillennialism in the first century.

In the second century, likewise, no trace of amillennialism can be found until about A.D. 190. In this period Justin Martyr, Melito, Hegesippius, Tatian, Irenaeus, Tertullian, Hippolytus, and Apollinarus can be pointed to as premillenarians. Although some of their teachings may not be shared in complete detail in modern interpretations, an overwhelming weight of premillennialism is seen in the second century.

With the rise of the Alexandrian school of theology, contention arose against premillenarians based on the supposed necessity of harmonizing biblical revelation with the idealism of Plato, a point of view that subverted all scriptural doctrines, not simply prophecy. Many think that the Alexandrian school of theology was heretical.

Though contention arose between the amillennial view and the premillennial view in the third century, other early church fathers can be cited as holding the premillennial view in the third century as well. Among them are Cyprian (c. A.D. 200–258), Commodius (A.D. 200–270), Nepos (A.D. 230–280), Coracion (A.D. 230–280), Victorinus (A.D. 240–303), Methodius (A.D. 250–311), and Lactantius (c. A.D. 240–320). The clear teaching of premillennialism in the early church before it was overtaken by the amillennial interpretation is sufficient evidence that the apostolic view was not amillennial and that the early church, following their teaching, expected Christ's return and a kingdom on earth.

Following the third century, however, premillennialism became less evident and the amillennial interpretation took over. This coincided, of course, with the advance of the church and its growing ritualism and, in some instances, departure from pure doctrine. Following Augustine in the fourth and fifth centuries, the Roman Catholic Church became largely amillennial, but through the centuries there have always been small groups, at least, that held a premillennial doctrine.

Premillennialism came to the fore in the nineteenth and twentieth centuries, among other things, as a defense against liberalism, evolution, and departure from historic doctrine. Premillenarians generally uphold the infallibility of Scripture and the inspiration of the Bible. Liberalism has never gained a foothold within premillennialism. Premillennial doctrine also carried with it other evangelical doctrines, so it went almost without dispute that a premillenarian was generally orthodox in other areas. Premillennialism was not embraced by most of the organized church which followed doctrine which often left out prophecy. The great prophetic conferences of the nineteenth and twentieth centuries designed to attack liberalism, though at the beginning including other millennial views, gradually became entirely premillennial. Premillennialism unquestionably came into its own in the twentieth century, with denominations, seminaries, colleges, and the Bible institute movement embracing the doctrine of the premillennial return of Christ.

Evidence from the principles of interpretation. Evangelical theology generally recognizes that Scripture as a whole should be interpreted from the grammatical-historical point of view in which Scripture is taken as a factual declaration of truth. This has yielded the orthodox creeds of the church, including also the doctrine of the Second Coming.

The idea that prophecy is an exception to this rule is an arbitrary decision motivated by unwillingness to accept what the Bible teaches about a future Millennium. Even in the interpretation of prophecy, the nonliteral interpretation is limited to doctrines that are not acceptable to amillennialism. The amillennial point of view may accept a literal Second Coming, a literal heaven, and a literal hell, but it rejects a literal millennial reign of Christ on earth. On the face of it, this viewpoint is arbitrary and without sufficient basis.

The spiritualizing interpretation of prophecy is contradicted by the prophecies that have already been fulfilled. Hundreds of prophecies throughout the Old and New Testaments are recorded as fulfilled prophecy. For example, such important prophecies as the birth of Christ in Bethlehem, his divine-human nature, his miracles on earth, his death on the cross, his bodily resurrection, and his bodily ascension into heaven all fulfill prophecy in a literal fashion. Likewise, in the Old Testament God's dealings with Israel again and again fulfilled prophecy. These include Israel's dispersions and regatherings and God's blessings and judgments on them. In a list of Old Testament prophecies it is rare to find a prophecy that is not fulfilled literally. Accordingly, the history of prophetic fulfillment ought to be a guideline. Just as even the most unusual prophecies were fulfilled literally in the past, so prophecies of the future, though seemingly strange and unlikely, are also subject to literal fulfillment. If this is the case, then the messianic kingdom of Christ, so clearly predicted in many Old Testament passages and also in the New Testament, should be accepted at face value. Standard principles of interpretation lead to the premillennial, not to the amillennial, interpretation.

The promised restoration of Israel. A familiar theme in both the Major and Minor Prophets is the anticipation of the restoration of Israel. Jeremiah 31 is a complete picture of this hope. Written in the time of Israel's apostasy when all seemed to be lost, Jeremiah describes the bright hope of God's gracious restoration of Israel in the future:

The LORD appeared to us in the past, saying:

> *"I have loved you with an everlasting love;*
> *I have drawn you with loving-kindness.*
> *I will build you up again*
> *and you will be rebuilt, O Virgin Israel.*
> *Again you will take up your tambourines*
> *and go out to dance with the joyful.*
> *Again you will plant vineyards*
> *on the hills of Samaria;*
> *the farmers will plant them*
> *and enjoy their fruit." (vv. 3–5)*

Though this prophecy was to some extent fulfilled in the return from the Babylonian captivity, it goes far beyond this to the ultimate messianic kingdom. God said through Jeremiah:

> *"See, I will bring them from the land of the north*
> *and gather them from the ends of the earth.*
> *Among them will be the blind and the lame,*
> *expectant mothers and women in labor;*
> *a great throng will return.*
> *They will come with weeping;*
> *they will pray as I bring them back.*

I will lead them beside streams of water
on a level path where they will not stumble,
because I am Israel's father,
and Ephraim is my firstborn son.
Hear the word of the LORD, O nations;
proclaim it in distant coastlands:
'He who scattered Israel will gather them
and will watch over his flock like a shepherd.'"

(31:8–10)

Likewise, Jeremiah predicted Israel's restoration, " 'The days are coming,' declares the LORD, 'when I will plant the house of Israel and the house of Judah with the offspring of men and of animals. Just as I watched over them to uproot and tear down, and to overthrow, destroy and bring disaster, so I will watch over them to build and to plant,' declares the LORD" (31:27–28).

As will be discussed in the chapter on the new covenant, God promised that Israel would operate under a gracious new covenant that would be in contrast to the Mosaic Law (Jer. 31:31–34).

Jeremiah declared emphatically that Israel would continue as long as our present earth lasts.

This is what the LORD says,

he who appoints the sun
to shine by day,
who decrees the moon and stars
to shine by night,
who stirs up the sea
so that its waves roar—
the LORD Almighty is his name:
"Only if these decrees vanish from my sight,"
declares the LORD,
"will the descendants of Israel ever cease
to be a nation before me."

This is what the LORD says:

"Only if the heavens above can be measured
and the foundations of the earth below be searched out
will I reject all the descendants of Israel

because of all they have done,"
declares the LORD. *(31:35–37)*

A more condensed statement of the same hope is given in Jeremiah 30:5–11, where Jeremiah predicts that Israel will have a terrible time of trouble. This prophecy coincides with other biblical prophecies of the Great Tribulation. Jeremiah adds, however, that Israel will survive this period of trouble and will be restored to serve her Lord God as well as David her king, who will be resurrected at the time of the Second Coming (v. 9). Jeremiah affirms that those scattered to distant lands will be brought back and that God will not destroy the nation Israel (v. 11).

In view of this clear statement by Jeremiah concerning the restoration of Israel, what do the amillenarians have to say? Some take the extreme view that Israel is unidentifiable today due to intermarriage. This, of course, is hardly recognized by anyone. Israelites know of their lineage even though they sometimes do not know from which tribe they have come. Some hold that Israel has been cast off. As has already been demonstrated, the Bible expressly says that Israel will not be cast off. Another avenue of dispute is to claim that Israel is the church and the promises are fulfilled in the church. Here again, only a segment of amillenarians hold this viewpoint, and, significantly, they want the promises of blessing that God gave Israel but not the threats. Actually, there is no real support for the concept that Israel has its promises fulfilled in the church, for the promises differ in character from what the church is experiencing in the present age. A more biblical approach to this on the part of postmillenarians is that Israel will be restored in the sense that they are converted in the church. This would constitute a partial spiritual restoration but would not satisfy the many passages that speak of their restoration to the land and their political restoration. The premillennial interpretation, which takes the passages literally and finds them fulfilled in the future kingdom which Christ will bring at his second coming, is far superior as a clear explanation of the revelation of God and these promises. The promises of Jeremiah 31 state explicitly that Israel will not be cast off nor lose its identity as a nation, and it will continue as a recognized entity in the world as long as the sun and moon endure (vv. 35–36).

Just as Israel literally went down into Egypt and literally

came back, the people were literally carried off into the Babylonian and Assyrian captivities and came back; and just as literally as they were scattered all over the world, so the Bible also predicts their return. As promised in Ezekiel 39:25–29, Israel is to be regathered to the last person (something that has never occurred in history), and once regathered will never be scattered again (Amos 9:15). This obviously refers to a geographic entity, the Promised Land, and to something that belongs to history rather than to life after death.

As brought out previously, Israel's restoration is implicit in the discussion of Paul in Romans 11 where Israel is pictured as being ultimately delivered by Jesus Christ at the time of his second coming. The basic promises of the Abrahamic covenant also require the restoration of Israel, because the promise that they will continue as a nation forever at the end of human history implies a recognizable and restored status that would coincide with the messianic kingdom. In Scripture the restoration of Israel clearly follows, rather than precedes, the second coming of Christ, and its restoration provides the final chapter of God's dealings with the earth prior to the new heaven and the new earth.

11

World History in
Prophetic Outline

The earth has become a global community with events of a world-transforming nature rapidly taking place. In these circumstances it is important to ask if the prophecies of the Bible cast any light on present world events and if they chart a course for the future.

As students of prophecy believe, the Bible offers a comprehensive view of the world, both in its history and in its future. The study of biblical prophecy casts an amazing beam of light on the significance of world events. In fact, the Bible offers an outline of world history that has already had dramatic fulfillment and clearly implies that dramatic events may soon fulfill prophecies as yet unfulfilled. The prophecies of the Bible will help one to understand what is happening in the world.

Introduction

In the prophecies of Daniel an amazing revelation is given of world history in outline. To Daniel the prophet was given the rare privilege of outlining not only Gentile history from his day until the second coming of Christ but also the parallel pathway of Israel, beginning with the rebuilding of Jerusalem in the time of Nehemiah and culminating in the second coming of Christ. Daniel 9:24–27 provides the outline of Israel's future and Daniel 2, 7–8, and 11–12 provide many details of the future of the nations in relationship to Israel. In particular, Daniel 2, in the imagery of Nebuchadnezzar's dream, reveals the history of the future world in outline until the Second Coming. Though other passages contain prophecies relating to Israel and the Gentiles, no other Old Testament prophet was given the comprehensive view that God revealed to Daniel. (For a commentary on the book of Daniel, see the author's *Daniel, the Key to Prophetic Interpretation* [Moody Press, 1971], 320 pages.)

Nebuchadnezzar's Dream

As the first chapter of Daniel indicates, Daniel was given an amazing preparation for his work as a prophet. He had been carried away to Babylon in the first conquest of Jerusalem by the Babylonians in 605 B.C. He and a number of other teenagers from royal families were selected to be carried off to Babylon, there to become future servants of King Nebuchadnezzar. As Daniel 1 records, Daniel stood true to his God and to his dietary restrictions. In chapter 1, which paves the way for Daniel's elevation to fame in chapter 2, Daniel was joined in his devotion to God and to the law of Moses by his three companions— Shadrach, Meshach, and Abednego. The many other captives, who, no doubt, were also carried from Jerusalem to Babylon, were not mentioned because they may have gone the way of the Babylonians, not maintaining their faith in the God of Israel.

Inability of the Wise Men to Interpret the Dream

Daniel 2 records the amazing revelation God gave to Nebuchadnezzar in the form of a dream or perhaps in more than one dream (Dan. 2:1). Even though it was still night, King Nebuchadnezzar summoned his wise men to determine the meaning of the dream. Upon learning of the dream, the astrologers exclaimed, "O king, live forever! Tell your servants the dream, and we will interpret it" (v. 4).

Nebuchadnezzar's wise men were faced with an unusual problem in that the king refused to tell them what the dream was and expected them to tell him the dream as well as its interpretation. Scholars are divided as to whether the king actually had forgotten the dream or at least did not have it clearly in mind, or was testing the supernatural claims of his wise men to have insight and wisdom beyond that which was natural.

Nebuchadnezzar was a young man who had just come into his kingdom when the dream occurred. According to 2:1, it took place "in the second year of his reign." He had inherited the cabinet of older men who had served as his father's advisers. The various classes of wise men claimed to have supernatural powers. It is possible that Nebuchadnezzar had some question as to whether these claims were valid, and wanted to put forth a test that would demonstrate clearly whether they had insight that could be given only by God.

King Nebuchadnezzar answered them roughly, "This is what I have firmly decided: If you do not tell me what my dream was and interpret it, I will have you cut into pieces and your houses turned into piles of rubble. But if you tell me the dream and explain it, you will receive from me gifts and rewards and great honor. So tell me the dream and interpret it for me" (Dan. 2:5–6).

The wise men, however, were unable to tell the king the dream, and they pleaded with him to tell them the dream so that they could interpret it. But the king was adamant and answered, "I am certain that you are trying to gain time, because you realize that this is what I have firmly decided" (2:8). He repeated his decree that, if they did not come forth with the dream and its interpretation, they would be executed.

This left the astrologers in a difficult position, and they pleaded with the king to give them the necessary information. They said, "There is not a man on earth who can do what the king asks! No king, however great and mighty, has ever asked such a thing of any magician or enchanter or astrologer. What the king asks is too difficult. No one can reveal it to the king except the gods, and they do not live among men" (2:10–11).

When the king received no further answer from the astrologers, he angrily ordered their execution. Unfortunately, as the decree went out to gather the men for execution, it included

Daniel and his friends who were classified as wise men even though they had not been present at this scene in the palace.

When Daniel was informed about the problem by Arioch, the commander of the king's guard, he went in to Nebuchadnezzar and asked for time (2:16). By then Nebuchadnezzar had cooled off somewhat and, no doubt, was intrigued that Daniel, a lad probably still in his teens, would come in and ask for time to interpret the dream instead of denying that the dream could be recalled and interpreted. Upon being granted permission, Daniel went to his three friends, Hananiah, Mishael, and Azariah, and with them pleaded with God to reveal to them the secret (vv. 17–18). It is interesting that Daniel here uses their Hebrew rather than their Babylonian names.

The Dream Revealed to Daniel

Verse 19 reports, "The mystery was revealed to Daniel in a vision." What followed was a demonstration of the maturity and brilliance of Daniel, for, instead of rushing in to the king immediately, he paused first to praise the God of heaven.

In 2:20–23 Daniel disclosed an amazing comprehension of the nature of God, his power and wisdom, and his ability to reveal secrets and to answer the prayers of Daniel and his friends by making known to them Nebuchadnezzar's dream and its interpretation. It was only after praising God in this fitting way that Daniel reported that he had the interpretation.

According to verse 24, Daniel reported to Arioch, under whose charge he was, that he knew the dream. He said, "Do not execute the wise men of Babylon. Take me to the king, and I will interpret his dream for him."

Arioch lost no time in going to the king to say, "I have found a man among the exiles from Judah who can tell the king what his dream means" (2:25). Arioch wanted, if possible, to collect some benefit from the king for having discovered Daniel even though he had done nothing beyond letting Daniel have time to pray.

Daniel Reported to Nebuchadnezzar

Upon Daniel's arrival in Nebuchadnezzar's court, he was asked by the king, "Are you able to tell me what I saw in my dream and interpret it?" (2:26). No doubt, the king was excited. Was this going to be proof that there was a supernatural God who could interpret a dream? And could Daniel be told what the dream was?

Daniel replied with a great deal of wisdom and maturity: "No wise man, enchanter, magician or diviner can explain to the king the mystery he has asked about, but there is a God in heaven who reveals mysteries. He has shown King Nebuchadnezzar what will happen in the days to come" (2:27). In this statement to Nebuchadnezzar Daniel was preparing the way for a testimony of the greatness of his God as the true God of heaven that would continue on for many years. Because the Babylonians also claimed that their gods were gods of the heavens, Daniel's testimony set forth for Nebuchadnezzar the truth that the God of Daniel was far greater than the gods of Babylon who had failed his wise men in regard to revealing the dream.

Daniel then told the king, "As you were lying there, O king, your mind turned to things to come, and the revealer of mysteries showed you what is going to happen. As for me, this mystery has been revealed to me, not because I have greater wisdom than other living men, but so that you, O king, may know the interpretation and that you may understand what went through your mind" (2:29–30). Daniel, with great wisdom and care, made it plain that his ability to interpret the dream was not normal wisdom but was supernatural and had come directly from Daniel's God.

The Contents of the Dream

The head of gold. Daniel reported to the king that what he saw was "a large statue—an enormous, dazzling statue, awesome in appearance. The head of the statue was made of pure gold" (2:31–32). It was implied in this revelation that the statue was larger than human life, possibly standing ten or more feet tall, and that it stood so close to Nebuchadnezzar's bed that it was a terrifying experience.

The chest of silver and body of bronze. Daniel quickly described the upper and lower parts of the body: "Its chest and arms [were] of silver, its belly and thighs of bronze" (2:32).

The legs of iron and feet of iron and clay. Daniel then described the legs and the feet: "Its legs [were] of iron, its feet partly of iron and partly of baked clay'" (v. 33). It should be obvious that the image was top-heavy, since the specific gravity of gold is greater than silver, and, in turn, the metals became lighter and lighter down to the feet of iron and clay, which did not constitute a firm base for the image.

The destroying rock. As Daniel contemplated the image, he said:

> While you were watching, a rock was cut out, but not by human hands. It struck the statue on its feet of iron and clay and smashed them. Then the iron, the clay, the bronze, the silver and the gold were broken to pieces at the same time and became like chaff on a threshing floor in the summer. The wind swept them away without leaving a trace. But the rock that struck the statue became a huge mountain and filled the whole earth. (2:34–35)

By this time Nebuchadnezzar was fascinated by Daniel's accurate picture of his dream, and he eagerly awaited the interpretation.

The Interpretation of Nebuchadnezzar's Dream

Babylon, the head of gold. Daniel began his interpretation by pointing out that the head of gold represented Nebuchadnezzar and the Babylonian Empire. "This was the dream, and now we will interpret it to the king. You, O king, are the king of kings. The God of heaven has given you dominion and power and might and glory; in your hands he has placed mankind and the beasts of the field and the birds of the air. Wherever they live, he has made you ruler over them all. You are that head of gold" (2:36–38). Although Nebuchadnezzar did not reign over the entire earth, from the standpoint of Babylon at the time in which Daniel lived it seemed as if the whole inhabited earth around them was under his dominion. Nebuchadnezzar reigned not only over his human subjects, but even the beasts of the field and the birds of the air were to some extent under his control. All of this is captured in the concept that the head of gold was Nebuchadnezzar.

The Medes and the Persians and Greece. In 2:39 Daniel said that the upper part of the body and the lower part of the body constituted two other kingdoms: "After you, another kingdom will arise, inferior to yours. Next, a third kingdom, one of bronze, will rule over the whole earth." Daniel was not given the identity of the second and third kingdoms at this time. Later on in Daniel 7 and 8 it became clear that the second kingdom was that of Medo-Persia and the third kingdom that of Greece, as identified in Daniel 8:5–8, 20–21.

The final world empire: Rome. In chapter 2 as well as in chapter 7, major attention was given to the fourth empire which, though not identified in the book of Daniel, is clearly the empire of Rome, which succeeded the Grecian Empire. This was represented in Nebuchadnezzar's vision by the legs of iron and feet of iron and baked clay. Daniel described it:

> Finally, there will be a fourth kingdom, strong as iron—for iron breaks and smashes everything—and as iron breaks things to pieces, so it will crush and break all the others. Just as you saw that the feet and toes were partly of baked clay and partly of iron, so this will be a divided kingdom; yet it will have some of the strength of iron in it, even as you saw iron mixed with clay. As the toes were partly iron and partly clay, so this kingdom will be partly strong and partly brittle. And just as you saw the iron mixed with baked clay, so the people will be a mixture and will not remain united, any more than iron mixes with clay. (2:40–43)

The Roman Empire fulfilled this description and later details in Daniel 7 as well. Through verse 43 the scene is prophetically what was true at the time of Christ.

Daniel went on, however, to reveal the time when the kingdom would be destroyed by a fifth kingdom which would come from heaven:

> In the time of those kings, the God of heaven will set up a kingdom that will never be destroyed, nor will it be left to another people. It will crush all those kingdoms and bring them to an end, but it will itself endure forever. This is the meaning of the vision of the rock cut out of a mountain, but not by human hands—a rock that broke the iron, the bronze, the clay, the silver and the gold to pieces. The great God has shown the king what will take place in the future. The dream is true and the interpretation is trustworthy. (2:44–45)

A rock described as one that was not cut out with human hands—that is, was prepared by God himself—struck the image at its feet and shattered the iron and the clay of the feet, resulting in the whole image disintegrating and fulfilling the description Daniel gave in 2:35. Once the statue was destroyed, it disappeared, and the rock that destroyed it, referring to the fifth kingdom, filled the whole earth.

The Roman Empire did not fall suddenly but rather hung on for many centuries after Christ and only gradually disappeared from human history. Accordingly, the destruction of the fourth empire, as described here, has never been fulfilled. This has been variously explained, but the best explanation is that it will be fulfilled by a revived Roman Empire that will occupy the stage at the end of human history. This is brought out more clearly in Daniel 7.

In these prophecies, as is often the case in the Old Testament, the prophetic foreview does not take into consideration the period between the first coming of Christ and the period immediately preceding his second coming. This is illustrated in the many cases where the first and second coming of Christ are referred to in the same breath, as in Isaiah 61:2. The present age involving the calling out of the church was not the subject of Old Testament prophecy, and God's plan for the present age was not revealed until the New Testament.

Nebuchadnezzar's dream and the statue's destruction by the rock cut out without hands makes clear that neither the amillennial nor postmillennial interpretation of the kingdom is supported by the Old Testament.

According to amillennial interpretation, the kingdom is in the world today and is being fulfilled by the progress of the church. This viewpoint implies at least a partial conquering of the world by the Gospel. But Nebuchadnezzar's dream does not indicate this. Neither is the postmillennial view—that the world is going to get better and better through the preaching of the Gospel and climax in the second coming of Christ—supported. Instead, the power of the Gentile kingdoms as described in Daniel, including the revival of the great Roman Empire and the final great world empire, will be destroyed by the second coming of Christ, not by a gradual process of human effort. Accordingly, we have here a preliminary revelation to which Daniel later added information concerning the outline of world events, including details about the four great empires of the past as well as the revived Roman Empire of the end time. At the second coming of Christ these kingdoms will be completely destroyed and replaced by the kingdom from heaven, represented here by the rock cut out without hands.

Nebuchadnezzar's Reaction

The Scriptures record that Nebuchadnezzar, mesmerized by Daniel's interpretation, bowed down before Daniel and testified to the greatness of his God. "Then King Nebuchadnezzar fell prostrate before Daniel and paid him honor and ordered that an offering and incense be presented to him. The king said to Daniel, 'Surely your God is the God of gods and the Lord of kings and a revealer of mysteries, for you were able to reveal this mystery'" (2:46–47).

Having given this preliminary recognition of the God of Daniel, Nebuchadnezzar showered gifts and privileges upon Daniel. According to verses 48–49, "Then the king placed Daniel in a high position and lavished many gifts on him. He made him ruler over the entire province of Babylon and placed him in charge of all its wise men. Moreover, at Daniel's request the king appointed Shadrach, Meshach and Abednego administrators over the province of Babylon, while Daniel himself remained in the royal court." Nebuchadnezzar's reaction to the revelation from God was astonishing. Remarkably the king elevated Daniel, though a foreigner and probably still a teenager, to be his right-hand man in authority. He also appointed Daniel's three companions as administrators over the province of Babylon, the capital province. These actions began a long and prominent career for Daniel in Nebuchadnezzar's government. He served Nebuchadnezzar until the king's death about forty years later. As in the case of Joseph in Egypt and Mordecai in the book of Esther, God honored those who honored him and gave them prominent places in Gentile government. In the process, God gave a wonderful testimony to his greatness as God and his superiority over the gods of the Babylonians.

12

Babylon in Old Testament Prophecy

The book of Daniel provides a remarkable overview of the four empires that would dominate the world scene before Christ's second coming. Other Scriptures add a great deal to Daniel's prophecies. Most of these prophecies already have been fulfilled, and their literal fulfillment is the evidence that the prophecies yet unfulfilled will also have literal fulfillment. Knowing this helps a great deal in answering questions about the future of our modern world.

Ancient Babylon

The first mention of Babylon in Scripture is found in Genesis 11:1–8, where people in rebellion against God built a tower, or ziggurat, which had the significance of reaching up into the heavens in rebellion against the true God. The tower was built of brick because there was no stone in the area, and tar was used for mortar (v. 3). Their purpose was stated in v. 4: "Then they said, 'Come, let us build ourselves a city, with a tower that reaches to the heavens, so that we may make a name for ourselves and not be scattered over the face of the whole earth.'" Instead of bringing the human race together, however, God pronounced a judgment on the project and confused their languages (vv. 5–7), with the result that they were scattered over the earth (v. 8). The building of the tower and the city, which later became Babylon, ceased. Accordingly, the city was given the name "Babel" (v. 9), similar to a Hebrew word for "confused."

Scriptures are silent on the history of Babylon except for the reference to "a beautiful robe from Babylonia," which was part of the plunder of Achan as recorded in Joshua 7:20–21. It was not until Isaiah, Jeremiah, Ezekiel, and Daniel mentioned Babylon in their prophecies and the Babylonian captivity took place (2 Kings 17–25; 1 Chron. 9:1; 2 Chron. 32–36) that Babylon became a prominent subject of biblical revelation. Between Genesis 11 and the time of the captivities, however, secular history provides considerable details concerning the progress of this civilization.

Some traces of civilization go back to the period before 3000 B.C., with written history beginning about 2800 B.C. The area of Babylon in the Mesopotamian Valley was the scene of advanced civilization, including canals and large buildings, especially temples.

From 2360 to 2180 B.C. the empire of Sargon reached from Persia all the way to the Mediterranean Sea. Abraham was born in what is known as the Neo-Sumerian period (2070–1960 B.C.). Following this, the land was overrun by the Elamites and the Amorites until 1830 when Babylon began once again to assert power. This period, known as the Old Babylonian period (1830–1550 B.C.), included the reign of Hammurabi (1726–1686 B.C.). Though we do not know too much about the personal life of Hammurabi, his famous code was discovered, which gave significant insight into the civilization of his day. The code was found on an eight-foot-high stele of black diorite discovered in 1901–1902 at Susa. It contained 282 paragraphs dealing with criminal law and did much to reveal the times in which Hammurabi lived. It also revealed an advanced Akkadian language which by that time was well organized.

Babylon had its ups and downs, however, and was invaded by the Kassites (1550–1169) following the Old Babylonian period (1830–1550 B.C.). Another dynasty, known as Dynasty II of Isin

(1169–1039 B.C.), recorded another period of Babylonian ascendancy. Babylon began to decline in 1100 B.C. until the Neo-Babylonian period began about 625 B.C. with Nabopolassar, the father of Nebuchadnezzar. In the period before Nabopolassar, however, Tiglath-Pileser became king of Babylon in 729 B.C. but was attacked by Sennacherib in 689 B.C., resulting in the destruction of Babylon by fire. It was later rebuilt by Esarhaddon and finally won its freedom from Assyria in 625 B.C. when Nabopolassar was able to establish his authority over Babylon, and the Neo-Babylonian Empire began.

Nabopolassar proved to be an able king who, cooperating with the Medes, attacked and destroyed Nineveh, the capital of Assyria (612 B.C.). It was so thoroughly destroyed that it was not rediscovered until the nineteenth century. Nebuchadnezzar, as a Babylonian general, after defeating Egypt the same year his father died, not only conquered Egypt but also Jerusalem (605 B.C.), beginning the biblical captivity of Israel.

Prophecies Concerning Babylon in Isaiah

Though Babylon was still an obscure nation and there was no hint of its later greatness, Isaiah the prophet began his predictions concerning Babylon, especially in chapters 13, 14, and 47. Babylon is also mentioned in Isaiah 21:9; 39:1, 3, 6, 7; 43:14; and 48:14, 20.

It is remarkable that Isaiah wrote before Babylon had become a prominent empire, and his predictions covered the wide scope of the earlier capture of Babylon by the Medes and the Persians (539 B.C.) as well as the ultimate destruction of Babylon at the time of the second coming of Christ.

One of the outstanding predictions of Isaiah is found in Isaiah 13. Babylon is pictured in verses 1–16 as sharing in the destruction of God visited upon all Gentile powers at the time of the second coming of Christ. In verses 17–19, however, specific reference is made to the fact that the Medes and the Persians would conquer Babylon in 539 B.C.:

> See, I will stir up against them the Medes,
>   who do not care for silver
>   and have no delight in gold.
> Their bows will strike down the young men;
>   they will have no mercy on infants

nor will they look with compassion on children.
Babylon, the jewel of kingdoms,
the glory of the Babylonians' pride,
will be overthrown by God like Sodom and Gomorrah.

In verses 20–22, however, the distant view is again the subject of prophecy. Isaiah wrote:

She will never be inhabited
or lived in through all generations;
no Arab will pitch his tent there,
no shepherd will rest his flocks there.
But desert creatures will lie there,
jackals will fill her houses;
there the owls will dwell,
and there the wild goats will leap about.
Hyenas will howl in her strongholds,
jackals in her luxurious palaces.
Her time is at hand,
and her days will not be prolonged.

The judgments on Babylon in verses 17–19 have now become history, but they did not fulfill verses 20–22, as Babylon has continued to be inhabited even down to modern times. At the present time Babylon in Iraq is being partially rebuilt as a tourist attraction, and some of the historic monuments are being reconstructed. As verses 20–22 make clear, when Babylon has its final destruction, as recorded in Revelation 18, it will never rise again.

Under Nebuchadnezzar who assumed the throne in 605 B.C., the same year he conquered Jerusalem, Babylon became one of the wonders of the world with great palaces, temples, and other buildings. Though conquered by the Medes in 539 B.C., as Isaiah predicted, Babylon was not destroyed. It continued to be a flourishing city long after the time of Christ, and included a large colony of Jews.

In Isaiah 14 the ultimate downfall of Babylon is related to the downfall of Satan. Many since the early Fathers have felt that Isaiah 14:12–17 goes far beyond any judgment on Babylon and records the fall of Satan at the time of his first sin. The passage also records his pride and his desire: "I will make myself like the Most High" (v. 14). In this chapter the wicked kings of Babylon join in death other monarchs who were far from God.

In Isaiah 47 the judgment on Babylon was likened to judgment on a wicked woman, described in verse 1 as the "Virgin Daughter of Babylon."

When Hezekiah showed visitors from Babylon all his storehouses, silver and gold, and the plunder of his kingdom, Isaiah told him: "Hear the word of the LORD Almighty: The time will surely come when everything in your palace, and all that your fathers have stored up until this day, will be carried off to Babylon. Nothing will be left, says the LORD. And some of your descendants, your own flesh and blood who will be born to you, will be taken away, and they will become eunuchs in the palace of the king of Babylon" (39:5–7). This was, of course, fulfilled in the Babylonian captivity. Brief mention of the future destruction of Babylon is also made in Isaiah 43:14 and 48:14, 20.

History has not recorded the ultimate destruction of Babylon, as it continued to be a noteworthy city as late as A.D. 1000. Because the destruction of Babylon has not been completely fulfilled, the prophecy has given rise to the idea that Babylon will be rebuilt and become a major city in the end time.

Much confusion exists in scholarly interpretation of the prophecies of Babylon because of the varied references to the city of Babylon as Babylon, to the empire as Babylon, and to the religions of Babylon as Babylon. Each of these areas has its own line of prophecy and fulfillment.

Prophecies Concerning Babylon in Jeremiah

Jeremiah lived in the time of the Babylonian captivity and faithfully predicted that it would come. Because Jeremiah's prophesying brought disfavor from the king of Judah, Jeremiah almost lost his life. In addition to the prophecies concerning the captivity, Jeremiah devoted two long chapters (Jer. 50 and 51) to revelation concerning Babylon.

The prophecies of Jeremiah 50–51 concern almost entirely the fall of Babylon to the Medes and the Persians. Jeremiah used poetic language to dramatically describe it. A few instances, however, seem to go beyond the destruction of the empire in 539 B.C., because the city itself was not destroyed. Jeremiah 50:39–40 reaches to the end time and the second coming of Christ. Here Jeremiah wrote, "'So desert creatures and hyenas will live there, and there the owl will dwell. It will never again be inhabited or lived in from generation to generation. As God overthrew Sodom and Gomorrah along with their neighboring towns,' declares the LORD, 'so no one will live there; no man will dwell in it.' " Like the references in Isaiah 13, this refers to the ultimate destruction of Babylon in the end time.

Likewise, in Jeremiah 51:25–26 the prophecy seems to be beyond anything that has been fulfilled: " 'I am against you, O destroying mountain, you who destroy the whole earth,' declares the LORD. 'I will stretch out my hand against you, roll you off the cliffs, and make you a burned-out mountain. No rock will be taken from you for a cornerstone, nor any stone for a foundation, for you will be desolate forever,' declares the LORD." This has not been fulfilled in history and awaits the destruction prior to the second coming of Christ.

Most of the prophecies of Babylon are in the light of what the Babylonians did in carrying Judah into captivity. Jeremiah predicted that those who anticipated victory over Babylon, as promoted by the false prophets (cf. Jer. 28:1–17), were wrong and that Babylon would conquer Judah and destroy it. Though this resulted in imprisonment for Jeremiah, he was vindicated, of course, when their captivity took place.

Of major interest to Bible students are the prophecies of Jeremiah concerning the duration of the Babylonian captivity. In Jeremiah 25:11 and 29:10 he anticipated the length of the Babylonian captivity as seventy years. Concerning the destruction of Judah, Jeremiah wrote, " 'This whole country will become a desolate wasteland, and these nations will serve the king of Babylon seventy years' " (25:11). In Jeremiah 29:10 further revelation was given: "This is what the LORD says: 'When seventy years are completed for Babylon, I will come to you and fulfill my gracious promise to bring you back to this place.' " It was on the basis of this prophecy that Daniel in 9:1–3 was impelled to turn to the Lord in prayer for the restoration of Jerusalem. His prayers were answered as recorded in Ezra and Nehemiah.

In addition to predicting the downfall of Judah at the hands of the Babylonians, Jeremiah also described in detail that Egypt would be conquered by the Babylonians and destroyed (43:10–13; 44:30; 46:1–26). Because of this prophetic revelation, Jeremiah warned the Jews in Egypt to escape before the

Babylonian armies overtook Egypt (44:30). These prophecies were fulfilled.

Prophecies Concerning Babylon in Ezekiel

As a contemporary of Jeremiah, Ezekiel added his revelation to the same themes that occupied Jeremiah. Like Jeremiah, he predicted the Babylonian captivity (17:12–24) and Egypt's fall to the Babylonians (29:18–19; 30:10–25; 32:1–32). Ezekiel also predicted the downfall of Tyre (26:7–28:19).

Prophecies Concerning Babylon in Daniel

The many prophecies of Isaiah and Jeremiah are brought together in the book of Daniel as Daniel himself experienced captivity, revealed the future of the Gentiles, and lived to see the Medes and the Persians fulfill the prophecy of conquering Babylon.

As a captive and among the first to be carried off from Jerusalem to Babylon, Daniel experienced what Jeremiah had predicted. Probably nearing the close of his training as a servant of the king, Daniel revealed to Nebuchadnezzar the meaning of a prophetic dream the king had had. As previously considered, the head of gold of the image (2:32, 38) represented Babylon as headed by Nebuchadnezzar the king.

In Daniel's vision of the four beasts in Daniel 7, representing the same four Gentile powers, beginning with Babylon, he described the Babylonian Empire as a lion with eagle's wings: "The first was like a lion, and it had the wings of an eagle. I watched until its wings were torn off and it was lifted from the ground so that it stood on two feet like a man, and the heart of a man was given to it" (Dan. 7:4). The lion as the king of beasts was a good representation of Babylon, and the eagle, the king of the birds, likewise, was a fitting simile. The reference to the wings being plucked and standing like a man refer to Nebuchadnezzar's experience in Daniel 4 when he went through seven years of insanity in fulfillment of Daniel's prophecy (vv. 24–26). The destruction of the great tree in Daniel 4 was a suitable vehicle for describing Nebuchadnezzar's temporary downfall. Through the amazing experience of Daniel 4, however, many believe that Nebuchadnezzar came to faith in the true God of Israel.

In both Daniel 2 and 7 the Babylonian Empire was to be succeeded by the empire of the Medes and the Persians. This is recorded historically in Daniel 5, which chronologically comes between Daniel 8 and 9.

The fall of Babylon to the Medes and the Persians in October 539 B.C. was shocking evidence of the power of God to bring down the mighty. The long reign of Nebuchadnezzar from 605 to 562 B.C. had prospered, and in it Daniel had had a major role as executive under Nebuchadnezzar. The reigns of kings following Nebuchadnezzar were short-lived. The reign of his son and successor, Amel-Marduk, lasted only two years before he was assassinated. Neriglissar reigned from 560 B.C. to 556 when he died, but his son, who assumed the throne after Neriglissar's death, was almost immediately assassinated. In 556 B.C. Nabonidus, with the help of others, usurped the throne. Three years later he named Belshazzar as co-ruler in an attempt to authenticate his rule. Belshazzar is variously regarded as the grandson or some other relation to Nebuchadnezzar.

In the background of Daniel 5, before the city of Babylon fell, Nabonidus—who was not in Babylon—and his army had already been captured and the entire area of Babylonia had been taken over by the Medes and the Persians, with the exception of the city of Babylon itself.

Herodotus gives a glorified picture of the city as being fourteen miles square with the Euphrates River running through it from north to south. According to Herodotus, the walls were 350 feet high and 87 feet thick with 250 watchtowers 100 feet higher than the wall itself. The city was surrounded by a deep water moat which made attacking it difficult. Babylon was a large enough area to sustain itself for many years. Provisions were such that the claim was made that it could last for twenty years of siege. From other sources the grand description of Herodotus is whittled down to a city about one-third the size pictured by him, but it still remained that Babylon was a formidable city and that the Medes and the Persians had tried for months to conquer it without success.

The plan was finally conceived, however, to divert the water of the Euphrates River, which ran underneath the wall, in order to lower the level of the water sufficiently to permit the armies to wade underneath the opening into the city both on the north and the south sides. This effort was underway on the very night of Belshazzar's feast as he gathered to encourage his lords and himself about the invincibility of the gods of Babylon. The graphic picture of the handwriting on the wall (Dan. 5:5) and Daniel's interpreting it as prophesying the downfall of Babylon were fulfilled only hours later as the Medes and the Persians overwhelmed the city of Babylon. Overnight, the city that could not fall fell to the second empire just as Daniel had predicted in chapters 2 and 7 and had implied in chapter 8.

The downfall of Babylon ended her political power and to some extent also affected her religious life, because the Medes and Persians put an end to much of the religious corruption that had characterized Babylon. However, the Babylonian religion moved first to the city of Pergamum in Asia Minor (Rev. 2:12–17) and later to Rome, where it was a major influence in corrupting the Christian church. Many of the objectionable rituals taken over by the Roman Catholic Church had their origin in Babylonian religion.

Through the centuries the influence of Babylon has been that of satanic perversion of biblical religion. This will continue until the end time. Babylon's influence in Revelation 17 and 18 is the subject of final prophecy. Revelation 17 portrays Babylon as a wicked woman astride a scarlet-colored beast, thus describing the final form of the apostate church in the end time. Revelation 18 pictures Babylon as the capital city of the end time which is destroyed by the gigantic earthquake of Revelation 16:19. Further attention will be given to this in consideration of the end time (Chapters 30–31). Much hangs on the issue as to whether the city of Babylon will be literally rebuilt as the capital of the Roman Empire and the world empire in the period before the second coming of Christ. Its evil influence, both politically and religiously, is too well chronicled in the Bible to deny that this influence will not be terminated until the second coming of Christ.

13

Medo-Persia in Old Testament Prophecy

The history of the Medes and the Persians forms an important background for the history of Israel during the period of Assyrian and Babylonian power. Their empires eventually stretched to the south of the Caspian Sea and somewhat to the east of Babylonia and included an area of about 250 miles east and west and 600 miles north and south. Their rise to power was hindered by the dominance of Assyria. They are mentioned in the inscriptions describing the reign of Shalmaneser III who was one of the brilliant kings of Assyria (859–824 B.C.).

As Assyria began to decline in the seventh century, the Medes and the Persians increased in strength. They moved into a place of power when the Medes captured Asshur, the capital city of Assyria in 610 B.C. Two years later, in 612 B.C., with the help of Chaldeans, they captured and destroyed Nineveh, the major city of the Assyrian Empire.

When the Babylonian Empire began to weaken after Nebuchadnezzar's death, the Persians became more and more power-

ful and during the reign of Cyrus II the Persians conquered
Media in 549 B.C. and combined the two countries into the
Medo-Persian Empire.

As the Medes and Persians grew in strength, they conquered
Babylonia, except for the city of Babylon; it fell in October of
539 B.C. The Medes and Persians dominated the Middle East
until the rise of Alexander the Great, who conquered Medo-
Persia in 331 B.C. The history of this period is the background of
the return of Israel to her land and the rebuilding of the temple
and the city of Jerusalem.

Early Prophecy Concerning Medo-Persia in Isaiah and Jeremiah

Isaiah the prophet, in predicting the fall of Babylon about 175
years before it happened, also prophesied that the Medes and
the Persians would be God's avenging instrument. In Isaiah
13:17–19 he predicted that the Medes would overthrow Babylon: "See, I will stir up against them the Medes, who do not care
for silver and have no delight in gold. Their bows will strike
down the young men; they will have no mercy on infants nor
will they look with compassion on children. Babylon, the jewel
of kingdoms, the glory of the Babylonians' pride, will be
overthrown by God like Sodom and Gomorrah." Isaiah added a
further word in Isaiah 21:2 where Media was urged to attack
Babylon.

Jeremiah, who came later during the time of the Babylonian
captivity, pronounced judgment on Babylon and the other
nations of his time, including Media. In Jeremiah 25:25 Media is
one of the nations that would be punished by God. The
extended prophecy of Jeremiah concerning Babylon in Jeremiah
50–51 also predicted that the Medes would destroy Babylon
(Jer. 51:11, 28). Actually, the prophecies of judgment on the
Medes and the Persians were not as severe as those on Babylon,
because Babylon had been the instrument of the destruction of
Jerusalem and the captivity of the kingdom of Judah while the
Medes and the Persians were God's instrument to allow them to
go back after the captivity and rebuild Jerusalem.

Prophecy Concerning the Medes and Persians in Daniel

Daniel, however, provides the most extensive prophetic
revelation concerning the Medes and the Persians. His revela-

tion is introduced in Daniel 2:39 in connection with the interpretation of Belshazzar's great image. The Medes and the Persians are not mentioned by name but are described in Daniel 2:39 as "another kingdom" which "will rise, inferior to yours." Medo-Persia was represented in the image by the chest of silver and the two arms, indicating the dual character of the kingdom, including the Medes and the Persians. As silver is less valuable than gold, so the Medes and the Persians lacked the glory of the Babylonian Empire.

A more detailed revelation of the place of Medo-Persia in prophecy was provided in chapter 7 in Daniel's vision, which occurred in 553 B.C., about fifty years after the revelation of the image of Nebuchadnezzar. In Daniel 7 the four great empires anticipated in the image of Daniel 2 were described as four beasts, the first being a lion representing Babylon, and the second a bear representing Medo-Persia. Daniel recorded the substance of his vision concerning Medo-Persia in these words: "And there before me was a second beast, which looked like a bear. It was raised up on one of its sides, and it had three ribs in its mouth between its teeth. It was told, 'Get up and eat your fill of flesh!' " (7:5). The representation of Medo-Persia as a bear, a strong lumbering beast, in contrast to the lion, which represented Babylon, was apt, as the Medo-Persian Empire was not brilliant in its history. It also is in contrast to the empire of Greece which followed and which was represented as a leopard with four wings (v. 6). Daniel did not reveal the significance of the three ribs, but one plausible explanation is that it represents the three geographical areas embraced in the Medo-Persian Empire—Persia, Media, and Babylonia. Medo-Persia was urged to expand its borders in the statement, "Get up and eat your fill of flesh!" (v. 5).

A more complete revelation of the place of the Medo-Persian Empire in the prophetic program was provided in Daniel 8, where there is a dual revelation of the Medo-Persian Empire and the Grecian Empire. Two years after Daniel had the vision of chapter 7, he received his second vision. He wrote:

> In the third year of King Belshazzar's reign, I, Daniel, had a vision, after the one that had already appeared to me. In my vision I saw myself in the citadel of Susa in the province of Elam; in the vision I was beside the Ulai Canal. I looked up, and there before me was a ram with two horns, standing

> beside the canal, and the horns were long. One of the horns
> was longer than the other but grew up later. I watched the
> ram as he charged toward the west and the north and the
> south. No animal could stand against him, and none could
> rescue from his power. He did as he pleased and became
> great. (8:1–4)

It is not clear from the text whether Daniel was actually in
Susa, which later became the capital of Persia, or whether he
pictured himself there in his vision, but the probability is that it
was only in vision. In Daniel's time Susa was not a significant
city, and he must have been astounded to find himself there in
this province of Elam. The ram with two horns, one of which
was greater than the other, was an apt description of the Medo-
Persian Empire, as Persia was much stronger than Media.
During the 280 years that the Medo-Persian Empire had power,
it went to the west, north, and south, since the Scriptures
indicate, and no force was strong enough to stand against it.

In the vision that followed, Greece was represented by the
goat with the prominent horn, referring to Alexander in his
conquest as supplanting and conquering Medo-Persia (Dan.
8:5–8). This occurred about 331 B.C. when Medo-Persia was
overrun by Alexander's armies. Significantly, the Medo-Persian
Empire extended to the west, north, and south, but not to the
east since it was already in the east, in contrast to the Grecian
Empire which came from the west and went east all the way to
India. Daniel lived to see the beginning of the Medo-Persian
Empire and the fall of Babylon in 539 B.C. But the advent of the
Grecian Empire, more than two hundred years later, was
entirely by prophetic revelation. Even at the time the vision was
given, about 550 B.C., the prophecy about the domination of the
Medo-Persian Empire was still eleven years away.

Israel's Restoration Under Medo-Persia

Though the particular events of the Medo-Persian Empire
were not all detailed by Daniel, except as prophesied in Daniel
11:1–2, the significance of the Medo-Persian Empire was
largely in its relation to Israel's restoration. Under Babylon,
Israel had experienced her destruction as a nation and the ruin
of Jerusalem and the beautiful temple. Under the Medes and the
Persians, Israel's restoration was to take form.

During the Medo-Persian Empire the last six books of the Old

Testament were written—Ezra, Nehemiah, and Esther, giving the history of the period; Haggai, Zechariah, and Malachi, recording the prophecy of the period.

The early events of the Medo-Persian Empire following the conquest of Babylon in 539 B.C. concerned the new ruler of Babylon described as "Darius son of Xerxes (a Mede by descent), who was made ruler over the Babylonian kingdom" (Dan. 9:1). Though some identify Darius as Cyrus, known as Cyrus II or Cyrus the Great (ruler of Persia, 559–530 B.C.), it is more probable that Darius was either Gobryes or Gubaru and that he was an appointee by Cyrus to govern Babylon itself, probably having control of the southern portion of Medo-Persia. In any case, we read, "So Daniel prospered during the reign of Darius and the reign of Cyrus the Persian" (6:28).

The events of the Medo-Persian Empire are important for their relationship to the restoration of Israel. In the very first year of Cyrus the captives of Israel were given permission to return to Jerusalem and rebuild the temple (2 Chron. 36:22–23; Ezra 1:1–4). Generally speaking, the Medo-Persian Empire was kinder to the Jewish faith than the Babylonians had been, and the building of a temple for the God of Israel was seen as a favorable project by the Medes and Persians. Religion in Medo-Persian was not tied into the political structure as it was at Babylon, and generally speaking, there was freedom of worship. Because of delays in the rebuilding of the temple, it was not completed until about 515 B.C. during the reign of the Medo-Persian ruler Cambyses II (530–522 B.C.) who succeeded his father who was killed in battle in 530 B.C. Persian rulers had the common title of Artaxerxes, and in Ezra 7:1 Artaxerxes I Longimanus was mentioned (465–425 B.C.). In the book of Esther, Xerxes was also referred to as Ahasuerus (Esth. 1:1), one of the great rulers who reigned from 486–465 B.C. Another prominent ruler of Persia was Darius I, or Darius the Great, not to be confused with Darius the Mede of Daniel 5:30.

As mentioned previously in Daniel 11:2, three kings of Medo-Persia were mentioned, the first probably being Cambyses II who succeeded Darius the Mede. Next to rule was Smerdis, who reigned for only eight months before he was murdered. Then Darius the Great (522–486 B.C.), mentioned in Ezra 4:24, assumed the throne. It was this Darius who approved the final building of the temple. The fourth king, mentioned in Daniel

11:3, was probably Xerxes (486–465 B.C.), the one who appointed Esther as his queen.

Taken as a whole, the Medo-Persian Empire provides the connection between Babylon and the conquests of Alexander the Great.

The Rebuilding of Jerusalem

Most important in the Medo-Persian period was the reconstruction of the city of Jerusalem. The temple was built first in 515 B.C. Many years later, under Nehemiah in 444 B.C., the wall of Jerusalem was rebuilt. In the fifty years following the rebuilding of the wall, the city of Jerusalem itself was rebuilt. Accordingly, Jesus was born, not in Babylon, but in Bethlehem, a village near Jerusalem. By the time of his birth Israel was once again a thriving nation.

The prophecies concerning the Medes and the Persians as they came from the pen of Daniel, however, provide another illustration of the accuracy of prophecy and the fact that prophecy, when fulfilled, meticulously corresponds to the prophecy itself. Though Babylon and Rome both reappear in the future in connection with God's prophetic program, Medo-Persia largely passed from the scene once the Grecian Empire was established.

The Fall of Medo-Persia

Medo-Persia probably somewhat lost its original power and strength in the years that followed its domination of the Middle East. By the time Alexander the Great began his conquest, Medo-Persia was no longer a formidable military power and quickly fell to his armies. By 331 B.C. Medo-Persia was incorporated in the empire of Alexander.

14

Greece in Old Testament Prophecy

In Daniel's prophecy of the four great world empires, the third
of the four was the Grecian Empire which followed the Medo-
Persian period. At the time Daniel was written, Greece was the
small country of Macedonia, and gave little promise of becoming a world power. After the Medo-Persian Empire had flour-
ished from 539 B.C. to 331 B.C., it was succeeded by the Grecian
Empire. Alexander the Great, their king and general, had begun
a campaign to conquer Western Asia in 336 B.C. The Persians fell
to his power in 331 B.C. The prophecies of Scripture relating to
this are so accurate that liberal scholars who deny the possibility
of prophecy have adopted the theory of Porphyry, an atheist of
the third century A.D., that Daniel was a forgery, actually written
in the second century by a pseudo-Daniel. This is an uninten-
tional compliment to the accuracy of Daniel's prophecies. There
was no possibility of Daniel's guessing that two hundred years
after his approximate death the Grecian Empire would become
great. The theory that Daniel is a second-century forgery has

been undermined by the discovery of a copy of Daniel in the Dead Sea Scrolls, though liberals are slow to admit it.

There is relatively little about the Grecian Empire in the Bible because it existed in the period between Malachi and Matthew, after the Old Testament had already been written. By the time of Christ, however, the Roman Empire had already succeeded the Grecian Empire, and there was no need for additional prophecy.

Identification of the Grecian Empire

The modern word *Greece*, or *Grecia*, does not appear in the Hebrew Bible. Instead, the word *yawan* (English *javan*) is mentioned in Genesis 10:2, and the name is assigned to one of the sons of Japheth who was a grandson of Noah. Though the Bible does not explicitly say so, it is commonly believed that Javan was the father of the Greek race and that his descendants not only occupied Greece but also the islands related to it. Accordingly, in Scripture his name in the Old Testament is translated "Grecian" (cf. Isa. 66:19; Ezek. 27:13, 19; Dan. 8:21; 10:20; 11:2; Joel 3:6; Zech. 9:13).

The Prophecies of Daniel 2, 7

Though mentioned by Isaiah (66:19), who lived a hundred years before Daniel, no specific prophecies are related to the empire of Greece until Nebuchadnezzar's image. Daniel interpreted the lower part of the body made of brass and the upper part of the legs as another kingdom that would succeed the first two kingdoms. In the interpretation of Nebuchadnezzar's image, scant attention was given to the place of Greece.

Daniel's first vision occurred many years later in 556 B.C. during the first year of the reign of Belshazzar, king of Babylon (Dan. 7:1). In this vision, in addition to describing Babylon as a lion and Medo-Persia as a bear, the Grecian Empire was described as a leopard with four wings and four heads: "After that, I looked, and there before me was another beast, one that looked like a leopard. And on its back it had four wings like those of a bird. This beast had four heads, and it was given authority to rule" (v. 6). The accuracy of this prediction is made clear when the history of the Grecian Empire is examined. The four wings of the leopard imply that a leopard, already swift of foot, would have great speed. This characterized all of Alexander's conquests. Likewise, the four heads illustrate the division of the Grecian Empire after Alexander's death. The accuracy of the description is that there were four, not three or five, and that the Grecian Empire, because of the swiftness of its conquests, was totally unlike that of the Medes and the Persians, which was described as a lumbering bear (v. 5).

Alexander the Great's Conquests

A detailed study of the conquests of Alexander illustrates how quickly he was able to conquer Western Asia. Originally possessing only a small part of Europe known as Macedonia, Alexander was intent upon erasing whatever memory there was of the Persian king Xerxes' attempted conquest of Greece a century earlier. Though Xerxes had failed, at that time it did not result in the expansion of Greece.

Alexander began by conquering Troy in Asia Minor. He then attacked the Persian army at Granicus and succeeded in annihilating it at Issus. Further opposition to Alexander in Persia was useless, and most of these cities were conquered without a fight. Only Tyre and Gaza required an extensive siege. The conquest of Tyre involved building a causeway from the mainland to the island. The city of Tyre itself was razed, and its ruins were used to build the causeway, a fulfillment of prophecy (Ezek. 26:3–5). Though conquered originally by Nebuchadnezzar, Tyre's final destruction was by Alexander in 332 B.C. Tyre never recovered from this war, although a new city was in place in the time of Christ.

Alexander then proceeded south to Egypt and was able to conquer the whole nation without a serious fight. In the process he established Alexandria, which became one of the largest cities of Egypt and held a significant place in Egypt's future.

Coming from Egypt, Alexander engaged in a battle at Issus, and again he won a decisive victory. With this behind him, his armies proceeded east to India. When they arrived they were weary and refused to go on, and it seemed best to return.

While in Babylon in 323 B.C., during a great feast in celebration of his victory, Alexander passed away, a victim of overeating, drunkenness, and malaria. He remains an outstanding example of a man who could conquer the world but could not conquer himself.

Though the conquests of Alexander were rapid and short in duration, he left the imprint of Greek culture in the areas he conquered. As a result, the Greek culture has persisted to modern times.

Following Alexander's death, his empire was divided into four parts as illustrated in the four wings and the four heads of Daniel 7:6.

The Grecian Empire Described as a Goat with a Principal Horn

Though mentioned only briefly in Daniel 2:39 and 7:6, all of chapter 8 is devoted to describing the conquest of Medo-Persia and the rise of the Grecian Empire. A vision was given to Daniel in 553 B.C., the third year of Belshazzar (8:1). While in Susa he had a vision of a ram with two horns being destroyed by a goat with one large horn: "I looked up, and there before me was a ram with two horns, standing beside the canal, and the horns were long. One of the horns was longer than the other but grew up later. I watched the ram as he charged toward the west and the north and the south. No animal could stand against him, and none could rescue from his power. He did as he pleased and became great" (vv. 3–4). This prophecy clearly refers to the Medes and the Persians, with the larger of the two horns referring to the Persian Empire, as stated in Daniel 8:20. During the two centuries of its sway, from 539–331 B.C., the Persian Empire was unopposed.

Having set the stage describing the Persian Empire, Daniel was then given a vision of the Grecian Empire under the figure of a goat:

> As I was thinking about this, suddenly a goat with a prominent horn between his eyes came from the west, crossing the whole earth without touching the ground. He came toward the two-horned ram I had seen standing beside the canal and charged at him in great rage. I saw him attack the ram furiously, striking the ram and shattering his two horns. The ram was powerless to stand against him; the goat knocked him to the ground and trampled on him, and none could rescue the ram from his power. The goat became very great, but at the height of his power his large horn was broken off, and in its place four prominent horns grew up

toward the four winds of heaven (8:5–8). The goat is identified in Daniel 8:21 as Greece.

This prophetic vision had correspondingly accurate fulfillment. The goat with one large horn pictured Alexander, and the two-horned ram depicted the Persian Empire. Though it is clear that the ram was destroyed, the goat at the height of its power had his large horn broken off—that is, Alexander the Great himself died. The four prominent horns that grew up after the major horn was broken off represent the four generals of Alexander.

Following Alexander's death in 323 B.C., the Grecian Empire was divided under the four generals of Alexander. Ptolemy was given Egypt and the surrounding territories; Seleucas was given Syria, Asia Minor, and lands to the east; Lysimachus was given Thrace and the surrounding territories; and Cassander was given Macedonia and Greece itself. Following the division of the empire, various changes took place, and eventually Thrace and the surrounding territories were joined to Greece, leaving three major kingdoms—that is, Macedonia, Syria, and Egypt. Later in prophecy Syria and Egypt become important.

The Prophecy Concerning Antiochus Epiphanes

After this concise and graphic picture of the destruction of the Medo-Persian Empire and of the division of the Grecian Empire split into four parts, attention was given to what was a relatively minor aspect of this period which was described as a "little horn" (Dan. 8:9–14). This "little horn" was said to grow in power toward the south and east and toward the beautiful land—that is, Israel (v. 9). There follows a revelation of a conflict of this "little horn" with the hosts of heaven: "It grew until it reached the host of the heavens, and it threw some of the starry host down to the earth and trampled on them. It set itself up to be as great as the Prince of the host; it took away the daily sacifice from him, and the place of his sanctuary was brought low. Because of rebellion, the host of the saints and the daily sacrifice were given over to it. It prospered in everything it did, and truth was thrown to the ground" (vv. 10–12).

It should be noted first that this "little horn" comes out of the Grecian Empire and not the Roman Empire. Therefore, it should not be confused with Daniel 7:8, referring to a "little horn" in the Roman Empire. In comparing the history of the period to what the Scriptures reveal, one clearly concludes that it refers to Antiochus Epiphanes, the ruler of Syria from 175 to 164 B.C.

Secular history, especially in 1 and 2 Maccabees, reveals that Antiochus was a determined foe of the Jewish religion and did what he could to stamp it out. In the process, as Daniel 8:11–12 indicated, he stopped the sacrifices of the temple and caused its desolation (vv. 11–13). According to the Scriptures, the temple would be desecrated for 2,300 evenings and mornings before it would be reconsecrated (v. 14). Antiochus stopped the temple sacrifices; set up an idol of a pagan god in the temple; and attacked the people of Israel who persisted in worshiping God, killing thousands of men, women, and children. This precipitated the Maccabean Revolt, which he was unable to contain. The period of 2,300 mornings and evenings should be considered as 2,300 days of twenty-four hours each, not years, as some cults have taught, attempting to mark the year 1844 as a prophetic date. This was the period during which the temple was desecrated from 171 to 165 B.C.

Antiochus eventually had to give in, and the temple was reconsecrated and the Jewish religion renewed. Antiochus himself died of natural causes while conducting a war in 164 B.C.

Because the action of Antiochus in desecrating the temple and stopping the sacrificial system seems to parallel what is described of the "little horn" of Daniel 7, of whom it is said that he also would abolish the daily sacrifice and cause an abomination in the temple (Dan. 12:11), some have attempted to bring the two prophecies together. It is preferable to observe the guidelines of Scripture here. Though Antiochus and his reign are now history, along with his desecration of the temple, these passages seem to be in anticipation of the ultimate desecration of the temple and the stopping of the sacrifices by the future world ruler, the little horn of Daniel 7:8, who will dominate the world in the last three and a half years before Christ's second coming. The future ruler will fulfill the prophecies of Daniel 12:11 as well as the related prophecies of 2 Thessalonians 2:4 and Revelation 13:14–16.

Further Prophecies of the Grecian Empire in Daniel 10 and 11

Daniel's fourth and final vision is recorded in chapters 10, 11, and 12. The first two chapters relate to the Grecian Empire.

Daniel 10 describes Daniel's further revelation about the Grecian Empire. Daniel was prepared for the vision by three weeks of fasting, after which he saw a vision of a man dressed in linen. Eventually, an angelic messenger, who had been delayed by demonic opposition for three weeks, arrived to describe the final revelation to him.

The revelation was given in Daniel 11:1–35, one of the most amazing prophecies in the Bible. A close examination of this passage reveals that approximately 135 prophecies were made, describing the course of the empire of Medo-Persia and Greece over an extended period of time. As stated earlier, these prophecies are so accurate and so detailed that liberal interpreters reject the possibility that this was written by Daniel in the sixth century B.C. Accordingly, liberal scholars have followed the Neoplatonic philosopher Porphyry, who claimed that Daniel was a forgery written in the second century B.C. by a pseudo-Daniel and written after the events described. This theory, however, has now been exploded by the discovery of a complete copy of Daniel in the Qumran papers written 700 years earlier than the previous Daniel manuscript. This makes the forgery theory untenable. Liberals now are attempting to answer this problem but, so far, have been largely silent. The prophecies of Daniel 11:1–35 cover the period of the later Persian emperors and the Alexandrian or Grecian period, culminating in Antiochus Epiphanes, who reigned from 175 to 164 B.C. over Syria. Beginning in verse 36, however, the prophecy leads to the end time.

Four kings of Persia are described in the opening portion of Daniel's prophecy: " 'Now then, I tell you the truth: Three more kings will appear in Persia, and then a fourth, who will be far richer than all the others. When he has gained power by his wealth, he will stir up everyone against the kingdom of Greece' " (Dan. 11:2). The four kings mentioned are references to Cambyses (529–522 B.C.), a ruler whose reign was not mentioned in the Old Testament; Pseudo-Smerdis (522–521 B.C.); Darius I, Hystaspes (521–486 B.C.; cf. Ezra 5–6); and Xerxes I (486–465 B.C.; cf. Ezra 4:6). Of these, Xerxes I was the most prominent because he was the one who attempted to conquer Greece in 480 B.C. Although he raised an immense armada of ships and many troops, he was defeated, largely due to a storm that destroyed his fleet of ships. Esther apparently was his queen. It is possible that the disaster that took place when his army attacked Greece occurred between Esther 1 and 2, which would account for the need for something to cheer him up, such as a new queen. The historical background is supplied by Ezra, Nehemiah, and Esther, with references to Haggai, Zechariah, and Malachi. Daniel probably died about 530 B.C., near the time of the close of the rule of Darius the Mede and Cyrus II (550–530 B.C.), who was not mentioned in Daniel 11.

The revelation of the coming of Alexander the Great is indicated in Daniel 11:3–4: " 'Then a mighty king will appear, who will rule with great power and do as he pleases. After he has appeared, his empire will be broken up and parceled out toward the four winds of heaven. It will not go to his descendants, nor will it have the power he exercised, because his empire will be uprooted and given to others.' " This prophecy was literally fulfilled in the life and conquest of Alexander the Great. It anticipated his untimely death and the division of his kingdom among his four generals. Earlier, in Daniel 8:5–8, as interpreted by Daniel in 8:21–22, the same events are prophesied. During Daniel's lifetime it would have been unusual to anticipate the greatness of the Grecian Empire.

In Daniel 11:5–6 the warfare between Egypt, the king of the South, and Syria, the king of the North, is spelled out:

"The king of the South will become strong, but one of his commanders will become even stronger than he and will rule his own kingdom with great power. After some years, they will become allies. The daughter of the king of the South will go to the king of the North to make an alliance, but she will not retain her power, and he and his power will not last. In those days she will be handed over, together with her royal escort and her father and the one who supported her."

Though Syria was not mentioned because it did not exist as a nation at the time of Daniel's writing, it is clear that Egypt and Syria are the two countries involved. At the time this prophecy was fulfilled, Ptolemy I Soter (323–285 B.C.) was the king of Egypt, and the one who was described as stronger was Seleucus I Nicator (312–281 B.C.). Seleucus had been forced to flee from Antigonus, another general under Alexander the Great; but later, with the help of Ptolemy I of Egypt, he defeated Antigonus, making it possible for Seleucus to seize control of an area of land extending all the way from east Asia Minor to India. This was the fulfillment of the prophecy that he would be stronger than the king of Egypt.

The power of Egypt and Syria was joined, as indicated in the marriage of the daughter of the king of the South, Egypt, to the king of the North, Syria. Marriage alliances were common in the ancient world. The daughter referred to was Berenice, the daughter of Ptolemy II Philadelpus (285–246 B.C.), who was king of Egypt at that time. The king of the North mentioned in 11:6 was Antiochus II Theos (261–246 B.C.). This marriage alliance did not last, however, as indicated in verse 7. Both Berenice and Antiochus were killed following a conspiracy conducted by Laodiceia, the wife of Antiochus, while Berenice's father, Ptolemy, died at the same time. This amazing sequence of events, described so accurately by Daniel here in this prophecy, corresponds precisely to the history of the period.

These events were followed by the rise of Ptolemy III Euergetes(246–222 B.C.), a later king of Egypt who conquered the northern kingdom of Syria and carried off a great deal of booty (Dan. 11:7–8).

Further wars between the North and the South are mentioned in 11:9, with temporary victories on each side, as prophesied in verses 9–13. Seleucus II Callinicus, a king of the North, attacked the king of the South in 240 B.C. but was defeated without conquering Egypt.

The prophecy in verses 11–12 anticipated a challenge of Egypt by Antiochus the Great in 217 B.C. but with the result that Egypt destroyed the army of Antiochus.

The prophecies of verses 13–16 correspond precisely to the history of the period, describing various wars and the success of the king of the North. Subsequent counterattacks by Egypt did not succeed.

A new power, however, emerged in the expanding control of Rome, and in Daniel 11:17–20 the northern kingdom had to give up its hope of conquering Egypt. Syria and Egypt formed an alliance with the marriage of Cleopatra to Ptolemy V Epiphanes, as indicated in verse 17. Antiochus turned his attention to Greece, attempting to conquer it, but was defeated in 191 B.C. at Thermopylae and again later in 189 B.C. at Magnesia, southeast of Ephesus, this time by Roman soldiers. This is described accurately in verses 18–19.

The accurate detail of Daniel 11:1–35, corresponding so

precisely to the tangled history of the period, is one of the most amazing passages in the Bible of detailed prophecy concerning the future, and demonstrates clearly the inspiration of Scripture as well as the divine revelation involved.

Daniel's Fourth Vision Continued: Antiochus Epiphanes

Two famous persecutors of Egypt are mentioned in 11:20–21. The first of these was Seleucus IV Philopater (187–175 B.C.) and his successor Antiochus IV Epiphanes (175–164 B.C.), the person referred to in Daniel 8:23–25 as a persecutor of Israel and as the "little horn" of Daniel 8:9–14.

The tax collector mentioned in 11:20 was Heliodorus (2 Macc. 3:7), a man appointed by Seleucus IV Philopater who had the task of raising a thousand talents a year to be paid to Rome. Seleucus IV Philopater died, however, in 175 B.C. Some believe he was killed by poison to pave the way for Antiochus IV Epiphanes, who began his reign in 175 B.C. Antiochus IV was able to secure the throne through the murder of possible candidates and by intrigue. Accordingly, he was described by Daniel as "a contemptible person who has not been given the honor of royalty" (v. 21). He was able for a time, however, to have considerable power in the kingdom.

Antiochus IV's claim to the throne was based on such a tangled history of the times that it is amazing how accurate the prophecy is. Seleucus IV was poisoned to death, and his younger brother, Dimetrius, was out of the way as a prisoner in Rome. Their infant brother, Antiochus, was also a possible contender for the throne. Antiochus IV Epiphanes was helped to the throne by the murder of the baby Antiochus by Andronicus, but Antiochus IV also put Andronicus to death. Thus the way was clear for Antiochus to secure the kingdom.

Antiochus IV took the title of Epiphanes, meaning "the glorious one." His enemies, however, mimicking the spelling, called him "Epimanes," which meant "madman." Antiochus IV survived an attack by a large army from Egypt, as indicated in 11:22. The statement that "a prince of the covenant will be destroyed" probably refers to the deposing of Onias III as the Jewish high priest, an event that began the persecution of the Jews by Antiochus IV.

Within five years after Antiochus IV took the throne, he was able to consolidate his power in his own area as well as wage a war against a large army of Egypt, which Daniel referred to as the king of the South in 11:25–26. The aftermath of the battle was that while Antiochus was king of Assyria and he and the king of Egypt, Ptolemy V Epiphanes (203–181 B.C.), had a conference, as described in 11:27: "The two kings, with their hearts bent on evil, will sit at the same table and lie to each other, but to no avail, because an end will still come at the appointed time." The conference did not achieve peace, but Antiochus IV returned to his home base with great wealth, and this aggravated his irritation at the Jews who had not supported him. According to verse 28, he began his persecution of them.

As recorded in 1 and 2 Maccabees, Antiochus IV desecrated the Jewish temple by offering a sow upon the altar and putting a statue of a Greek pagan god in the Holy Place. This precipitated the Maccabean Revolt, with the tragic result that thousands of Jews—men, women, and children—were killed, but the revolt was not suppressed. The desecration of the altar itself is mentioned in 11:31–32. The final stage of this desecration of the temple was part of his frustration at an attack on Egypt which had failed because of the power of Rome, and Antiochus IV wisely decided it was not a good time to attempt to invade Egypt. This change of situation was mentioned in verses 29–30: " 'At the appointed time he will invade the South again, but this time the outcome will be different from what it was before. Ships of the western coastlands will oppose him, and he will lose heart. Then he will turn back and vent his fury against the holy covenant. He will return and show favor to those who forsake the holy covenant.' " The reference to "ships of the western coastlands" was a reference to the power of Rome.

In this time of distress for the people of Israel, Daniel said, "Those who are wise will instruct many, though for a time they will fall by the sword or be burned or captured or plundered. When they fall, they will receive a little help, and many who are not sincere will join them. Some of the wise will stumble, so that they may be refined, purified and made spotless until the time of the end, for it will still come at the appointed time" (11:33–35). Verse 35 concludes the prophetic foreview of Antiochus IV, and from here on in the chapter, the end time, which is still future, is anticipated.

The comprehensive prophecy concerning amazing details of the Grecian Empire is a sensational proof that prophecy can deal with details—and with perfect accuracy. The prophecies would be impossible to invent, and they demand the supernatural inspiration of the Holy Spirit.

15

Rome in Old Testament Prophecy

Importance of Rome

The Roman Empire is important to Christians because it was the political power that dominated the world during the lifetime of Jesus Christ and the apostles. Its political power began 250 years before Christ was born, and the final Roman ruler was not killed until A.D. 1453—a span of 1,700 years.

In history as well as in the Bible, the Roman Empire was important. It was the greatest empire of all time in territory possessed and in duration of political power. It is necessary to know something about Rome in order to understand the Bible.

The course of the Roman Empire was prophesied in great detail, and many of those prophecies have been fulfilled. However, unlike the preceding world empires of Babylon, Medo-Persia, and Greece, the final chapter of the Roman Empire has not been fulfilled. Accordingly, many interpreters of prophecy believe the future holds a revival of Rome and its ultimate expansion into a global empire. This will occur during the ten-nation confederacy prophesied in Daniel 7:7, 24 and the last seven years preceding the Second Coming. The final destruction of revived Rome will be fulfilled when Christ returns. For these reasons the study of prophecy relating to Rome is important to Bible students.

Rome in Fulfilled Prophecy

Though mentioned in Acts, Romans, and 2 Timothy, Rome was never referred to by name in the Old Testament. Yet Old Testament prophecies concerning Rome are unmistakable, especially in the revelations given through Daniel. The great majority of evangelical Bible expositors who find Daniel predicting the course of Babylon, Medo-Persia, and Greece recognize that the fourth empire, though unnamed, is clearly Rome. Of all the world empires of Scripture, including Egypt and Assyria, Rome was by far the most powerful, the most extensive in territories subdued, and the longest in duration. For more than a thousand years the Roman Empire was a major factor in Southern Europe, Western Asia, and Northern Africa, leaving its imprint on every aspect of culture and life. The rise of this fourth empire was depicted in Daniel 2 in the legs and feet of the great image of Nebuchadnezzar (v. 33) and the fourth beast of Daniel 7 (v. 7).

The rise of the Roman Empire was already underway about seventy years before the predicted wars between Syria and Egypt, during the time of Antiochus Epiphanes (175–164 B.C.). In its first stage Rome conquered Italy itself. Sicily was conquered in 242 B.C. Though Carthage for a time challenged Roman power and conquered Spain in 202 B.C., when Rome later conquered Spain, Carthage became a tributary under Rome. This occurred after the battle of Zama in North Africa. Carthage was eventually destroyed in 146 B.C.

Following this conquest the Mediterranean soon became a Roman lake as the Roman Empire, after extending its authority north of the Alps, began to conquer nations to the east, including Macedonia, Greece, and Asia Minor. As Daniel 7:7 anticipated, Rome devoured its conquered peoples, carrying off thousands into slavery and superimposing her own rigid government upon them: "After that, in my vision at night I looked, and there before me was a fourth beast—terrifying and frightening and very powerful. It had large iron teeth; it crushed and devoured its victims and trampled underfoot whatever was left. It was different from all the former beasts, and it had ten horns." Antiochus Epiphanes had to recognize the power of Rome in the latter days of his reign. Jerusalem and Israel came under Roman power in 63 B.C. when Pompey, known as Pompey the Great (106–48 B.C.), conquered Jerusalem.

Roman power continued to expand to the north throughout what is today Switzerland, France, and Belgium and lands south of the Rhine and the Danube. The southern part of Great Britain also came partially under Roman power. To the East, Roman power extended all the way to the Euphrates, including the Mesopotamian Valley as well as all of North Africa. As anticipated in Daniel 2:40, " 'Finally, there will be a fourth kingdom, strong as iron—for iron breaks and smashes everything—and as iron breaks things to pieces, so it will crush and break all the others.' " Nothing could be made clearer than that the Scriptures concerning the fourth empire of Daniel were fulfilled literally in the expansion of Rome's power.

Unfulfilled Prophecy Concerning Rome

As predicted in Daniel 2 and 7, however, the final outcome of the Roman Empire has never been fulfilled. The explanation here, as it is for many prophecies in the Old Testament, is that the prophetic vision of the Old Testament did not include the two thousand years since Christ. Instead, the prophecies leap from the time of the first coming to the time of the second coming of Christ. Accordingly, in Daniel 2, though the two legs of iron clearly represent the eastern and western territories of the Roman Empire, nothing has occurred in history to correspond to the statue's feet of clay and iron. The fact that the eastern portion of the Roman Empire existed much longer than the western portion was not indicated in the image of Daniel 2. It is as if a curtain fell on the prophetic scene at the time of the first coming of Christ, a curtain that is not lifted until the present church age is over and the end time preceding the Second Coming begins.

Nothing in history corresponds to the prophecy of Daniel 2:34–35: "While you were watching, a rock was cut out, but not by human hands. It struck the statue on its feet of iron and clay and smashed them. Then the iron, the clay, the bronze, the silver and the gold were broken to pieces at the same time and became like chaff on a threshing floor in the summer. The wind swept them away without leaving a trace. But the rock that struck the statue became a huge mountain and filled the whole earth."

In history, instead of being suddenly destroyed, the Roman Empire gradually ebbed away over many centuries. Rome first lost her control over territories most distant from Italy, including Great Britain, France, and areas of Germany. But Italy was not spared, and Attila led the Huns in an invasion of Italy in A.D. 451. A few years later in A.D. 455, Italy also succumbed to the Vandals and the Moors.

Portions of the Roman Empire, however, continued to exist in one way or another. The eastern territory of the Roman Empire was gradually conquered by the followers of Mohammed, who first conquered Persia, then Syria, Israel, and Europe, and also swept across North Africa into Spain. These were followed later by the Turks, who conquered Persia, Armenia, and Asia Minor.

The final blow came in A.D. 1453 when Mohammed II's forces conquered Constantinople and killed the last of the Roman emperors in the battle. Turks continued to control Asia Minor and the Holy Land until well into the twentieth century, and the Holy Land was freed of Turkish and Moslem control only by the events of World War I. Nothing of this long, drawn-out process was indicated in Old Testament prophecy. The reason for this is quite clear. The final blow to the image of Daniel 2 will be by the "rock," representing Jesus Christ in his second coming, and the millennial kingdom will follow. This prophecy gives no comfort to the postmillennial interpretation of prophecy which follows the premise that the church conquered Rome, a view that is historically inaccurate.

Just as the image of Daniel 2 was destroyed suddenly by the kingdom from heaven, so also, according to Daniel 7, the final destruction of the Roman Empire has not been fulfilled and awaits the Second Coming.

Many have attempted to find the ten-horned stage of Daniel 7:7 fulfilled in ten kings of the Roman Empire, but there is nothing in history that corresponds to this. Never have ten Roman kings reigned simultaneously as this prophecy is interpreted in Daniel 7:24. Likewise, the ruler of Daniel 7:8 who conquers three, then apparently all ten kingdoms, and later becomes a world ruler (Dan. 7:23), has no correspondence to anything that has occurred in history.

The requirement for fulfillment of both Daniel 2 and 7 is a revival of the Roman Empire in relation to the end of the age. The New Testament adds many prophecies along this line. The final ruler will be politically Roman, as were the people who destroyed Jerusalem in A.D. 70 (Dan. 9:26). The Roman Empire fulfilled the prophecies precisely as in Daniel 2 and 7 right at the time of the first coming of Christ. From there on, however, there is no correspondence to history, and the final stage of the Roman Empire, which will be destroyed by the kingdom that comes from heaven, has never been fulfilled.

In Daniel's vision he sees the fall of Rome as related to the second coming of Christ: "In my vision at night I looked, and there before me was one like a son of man, coming with the clouds of heaven. He approached the Ancient of Days and was led into his presence. He was given authority, glory and sovereign power; all peoples, nations and men of every language worshiped him. His dominion is an everlasting dominion that will not pass away, and his kingdom is one that will never be destroyed" (7:13–14). The final kingdom, which is from heaven and will come with Christ's second coming, according to premillenarians, is most in line with these portions of Scripture. The final chapter of the Roman Empire is found in the enlarged picture given in the book of Revelation.

16

The 490 Years of Israel's Prophetic Destiny

Israel, the Key to Interpreting Prophecy

For a Gentile Christian, the subject of Israel in prophecy does not immediately have an appeal as an important doctrine. When one begins to study prophecy in the Bible, however, it soon becomes evident that Israel is in the center of biblical prophecy and that to understand prophecy as a whole one must understand God's purpose for Israel.

In the history of prophetic interpretation the study of Israel often has been neglected, with the result that prophecy as a whole has not been understood. The many attempts to twist prophecies about Israel as referring to the church, and the widespread neglect of biblical revelation about Israel, resulted in inattention to Israel until revived interest in prophecy in the twentieth century directed attention once again to Israel's prophesied future.

Revived study of Daniel 9:24–27 has focused on the question of Israel's future. Though the passage is difficult, and many divergent interpretations tend to confuse the interpreter, careful exegesis will reward the interpreter with Daniel's summary of Israel's prophetic history as culminating in the Second Coming. What follows the Second Coming is not in Daniel's revelation but is found in other prophets such as Isaiah and Jeremiah.

Importance of this prophecy. Few passages in the Old Testament are more important to prophetic understanding than Daniel 9:24–27. Interpretation of this passage depends largely on whether the interpreter is a liberal who denies the reality of prophecy, a conservative amillenarian who recognizes the legitimacy of prophecy but denies that it is to be interpreted literally, or a premillennialist who attempts a literal interpretation of the passage. Also worthy of consideration is the Jewish interpretation. Interpreters are influenced largely by their presuppositions, and because only the premillennialists provide a literal interpretation, all nonliteral interpretations are characterized by great diversity and disagreement.

Questions concerning the prophecy. Some major questions are: What people are in view in the prophecy? What is meant chronologically by the seventy "sevens"? What are the major six events described in Daniel 9:24, the events described for the first seven "sevens"? What is meant by the sixty-two "sevens"? and, most important, what is prophesied in the seventieth "seven"? Involved in all these considerations is the question of whether some of the prophecies have already been fulfilled and whether some are yet subject to future fulfillment.

Background of the prophecy. The background of this prophecy was the fulfillment of Daniel's predictions that the Babylonian Empire would be succeeded by the Medes and the Persians. Fulfillment took place (Dan. 9:1) when Babylon fell to the Medo-Persians. At the time the Persians conquered Babylon, Daniel apparently discovered for the first time the prophecy of Jeremiah 25:11 that the desolations of Jerusalem would take seventy years, and the prophecy of Jeremiah 29:10 that after the seventy years Israel would be able to go back to their homeland.

Daniel's prayer. Because approximately sixty-seven years had already elapsed, Daniel's comprehension of these prophecies of Jeremiah caused him to pray for fulfillment of the restoration of Israel. In this beautiful prayer Daniel expressed sorrow for the sins of Israel which had caused her captivity, and he appealed to God for his grace in restoring them in keeping with the prophetic word. Daniel clearly expected a literal fulfillment of the prophecy. The answer to Daniel's prayer is found in the book of Ezra, when about 50,000 returned from Babylon to Israel and began the important work of restoration.

Though the prayer of Daniel as recorded is comparatively brief, his actual prayer probably went on for some time, and while he was still praying, God sent Gabriel with a vision concerning the 490 years. Daniel wrote, "while I was still in prayer, Gabriel, the man I had seen in the earlier vision, came to me in swift flight about the time of the evening sacrifice. He instructed me and said to me, 'Daniel, I have now come to give you insight and understanding. As soon as you began to pray, an answer was given, which I have come to tell you, for you are highly esteemed. Therefore, consider the message and understand the vision'" (9:21–23).

Gabriel's prophecy. The prophetic utterance of Gabriel followed:

> Seventy "sevens" are decreed for your people and your holy city to finish transgression, to put an end to sin, to atone for wickedness, to bring in everlasting righteousness, to seal up vision and prophecy and to anoint the most holy. Know and understand this: From the issuing of the decree to restore and rebuild Jerusalem until the Anointed One, the ruler, comes, there will be seven "sevens," and sixty-two "sevens." It will be rebuilt with streets and a trench, but in times of trouble. After the sixty-two "sevens," the Anointed One will be cut off and will have nothing. The people of the ruler who will come will destroy the city and the sanctuary. The end will come like a flood: War will continue until the end, and desolations have been decreed. He will confirm a covenant with many for one "seven." In the middle of the "seven" he will put an end to sacrifice and offering. And on a wing of the temple he will set up an abomination that causes desolation until the end that is decreed is poured out on him. (Dan. 9:24–27)

The Seventy "Sevens"

The prophecy opens by stating that the period of the prophecy is 70 times 7, or 490. Both liberal and conservative interpreters are in general agreement that the unit is years rather than twenty-four-hour days. The word *weeks* (KJV) is not in the original text. As the prophecy unfolds, the seventy "sevens" are divided into three units. First, seven "sevens," then a second period of sixty-two "sevens," and a final period of one "seven." Each of these three periods has been subject to different interpretations.

The People Addressed: Israel

An important decision at the outset is the identification of the people addressed who were described as "your people and your holy city" (v. 24). Those determined to identify the church and Israel as the same people attempt to apply this to the church. It is obvious, if one comes to this passage with an open mind, that Daniel would clearly understand "your people" as the people of Israel, for whom he had just completed an agonizing prayer, and "your holy city" as Jerusalem, which had been the object of his petition in 9:16–19.

The revelation here of God's plan and purpose for Israel is obviously in contrast to what he had revealed to Daniel earlier concerning the four great world empires. Daniel was given the unusual privilege, more so than any other Old Testament prophet, of outlining the major program for the nations, or the Gentiles, and God's major program for Israel. It is questionable whether there would be any doubt expressed that the passage refers to Israel if it were not for the amillennial conclusion that Israel has no future politically or nationally. On the other hand, as premillennial interpretation of Old Testament prophecies makes clear, God's revelation in many passages of a future for Israel becomes a keystone in understanding God's program for the future, as well as for fulfillment of prophecy in the past.

The Six Major Events Prophesied in Daniel 9:24

The period involved in the prophecy embraces six major elements described in the phrases: (1) "to finish transgression," (2) "to put an end to sin," (3) "to atone for wickedness," (4) "to bring in everlasting righteousness," (5) "to seal up vision and prophecy," and (6) "to anoint the most holy." No explanation is offered for these six prophecies, and this poses a problem for the interpreter.

Finishing transgression. As the period involved in this prophecy apparently brings Israel to her point of restoration, the concept of finishing transgression probably is best interpreted as bringing Israel's apostasy to judgment and conclusion and to begin her period of spiritual restoration—that is, her restoration in the millennial kingdom.

Ending sin. The concept of ending sin, likewise, leads to forgiveness and restoration and the beginning of a new spiritual plateau.

Atoning for wickedness. The promise of atoning for wickedness undoubtedly refers to the death of Christ as the basis of God's grace and the application of this at the time when Jesus Christ comes again.

Bringing everlasting righteousness. "Everlasting righteousness" is accomplished by the grace of God through the death of Christ and is embodied in the prophecy of Jeremiah 23:5–6: " 'The days are coming,' declares the LORD, "when I will raise up to David a righteous Branch, a King who will reign wisely and do what is just and right in the land. In his days Judah will be saved and Israel will live in safety. This is the name by which he will be called: The LORD Our Righteousness.' " Just as Daniel indicated that the culmination of history would be in the coming of the kingdom from heaven (Dan. 7:13–14), the climax intended here no doubt relates to the second coming of Christ and the beginning of his kingdom on earth.

Sealing up vision and prophecy. Sealing up vision and prophecy, no doubt also relates to the second coming of Christ, though earlier the Bible was rendered complete and no additional books of the Bible can now be written. Vision, however, will continue and will be a feature of the end time, but it too will end when Christ himself returns in his visible presence on earth. At that time no additional prophecy will be necessary.

Anointing the most holy. The final step, "to anoint the most holy," probably poses the greatest problem. Though it could be related to some events in the past, it could be in relation to the Most Holy Place in the millennial temple described in Ezekiel 40–43. Some would make it extend to the New Jerusalem in the eternal state. Taken as a whole, these prophecies occur just before or at the time of the second coming of Christ.

The Beginning of the Seventy "Sevens"

Probably no aspect of the seventy "sevens" has caused more controversy than the question as to when the seventy "sevens" were prophesied to begin. According to the prophecy itself, it would be "From the issuing of the decree to restore and rebuild

Jerusalem" (9:25). Daniel was told that he should "know and understand this" (v. 25). Daniel, however, probably did not have it clearly in mind any more than we do today.

The theological position of the interpreter again comes into play. Amillenarians generally attempt to begin the series at a time that would lead to a nonliteral fulfillment. For instance, some would begin the 490 years in 486 B.C. when, in fulfillment of Daniel's prophecies, Jerusalem was destroyed. The fulfillment obviously does not coincide with the prophecy itself.

If the decree refers to the decree of a human ruler instead of a decree of God, at least four different decrees are mentioned in Scripture. (1) The decree of Cyrus was relative to rebuilding the temple in 538 B.C. (2 Chron. 36:22–23; Ezra 1:1–4; 6:1–5). (2) Darius issued a decree that confirmed the decree of Cyrus (Ezra 6:6–12). This was in answer to the request of the enemies of Israel as to whether there ever was a decree of Cyrus. A search in the archives revealed the scroll (Ezra 6:1), which accordingly allowed the children of Israel to complete the tabernacle. (3) Artaxerxes gave Ezra authority to build a temple to God in Jerusalem (Ezra 7:11–26). (4) A final decree was given by Artaxerxes to Nehemiah to build the city and the walls in keeping with Nehemiah's request (Neh. 1:3; 2:4–8). This final decree is the only one that actually relates to the restoration and building of the city itself.

Each of these decrees, however, has been used as a starting point by various expositors for the seventy "sevens". Only the final decree of Nehemiah actually fits the detail of the prophecy that predicted the rebuilding of the city. In any case, there was no actual rebuilding of the city until the time of Nehemiah, with the decree being issued either in the last month of 445 B.C. or the first month of 444 B.C. Views other than the premillennial interpretation tend to avoid this conclusion because it lends too much literalness to the prophecy which would contradict the concept that prophecy cannot be taken literally.

Fulfillment of the Seventy "Sevens"

If the 490 years begin in 445 B.C., it would provide fulfillment for the 483 years by A.D. 33. In the computation, the prophetic year of 360 days must be understood in keeping with scriptural prophecy where this is consistently used. The Jewish calendar consisted of 12 months of 30 days each, with provision that after enough days had accumulated a thirteenth month would be added to correct the calendar. In prophecy, however, this thirteenth month is not considered. In Revelation 11:3 and 12:6, for instance, the 3½ years of 360 days is confirmed by the use of 1,260 days. Also, 42 months cover the same period (Rev. 11:2; 13:5). The expression, "a time, times, and half a time" is also considered as 3½ years: a "time" equals 1 year, "times" equals 2 years, and "half a time" equals 6 months, for a total of 3½ years in keeping with other prophecy (Dan. 7:25; 12:7; Rev. 12:14). Until recently it was assumed that the death of Christ occurred several years earlier, but modern scholarship has given credence to the conclusion that the death of Christ occurred in 33 A.D., which would fit precisely into the pattern of 483 years, leaving the last 7 years to be fulfilled some time after the death of Christ. Premillenarians generally adopt the view that the 483 years have now been fulfilled. This leaves the question as to whether the final seven years have also been fulfilled.

The Seventy "Sevens": The First Seven Years

As the prophecy indicates, the 490 years are divided into three parts, the first consisting of 49 years. If the 490 years begin with the work of Nehemiah on the city of Jerusalem, it fits naturally into what the prophecy states—that the city would be rebuilt with streets and a trench. According to Nehemiah 11:1, one out of ten was ordered to build a house in Jerusalem. This involved spreading out the rubble and building a new city on top of the old. In any case, when Christ was born in Bethlehem, a village near Jerusalem, Jerusalem was a thriving city.

The Sixty-Two "Sevens," 434 Years

The second segment of sixty-two "sevens," or 434 years, apparently followed immediately after the first seven "sevens," and practically all commentators agree on this sequence. Nothing specific is indicated as occurring in this period, but apparently the rebuilding of Jerusalem continued.

The Final Seven Years

Two major events prophesied. The climax of the prophecy concerns two events that will occur after the sixty-ninth "seven" and apparently not in the seventieth "seven." This introduces a major controversy in the interpretation of this passage. The two events mentioned are, first, that "the Anointed One will be cut off and will have nothing" (Dan. 9:26), which seems to be a clear reference to the death of Jesus Christ as the Messiah. Second, "the people of the ruler who will come will destroy the city and the sanctuary. The end will come like a flood: War will continue until the end, and desolations have been decreed" (v. 26). This occurred in A.D. 70, or 37 years after the death of Christ, which is too long a period to be described as 7 years. The problem of interpretation is that these two events are said to be after the sixty-two "sevens," or the 483 years, but apparently not in the final 7 years. The implication is that there is a time period between the end of the 483 years and the beginning of the final 7 years.

Amillennial interpretation. The interpretation of an intervening time period has been strenuously opposed by the amillenarians who do not believe a future 7-year period will be literally fulfilled. They attempt to find the final 7 years fulfilled in history. Generally speaking, this is accomplished by ignoring literal fulfillment. One popular approach of the amillenarians is to consider that the last 7 years began when the Messiah began his public ministry. The first 3½ years of the last 7 would then correspond to the life of Christ, and he would be cut off in the middle of the last 7 years, not after the sixty-ninth "seven." The covenant that is mentioned (Dan. 9:27) is held to be the new covenant of grace brought in through the death of Christ.

Numerous problems hinder this interpretation. In order to get in the 69 times 7 years, or 483 years, it is necessary to begin the 490 years before 444 B.C., requiring an interpretation that the earlier decrees authorize the building of the city. This does not seem to be sustained by the text. Appeal is made to Isaiah 44:28 where Cyrus is quoted as saying of Jerusalem, "Let it be rebuilt," and of the temple, "Let its foundations be laid." In stating the contents of the decree of Cyrus in Ezra 1:2–4, no mention is made of the rebuilding of the city, but only of the temple. It is clear that the city itself was left in ruins until the time of Nehemiah in 445 B.C. When the decree was searched out, as recorded in Ezra 6:3–5, the decree related only to the rebuilding of the temple. For these reasons, the interpretation that the rebuilding of the city relates to the decree of Artaxerxes given to Nehemiah in 445 B.C. is preferable. This also makes impossible the amillennial interpretation that the 483 years ended with the beginning of the public ministry of Christ.

Objections to the amillennial interpretation. Numerous objections can be raised to identifying the new covenant brought in by the death of Christ with a seven-year covenant mentioned in Daniel. The covenant of grace as instituted by Christ does not exist for 7 years but continues forever. It does not seem to be the reference of Daniel 9. A further difficulty follows in that the last 7 years do not bring in any sense of culmination, as 3½ years after the death of Christ brought no restoration to Israel and no fulfillment of the other precious promises that are related to the Second Coming. Accordingly, the terminus of the 483 years is better identified with the death of Christ in A.D. 33, and the last 7 years are still future, with a time period of indeterminate length between the end of the 483 years and the beginning of the last 7 years.

Premillennial interpretation. In this time period two events, the death of Christ and the destruction of Jerusalem, occur at least 33 years apart. It would be impossible to compact these two events into the last 3½ years of the prophecy. For these and other reasons, the premillennial interpretation is considered preferable as providing a more literal interpretation of the prophecy.

A study of the events recorded for the last 7 years of the 490 years also seems to relate clearly to events that are yet future. The pronoun "he" of Daniel 9:27, if it refers to the nearest antecedent, would refer to the ruler of verse 26 rather than to the Messiah. This is in keeping with other prophecies that picture the last 7 years as a time of trouble leading up to the second coming of Christ. In the premillennial interpretation during the first half of this period, according to Daniel 9:27, a covenant with Israel will be made and observed. This apparently will be a covenant of peace, which helps explain Israel's brief time of peace in Ezekiel 38. In the middle of the last 7 years, however, the covenant will be broken. This refers to a covenant made with a political ruler, and it will begin a period of Israel's trouble. This will be characterized by the ending of the sacrifice and offering in the temple, further confirmed in Daniel 12:11: "From the time that the daily sacrifice is abolished and the abomination that causes desolation is set up, there will be 1,290 days." This coincides with the prophecy of Christ that the desecration of the temple would take place at the beginning of the Great Tribulation (Matt. 24:15–22). The abomination that causes desolation is the desecration of the temple at a future time when the statue of the ruler mentioned in Daniel 9:26 will be placed in the temple as an object of worship (2 Thess. 2:4; Rev. 13:14–15). The Great Tribulation is still future from the viewpoint of the book of Revelation. It is impossible to identify it as something that occurred in the immediate aftermath of the death of Christ as amillenarians contend.

The prophecies yet to be fulfilled coincide with what occurred at the time of Antiochus, who desecrated the temple in the second century B.C. He, likewise, stopped the sacrifice and set up a pagan idol in the temple. This was an abomination, and explains why the future desecration of the temple is also described as an abomination.

Further examination of the text indicates that the ruler who introduces the final 3½ of Great Tribulation will also be judged at Christ's second coming (Rev. 13), which again makes it clear that the events described are future instead of past.

Conclusion

Accordingly, when all the various views are considered and the arguments pro and con are evaluated, the only point of view that really satisfies the passage and provides a literal fulfillment is the view that begins the 490 years at 445 B.C., concludes that first 483 years in 33 A.D. at the time of Christ's death, and then postpones the last 7 years until the 7 years preceding the second coming of Christ, which is obviously still future. A future ruler will observe a covenant with Israel during the first 3½ years of that period and will become the world ruler in the final years before the Second Coming. He will break this covenant with Israel after 3½ years, and great tribulation will be brought upon the entire world as well as on the people of Israel, climaxing in the Second Coming. Christ will judge the world and bring in his millennial kingdom. This literal interpretation accounts for the various details of the passage and is far superior to any of the many other views.

In contemplating the prophecy of Daniel 9:24–27, it becomes evident that Daniel was given the broad sweep of prophecy, not only embracing the four final Gentile kingdoms and climaxing in the kingdom from heaven at the Second Coming, but also covering the 490 years for Israel and likewise terminating at the

Second Coming. Daniel also describes Israel's place in the world and events leading up to the Second Coming. The present age is not included in this prophecy concerning Israel any more than it is included in the prophecies concerning the Gentiles. The present age of grace is an interpolation into the prophetic sequence of events given in the New Testament concerning the church, the body of Christ.

World events are shaping up into a situation that is similar to what one would expect if the rapture of the church were about to occur. Just as prophecy was literally fulfilled at the first coming of Christ in hundreds of particulars, so will the Word be fulfilled in connection with the second coming of Christ.The practical exhortation related to this is that if the coming of Christ for his church is near, it behooves Christians to evaluate their lives in keeping with the eternal values of God.

17

The New Covenant

The Old and New Testaments Contrasted

One of the most obvious facts about the Bible is that it is divided
into the Old and New Testaments, or the old and new
covenants. Though the entire Bible bears witness to a gracious,
loving God, there is a sharp contrast between the basic
revelation of the Old Testament as compared to the New. This is
captured in the simple statement of John 1:17, "For the law was
given through Moses; grace and truth came through Jesus
Christ." The Old Testament is not entirely law, nor is the New
Testament entirely grace, but there is a broad contrast between
the two. The Mosaic Law with its more than six hundred laws
dominated the Old Testament from the time of Moses until the
time of Christ. The law was basically a works situation where, in
order to be blessed, people had to obey the law of God. The law
was not devoid of grace, for salvation was by grace and
forgiveness was available even under the law, but the Old

Testament lacked the clear revelation of what constituted the grace of God and of how a righteous God could forgive sin.

In contrast, the New Testament emphasizes the doctrine of grace. The New Testament plainly discloses that Jesus Christ died on the cross for the sins of the whole world and has made grace possible. God can now forgive those who trust in Christ because the price has been paid. According to Hebrews 12:24, Jesus is the Mediator of a new covenant that is based upon shed blood. Though blood redemption was clearly revealed in the Old Testament, it is doubtful that anyone understood that Jesus, the Messiah, was to die on the cross for the sins of the whole world and that this would be the basis of God's grace to them.

Grace, the Central Feature of the New Covenant

A covenant is a solemn pledge to fulfill a promise. Sometimes it is unilateral in the sense that one promises to do something for someone else regardless of the circumstances. In other cases it is a mutual covenant where two parties agree on a course of action and the promises related to it. Basically, grace is a unilateral covenant and God promises to extend grace to those who trust him. The New Testament, accordingly, abounds with references to and explanations of the doctrine of grace. The basic concepts of grace are revealed in Romans, where justification by faith is defined.

Righteousness apart from the law. In contrast to the Old Testament, where keeping the law was recognized as a form of righteousness, God has provided a righteousness which is not based on the Mosaic Law but which comes as a gift of God. Paul wrote, "But now a righteousness from God, apart from law, has been made known, to which the Law and the Prophets testify. This righteousness from God comes through faith in Jesus Christ to all who believe. There is no difference, for all have sinned and fall short of the glory of God" (Rom. 3:21–23). This is a dramatically different revelation than was given in the Old Testament, though the law was never offered as a way of salvation. The righteousness that comes from God's unmerited favor, or grace, is realized through faith in Christ, because all have sinned and fallen short of infinite perfection such as characterizes the glory of God. All have to come on the same basis of belief in Christ in order to be received in grace.

Grace is explained as coming through the redemption that is

in Christ Jesus. Believers "are justified freely by his grace through the redemption that came by Christ Jesus" (Rom. 3:24). A believer in Christ is declared righteous by faith in Christ, and this is without cost because it is through God's grace, or unmerited favor, accomplished by the redemption which Christ wrought on the cross. By redemption it is meant that Christ paid the price of judgment on sin and became the Lamb of God which takes away the sin of the world.

This is further explained by the statement that "God presented him as a sacrifice of atonement, through faith in his blood. He did this to demonstrate his justice, because in his forbearance he had left the sins committed beforehand unpunished—he did it to demonstrate his justice at the present time, so as to be just and the one who justifies those who have faith in Jesus" (Rom. 3:25–26). According to this passage, Christ in his sacrifice on the cross provided an atonement or a satisfaction of God's righteous demands. Believers in Christ accept this revelation that through Christ's shed blood and his death on the cross they can have forgiveness of sins. The death of Christ is not only the basis for salvation now, but it also reaches back into the Old Testament and justifies God's extending grace in the Old Testament before the sacrifice of Christ took place. This is what is meant by God's demonstrating his justice concerning the sins committed in the Old Testament era. On the basis of the death of Christ, because it is of infinite value, God can now justly forgive both the Old Testament saints and those who live now in the period after the New Testament. The promise of this glorious salvation is the new covenant that characterizes salvation in Christ.

Another statement of this same great truth is found in Ephesians 2 where Paul writes, "But because of his great love for us, God, who is rich in mercy, made us alive with Christ even when we were dead in transgressions—it is by grace you have been saved. And God raised us up with Christ and seated us with him in the heavenly realms in Christ Jesus, in order that in the coming ages he might show the incomparable riches of his grace, expressed in his kindness to us in Christ Jesus" (Eph. 2:4–7). Here, as in the epistle to the Romans, a Christian is declared to be saved by grace, God's unmerited favor. We also see here God's purpose in eternity to demonstrate what grace is by exhibiting Christians in heaven who have been saved by grace, righteous apart from works.

This purpose is explained further in the verses that follow: "For it is by grace you have been saved, through faith—and this not from yourselves, it is the gift of God—not by works, so that no one can boast. For we are God's workmanship, created in Christ Jesus to do good works, which God prepared in advance for us to do" (Eph. 2:8–10).

This passage makes clear that we are saved not by our works but by Christ's death on the cross, which makes it possible for God to extend grace, or forgiveness and favor, to those who trust in Christ. Our salvation is a gift of God, not something that is earned or is a subject of reward. It is made plain that salvation is not by works; no one will be able to boast that he or she reached heaven on the basis of good works. Rather, good works eventuate because persons become Christians as a result of God's working in them—that is, they are "God's workmanship," and as new creatures in Christ they are created to do the good works which God anticipated in saving them.

The New Testament abounds in additional passages that bear upon the subject of God's wonderful grace for Christians, which includes their place in the body of Christ, the spiritual gifts God has given them, their inheritance as coheirs with Jesus Christ, and all the promises of God that extend from time to eternity for them. Salvation is based on God's unmerited favor, secured for the believer by Christ's death on the cross. As such, the new covenant is the central feature of the New Testament and is the central truth that is revealed in the New Testament writings.

Problems in the Doctrine of the New Covenant

Though the new covenant of grace is preeminently revealed in the New Testament, the Old Testament also predicted a new covenant.

Jeremiah predicted that God had a new covenant for the house of Israel:

> *"The time is coming," declares the LORD,*
> *"when I will make a new covenant*
> *with the house of Israel*
> *and with the house of Judah.*
> *It will not be like the covenant*
> *I made with their forefathers*
> *when I took them by the hand*

to lead them out of Egypt,
because they broke my covenant,
   though I was a husband to them,"
declares the LORD.
   "This is the covenant I will make
with the house of Israel
   after that time," declares the LORD.
"I will put my law in their minds
   and write it on their hearts.
I will be their God,
   and they will be my people.
No longer will a man teach his neighbor,
   or a man his brother, saying, 'Know the LORD,'
because they will all know me,
   from the least of them to the greatest,"
declares the LORD.
"For I will forgive their wickedness
   and will remember their sins no more."

This is what the LORD says,

he who appoints the sun
   to shine by day,
who decrees the moon and stars
   to shine by night,
who stirs up the sea
   so that its waves roar—
   the LORD Almighty is his name:
"Only if these decrees vanish from my sight,"
   declares the LORD,
"will the descendants of Israel ever cease
   to be a nation before me."

This is what the LORD says:

"Only if the heavens above can be measured
   and the foundations of the earth below be
searched out will I reject all the descendants
   of Israel because of all they have done,"
declares the LORD. (31:31–37)

It is significant that this revelation was given in a time of Israel's complete apostasy just before the Babylonian captivity took place. The promises were not given, therefore, as a reward for faithfulness, nor did they stem from the provision of the Mosaic Law. It was, rather, a new statement from God of his settled purpose of dealing graciously with Israel in spite of their sins even though at times judgment had to be inflicted, as in the case of the Babylonian captivity.

The provisions of the covenant are detailed.

1. The covenant is made specifically with the nation Israel, and the detailed provisions of this covenant do not relate to anyone who is not a descendant of Jacob.

2. The new covenant as revealed here is in contrast to the Mosaic covenant. The Mosaic covenant was meritorious—that is, blessing depended upon obedience with provision for punishment if the people did not obey. The new covenant stems from the grace of God and is announced in spite of Israel's apostasy. The new covenant, therefore, was predicted to replace the Mosaic covenant which was temporary and would terminate in the death of Christ. The new covenant was to extend throughout history as well as in eternity to come.

3. The major provision of the new covenant will be fulfilled after Israel's time of trouble, specifically the Great Tribulation described in many Old Testament passages and in Revelation 6–18. The promised fulfillment, accordingly, is after the time of trouble (Jer. 30:7) and after what Christ referred to as the time of Israel's "great distress, unequaled from the beginning of the world until now—and never to be equaled again" (Matt. 24:21). In terms of time of fulfillment, the provisions of the covenant are a part of God's program to regather Israel and bring them back to their ancient land (Jer. 30:10–11, 18–21; 31:8–14, 23–28).

4. The new covenant will take the place of the Mosaic covenant and will be written "on their hearts" instead of on tables of stone (Jer. 31:33).

5. The new covenant will feature great spiritual blessing for the people of Israel and their exaltation to a place of prominence when God will be identified with them (Jer. 31:33).

6. The new covenant will bring with it the revelation of the glory of God so that it will no longer be necessary to bear witness to a neighbor or a brother, because all will know that Jesus Christ is indeed King of Kings and Lord of Lords (Jer. 31:34). Isaiah refers to this same period as a time when "the

earth will be full of the knowledge of the LORD as the waters cover the sea" (Isa. 11:9). In brief, it refers to the kingdom Christ will bring in his second coming. This circumstance has never been fulfilled in the past or the present and will take the place of the constant missionary effort that is extended at the present time to take the Gospel to those who have not heard.

7. The new covenant will feature forgiveness, grace, and blessing. God promises "I will forgive their wickedness and remember their sins no more" (Jer. 31:34).

The provisions of the new covenant are so detailed that it should be apparent to any careful observer that this covenant has never been fulfilled in the past and is not being fulfilled in the present. It therefore becomes a major cornerstone of the belief in a millennial kingdom to follow the second coming of Christ. Accordingly, amillenarians, who deny a future millennial reign, must attempt to prove that the covenant is presently fulfilled even though, obviously, the details are not.

Although the main passage concerning the covenant is found in Jeremiah 31, other references in the Old Testament are equally explicit. More than a century before Jeremiah, Isaiah had declared:

> *"For I, the LORD, love justice;*
> *I hate robbery and iniquity.*
> *In my faithfulness I will reward them*
> *and make an everlasting covenant with them.*
> *Their descendants will be known among the nations*
> *and their offspring among the peoples.*
> *All who see them will acknowledge*
> *that they are a people the LORD has blessed." (61:8–9)*

Isaiah anticipated an everlasting covenant that would result in the world's recognizing that the people of Israel are a people of God. The context of this prophecy is the same as that of Jeremiah, that the fulfillment of the covenant will follow a time of sorrow and difficulty for Israel and will involve the regathering of Israel.

Another of God's purposes stated in the new covenant is the regathering of Israel.

> "I will surely gather them from all the lands where I banish them in my furious anger and great wrath; I will bring them

back to this place and let them live in safety. They will be my people, and I will be their God. I will give them singleness of heart and action, so that they will always fear me for their own good and the good of their children after them. I will make an everlasting covenant with them: I will never stop doing good to them, and I will inspire them to fear me, so that they will never turn away from me. I will rejoice in doing them good and will assuredly plant them in this land with all my heart and soul." (Jer. 32:37–41)

The regathering of Israel following God's judgment on them in dispersing them over the world will include bringing them back to their ancient land and allowing them to "live in safety" (v. 37). His covenant with them will be "an everlasting covenant" (v. 40). The fulfillment of the covenant will involve that God "will never stop doing good to them" (v. 40). The conclusion of the matter will be that God will "plant them in this land with all [his] heart and soul" (v. 41).

The prophet Ezekiel, writing after Jeremiah during the Captivity, confirmed the new covenant and gave further detail:

"'This is what the Sovereign LORD says: I will take the Israelites out of the nations where they have gone. I will gather them from all around and bring them back into their own land. I will make them one nation in the land, on the mountains of Israel. There will be one king over all of them and they will never again be two nations or be divided into two kingdoms. They will no longer defile themselves with their idols and vile images or with any of their offenses, for I will save them from all their sinful backsliding, and I will cleanse them. They will be my people, and I will be their God. My servant David will be king over them, and they will all have one shepherd. They will follow my laws and be careful to keep my decrees. They will live in the land I gave to my servant Jacob, the land where your fathers lived. They and their children and their children's children will live there forever, and David my servant will be their prince forever. I will make a covenant of peace with them; it will be an everlasting covenant. I will establish them and increase their numbers, and I will put my sanctuary among them forever. My dwelling place will be with them; I will be their God, and they will be my people. Then the nations will know that I the LORD make Israel holy, when my sanctuary is among them forever.'" (37:21–28)

Here are detailed the same elements that entered into the new covenant in other passages—that is, the regathering of Israel, the reuniting of Israel and Judah, the elevation of one king over them, their deliverance from idols, and their cleansing from sin (Ezek. 37:21–23). Featured in their new kingdom situation following the Second Coming will be the resurrection of David to be king over them (v. 24). David will reign with Christ and will be Israel's "prince forever" (v. 25). The new covenant is an everlasting covenant in contrast to the Mosaic covenant, which was terminated at the death of Christ (v. 26). In this period of the new covenant, God will dwell among his people, and the nations will know that Israel is a people set apart for God's holy use (vv. 27–28). It should be apparent that there is no literal fulfillment of this prophecy at the present time, for it includes too many elements that are not true in the world today. Accordingly, these passages support the contention that there must be a kingdom on earth following the second coming of Christ according to the premillennial interpretation. At the present time Israel has not been regathered, the nation Israel has not been restored to one kingdom, David has not been resurrected to be king over them, not everyone knows the Lord, and the people of Israel are not clearly identified as the people of God. The time of Israel's trouble which precedes these events has not yet taken place.

Taken in their natural meaning, these promises of the new covenant are so specific that it is obvious that they have not been fulfilled at the present time. Amillenarians will sometimes admit this, contending that the promises, if interpreted literally, have not been fulfilled but that it is God's intent that they be fulfilled spiritually. It is the amillennial contention that the Jewish expectation of a kingdom on earth is in error; and in their treatment of these passages, amillenarians consistently avoid detailing the promises given as requiring fulfillment. For the most part, they ignore the promises and go to the new covenant in the New Testament for their interpretation, trying to find present fulfillment. There is no intimation that the Old Testament saints expected or that the passages permitted other than a literal interpretation.

The New Covenant in the New Testament

The extent of references to the new covenant in the New Testament. The many New Testament references to the new covenant make evident that this is an important and central doctrine of the New Testament. At least five direct references are found to the new covenant (Luke 22:20; 1 Cor. 11:25; 2 Cor. 3:6; Heb. 8:8; 9:15). A number of other references refer to the covenant without necessarily using the word "new" (Matt. 26:28; Mark 14:24; Rom. 11:27; Heb. 8:10, 13; 10:16; 12:24). In some of these passages there is a textual variation with the word "new" in some texts and not in others, but the reference is clearly to the same concept.

The New Testament references to Israel. In the New Testament, as in the Old, the new covenant is sometimes traced to the promises given to Israel. As such, they point to a future fulfillment.

Paul wrote in Romans 11:26–27, "And so all Israel will be saved, as it is written: 'The deliverer will come from Zion; he will turn godlessness away from Jacob. And this is my covenant with them when I take away their sins.'"

This passage does much to date the time of fulfillment of the new covenant for Israel—that is, it points to the time of Christ's return when the Deliverer will come. It is significant that in amillennial treatments of the new covenant this passage is generally ignored.

One of the most prominent references to the new covenant of Israel is found in Hebrews 8. In understanding this passage it is important to note that the writer is attempting to prove that the new covenant is better than the Mosaic covenant. In Hebrews 8:6 he says, "But the ministry Jesus has received is as superior to theirs as the covenant of which he is mediator [the new covenant] is superior to the old one [the Mosaic Covenant], and it is founded on better promises."

The writer then quotes Jeremiah 31:31–34:

> For if there had been nothing wrong with that first covenant, no place would have been sought for another. But God found fault with the people and said:

> *"The time is coming, declares the Lord,*
>   *when I will make a new covenant*
> *with the house of Israel*
>   *and with the house of Judah.*
> *It will not be like the covenant*
>   *I made with their forefathers*

when I took them by the hand
* to lead them out of Egypt,*
because they did not remain faithful to my covenant,
* and I turned away from them,*
declares the Lord.
This is the covenant I will make with the house
*   of Israel*
* after that time, declares the Lord.*
I will put my laws in their minds
* and write them on their hearts.*
I will be their God,
* and they will be my people.*
No longer will a man teach his neighbor,
* or a man his brother, saying, 'Know the Lord,'*
because they will all know me,
* from the least of them to the greatest.*
For I will forgive their wickedness
* and will remember their sins no more." (Heb. 8:7–12)*

The use of this quotation should be noted along with the context of the passage. Amillenarians jump to the conclusion that this passage proves that the church is inheriting the covenant with Israel as declared by Jeremiah. A careful examination of Hebrews 8, however, reveals that this is not the case. In Hebrews 8:13 the application is made, "By calling this covenant 'new,' he has made the first one obsolete; and what is obsolete and aging will soon disappear." The only application made of the Jeremiah passage is to show that the Old Testament itself had anticipated that the Mosaic Covenant would become obsolete and would be succeeded by the fulfillment of the new covenant. The passage does not state nor is it the purpose of the author of Hebrews to state that Jeremiah's prophecy is being fulfilled today. Rather, the interpretation is that the Old Testament predicted that the Mosaic covenant would cease. Amillenarians attempt to derive from the passage something it does not state.

It is most significant that the writer of Hebrews does not interpret the passage as being fulfilled today. If this were the case, it would be a crushing blow to the premillennial contention that there is a future kingdom. The writer, however, carefully avoids this and instead says that the Old Testament itself anticipated that the Mosaic covenant would become obsolete. This supports the concept that the people should no longer live under the Mosaic covenant but should move away from it.

The details of the covenant relate primarily to Israel's future in the millennial kingdom. At that time Israel will experience spiritual revival. The knowledge of Christ will be universal, as Christ will be dwelling bodily on the earth. Evangelism, as it is now undertaken, will be unnecessary. Israelites regathered to their own land will fulfill God's purpose of the nation's continuing as long as the sun and moon exist—that is, during the millennial kingdom.

The attempts of amillenarians to apply this passage to the church are unsupported by the facts revealed. Today not everyone knows the Lord. Today there is departure from God, not widespread spiritual revival. If close attention is given to the details of this prophecy, one can see the futility of trying to regard the church as fulfilling Israel's prophetic destiny. Though the church is given the eternal role of demonstrating the grace of God (Eph. 2:7), Israel has the similar role of illustrating how a gracious God fulfills his covenant promises in both the judgments and restorations of Israel. The promise of the new covenant will be fulfilled in the Millennium for Israel as well as in eternity future.

Another passage in Hebrews that is usually not brought into the argument by amillenarians is Hebrews 10:16-17: "This is the covenant I will make with them after that time, says the Lord. I will put my laws in their hearts, and I will write them on their minds." Then the Lord adds, "Their sins and lawless acts I will remember no more." Here the principle is drawn from the prophecy that if sins are forgiven, it is not necessary to have further sacrifice for sin, thus justifying the discontinuance of Mosaic sacrifices. Accordingly, the reader is urged to enter into the new and living way in Christ, accepting the sacrifice that Christ has provided (Heb. 10:19-22).

It may be concluded that references to the new covenant as it relates to Israel are presented in the New Testament without claiming present fulfillment, but necessarily implying, and even stating, that the new covenant will be fulfilled at the time of Christ's second coming, as in Romans 11:27.

The New Testament references to the church. Most prominent are New Testament references to the church. Some of these references recognize the institution of the Lord's Supper as the memorial of the new covenant established by the sacrifice of Christ on the cross. In Luke 22:20 the new covenant was made a part of this memorial when Christ said, "This cup is the new covenant in my blood, which is poured out for you." Similar references are found in Matthew 26:28 and Mark 14:24. In 1 Corinthians 11:25 another reference is found relating the new covenant to the Lord's Supper. Paul claims in 2 Corinthians 3:6 to be competent as a minister of the new covenant. In Hebrews 12:24 Jesus is said to be the Mediator of the new covenant, and the expression "new" is used in the sense of "recent." The blood of Christ is contrasted with sacrificial offerings in the Old Testament and is said to be efficacious.

In references to the Lord's Supper and other references relating the new covenant to the church, it is obvious that what the covenant described for Israel is not being fulfilled. The New Testament, as well as the Old, traces the fulfillment of the new covenant for Israel as something that is related to the second coming of Christ and subsequent to it, which constitutes a confirmation of the premillennial interpretation.

Various Premillennial Interpretations of the New Covenant

Though premillenarians are united in insisting that the new covenant has its ultimate fulfillment in Israel, there has been some confusion as to how the new covenant of the Old Testament relating to Israel relates to the new covenant for the church. Some, like John Darby, attempt to make the new covenant for Israel relate exclusively to Israel and deny that there is a new covenant for the church. This, however, is clearly wrong, because the Lord's Supper and various references in the New Testament make clear that the church is operating under a new covenant of grace as indicated in the Lord's Supper.

Some, like C. I. Scofield, held that while the new covenant of the Old Testament was for Israel, it had an oblique application to the church, and in some sense the church inherited the grace that was involved. This view confuses the promises to Israel and the promises to the church.

Still another point of view is that there are two new covenants in the Bible: (1) a new covenant for Israel in the Old Testament, and (2) a new covenant for the church in the New Testament. For years I struggled with the problem of how to relate the new covenant in the New Testament to the new covenant for Israel.

Finally I arrived at a relatively simple solution. Because the new covenant for Israel as well as the new covenant for the church both stem from the death of Christ, his death on the cross is the single event that becomes determinative in grace. Accordingly, it simplifies the problem and clarifies the confusion, allowing one to arrive at the conclusion that there is one new covenant, commonly recognized as the covenant of grace in systematic theology, which stems from the death of Christ. In brief, it provides that God through the death of Christ is able to extend favor and salvation to those who do not deserve it.

This one covenant of grace, however, has a wide application. The death of Christ constitutes the ground of salvation for everyone from Adam to the last person who is saved. This grace extends to Israel and to the church and to any others who may partake of the grace of God. Accordingly, the concept of one covenant of grace with many applications serves to provide an intelligent understanding of the various provisions of the covenant in both the Old and New Testaments and preserves the distinction that should be observed between God's purpose and plan for Israel and God's purpose and plan for the church. Accordingly, the new covenant extends salvation to all people in all ages who believe. It also provides God's blessings for people who do not deserve them, regardless of whether they are Jew or Gentile, the church, or future believers in Christ. This point of view also makes clear that when Israel is restored in the millennial kingdom, it will be an act of grace, not something they deserve, and they will receive the blessing of the millennial reign of Christ on the basis of the death of Christ, just as the church receives its blessing.

This concept of one covenant of grace with many applications casts light upon the entire work of God in the Old Testament. In the Old Testament, prophecy extends to many individuals, peoples, and nations. It includes God's prophecies concerning Adam and Eve as well as subsequent descendants of the human race. It relates to both Jews and Gentiles. It deals with political entities as well as spiritual entities. Old Testament prophecy includes many diverse elements, but in all of this the doctrine of grace provides a unifying factor.

A major element in God's prophecy concerning Israel begins in Genesis 11 with prophecy concerning Abraham and his posterity; and from there through the rest of the Old Testament, Israel becomes a dominant factor in prophetic revelation. God's purpose for Israel is detailed in many Scriptures. Interwoven in these Scriptures, however, is the doctrine of grace as the basis of the new covenant and God's provision for Israel. Because the Mosaic Law is basically a legal relationship between Israel and God, the element of grace is often obscured. Even in a sacrificial system, God dealt with Israel in grace and gave them blessings they did not deserve. All of this, however, was made possible only by the death of Christ, on the basis of which God forgave sins in the Old Testament and extended grace to Israel as well as to present and future believers.

The doctrine of grace in the New Testament, as has already been pointed out, is related to God's new purpose of calling out from Jews and Gentiles a people for his name to form the body of Christ. Accordingly, the new covenant is found in its major provisions throughout the New Testament. As embodying the provisions of grace, it is a determinative element in prophecy and extends the provision of God not only to those who lived in the past but also to God's purpose for the church—its completion, rapture, and eternal blessing. As far as Israel is concerned, the doctrine of grace especially relates to the millennial kingdom.

Summary of the New Covenant in Relation to Salvation

Because the new covenant has a wide application to all the human race from Adam to the last human being in the future, it offers salvation by grace through faith as a work of God.

Salvation by faith, not works. In contrast to the universal non-Christian approach to religion which views humans as attempting to obtain favor with God through works, the Christian Gospel as contained in the new covenant makes clear that salvation comes by faith and not by works. Accordingly, persons who are obviously unqualified and do not merit salvation can receive salvation by faith in Christ. As previously noted, this is embodied in the familiar text of Ephesians 2:8–9: "For it is by grace you have been saved, through faith—and this not from yourselves, it is the gift of God—not by works, so that no one can boast." Though the doctrine of grace is difficult for the human mind to contemplate, God's plan and purpose for the church is founded in grace as is his plan and purpose for Israel. Salvation in every dispensation and in every situation must be by faith and not by works.

Salvation by grace, not merit. Not only works in general, but any meritorious work that humans may perform, is automatically eliminated as a basis for salvation. The grace of God depends on the work of Christ, not on the merit a person might achieve by doing something worthwhile. Those who come to Christ for salvation come without any redeeming feature, and even faith is not regarded as a meritorious work but is a channel through which the grace of God can flow.

Salvation is from God and not by human effort. It is fundamental to the Christian Gospel that salvation is a work of God. This is stated eloquently in John 1:12–13: "Yet to all who received him, to those who believed in his name, he gave the right to become children of God—children born not of natural descent, nor of human decision or a husband's will, but born of God." Because it is a work of God, it cannot be overturned, annulled, or changed. Salvation by its nature is a new birth, a new creation, and a new spiritual resurrection. In the nature of these aspects of salvation, salvation becomes a work that cannot be changed by humans; and humans, once saved, are rendered secure forever by the grace of God.

A proper understanding of the new covenant is therefore essential in understanding God's purposes both for the church and for Israel. It is founded on the basic fact that Christ died for our sins on the cross and that God is therefore free to redeem, to reconcile, and to transform quite apart from human merit or worthiness. The new covenant is a covenant of grace, a covenant that will be observed by God without end throughout eternity.

18

The Sermon on the Mount

Background of the Sermon on the Mount

The Sermon on the Mount is the first of Jesus' discourses recorded in the Gospels; it combines prophecy to be fulfilled with moral and ethical principles involved in the kingdom. In many respects it is the first major teaching of Christ concerning his kingdom.

The Birth and Early Life of John the Baptist
(Matt. 3:1–12; Mark 1:2–8; Luke 1:13–25, 57–80; 3:1–19;
John 1:6–8, 15–37)

The birth and early ministry of John the Baptist fulfilled the prophecy of Isaiah concerning the voice in the wilderness to prepare the way of the Lord (Isa. 40:3–5). For four hundred years there had been no prophet in Israel, and the emergence of John the Baptist caused great excitement and attracted huge crowds.

The Birth and Early Life of Jesus

The account of John the Baptist introduced the events that related to the birth and early life of Jesus (Matt. 1:1–2:12, 19–23; Luke 1:26–56; 2:1–40; 3:23–38; John 1:14). The accounts of Jesus' birth and early life along with the accounts of John the Baptist form the basis for the claim of Christ to be the Messiah of Israel, the Son of God, and the Savior. Jesus clearly came on the scene as the fulfillment of prophecy concerning Israel's Messiah and Savior.

The Kingdom Declared to be at Hand

In the early accounts about Jesus in the Gospels, announcement was made that the prophesied kingdom was at hand (Matt. 4:17; Mark 1:14–15). The kingdom was at hand in the sense that the King was now introducing himself to Israel. The kingdom referred to the prophesied kingdom on earth in which Christ would reign over the house of David and over the entire world (Dan. 7:13–14; Luke 1:31–33).

The Ethical Character of the Sermon

The Sermon on the Mount as the first major address delivered by Jesus is recorded principally in Matthew 5–7, but portions of the sermon were delivered on other occasions as recorded in Mark 4:21–23; Luke 6:20–49; 8:16–18; 11:1–4, 9–13, and 33–36. Because of the prominence of the promise of the kingdom in the Old Testament, the Jews expected that when their Messiah arrived, he would bring in the glory of the future kingdom. They anticipated emancipation from Rome and political independence, as well as the material blessings promised in the kingdom. Though they were correct in their anticipation of a future political kingdom, they did not understand that the kingdom brought with it certain ethical principles, and only those who were qualified would be able to enter the kingdom. The Sermon on the Mount was designed to correct the lack of ethical content in the expectation of the Jews and, accordingly, dwells upon the qualities that will characterize the kingdom from an ethical standpoint.

Many interpreters of the Sermon on the Mount have erred because of their failure to consider the character of the kingdom Christ was discussing. Coming as the Messiah promised in the

Old Testament who would bring a kingdom on earth over which he would reign from the throne of David, Christ here was declaring what the ethical qualities of this kingdom would be when it came about. Subsequent developments, of course, revealed that, because of the rejection of Christ, from a human viewpoint the kingdom was postponed and would not be fulfilled until after Christ's second coming. A proper understanding of this, however, will set the stage for an interpretation in keeping with the context.

Liberal interpreters have gone so far as to interpret the Sermon on the Mount as the Gospel message for the present age. Though some passages apply to the present age and the principles can be applied, the Sermon on the Mount does not provide the way of salvation. There is no reference to Christ's cross, crucifixion, death, resurrection, or the other elements that form the genuine Gospel of salvation. The Sermon on the Mount, however, deals with ethical principles, things that ought to be true of the children of the kingdom.

On the other hand, the extreme view should not be followed that the Sermon on the Mount is exclusively eschatological— that is, that it refers only to the millennial kingdom. As the Sermon on the Mount itself reveals, there are frequent applications of the principles of ethics that will be displayed in the future kingdom, and present application is made of these principles. Though basic rules of life differ in different dispensations, there also are similarities, and where the application is made of an ethical principle relating the future kingdom to the present situation, it is because these qualities are broader than those confined to one dispensation. In brief, though the Sermon on the Mount does not declare the way of salvation, it does declare the ethical evidences of salvation for the children of the kingdom. This kingdom will have its ultimate revelation in the future millennial kingdom, but it has present applications of the ethical character of the Christian life even in the present age.

Who is Qualified to Enter the Kingdom?

Having announced the kingdom at hand (Matt. 4:17), Jesus then addressed the question as to who is qualified to enter this kingdom.

The disciples who heard Jesus speak, probably a reference to the entire crowd and not just to the Twelve, were familiar with the legal standards set forth by the Pharisees that dealt mostly with outer conformity to the law. Here Jesus ignored the approach of the Pharisees and instead focused on matters that relate to inner character. He began by declaring a blessing on those who qualify:

> Blessed are the poor in spirit,
>   for theirs is the kingdom of heaven.
> Blessed are those who mourn,
>   for they will be comforted.
> Blessed are the meek,
>   for they will inherit the earth. (Matt. 5:3–5)

The description given here does not describe the Pharisees, who were anything but poor in spirit or meek, but rather the transformed hearts of those who have experienced the grace of God. Though it is true that followers of Jesus in this life may have many sorrows and troubles and will experience mourning and need for comfort, their future in the kingdom is assured.

Jesus went on,

> Blessed are those who hunger and thirst for
>   righteousness,
>   for they will be filled.
> Blessed are the merciful,
>   for they will be shown mercy. (Matt. 5:6–7)

Here again the righteousness demanded of those entering the kingdom far exceeds that of the Pharisees. Typical of the Pharisees was the desire to be recognized and called righteous by other people. Here those who enter the kingdom are those who have an inner hunger for righteousness that can never be completely satisfied in this life but will be satisfied in the kingdom to come. Likewise, the Pharisees often lacked mercy, but true children of the kingdom are merciful and will receive mercy.

The inner blessings of being a child of God are reflected in Christ's pronouncement upon those who are pure in heart and who are peacemakers:

> Blessed are the pure in heart,
>   for they will see God.

> *Blessed are the peacemakers,*
> *for they will be called sons of God. (Matt. 5:8–9)*

It is not only important to have our outward life righteous before God but also to be pure in our motivation, thought life, and love for God. When a person is a peacemaker instead of a trouble-maker, that is evidence that he or she truly is a child of God.

Jesus pronounced a final blessing on those who are persecuted:

> *Blessed are those who are persecuted because of*
>   *righteousness,*
> *for theirs is the kingdom of heaven.*

> Blessed are you when people insult you, persecute you and falsely say all kinds of evil against you because of me. Rejoice and be glad, because great is your reward in heaven, for in the same way they persecuted the prophets who were before you. (Matt. 5:10–12)

Though the Pharisees might under certain circumstances be subject to persecution, the problem was that they used their legal approach to persecute others, including those who were Christians. Though it is possible for Christians to suffer because of their sins, it is also a common experience to be persecuted because they are righteous and belong to God. Jesus here pronounced a special blessing on those who are persecuted without cause and instructed them to rejoice because they will receive reward in heaven. The promise here is greater than simply reward to those who are in the future millennial kingdom; it applies to anyone in any dispensation who qualifies with these characteristics.

True believers are the "salt of the earth" (Matt. 5:13), but pharisaical religion is like salt without saltiness and, as Christ states, is only fit to be thrown out.

Likewise, true believers are like lights in a dark place. They will let their light shine before others (Matt. 5:14).

The Kingdom in Relation to the Law of Moses

The people, of course, were astonished at Jesus' sayings because they were so different from what they heard from the

Pharisees. This introduced the question as to whether Jesus was upholding the Mosaic Law. He said plainly, "Do not think that I have come to abolish the Law or the Prophets; I have not come to abolish them but to fulfill them" (Matt. 5:17).

In confirmation of his recognition of the Mosaic Law, Jesus gave the most profound statement concerning the inspiration of Scripture: "I tell you the truth, until heaven and earth disappear, not the smallest letter, not the least stroke of a pen, will by any means disappear from the Law until everything is accomplished" (Matt. 5:18). As long as heaven and earth continue, the Law will continue to have its application. The inspiration of Scripture extends to the smallest letter, the Hebrew *yod*, and the smallest part of a letter that would change its meaning. This can be illustrated in the English capital letter *F*. If another horizontal line is added at the bottom of the letter, it changes it from *F* to *E*. This added stroke is what is meant by "the least stroke of the pen." In effect, Christ is affirming verbal inspiration, and that inspiration extends not only to the words but even to the letters.

Jesus then affirmed that it is important to observe the law and to teach others to do the same (Matt. 5:19). But even keeping the law is not enough. Jesus said, "For I tell you that unless your righteousness surpasses that of the Pharisees and the teachers of the law, you will certainly not enter the kingdom of heaven" (v. 20). A godly Jew would keep the law, but keeping the law did not save him, and he needed to have in addition the saving grace of God which transforms the inner as well as the outer life.

Jesus illustrated this in his command not to kill. He pointed out that murder is the result of anger, and the outer act is wrong just as the inner attitude which prompts it. An individual who takes a position of superiority in calling someone else a fool indicates that he has not been transformed in his inner life (Matt. 5:21-22).

In relation to fellow believers in Christ, reconciliation was declared to be most important. If one was involved in a controversy with a fellow believer, it was more important to be reconciled than to bring a gift to the altar (Matt. 5:23-26). A further appeal to inner purity was in regard to adultery. Here Jesus not only declared that adultery was wrong, but even looking " 'at a woman lustfully' " was a sin similar to adultery (vv. 27-28). This also introduced the question of divorce, which was prohibited except for unfaithfulness to the marriage vow

(vv. 31–32). All of these moral issues relate to whether one is worthy to enter the future kingdom.

In addition to these moral issues, perjury or revenge was also prohibited, and it was necessary to avoid oaths that might be broken (vv. 33–37). The principle of nonresistance was declared in Matthew 5:38–42. This can, to some extent, be applied to our present life but will be completely applicable to the kingdom situation when Christ rules on earth. The final requirement was that of loving not only your neighbor but also your enemy and thereby demonstrating that you are indeed a child of God with a future place in the kingdom. Jesus summed it up, "Be perfect, therefore, as your heavenly Father is perfect" (v. 48). By perfection he was not speaking of infinite perfection but rather of perfection in the sense of mature godliness that will manifest the work of grace in the heart of an individual.

The Life of Faith to Be Rewarded

Continuing the emphasis on inner righteousness rather than outward show characteristic of the Pharisees, Jesus instructed the disciples that when they gave a gift to the poor, they should not announce it to receive their reward from other people but rather from the Father who sees what they have done and "will reward [them]" (Matt. 6:4).

Likewise, there is a right and a wrong way to pray. Our prayers should not be a matter of public ostentation, such as standing on the street corners so that people will see us praying; rather, we are to pray in secret and be specific with our requests, not babbling vainly like pagans (Matt. 6:5–8).

Jesus gave us what is commonly called "The Lord's Prayer" as a model for how we should pray:

> "Our Father in heaven,
> hallowed be your name,
> your kingdom come,
> your will be done
>   on earth as it is in heaven.
> Give us today our daily bread.
> Forgive us our debts,
>   as we also have forgiven our debtors.
> And lead us not into temptation,
>   but deliver us from the evil one." (Matt. 6:9–13)

Some manuscripts add, "'for yours is the kingdom and the power and the glory forever. Amen.'"

In this simple prayer Jesus illustrated the kinds of prayers that God can answer. The prayer must begin with the recognition of who God is and of his greatness and powerfulness. The prayer should be primarily concerned about bringing in the kingdom of God so that all on earth will worship God as he is worshiped in heaven. Prayer includes requests for our daily needs, "our daily bread" (Matt. 6:11). In our prayers we should also be concerned about our sins and seek forgiveness as well as forgiving others. It is proper to pray that we will not be led into temptation—that is, led into temptation that will result in our sinning—and that we will be delivered from the wiles of the devil (v. 13).

It was customary for the Pharisees to fast and even disfigure their faces so that they would look as if they were suffering more than they really were. Jesus exhorted them to disguise the fact that they were fasting by putting oil on their heads and washing their faces so that only their heavenly Father would know that they were fasting, and he would reward them. Again, the emphasis is on inward piety and devotion rather than outward religious form.

Another area of testing a person's spiritual character is materialism. The Pharisees made much of an outward show of tithing but actually were covetous and materialistic. In view of this, Jesus exhorted them: "Do not store up for yourselves treasures on earth, where moth and rust destroy, and where thieves break in and steal. But store up for yourselves treasures in heaven, where moth and rust do not destroy, and where thieves do not break in and steal. For where your treasure is, there your heart will be also" (Matt. 6:19–21). Here the promise goes beyond reward in the kingdom to all who go to heaven, and it is a general principle that our real wealth is not in the material things of this world but in the treasures, or values, that will count in eternity.

Jesus used the eye as an illustration in his discourse. All light comes to the body through the eye. Jesus declared: "But if your eyes are bad, your whole body will be full of darkness. If then the light within you is darkness, how great is that darkness!" (Matt. 6:23). In contrast, he said, "If your eyes are good, your whole body will be full of light" (v. 22).

Likewise, there is a choice to be made in serving masters. Jesus declared: "No one can serve two masters. Either he will hate the one and love the other, or he will be devoted to the one and despise the other. You cannot serve both God and Money" (Matt. 6:24). One by one, Jesus was detailing the issues of the spiritual life, contrasting what the Pharisees did with what a spiritually minded person would do. When discussing the qualifications of entering the kingdom, inner virtues will be important, not outward religious show.

Another area of Jesus' listeners' concern was whether they would inherit the kingdom. Here, as elsewhere in Christ's ministry, he dealt with the subject of faith in God. He declared:

> Therefore I tell you, do not worry about your life, what you will eat or drink; or about your body, what you will wear. Is not life more important than food, and the body more important than clothes? Look at the birds of the air; they do not sow or reap or store away in barns, and yet your heavenly Father feeds them. Are you not much more valuable than they? Who of you by worrying can add a single hour to his life? (Matt. 6:25-27)

In their religious life the Pharisees were much concerned about what they ate and drank and what they wore. Here Jesus made clear that these things are comparatively unimportant and that God will care for us in these basic elements of life.

Using the illustration of lilies in a field, Jesus said, "I tell you that not even Solomon in all his splendor was dressed like one of these" (Matt. 6:29). Accordingly, the children of the kingdom are instructed not to worry about these things as the heathen world does. Jesus said, "But seek first his kingdom and his righteousness, and all these things will be given to you as well. Therefore do not worry about tomorrow, for tomorrow will worry about itself. Each day has enough trouble of its own'" (vv. 33–34). On the one hand, we should be concerned about what we do in preparation for the kingdom and pay attention to the spiritual verities of our life; on the other hand, we can trust God to be faithful in areas where we cannot take care of ourselves.

Continuing his contrast between the lifestyle of the children of the kingdom and the lifestyle of the Pharisees, Jesus said: "Do not judge, or you too will be judged. For in the same way you judge others, you will be judged, and with the measure you use, it will be measured to you" (Matt. 7:1-2). The Pharisees were notable for their severe judgment of others in contrasting their supposed life of piety to those who did not pay attention to the law as they did. Jesus used the illustration of an irritation in the eye. "Why do you look at the speck of sawdust in your brother's eye and pay no attention to the plank in your own eye? How can you say to your brother, 'Let me take the speck out of your eye,' when all the time there is a plank in your own eye? You hypocrite, first take the plank out of your own eye, and then you will see clearly to remove the speck from your brother's eye" (vv. 3–5). There is a sharp contrast here between the small speck and a piece of lumber, and the point that Jesus was making is that too often when persons judge another they fail to deal with the problems in their own lives, and therefore their judgment is warped. If we are to correct others, we must first of all correct ourselves. Then we will be able to understand clearly what is wrong with others.

Jesus gave a word of caution about dealing with sacred things in relation to those who will not value them. Jesus said, "Do not give dogs what is sacred; do not throw your pearls to pigs. If you do, they may trample them under their feet, and then turn and tear you to pieces" (Matt. 7:6). The reference here is to the common experience of rejection of one's efforts to help others spiritually. Caution must be taken that we do not throw pearls to pigs.

One of the important aspects of spiritual life is prayer. In contrast to the Pharisees who prayed in public to be seen, as Jesus had previously noted, it is important to have an effective prayer life. Here he instructed the children of the kingdom in this regard: "Ask and it will be given to you; seek and you will find; knock and the door will be opened to you. For everyone who asks receives; he who seeks finds; and to him who knocks, the door will be opened" (Matt. 7:7–8). Children of the kingdom are encouraged to pray for answers to prayers now even before the blessings of the kingdom are realized in the future.

To illustrate this, Jesus used the instance of a son who asked for bread. He said, "Which of you, if his son asks for bread, will give him a stone? Or if he asks for a fish, will give him a snake? If you, then, though you are evil, know how to give good gifts to your children, how much more will your Father in heaven give good gifts to those who ask him!" (Matt. 7:9–11). In seeking answers to prayer, we can be assured that God will give us what we really need though it may not be exactly what we ask.

Encouragements to prayer are very real even in our present life. In the kingdom to come there will be even more wonderful answers to prayer.

In summarizing the moral and ethical principles of life in the kingdom, Jesus stated, " 'In everything, do to others what you would have them do to you, for this sums up the Law and the Prophets' " (Matt. 7:12). This is sometimes called the Golden Rule because it applies to so many decisions in life. If we determine what is best for others, then we should also do for them what is best for them. The intent of the Law and the Prophets is to help people in ways they need to be helped.

The closing exhortations and prophecies relating to the Sermon on the Mount deal with the contrasts of the two ways, the one being that of the Pharisees and the other that of the child of the kingdom. As in Psalm 1, which begins with the blessed man as contrasted to the ungodly man, so here the two ways of life were before Jesus' listeners.

First, Jesus pointed out the necessity of salvation: "Enter through the narrow gate. For wide is the gate and broad is the road that leads to destruction, and many enter through it. But small is the gate and narrow the road that leads to life, and only a few find it" (Matt. 7:13–14). Even though the road to heaven is for "whosoever will" and "whosoever believes," relatively few find the road that leads to life. The broad road on which the world is traveling leads to ultimate destruction.

Jesus gave his hearers warning about false prophets:

> Watch out for false prophets. They come to you in sheep's clothing, but inwardly they are ferocious wolves. By their fruit you will recognize them. Do people pick grapes from thornbushes, or figs from thistles? Likewise, every good tree bears good fruit, but a bad tree bears bad fruit. A good tree cannot bear bad fruit, and a bad tree cannot bear good fruit. Every tree that does not bear good fruit is cut down and thrown into the fire. Thus by their fruits you will recognize them" (Matt. 7:15–20).

Here again Christ is referring to the essential goodness or badness of an individual. A false prophet is bad not simply for the false doctrines he teaches but because of the wrong attitude of his heart that causes him to be a false prophet. Like the Pharisees, false prophets often come in religious garb with the appearance of righteousness, but actually they are like ferocious wolves, devouring what they can. A good tree bears good fruit; a bad tree bears bad fruit. By fruit you can identify a tree and what its character is. False prophets can be identified in the same way.

Along with false prophets is the problem of false profession. Jesus showed that a superficial belief in addressing God is not sufficient to secure salvation. He said, "Not everyone who says to me, 'Lord, Lord' will enter the kingdom of heaven, but only he who does the will of my Father who is in heaven. Many will say to me on that day, 'Lord, Lord, did we not prophesy in your name, and in your name drive out demons and perform many miracles?' Then I will tell them plainly, 'I never knew you. Away from me, you evildoers!' " (Matt. 7:21–23). The Pharisees illustrated the danger of mere outward religion without inner transformation. All through the Sermon on the Mount Jesus emphasized inner transformation as a requirement for the kingdom. Jesus set the two ways before his listeners—the way of sincerity and truth stemming from a right attitude and faith toward God, and the way of the Pharisees, which was characterized by outward religious observances and self-promotion.

Finally, Jesus used the illustration of two houses, one built on sand and the other on rock, and the result that occurred when storms came:

> Therefore everyone who hears these words of mine and puts them into practice is like a wise man who built his house on the rock. The rain came down, the streams rose, the winds blew and beat against that house; yet it did not fall, because it had its foundation on the rock. But everyone who hears these words of mine and does not put them into practice is like a foolish man who built his house on sand. The rain came down, the streams rose, and the winds blew and beat against that house, and it fell with a great crash. (Matt. 7:24–27)

As the Scriptures make clear, true faith in Christ is the only foundation upon which one can safely build. Two houses can be equally well-built, but the one built on rock survives the storm, and the one built on sand does not. How important it is to have the certainty of faith in Christ, the certainty of being a child of the King. This alone will make it possible for people to enter the future kingdom.

Matthew 7 closes with a statement that the crowds were amazed because Jesus' teaching was so different from the teachings of the Pharisees who emphasized outer things.

Taken as a whole, the Sermon on the Mount emphasizes the importance of conversion and faith in Christ and the necessity of inner change as well as outward change as evidence of faith. Though the entire discourse focuses on ethical and spiritual realities, this does not contradict the fact that the kingdom Christ will bring in his second coming will be a political kingdom. Yet it will be one in which the spiritual verities will also be illustrated. Jesus' message served to correct the misunderstanding of the Jewish people who reduced the kingdom to a political issue, that of freedom from Roman oppression and freedom to govern themselves.

19

The Inter-Advent Age: Mysteries of the Kingdom of Heaven

Background of the Prophecy

After Jesus delivered his Sermon on the Mount on the ethical principles of the kingdom (Matt. 5–7), he began to perform hundreds of miracles, offering the credentials prophesied in the Old Testament, as illustrated in the prophecy of Isaiah 35:5–6: "Then will the eyes of the blind be opened and the ears of the deaf unstopped. Then will the lame leap like a deer, and the tongue of the mute shout for joy." Most of the prophecies in Isaiah 35 relate to the future millennial kingdom, but these verses also find fulfillment in the public ministry of Christ in his first coming. Christ's performance of so many miracles in the power of God should have alerted the Jews to the fact that he was indeed their Messiah and the prophesied Deliverer of Israel.

Though the miracles of Christ created a stir in Israel and caused many who wanted to be healed to follow him, the nation as a whole seems to have been untouched by these evidences, and continued in unbelief. Subsequent to the many miracles that Christ performed, he sent out his twelve disciples, giving them authority to perform miracles and to drive out evil spirits (Matt. 10:1–42).

When John the Baptist was in Herod's prison he began to wonder if Jesus was the One who was to bring deliverance from the Romans, and he sent his disciples to ask Jesus. Jesus told the disciples to go back to John and report to him the miracles they had seen him doing. Jesus then declared John to be a great prophet, the prophesied messenger who would come before the Messiah (Matt. 11:9–15), but he also noted that that generation had rejected John's message of repentance. Jesus took this as illustrative of his own rejection: "For John came neither eating nor drinking, and they say, 'He has a demon.' The Son of Man came eating and drinking, and they say, 'Here is a glutton and a drunkard, a friend of tax collectors and "sinners."'" But wisdom is proved right by her actions" (vv. 18–19).

Following the recognition of the rejection of both John's ministry and his own, "Jesus began to denounce the cities in which most of his miracles had been performed, because they did not repent" (Matt. 11:20). Jesus pronounced judgment on Korazin, Bethsaida, Tyre, Sidon, and Capernaum (vv. 21–24). In view of the national rejection of John and himself, Jesus then offered an invitation to individuals to become his disciples: "Come to me, all you who are weary and burdened, and I will give you rest. Take my yoke upon you and learn from me, for I am gentle and humble in heart, and you will find rest for your souls. For my yoke is easy and my burden is light" (Matt. 11:28–30).

After Jesus was rebuked by the Pharisees because the disciples' ate grain gathered on the Sabbath, Jesus deliberately healed others on the Sabbath, but he warned the people of Israel that the prophecy of Isaiah 42:1–4 concerning their hardness of heart and incapacity to receive the truth was being fulfilled. This was followed by the Pharisees' blaspheming the Holy Spirit by saying that Jesus' miracles were of Satan. Jesus declared that this was the unpardonable sin. His concluding word was that the sign of the prophet Jonah was to be fulfilled by Jesus' death, burial, and resurrection (Matt. 12:38–41).

With this background of rejection, Jesus recognized that the kingdom he was offering would not be fulfilled soon but would come about at his second coming. This is the theme of Matthew 13.

There has been much resistance to the idea that the kingdom was postponed. It must be understood that what is postponed from a human standpoint is not postponed from the divine standpoint. With God, all contingencies and seeming changes of direction are known from eternity past, and there is no change in God's central purpose.

Jesus had been offering the kingdom in the form of offering himself as the Messiah and King of Israel. This offer had been rejected, as God had anticipated, and ultimately this rejection would lead to the cross of Christ, which was part of God's plan for the redemption of the world. On the divine side this was no change of plan, but on the human side it was a change of direction regarding fulfillment of the kingdom promise. A comparison can be found in the experience of Israel at Kadesh-Barnea when the children of Israel were contemplating entering the Promised Land. When the spies reported that there were giants in the land, and ten of the twelve said that the land could not be conquered, the unbelief of Israel resulted in Israel's wandering in the wilderness for forty years (Num. 13:26–14:25). From a divine standpoint this was anticipated in the plan of God, but from a human standpoint it was a postponement of the promise of the possession of the land.

In a similar way the Israelites' widespread unbelief at this point in the life of Christ changed his message from one of offering the kingdom to one of contemplating what would result in view of Israel's rejection of him. In keeping with this, Matthew 13 reveals the general character of the present age between the first and second comings of Christ. This is done by revealing aspects of the mystery of the kingdom.

The Kingdom in Mystery Form

In the New Testament a mystery is a truth that was hidden in the Old Testament but revealed in the New. Generally speaking, it is not a truth that is difficult to understand but refers to New Testament revelation in contrast to the limitations of the Old Testament. In Colossians 1:26 a typical definition of mystery is found, "the mystery that has been kept hidden for ages and generations, but is now disclosed to the saints." A major aspect of this is the present purpose of God to call out from among Jews and Gentiles the church as the body of Christ and as God's present means of testimony in the world. During this period the promises to and concerning Israel are not progressing, and the promise of the millennial kingdom awaits future fulfillment.

In interpreting Matthew 13 the prophetic background of the interpreter comes into play. Postmillennialism, with its teaching that the world will progressively become more Christian and climax in the triumphant return of Christ, has done much to influence the interpretation of this chapter contrary to what it intended to convey. If anything, this chapter teaches definitely that the world, instead of getting better, will get worse and that evil will triumph until the time of Christ's second coming.

Another approach is the amillennial interpretation which attempts to find a certain amount of fulfillment of the kingdom promises of the Old Testament in the present age. Matthew 13, likewise, refutes the amillennial point of view, because what it reveals is not the Old Testament kingdom but a new form of the kingdom, a spiritual kingdom, which relates to the rule of Christ in the hearts of people. As each parable is unfolded, consideration needs to be given to the differing perspectives in the postmillennial, amillennial, and premillennial points of view.

According to the premillenarian, the fulfillment of the promises concerning the Davidic kingdom will follow the second coming of Christ. This view stands in contrast to the amillennial and postmillennial views, which generally see the kingdom as being fulfilled prior to the second coming of Christ in the present age. A few amillenarians are currently trying to find fulfillment of millennial prophecies in the New Jerusalem in eternity future.

A further word of introduction is necessary regarding the fact that the truth is presented here in parables. Up until this point Christ spoke plainly with the idea of communicating the truth to his audience. Now he is speaking in parables so that truth will be revealed to the believer but not to the unbeliever. The parables are not difficult to understand, but unless one comes with faith and spiritual understanding, one will not arrive at the full meaning of each parable.

The Parable of the Sower
(Matthew 13:1–9; Mark 4:1–20; Luke 8:4–15)

A large crowd had gathered to hear Jesus speak and to see him perform miracles. In order to be heard, Jesus got into a boat and pushed out a little way from the shore, sat down, and gave his discourse. It was customary for teachers of his day to sit down when teaching. The crowd sat or stood on the shore. The parables that Christ gave used situations familiar to a rural population. In presenting the parable of the sower, the emphasis was on reception of the truth.

Jesus began:

> A farmer went out to sow his seed. As he was scattering the seed, some fell along the path, and the birds came and ate it up. Some fell on rocky places, where it did not have much soil. It sprang up quickly, because the soil was shallow. But when the sun came up, the plants were scorched, and they withered because they had no root. Other seed fell among thorns, which grew up and choked the plants. Still other seed fell on good soil, where it produced a crop—a hundred, sixty or thirty times what was sown. He who has ears, let him hear. (Matt. 13:3–9)

After delivering the first parable, the disciples questioned Christ concerning his use of parables. Jesus explained, "The knowledge of the secrets of the kingdom of heaven has been given to you, but not to them. Whoever has will be given more, and he will have an abundance. Whoever does not have, even what he has will be taken from him. This is why I speak in parables" (Matt. 13:11–13). Jesus then quoted from Isaiah 6:9–10, where Isaiah deplored the hardness of heart and dullness of understanding of the people with whom he spoke. Jesus pronounced a blessing upon his disciples because they would see and understand (Matt. 13:16–17).

Jesus then explained the parable of the sower:

> When anyone hears the message about the kingdom and does not understand it, the evil one comes and snatches away what was sown in his heart. This is the seed sown along the path. The one who received the seed that fell on rocky places is the man who hears the word and at once receives it with joy. But since he has no root, he lasts only a short time. When trouble or persecution comes because of the word, he quickly falls away. The one who received the seed that fell among thorns is the man who hears the word, but the worries of this life and the deceitfulness of wealth choke it, making it unfruitful. But the one who received the

seed that fell on good soil is the man who hears the word
and understands it. He produces a crop, yielding a hundred,
sixty or thirty times what was sown. (Matt. 13:19-23)

The four types of soil represent four types of hearers. The first
represents the one who rejects the Word entirely. The second,
superficial reception of the Word, is like rocky soil. Ground that
has a thin layer of soil on top of a bed of rock welcomes the seed
but has no depth for it to develop, and the plant quickly withers
when the sun shines on it. The third type of soil is good but is
choked by weeds. The fourth soil is the type of hearer that is
receptive and produces thirty-, sixty-, and a hundredfold fruit.

This parable obviously is not referring to the millennial
kingdom when the law of God will be written on the hearts of
the people and when it will not be necessary for one to teach
another because all will know the Lord (Jer. 31:33-34). Likewise, this is not the postmillennial interpretation that the world
is getting better and better. The implication of this passage is
that most of the world will reject the message and continue in
unbelief, but a spiritual kingdom, including those genuinely
saved in the present age, will grow.

The Weeds Among the Wheat
(Matthew 13:24–30, 37–43)

The first parable concerned the hearing of the Word. The
second parable deals with the mingled seed, represented by the
wheat and the weeds. Here the kingdom of heaven is represented as a field in which good seed has been sown and wheat is
beginning to come up. However, in this case an enemy sows bad
seed, and weeds come up alongside the wheat. When the
servants asked, "Do you want us to go and pull them up?" (Matt.
13:28), they were told not to do so lest they pull up the wheat
also. Instead, Jesus said, "Let both grow together until the
harvest. At that time I will tell the harvesters: First collect the
weeds and tie them in bundles to be burned; then gather the
wheat and bring it into my barn" (v. 30).

Both truth and error will be proclaimed in the period before
the fulfillment of the kingdom. Here again there is no encouragement for the postmillennial view that the wheat gradually
overcomes the weeds; nor is it a fulfillment of the Old

Testament prophecies concerning the millennial kingdom as the amillenarians hold.

A further doctrinal problem arises from the postmillennial argument that this parable, indicating that the weeds are taken out first, contradicts the pretribulation rapture of the church, which would remove the church from the world before judgment falls upon the unbelievers. This argument is based upon a faulty assumption that the judgment at the second coming of Christ is a single event. Rather, as the Bible indicates, there will be a series of judgments in which God will deal in some cases with the righteous first and in some cases with the wicked first. This is illustrated in the final parable, where in the net the good fish are taken out first (Matt. 13:48). The real problem, however, is that this passage is not talking about the Rapture, as is presumed by posttribulationists. Rather, it is talking about the second coming of Christ, at which time there will be no rapture. According to pretribulationists, the Rapture occurs some years before the second coming of Christ and is not in view in Matthew. The argument that this parable relates to the Rapture is irrelevant as there is no rapture in view.

As in the case of the parable of the sower, in response to the questions of his disciples, Jesus explained the parable of the weeds in the field. He said:

> The one who sowed the good seed is the Son of Man. The field is the world, and the good seed stands for the sons of the kingdom. The weeds are the sons of the evil one, and the enemy who sows them is the devil. The harvest is the end of the age, and the harvesters are angels. As the weeds are pulled up and burned in the fire, so it will be at the end of the age. The Son of Man will send out his angels, and they will weed out of his kingdom everything that causes sin and all who do evil. They will throw them into the fiery furnace, where there will be weeping and gnashing of teeth. Then the righteous will shine like the sun in the kingdom of their Father. He who has ears, let him hear. (Matt. 13:37–43)

Again in this parable postmillenarians search in vain for confirmation that the Gospel is going to triumph over evil at the end of the age and that the church will be presented triumphantly to Christ at his second coming. Rather, there is the dual development of good and evil with, if anything, evil growing and good declining. Likewise, there is no justification for the amillennial contention that this parable fulfills the kingdom promises of the Old Testament. Rather, it describes the age between the first and second coming of Christ. It aptly describes what has happened in the two thousand years since the first coming of Christ—some have received the true message while others have followed false doctrine. Scripture implies an increase in wrong doctrine at the end of the age, as prophesied by Paul in 2 Timothy 3:1–9. The context of Matthew 13 is the revelation of the kingdom in its mystery form as the alternative to bringing in the millennial kingdom previously announced. The age being described is a mystery not revealed in the Old Testament but revealed in the New.

The Parable of the Mustard Seed
(Matthew 13:31–32; Mark 4:30–32)

The parable of the mustard seed illustrates another aspect of the kingdom of heaven—that is, that it will have a rapid and substantial growth. The plant here envisioned is one that has hundreds of tiny seeds, each of which has the capacity to produce a plant. Concerning this, Jesus said, "The kingdom of heaven is like a mustard seed, which a man took and planted in his field. Though it is the smallest of all your seeds, yet when it grows, it is the largest of garden plants and becomes a tree, so that the birds of the air come and perch in its branches" (Matt. 13:31–32).

The church, like a mustard seed, had a small beginning. Jesus and his disciples outwardly seemed like a small and insignificant beginning for a great undertaking. Yet in the centuries that have followed, the professing church has become a gigantic institution, including millions of individuals.

Some have pointed out that the mustard seed is not the smallest of all seeds, as, for instance, the orchid has even smaller seeds. However, in Christ's presentation it is not actually called the smallest but a comparative form, indicating that the seed is "smaller" than others (Gr. *mikroteron*). Though there are smaller seeds elsewhere in the world, in the Holy Land the mustard seed is the smallest of all seeds planted. The argument that this proves an inaccuracy in the saying of Christ is therefore without basis.

It is significant that in Mark 4:30–32 the same parable is

related to the kingdom of God. Most expositors regard the
kingdom of heaven as the equivalent of the kingdom of God, and
explain it on the grounds that Matthew, like many Jews, did not
like to use the word *God* and used *heaven* instead. Actually,
Matthew refers to the kingdom of God several times. In
Matthew's gospel there seems to be a difference in the usage of
"kingdom of heaven," justifying the conclusion that it refers to
the sphere of profession in contrast to "kingdom of God," which
always refers only to those who are saved or, in the case of
angels, holy. What is true of the sphere of profession, however,
is also true of those who are genuinely saved, as both the
professing church and the true church have grown tremendously
from a small beginning. Accordingly, the same parable can be
used to illustrate both.

A further note should be made of the fact that Jesus said that
"the birds of the air come and perch in its branches" (Matt.
13:32), indicating that related to the rapid growth of the church
are those who are not even professing believers. As in the case
of the parable of the sower and the parable of the seed,
imperfection is a major feature of the present age, contradicting
the postmillenarian concept that these parables picture a
growing spiritual conquest by the church. That the church, both
in its profession and true believers, has reached a large
proportion in the world is certainly true; that it has overcome
the unbelievers and the world as a whole is false.

The Parable of the Yeast
(Matthew 13:33; Luke 13:20–21)

In his comparison of the present age in his parables, Christ
used yeast as an illustration. "The kingdom of heaven is like
yeast that a woman took and mixed into a large amount of flour
until it worked all through the dough" (Matt. 13:33). It was
common practice in the Middle East for people to take out a
portion of dough previously fermented to add to a new batch of
dough in order to allow the yeast to spread. Here Christ used
this as an illustration of the character of the kingdom of heaven.
Most interpreters, influenced by the postmillenarian view
which was so dominant in the latter nineteenth century and
early twentieth centuries, identified the yeast as the Gospel
which spreads throughout the world. The concept that the yeast
is the Gospel, however, is an arbitrary deduction, since through-

out Scripture yeast always refers to something contrary to holiness and representing evil. In the Old Testament sacrifices unleavened bread was used to represent the holiness of God and was specifically kept from having any leaven in it. In the typical representation of the professing church (Luke 13:21), however, leaven is included because, as a part of the kingdom of heaven, the professing church does contain a strain of evil.

Just as yeast entering dough tends to puff it up and make it look much larger than it really is, though adding nothing to its value, so false doctrine—such as the teachings of the Pharisees—unbelief as it was found among the Sadducees; and the worldliness of the Herodians tended to puff up religion but actually was an evil force (Matt. 16:6–12; Mark 8:14–21). Even in the Epistles yeast was used to represent evil (1 Cor. 5:6–8; Gal. 5:7–10). The fact that there is evil in both the true church and in the professing church is recognized in Scripture and is the basis for many exhortations and rebukes. It is, accordingly, far better to interpret the yeast as this element of evil in the professing church, as is true in the actual fulfillment of the prophecy. While evil has penetrated the church, it is not true that the Gospel has penetrated the entire world. Much of the world today has not even heard the Gospel.

At this point in Jesus' unfolding of the parables, and before he explained the mystery of the parable of the weeds (Matt. 13:36–43), he again called attention to the fact that he was speaking in parables: "Jesus spoke all these things to the crowd in parables; he did not say anything to them without using a parable. So was fulfilled what was spoken through the prophet: 'I will open my mouth in parables, I will utter things hidden since the foundation of the world'" (vv. 34–35). Here Matthew was quoting from Psalm 78:2.

The Parable of the Hidden Treasure
(Matthew 13:44)

Continuing his revelation concerning the kingdom of heaven, Jesus likened it to a treasure hidden in a field. He described how a man finds a treasure, hides it to prevent anyone else from finding it, and then in his joy sells all that he has to buy the field.

This parable, like others, has been subject to diverse interpretations. A common idea is that the parable represents the salvation of an individual who, discovering Christ, sells all to obtain Christ. Though it is true that there is a putting aside of all earthly wealth in a sense in order to have Christ, this is not an accurate presentation of receiving Christ as Savior. It is true that Paul stated, "What is more, I consider everything a loss compared to the surpassing greatness of knowing Christ Jesus my Lord, for whose sake I have lost all things. I consider them rubbish, that I may gain Christ and be found in him, not having a righteousness of my own that comes from the law, but that which is through faith in Christ—the righteousness that comes from God and is by faith" (Phil. 3:8–9). In salvation, however, an individual coming to Christ comes bankrupt as far as any capacity to buy salvation. Christ is not for sale, and salvation is not earned or deserved but is bestowed as a gift of grace. It is far better, therefore, to explain the treasure in another sense.

In the Jewish background from which Jesus is speaking, Israel is God's treasure. According to Exodus 19:5, God declared of Israel, "You will be my treasured possession." Psalm 135:4 says, "For the LORD has chosen Jacob to be his own, Israel to be his treasured possession."

The fact that the treasure is hidden in a field is all too evident today. Though Israel is a recognized entity in the world, she is not regarded as a treasure of God, but her true nature is hidden in the mass of human population. From God's standpoint, however, Israel is the jewel in the midst of the world, and when Christ died on the cross, one of his essential purposes was to redeem Israel and provide grace to support the many promises God had given her. It was Jesus who sold all in order to secure his treasure in dying on the cross for the sins of the world. (Phil. 2:7–8; 1 Peter 1:18–19). It is contradictory to the concept of salvation by grace for an individual to secure Christ by selling what he himself possesses.

The Parable of the Pearl
(Matthew 13:45–46)

Like the parable of the treasure, the parable of the pearl represents a merchant selling all that he has in order to buy a pearl. As in the parable of the treasure, the common interpretation uses this as a description of what a person does when he forsakes all to be a believer in Christ. This interpretation again is derived from the faulty postmillennial idea that this chapter pictures a triumphant church leading up to the second coming of

Christ. This interpretation also raises questions about salvation by grace and where works enter in.

The merchant here is Christ, not the believer, and it is Christ who gives up all to purchase the pearl. A believer has nothing to justify identifying him with the merchant who sells all, as it is impossible for anyone to purchase salvation by anything he does or possesses.

Though this is not explained in the Bible, the pearl seems to represent the church as a jewel—unusual in the sense that it grows out of an irritation in an oyster. It can portray the role of the church as growing out of the wounded side of Christ. Just as the parable of the treasure pictures Christ's dying for Israel as his treasure, so this parable can be interpreted as referring to Christ's dying for his church. This interpretation has far fewer complications and is more in keeping with the doctrine of grace.

The Parable of the Net
(Matthew 13:47–50)

The parable of the net sums up the truth embodied in the preceding parables. Jesus here likened the kingdom of heaven to a net drawn in from the sea containing both good and bad fish:

> Once again, the kingdom of heaven is like a net that was let down into the lake and caught all kinds of fish. When it was full, the fishermen pulled it up on the shore. Then they sat down and collected the good fish in baskets, but threw the bad away. This is how it will be at the end of the age. The angels will come and separate the wicked from the right-eous and throw them into the fiery furnace, where there will be weeping and gnashing of teeth. (Matt. 13:47–50)

This parable again emphasizes that the kingdom of heaven includes both those who are saved and those who profess to be a part of the kingdom of heaven, in contrast to the universal usage of the term "kingdom of God," which refers only to those who are saved. The parable declares that the sphere of profession represented by the bad fish will be separated from the true fish, or true believers, at the end of the age.

The age in mind here, as in the previous parables, is the whole inter-advent period from the time of Christ on earth to the time of his second coming. The parables do not take into consideration the special character of the church age from

Pentecost to the Rapture. The climax, accordingly, is different from that at the Rapture. At the rapture of the church, believers will be caught out of the world and taken to heaven, but all others will be left on the earth. At the Second Coming, however, there will be a worldwide judgment, and those who are saved will be separated from those who are not saved, whether Jews or Gentiles, as the millennial kingdom does not allow unsaved adults to enter the kingdom. This is brought out later in Matthew 25:31–46 as well as in Ezekiel 20:33–38.

The illustration Christ used refers to a net that could be as long as a half mile. It would require several boats to carry it out to sea and as many to bring it back to land. The gathering of the fish would be much too large for any one boat to handle. Likewise, this refers to the worldwide judgment at Christ's second coming when those who are not worthy to enter the kingdom will be discarded and put to death.

At the Second Coming there will be a series of judgments dealing with those living on earth. Jews and Gentiles will be judged and unbelievers purged out. Old Testament saints will be resurrected and rewarded (Dan. 12:2–3). Also, the martyrs of the Great Tribulation, who died because they would not worship the beast, will be resurrected to share in Christ's millennial kingdom (Rev. 20:1–3).

The content of the Matthew 13 parables does much to illustrate what will happen between the first and second comings of Christ. Instead of bringing in the prophesied kingdom in his first coming, Christ here predicted a long period of time in which the prophecies of these parables would be fulfilled. The climax of the second coming of Christ will involve the divine judgments. Then, and only then, will Jesus fulfill the prophecies of a kingdom on earth which, according to Revelation 20, will go on for a thousand years before the present heaven and earth are destroyed and a new heaven and new earth are created. This revelation should have alerted the disciples to the fact that Jesus would not bring in the kingdom immediately; it seems, however, that they did not understand this even at the time of Christ's ascension, and still wanted to know when he would bring in the kingdom.

The content of these parables makes impossible the postmillennial concept that the present age is the Millennium in which Christ is going to rule in the hearts of people from sea to sea. It also does not in any sense justify the amillennial contention that the millennial kingdom prophecies are being fulfilled in the present age. Rather, it confirms that the fulfillment of the kingdom promise, as far as the millennial kingdom is concerned, will be postponed until the second coming of Christ. Meanwhile, in the present age the mystery form of the kingdom is being fulfilled—that is, the form of the kingdom not anticipated in the Old Testament, in which Christ rules spiritually in the hearts of believers without fulfilling the prophecies of the kingdom on earth.

20

The Death and Resurrection
of Christ

The death and resurrection of Christ are not only facts of history but have their roots in prophecy in both the Old Testament and in the Gospels. As one grows in comprehension of the meaning of Christ's death and resurrection, the truth emerges that all of God's eternal purposes depend on Christ's death and resurrection. This line of truth is the most important doctrine of Scripture and is at the heart of all God's purposes in time and eternity.

Because Jesus Christ is the central character of Scripture concerning whom both the Old and New Testaments reveal profound truths, the prophecies relating to his death and resurrection constitute an important line of Old and New Testament prophecy. As such, they form a part of the revelation of God's grand program for the earth from eternity past to eternity future.

Prophecies in the Old Testament of the Death and Resurrection of Christ

Prophecies concerning the death and resurrection of Christ were the occasion for intense questioning both by those living in the Old Testament and by Jesus' disciples. Peter wrote, "Concerning this salvation, the prophets, who spoke of the grace that was to come to you, searched intently and with the greatest care, trying to find out the time and circumstances to which the Spirit of Christ in them was pointing when he predicted the sufferings of Christ and the glories that would follow" (1 Peter 1:10–11).

Though the Old Testament bears witness to both the death and resurrection of Christ, it seems clear that even the writers of Scripture did not understand what they were predicting. They could not comprehend how one person could be a suffering, dying Messiah and at the same time a glorious, reigning Messiah. The New Testament, of course, solves this problem by separating the two situations—Christ's suffering and dying occur in his first coming and his glorious reign takes place in his second coming. The Old Testament bears witness to both. No other person in history has ever been the subject of the extensive predictions concerning his birth, life, death, and resurrection. Though some passages are devoted to each of these doctrines, the truth concerning Christ's coming is interwoven throughout the Old Testament from Genesis to Malachi. Jesus Christ is the main character of the Old Testament, and understanding this helps one to comprehend the prophecies relating to his death and resurrection.

Already considered are the genealogies and the birth of Christ and his life on earth. Passages that deal with his death and resurrection, however, are extensive, sometimes in direct prophecy, sometimes in typology, sometimes by inference.

Prophecies in Genesis of Christ's death. As early as Genesis 3:15, in anticipation of Christ's crucifixion, the prediction was recorded that Satan would strike Christ's heel. In the sacrificial system inaugurated by Abel there is typical anticipation of the death of Christ as the Lamb of God. This theme is carried through the whole sacrificial system of the Old Testament; wherever blood was shed, it referred ultimately to the coming of the Lamb of God who would take away the sin of the world. The concept of sacrificial blood being shed for sin permeates the Old

Testament and directs students of prophecy to the fulfillment in Christ's death on the cross.

Prophecies in the Psalms of the death of Christ. Several passages are particularly specific about the death of Christ. One of these is Psalm 22. The opening verse of the psalm includes precisely the words that Christ spoke on the cross, "My God, my God, why have you forsaken me? Why are you so far from saving me, so far from the words of my groaning?" (v. 1; cf. Mark 15:34). The Psalm anticipates light and darkness as it occurred on the cross (v. 2; cf. Matt. 27:45). Christ's humiliation at the hands of the unbelieving Jews is also described (vv. 6–8; cf. Matt. 27:39–44). Further, the psalm pictures Christ's agony on the cross: "I am poured out like water, and all my bones are out of joint. My heart has turned to wax; it has melted away within me. My strength is dried up like a potsherd, and my tongue sticks to the roof of my mouth; you lay me in the dust of death" (vv. 14–15).

Christ's suffering at the hand of his tormentors and the unbelievers that surrounded him is described in Psalm 22:16: "Dogs have surrounded me; a band of evil men has encircled me, they have pierced my hands and my feet." The fact that they would cast lots for Christ's clothing (Ps. 22:18; cf. Matt. 27:35) was fulfilled exactly as the Psalm anticipated. The description of the crucifixion of Christ in Psalm 22 is all the more significant because crucifixion was not invented as a method of execution until many years later. Other psalms add their contribution to the sufferings of Christ in his death. He was to be betrayed by a friend (41:9); his bones were not to be broken (34:20); and he was falsely accused and spit upon (35:11; Isa. 50:6).

Prophecies in Isaiah of the death of Christ. Another major passage dealing with the death of Christ is found in Isaiah 53. In this passage Christ is described as a man of sorrows and one acquainted with grief (v. 3). On the cross he carried our sorrows and infirmities (v. 4). The prophecy is specific:

But he was pierced for our transgressions,
    he was crushed for our iniquities;
the punishment that brought us peace was upon him,
    and by his wounds we are healed.
We all, like sheep, have gone astray,
    each of us has turned to his own way;
and the LORD has laid on him the iniquity of us all.

He was oppressed and afflicted,
　　yet he did not open his mouth;
he was led like a lamb to the slaughter,
　　and as a sheep before her shearers is silent,
　　so he did not open his mouth.
By oppression and judgment he was taken away.
　　And who can speak of his descendants?
For he was cut off from the land of the living;
　　for the transgression of my people he was stricken.
He was assigned a grave with the wicked,
　　and with the rich in his death,
though he had done no violence,
　　nor was any deceit in his mouth.

Yet it was the LORD's will to crush him and cause him to suffer,
　　and though the LORD makes his life a guilt offering,
he will see his offspring and prolong his days,
　　and the will of the LORD will prosper in his hand.
　　(vv. 5–10)

The crucifixion of Christ specifically fulfilled most of these predictions. His death was to be followed by his resurrection. The main point, of course, is that Christ as the Lamb of God constituted a sacrifice for sin. Upon him the sins of the whole world were laid. As the prophecy anticipated, he did not open his mouth but was like a lamb at the slaughter (Acts 8:32). After his death he was buried in the grave of a rich person, though judged to have died a criminal's death (Matt. 27:57–60; Mark 15:42–46; Luke 23:50–53; John 19:38–42). The death of no other man in history was predicted in its details as was the death of Christ. The precise fulfillment in the New Testament is a testimony to the supernatural inspiration of Scripture as well as to the deity of Jesus Christ himself.

Old Testament prophecy concerning Christ's resurrection. Along with prophecies of Christ's death, there are constant reminders that the Old Testament anticipated Christ's resurrection. Hebrews 11:17–19 gives an intimate account of Abraham's willingness to offer up his son Isaac in death even though the promises of the Abrahamic covenant required Isaac's life. This passage testifies that Abraham's faith in God was such that he believed that if he killed Isaac and burned his body to ashes on the altar, God would raise up Isaac to fulfill his prophesied role: "By faith Abraham, when God tested him, offered Isaac as a sacrifice. He who had received the promises was about to sacrifice his one and only son, even though God had said to him, 'It is through Isaac that your offspring will be reckoned.' Abraham reasoned that God could raise the dead, and figuratively speaking, he did receive Isaac back from death."

Psalm 22, which speaks so specifically of Christ's death, states, "I will declare your name to my brothers; in the congregation I will praise you" (v. 22). This implies the resurrection of Christ and his subsequent public ministry. The same is true of the close of the psalm:

> All the ends of the earth
>   will remember and turn to the LORD,
> and all the families of the nations
>   will bow down before him,
> for dominion belongs to the LORD
>   and he rules over the nations.
>
> All the rich of the earth will feast and worship;
>   all who go down to the dust will kneel before him—
>   those who cannot keep themselves alive.
> Posterity will serve him;
>   future generations will be told about the Lord.
> They will proclaim his righteousness
>   to people yet unborn—
>   for he has done it. (vv. 27–31)

This passage, as well as many others that anticipate Christ's future glorious reign on earth, necessarily requires resurrection from the dead not simply in the sense that all people are raised but in that Christ was raised on the third day to fulfill his role, first as the Mediator at the right hand of the Father, and then as King of Kings and Lord of Lords at his second coming.

After stating the facts concerning Christ's death in Isaiah 53, the writer goes on: "He will see his offspring and prolong his days, and the will of the LORD will prosper in his hand" (v. 10). The rest of the chapter likewise refers to his life after death (vv. 11–12).

The most specific prophecy of Christ's resurrection is found in Psalm 16:10: ". . . because you will not abandon me to the grave, nor will you let your Holy One see decay." Though David is speaking here of his own resurrection, the prophecy goes far beyond that of David and refers to Christ. In his Pentecostal sermon Peter said:

> But God raised him from the dead, freeing him from the agony of death, because it was impossible for death to keep its hold on him. David said about him:

> *"I saw the Lord always before me.*
>   *Because he is at my right hand,*
>   *I will not be shaken.*
> *Therefore my heart is glad and my tongue rejoices;*
>   *my body also will live in hope,*
> *because you will not abandon me to the grave,*
>   *nor will you let your Holy One see decay.*
> *You have made known to me the paths of life;*
>   *you will fill me with joy in your presence."*
>   *(Acts 2:24–28)*

As Peter went on to explain, the tomb of David was still with them a thousand years or more after David died, but the resurrection of Christ was proved by the fact that his tomb was empty. Undoubtedly, the Jews, upon hearing the story of Christ's resurrection, had gone to the tomb and seen for themselves, and this helps to explain how three thousand of them did not question the fact that Christ was indeed raised from the dead.

All the Old Testament prophecies that speak of Christ's future reign come into consideration here because all of them anticipated that Jesus Christ who would die would also be raised from the dead in order to assume his heavenly authority and ultimately his reign over the earth in the future kingdom.

Predictions in the Gospels of the Death and
Resurrection of Christ

As revealed in the Gospels, the death and resurrection of Christ are usually spoken of in the same passage. In Matthew 12:38–40 and Luke 11:29–30, Christ referred to Jonah as being an illustration of how he would die and be resurrected on the third day. Jesus repeatedly referred to his death and resurrection in subsequent Scriptures (Matt. 16:21; 17:9, 23; 20:19; 26:32; Mark 8:31; 9:9, 31; 10:33–34; Luke 9:22; 18:32–33; John 2:19–22). Even the Pharisees remembered the promise of his resurrection when the disciples did not (Matt. 27:63). Likewise, at Jesus' trial, his prediction that he would build the temple in three days was cited against him (Mark 14:58).

The death and resurrection of Christ, so prominent in the Christian faith and so essential to the doctrine of salvation, play a large part in the prophetic portions of the Old Testament and the Gospels, emphasizing their central place in the plan of God for the redemption of humankind. Later mentions of Christ's resurrection, both in the Gospels and the Epistles, refer back to the historical fact that Jesus Christ died, and in his death and resurrection fulfilled the prophecies of both the Old and New Testaments. Thus they constitute proof of Jesus Christ's deity, proof of the value of his death, and proof of his power to save.

The Death and Resurrection of Christ in Acts

Just as Christ's death and resurrection were the subject of many prophecies in the Old Testament and Gospels, so there is continued witness in Acts, the Epistles, and Revelation. In the opening verses of Acts the death and resurrection of Christ are mentioned as important doctrines: "After his suffering, he showed himself to these men and gave many convincing proofs that he was alive. He appeared to them over a period of forty days and spoke about the kingdom of God" (1:3–4). In this passage, as in many other references, the abundant evidences that Jesus Christ actually died and arose from the dead are offered as proof of the validity of the Christian Gospel. The faithful witness of the apostles to the death and resurrection of Christ is continued throughout the book of Acts (2:24–32; 3:15; 4:10; 5:30–31; 10:39–41; 13:29–37; 17:3, 31–32; 26:23–26). These many passages not only affirm the witness of the apostles to the death and resurrection of Christ but also confirm the importance of this truth in the Christian faith. If there had been no Resurrection, there would have been no book of Acts.

The Death and Resurrection of Christ in the Epistles

In expounding the importance of the death and resurrection of Christ, the apostle Paul included frequent reference to them in his revelation of the broad truth of Christian theology. He began in Romans 1:4 in referring to Jesus as "who through the Spirit of holiness was declared with power to be the Son of God by his resurrection from the dead." In Romans 4:23–25 the death and resurrection of Christ are declared to be essential to our justification: "The words 'it was credited to him' were written not for him alone, but also for us, to whom God will credit righteousness—for us who believe in him who raised Jesus our Lord from the dead. He was delivered over to death for our sins and was raised to life for our justification." The fact that Christ died gives God a basis for righteously justifying a believer, and Christ's resurrection confirms his death and confirms resurrection for believers. If Christ had died but had not risen from the dead, there would be no basis for justification.

The death and resurrection of Christ are also declared to be the basis of our reconciliation: "For if, when we were God's enemies, we were reconciled to him through the death of his Son, how much more, having been reconciled, shall we be saved through his life!" (Rom. 5:10). Here again Christ's death, resurrection, and life are necessary for our salvation. His death alone could not save apart from the confirming fact of his resurrection, providing life for believers in Christ.

Paul continued to refer to the resurrection of Christ as essential to our salvation (Rom. 6:9–10; 8:11, 34; 10:9). It is an essential aspect of the Christian Gospel, without which a person cannot be saved. Paul wrote, "If you confess with your mouth, 'Jesus is Lord,' and believe in your heart that God raised him from the dead, you will be saved" (Rom. 10:9).

References to the death and resurrection of Christ can be found in other epistles. The power of God that raised Christ from the dead is the same power that will cause us to be raised from the dead (1 Cor. 6:14). First Corinthians 15:3–4 says that the death of Christ for our sins, his burial, and his resurrection on the third day are the essential message of the Gospel. In 1 Corinthians 15:20–23 Christ is declared to be "the firstfruits of those who have fallen asleep" (v. 20). As the resurrected One, he is able to bring all under his authority and deliver them triumphantly to the Father (1 Cor. 15:24–27).

Paul also pointed out that if there is no resurrection of Christ, there is no resurrection for Christians and there is no Christian Gospel (1 Cor. 15:29–32). The resurrection of Christ is pointed out in 2 Corinthians 4:10; 5:15; and 13:4. The fact that Christ died for all is emphasized in 2 Corinthians 5:14.

In the opening of the epistle to the Galatians, Paul refers to God the Father as the One "who raised [Christ] from the dead" (1:1). In Ephesians 1:19–21 Paul describes the power of God manifested in raising Christ from the dead and exalting him to God's right hand above all other authority and power.

Paul states his ambition of sharing the sufferings of Christ as well as his power of resurrection in Philippians 3:10–11: "I want to know Christ and the power of his resurrection and the fellowship of sharing in his sufferings, becoming like him in his death, and so, somehow, to attain to the resurrection from the dead." In Colossians 1:18 Christ is referred to as "the firstborn from among the dead, so that in everything he might have the supremacy." In Colossians 2:12, because of the baptism of the Holy Spirit and identification of the believer with Christ, believers are considered as "having been buried with him in baptism and raised with him through . . . faith in the power of God, who raised him from the dead." The Thessalonians are described in 1 Thessalonians 1:10 as those who are waiting for God's "Son from heaven, whom he raised from the dead—Jesus, who rescues us from the coming wrath." In 1 Thessalonians 4:14 the certainty of the death and resurrection of Christ, now a historical fact, is the basis for the believers' faith and trust in his coming again for them at the Rapture.

Those who claim that the resurrection of all people has already taken place are declared to be teaching heresy (2 Tim. 2:18). The death and resurrection of Christ in relation to the eternal new covenant is mentioned in Hebrews 13:20–21: "May the God of peace, who through the blood of the eternal covenant brought back from the dead our Lord Jesus, that great Shepherd of the sheep, equip you with everything good for doing his will, and may he work in us what is pleasing to him, through Jesus Christ, to whom be glory for ever and ever. Amen."

In 1 Peter 1:3–4 the resurrection of Christ is the basis for our new birth and living hope in Christ and for our inheritance that will not fade away. The resurrection of Christ is also mentioned in 1 Peter 3:18: "For Christ died for sins once for all, the righteous for the unrighteous, to bring you to God. He was put to death in the body but made alive by the Spirit." The resurrection of Christ saves us from sin, much as the ark saved Noah and his family from the Flood (vv. 19–21).

The Death and Resurrection of Christ in Revelation

Salvation through the blood of Christ in his death on the cross is mentioned in Revelation 1:4–5: "Grace and peace . . . from Jesus Christ, who is the faithful witness, the firstborn from the dead, and the ruler of the kings of the earth. To him who loves us and has freed us from our sins by his blood."

In Revelation 1:18 Jesus speaks of himself as "the Living One; I was dead, and behold I am alive for ever and ever! And I hold the keys of death and Hades.'"

Throughout the book of Revelation, though the Resurrection of Christ is not specifically mentioned, Jesus Christ is revealed as the Lamb that "had been slain" but is now the Resurrected One who "has triumphed" (5:6). If Christ had not been raised from the dead, the second coming of Christ in Revelation 19:11–16 would be impossible. The New Testament bears unmistakable testimony to both the death of Christ on the cross for our sins and to his bodily resurrection. In this testimony we have proof of his person, support of his promises, and hope for salvation and resurrection.

21

The New Program for the Church

The Increasing Opposition to Christ

Toward the close of Christ's ministry on earth it became apparent that the messianic kingdom predicted in the Old Testament would not be fulfilled in the first coming of Christ. The disciples realized that there was increased opposition to Christ on the part of the religious rulers and that there was a movement underway to kill Christ. On several occasions Christ had predicted that he would be crucified and resurrected. The disciples not only refused to accept this but erased it from their memories so thoroughly that when Christ died they did not realize that he was fulfilling this prophecy.

On the other hand, Christ had affirmed that God would exalt the twelve apostles and put them on thrones, judging the twelve tribes of Israel. Matthew 19:28–30 records:

> Jesus said to them, "I tell you the truth, at the renewal of all things, when the Son of Man sits on his glorious throne,

you who have followed me will also sit on twelve thrones, judging the twelve tribes of Israel. And everyone who has left houses or brothers or sisters or father or mother or children or fields for my sake will receive a hundred times as much and will inherit eternal life. But many who are first will be last, and many who are last will be first."

In Mark 10:28–31 and Luke 18:28–30 Jesus assured his disciples that they would be richly rewarded in heaven for their trials and troubles. All of this tended to kindle their anticipation of the prospect that they would sit on thrones and receive blessing from God because of their relationship to Jesus Christ. However, as Jesus made plain in all these quotations, the fulfillment was not to come in this life but in the future kingdom. The problem was that the disciples thought the kingdom was going to come immediately.

Revelation of the New Program at the Last Passover

Christ's rejection by the religious rulers was to come to a head with his crucifixion. On the night before his crucifixion, Jesus met with his disciples for their last Passover, and in the Upper Room Discourse (John 13–17) he initiated the revelation that pointed to a new program to be introduced prior to the fulfillment of the millennial kingdom. In this new program the disciples, instead of sitting on thrones, would be working as servants of God. This is brought out in the opening of the Passover celebration when Jesus washed the disciples' feet.

It was customary for a slave to wash the feet of guests who came to a dinner. No slave, however, was available, and none of the disciples wanted to volunteer for this task because it would be an admission of inferiorty to the other disciples. According to Mark 9:33–34 and Luke 9:46, the disciples had been arguing for some months as to which one of them would be the greatest. Under the circumstances, none of them wanted to take the role of a slave. When Christ took a basin of water and began to go around washing the disciples' feet, conversation probably ceased and the room became deadly quiet.

He came to Simon Peter, who said to him, "Lord, are you going to wash my feet?"

Jesus replied, "You do not realize now what I am doing, but later you will understand."

"No," said Peter, "you shall never wash my feet."

Jesus answered, "Unless I wash you, you have no part with me."

"Then, Lord," Simon Peter replied, "not just my feet but my hands and my head as well!"

Jesus answered, "A person who has had a bath needs only to wash his feet; his whole body is clean. And you are clean, though not every one of you." For he knew who was going to betray him, and that was why he said not every one was clean." (John 13:6–11)

In this dramatic incident on the night before Jesus' crucifixion, he was making clear that the disciples' future role for this life was one of being servants, not rulers on thrones. This further challenged their hope of soon being in a place of exalted privilege in the kingdom of Christ. It also served to cement Judas Iscariot's resolve to betray Christ.

Judas had been impressed with the growing opposition of the Jewish rulers and began to see the light of a glorious kingdom fading. He argued to himself that if he betrayed Jesus to the Jewish authorities, nothing would happen to Jesus if indeed he was the Messiah. On the other hand, if he was not the Messiah, then it would not matter if he was betrayed. Judas thought it was a situation where he could not lose. Instead, it was a situation where he could not win. Later in the feast Jesus identified Judas as his betrayer by saying that his betrayer was the one who dipped his bread into the same dish as he (John 13:26), and after this Satan entered into Judas (v. 27) and he left (v. 30).

Departure of Jesus Announced

In keeping with the concept of a new program being introduced, Jesus told his disciples that he was going to leave them. He said, "My children, I will be with you only a little longer. You will look for me, and just as I told the Jews, so I tell you now: Where I am going, you cannot come" (John 13:33). Following this announcement he gave them a new commandment: "A new commandment I give you: Love one another. As I have loved you, so you must love one another. By this all men will know that you are my disciples, if you love one another" (vv. 34–35).

Jesus' command to his disciples that they should love one another fell on deaf ears. Obviously their contention as to which one of them was the greatest was not a suitable basis for their love for one another. They were concerned, however, that Jesus was going to leave them. After all, the disciples had left their homes and their families for more than three years under the supposition that Jesus was the Messiah and that he was going to bring in the glorious prophesied kingdom. At this point they still did not understand that this related to his second coming and not to his first coming.

Accordingly, Simon Peter immediately asked, "Lord, where are you going?" (John 13:36). When Jesus answered, "Where I am going, you cannot follow now, but you will follow later" (v. 36), Peter replied, "Lord, why can't I follow you now? I will lay down my life for you" (v. 37). In reply, Jesus said, "Will you really lay down your life for me? I tell you the truth, before the rooster crows, you will disown me three times!" (v. 38).

Message on Trusting God

The events of the Upper Room that signaled God's new program left the disciples in complete consternation. They were disturbed by Christ's example of servanthood. They were dismayed at the thought that one of them would betray him. And now when Jesus said that he was going to leave them and Peter said that he would die for him, Jesus revealed that Peter would disown him three times before morning. It was obvious to all the disciples that they were coming to a major crisis.

To the disciples it seemed as if all was lost. They were losing their hope of a future kingdom on earth, their support of Jesus was disintegrating in betrayal and denial, and they were being vehemently opposed by the scribes and Pharisees. In addition to all this, Jesus was going to leave them.

It is significant that at this point in his Upper Room Discourse Jesus revealed to his disciples a lesson on the abiding work of God in his absence. Though the disciples' hope of the future kingdom would not be immediately realized, there was much that did not change and much that would constitute additional blessing. On the basis of this, Jesus said, "Do not let your hearts be troubled" (John 14:1). He had good solid reasons for not being troubled.

Jesus exhorted his disciples, "Trust in God; trust also in me" (John 14:1). In referring to continued trusting in God, Jesus gathered in all the evidence from the Old Testament of the faithfulness of God to the people of Israel. In spite of their sins and shortcomings, God had been faithful to every promise he had given them. The God of Israel would still be on the throne.

It is significant that Jesus added, "Trust also in me" (John 14:1). The disciples had learned in their three and a half years with Christ that he could be trusted. In every situation Jesus was in command. He could feed the five thousand. He could heal the sick, the blind, and the lame and could restore hearing to the deaf. He could cast out demons, and on several occasions he raised people from the dead. They could learn from these experiences the wonderful fact that Jesus never fails. In a sense, the whole of this chapter, dealing with the basis for comfort in God, finds its key in this opening exhortation. In keeping with God's willingness to stoop to human levels to give additional facts, Jesus went on.

The First Promise of the Rapture

In justifying the fact that he was going to leave them, Jesus said, "In my Father's house are many rooms; if it were not so, I would have told you. I am going there to prepare a place for you. And if I go and prepare a place for you, I will come back and take you to be with me that you also may be where I am" (John 14:2–3).

Previously Jesus had announced his second coming (Matt. 24:27). Here, however, is the first mention in Scripture of the rapture of the church. Though actually recorded by John long after Paul's revelation on this subject, in the order of canonical revelation, it comes the night before the crucifixion of Christ.

The disciples, however, were in no position to understand what Jesus was saying. In view of the fact that they did not understand the difference between the first and second coming of Christ, they certainly were in no frame of mind to understand the difference between the second coming of Christ to bring in his kingdom and the Rapture to take the church to heaven. Accordingly, it was not until later when Paul was given added revelation on this subject that the whole truth concerning the Rapture was revealed.

Jesus' statement, however, was most significant, for it indicated the major difference between the Rapture and the second coming of Christ. At the Rapture the church will be taken from earth to the Father's house, which, in this context, refers to heaven. At the Second Coming, Jesus will come from heaven to earth to remain on earth for a thousand years in his millennial kingdom. The two events are totally different in their timing, circumstances, and purpose.

The Certainty of Salvation

In connection with Jesus' statement concerning coming for his disciples to take them to the Father's house, he went on to say, "You know the way to the place where I am going" (John 14:4). This posed a new problem for the disciples. They did not know where Jesus was going, and Thomas spoke up, probably voicing the question that was on all of their minds: "Lord, we don't know where you are going, so how can we know the way?" (v. 5).

In answer to Thomas's question, Jesus said, "I am the way and the truth and the life. No one comes to the Father except through me" (John 14:6).

No pronouncement could be more simple and yet more profound than this statement of Jesus. He alone is the way, or the road, to heaven. He alone is the truth as all truth is measured by him. And he alone is the source of eternal life. The path to heaven is through Jesus, and no one can come to heaven or to the Father in salvation apart from Jesus Christ. No matter what their future might hold, the disciples were certain of their salvation through their faith in Christ.

The Assurance That God Is Their Father

Having heard that he could come to the Father only through Christ, Philip said "Lord, show us the Father and that will be enough for us" (John 14:8). In reply Jesus called attention to the fact that he himself was the revelation of the Father: "Anyone who has seen me has seen the Father. How can you say, 'Show us the Father?' " (v. 9). Jesus was the living embodiment of the attributes of God the Father. Jesus then asked, "Don't you believe that I am in the Father, and that the Father is in me?" (v. 10). In other words, not only is Jesus the revelation of who God is, but the Father is in him and he is in the Father. This is a subtle preparation for the truth Jesus would later reveal—that believers are declared to be in Christ. The fact that believers in Christ have a heavenly Father who is infinitely rich, wise, powerful, and gracious is one of the major reasons why a Christian can be untroubled in a troubled world.

The Son As Our Mediator and High Priest

In addition to having a wonderful heavenly Father, believers have a representative on the throne of God in the person of Jesus Christ, who is our High Priest and Mediator before God. This is the basis for Christ saying, "I tell you the truth, anyone who has faith in me will do what I have been doing. He will do even greater things than these, because I am going to the Father" (John 14:12). The thought that a believer in Christ can do greater miracles than Christ did is astounding, to say the least. What Jesus was saying, however, was not that the believer alone can do greater things than Christ but that the partnership of Jesus at the right hand of the Father and the believer on earth laboring together will accomplish more for the Lord than if Jesus had remained on earth in his physical presence. When he was on earth, Jesus could be at only one place at a time, but now that he is in heaven representing believers, he can carry on partnerships with believers all over the world and, in effect, be everywhere in his influence and his work. This constitutes a greater work than what he did on earth.

It is also true that what believers accomplish through this partnership, such as leading people to eternal life and discipling them, is a work that is infinite in its scope and far greater than a work of creation even though both are supernatural.

A result of the partnership that believers have with Christ is to magnify our privilege in prayer. Jesus said, "I will do whatever you ask in my name, so that the Son may bring glory to the Father. You may ask me for anything in my name, and I will do it" (John 14:13–14).

On the surface this seems to be an unlimited pledge from Jesus to believers that he will grant answers to their prayers. This statement, however, must be understood in the larger revelation of the Word of God, such as in 1 John 5:14, "This is the confidence we have in approaching God: that if we ask anything according to his will, he hears us." If it were possible for a disciple to ask for something contrary to the will of God, God would not hear and answer that prayer. Every prayer request must be subject to the will of God.

A prayer request that will be honored must, on the one hand, be a request on the part of the believer and, on the other hand, be approved by Jesus Christ. It is comparable in business life to a check with two signatures. The prayer request has the signature of the believer who makes it. If it bears the signature also of Jesus Christ, it does not make any difference how impossible, supernatural, or tremendous the request may be. God will answer.

This is also a corrective to us and magnifies the prayer life of the believer. It encourages us to present our petitions to the Lord; and if our petition is not answered, it then places our situation, such as it is, under the will of God. It is a situation we should endure or work with until such time as God sees fit to change it. Because the matter has been presented to God, even unanswered prayer changes the situation.

The Holy Spirit Indwelling

In addition to the work of the Father and the Son, the Holy Spirit is also a part of the new program of God for believers. Jesus promised that the Holy Spirit would come and indwell the believer: "If you love me, you will obey what I command. And I will ask the Father, and he will give you another Counselor to be with you forever—the Spirit of truth. The world cannot accept him, because it neither sees him nor knows him. But you know him, for he lives with you and will be in you" (John 14:15–17). This tremendous declaration indicates the great change in the future program as compared to the past. The Holy Spirit had been "with" believers throughout the Old Testament and Gospels, but in the future he would be "in" them (v. 17). Though Christ will be bodily absent, the Holy Spirit will indwell every believer.

In the Old Testament believers were born again by the Spirit, but they did not universally have the indwelling of the Spirit. This is why in Christ's post-resurrection ministry it was recorded that he gave his disciples a special bestowal of the Holy Spirit: "And with that he breathed on them and said, 'Receive the Holy Spirit' " (John 20:22). Christ did this in recognition of the fact that the disciples, though they were born again and saved, were not indwelt by the Spirit. His purpose was to enable them to comprehend the truth he was presenting. On the Day of Pentecost this indwelling became permanent.

The indwelling of the Holy Spirit is mentioned often in other books of the New Testament (e.g., John 7:37–39; Acts 11:16–17; Rom. 5:5; 8:9, 11; 1 Cor. 2:12; 6:19–20; 12:13; 2 Cor. 5:5; Gal. 3:2; 4:6; 1 John 3:24; 4:13). Because the Holy Spirit indwells believers, their spiritual lives, effectiveness and service, use of spiritual gifts, and understanding of the will of God, all stem from the fact that the Holy Spirit has been given to them to minister to them. This is a change from the situation in the Old Testament where the Spirit of God could be taken away from a person, as in the case of Saul (1 Sam. 16:14). David prayed that the Spirit would not be taken from him (Psa. 51:11). By contrast, all Christians in this age are permanently indwelt by the Spirit (John 16:17; Rom. 5:5, 8:9,11; 1 Cor. 2:12, 6:19–20; 2 Cor. 5:5; Gal. 3:2, 9:6; 1 John 3:24, 4:13).

Because the Holy Spirit indwells believers, it is possible for every believer to be filled with and empowered by the Spirit. This is a most important aspect of God's program for the present age.

Christ and the Father to Indwell Believers

In addition to the indwelling of the Holy Spirit, Jesus also revealed that God the Father as well as he himself would indwell believers: "If anyone loves me, he will obey my teaching. My Father will love him, and we will come to him and make our home with him" (John 14:23). The Father, Son, and Holy Spirit will combine in their witness to believers and make it possible for them to understand God's truth and to teach it (vv. 25–26).

Supernatural Peace

One of the great legacies Christ left behind at his ascension to heaven was the infinite and supernatural peace of God which believers in Christ can experience in our present evil world. Jesus said, "Peace I leave with you; my peace I give you. I do not give to you as the world gives. Do not let your hearts be troubled and do not be afraid" (John 14:27). Peace is one of the fruits of the Spirit (Gal. 5:22). All the factors that Jesus mentioned in this discourse constitute the ground of a believer's peace in a troubled world.

In Christ

To the marvelous provision of the Holy Spirit indwelling believers (John 14:17), Christ added another distinctive factor in his new program for the church: believers would be "in Christ." In John 14:20 he said, "On that day you will realize that I am in my Father and you are in me, and I am in you." The simple statement "you are in me," embodies a feature of the new relationship in the present age that was never possible in Old Testament times.

The Baptism of the Holy Spirit

Though not mentioned in John 14, the work of God in placing the believer in Christ is called the baptism of the Holy Spirit, mentioned eleven times in the New Testament (Matt. 3:11; Mark 1:8; Luke 3:16; John 1:33; Acts 1:5; 11:16; Rom. 6:1–4; 1 Cor. 12:13; Gal. 3:27; Eph. 4:5; Col. 2:12). The references prior to Pentecost, as found in the Gospels, were prophetic, announcing a future work of God that had never been done in the past. The baptism of the Spirit, however, took place on the Day of Pentecost in fulfillment of the promise of Christ in Acts 1:4–5: "Do not leave Jerusalem, but wait for the gift my Father promised, which you have heard me speak about. For John baptized with water, but in a few days you will be baptized with the Holy Spirit." Though believers in Christ had been born again and in some cases had been filled with the Spirit, the baptism of the Spirit was a work that occurred for the first time on the Day of Pentecost. On that day every living person who had believed in Christ was baptized into the body of Christ (1 Cor. 12:13).

Specific attention was also given to the fact that the baptism of the Spirit occurred again for believers in the house of Cornelius (Acts 10:44–47). When these believers were saved they not only were indwelt and filled with the Spirit, they were also baptized by the Spirit. They spoke in tongues, which occurred at the time in relation to the filling of the Spirit. The baptism of the Spirit resulted in their being joined in a living union in Christ.

Another instance occurred in Acts 19 when the followers of Apollos were led to Christ and, like those in Acts 10, spoke in tongues, indicating their salvation and the infilling of the Spirit but also the baptism of the Spirit. The fact that every believer is baptized by the Spirit at the moment of faith is brought out in 1 Corinthians 12:13: "For we were all baptized by one Spirit into one body—whether Jews or Greeks, slave or free—and we were all given the one Spirit to drink." Though not all believers are filled with the Spirit, all believers are baptized by the Spirit, indwelt by the Spirit, and born again by the Spirit. In the early church, if one was filled with the Spirit, it automatically was evidence that the permanent works of the Spirit had already taken place.

The baptism of the Holy Spirit sets apart believers in the present age from those who were believers in previous dispensations and also from those who believe in Christ in the millennial kingdom.

In the baptism of the Spirit, not only are believers placed in Christ, but Jews and Gentiles are joined together on a common basis that wipes out the distinction between them. This truth is declared to be a mystery—that is, a truth that was not taught in the Old Testament but is now taught in the New Testament. Paul wrote to the Ephesians:

> Surely you have heard about the administration of God's grace that was given to me for you, that is, the mystery made known to me by revelation, as I have already written briefly. In reading this, then, you will be able to understand my insight into the mystery of Christ, which was not known to men in other generations as it has now been revealed by the Spirit to God's holy apostles and prophets. This mystery is that through the gospel the Gentiles are heirs together with Israel, members together of one body, and sharers together in the promise in Christ Jesus. (3:2–6)

The fact that believers—whether Jews or Gentiles—are in Christ is one of the outstanding evidences that a new program has been instituted. In the Old Testament the Jews were treated separately from Gentiles, and God's purposes for the Jews were limited to them. In the future millennial kingdom Jews and Gentiles again will be treated separately, though both can be saved and both can enjoy the blessings of God. In the present age the new program for the church puts aside the distinctions of race, and Jews and Gentiles alike share in the abundant riches of grace in Christ Jesus.

The baptism of the Spirit, according to the Scriptures, now

occurs at the moment of saving faith and is not a subsequent work of the Holy Spirit in contrast to the filling of the Spirit, which can come after salvation. The baptism of the Spirit occurs once for all and is never repeated. Accordingly, Christians are never exhorted to seek the baptism of the Spirit as it is automatically a part of their salvation. Though they may lack the filling of the Spirit, the baptism of the Spirit is assured every Christian. The baptism by its nature is a positional matter as a believer is in Christ and in the body of Christ, and it is not directly related to human experience, though human experience may come as a result of it. All the experiences of being a Christian are a result of the salvation of which baptism is a part. As a result of the baptism of the Spirit, believers have a new union with Christ and with fellow believers. They have a new position of being in Christ rather than in Adam, and they have a new relationship in that they are related to God and to all other believers in this special way.

In the new program for the church the relationship of believers to Jesus Christ is illustrated in two figures, that of the vine and the branches and that of the body and the Head of the body.

The Vine and the Branches

In the figure of the vine, representing Christ, and the branches, representing the believer, truth is taught concerning the living relationship between the two as it relates to bearing fruit. Jesus said: "I am the true vine, and my Father is the gardener. He cuts off every branch in me that bears no fruit, while every branch that does bear fruit he prunes so that it will be even more fruitful" (John 15:1-2).

Two kinds of branches are named in the illustration, branches that abide in the vine and bear fruit and branches that do not abide in the vine and do not bear fruit. The implication is that branches that have a real and vital connection to the vine are fruitful branches. Jesus said: "I am the vine; you are the branches. If a man remains in me and I in him, he will bear much fruit; apart from me you can do nothing. If anyone does not remain in me, he is like a branch that is thrown away and withers; such branches are picked up, thrown into the fire and burned" (John 15:5-6). In attempting to understand this figure, one should bear in mind that Jesus is not talking about salvation but about fruitbearing. The implication is that branches that do not bear fruit are not true branches and need to be cut off and burned because they do not add to the fruit of the vine.

An important part of a branch's abiding in the vine is the promise of answered prayer: "If you remain in me and my words remain in you, ask whatever you wish, and it will be given you" (John 15:7).

Three levels of fruitbearing are mentioned—"fruit" (John 15:2), "more fruitful" (v. 2), and "much fruit" (vv. 5, 8). A byproduct of bearing much fruit is joy in serving the Lord (v. 11).

The central thought in the figure of the vine and the branches is that individual Christians cannot expect to accomplish much for God unless they are living in fellowship with the Savior and drawing from his life and strength. If they draw on the vine and bear fruit, the fruit will have the same characteristics as the vine from which its life came.

The Head and the Body

As brought out in the previous study on the baptism of the Spirit, the body of Christ is formed at the time believers are saved, and they are placed into a living union in which all believers are joined to Christ as the Head of the body. This was not true in the Old Testament. Although there was a body of believers composed of Israelites as well as Gentiles who were saved, they did not have an organic union. In the new program for the church, Jew and Gentile are brought together in one living union with any racial tensions between them eliminated. Ephesians 2:14 says, "For [Christ] himself is our peace, who has made the two one and has destroyed the barrier, the dividing wall of hostility." Paul goes on, "His purpose was to create in himself one new man out of the two, thus making peace, and in this one body to reconcile both of them to God through the cross, by which he put to death their hostility" (vv. 15–16). As a result of this, in the new order Gentiles are now one with Jews in the household of God:

> Consequently, you are no longer foreigners and aliens, but fellow citizens with God's people and members of God's household, built on the foundation of the apostles and prophets, with Christ Jesus himself as the chief cornerstone.

In him the whole building is joined together and rises to
become a holy temple in the Lord. And in him you too are
being built together to become a dwelling in which God
lives by his Spirit. (vv. 19–22)

In addition to the analogy of the human body, the thought of
the church being a building built upon foundations of which
Christ himself is the chief foundation is introduced. The point is
that all believers, regardless of their background, are now a
dwelling place for the Spirit of God.

As previously brought out, this is the mystery—that is, the
truth not revealed in the Old Testament that Jew and Gentile
would have the same spiritual heritage in the new program for
the church.

Ephesians 4:4–6 says that there should be unity in the body
of Christ: "There is one body and one Spirit—just as you are
called to one hope when you were called—one Lord, one faith,
one baptism; one God and Father of all, who is over all and
through all and in all." However, the figure of the body
illustrates the diversity of believers as well as their unity. In the
human body different parts have different functions and different abilities. So also in the body of Christ individual believers
have different qualities yet are joined together. Ephesians 4:16
says, "From [Christ] the whole body, joined and held together
by every supporting ligament, grows and builds itself up in love,
as each part does its work."

The Gifts of the Body: Spiritual Gifts

Members of the body are also endowed with special spiritual
gifts. Some of the miraculous gifts given in the early church
declined once the New Testament was written and the special
purposes of these gifts ceased. In the early church there was the
gift of apostleship, such as possessed by Paul (Rom. 1:1; 1 Cor.
1:1; et al.), Barnabas (Acts 14:14; cf. Gal. 2:9), Matthias (Acts
1:23–26), and others. Apostles were chosen by God and sent
forth to represent God.

Some early Christians had the gift of prophecy—that is, they
could communicate truth from God in an authoritative and
accurate way (Rom. 12:6; 1 Cor. 12:10, 28; 14:1–40). A prophet
needed to receive the Word accurately and be able to communi-

cate it effectively. It would include not only future events but also God's instruction concerning special needs of the church.

Another important gift was the gift of miracles, which was often used as a sign of the accuracy of the Gospel and of the fact that a person came from God (1 Cor. 12:28). Though God continues to do miracles even in modern times, the gift of miracles, as a proof that the message given was from God, ceased. The same can be said of the gift of healing, which was a form of miracles (1 Cor. 12:9, 28, 30). God can continue to heal supernaturally today but not as a confirming sign of the gospel.

One of the prominent gifts in the apostolic period was the gift of tongues, the ability to speak in languages that the people did not know naturally. Three important passages are found in the book of Acts (Acts 2:1–13; 10:46; 19:6). Tongues are not mentioned elsewhere in Scripture except in the account in 1 Corinthians where Paul rebuked the church for misusing the gift (12:10, 28, 30; 14:1–40). Though in modern times some have claimed to have the gift of tongues, many others believe that the modern use of tongues is not what the Scriptures reveal, as the need for support for the message from God no longer exists now that the New Testament has been completed.

In 1 Corinthians 14 the gift of tongues is expounded and its limitations indicated. Tongues was declared to be one of the lesser gifts and inferior to prophecy (vv. 1–12). In this connection Paul said that while he did have the gift of tongues, he preferred to speak five words that could be understood rather than ten thousand words in tongues (v. 19). The exercise of tongues was forbidden unless an interpreter was present (vv. 13–20). The purpose of tongues was primarily as a sign to unbelievers that the message, given in language they could understand, was from God (vv. 21–22). The exercise of the gift of tongues, when permitted, was to be regulated with only two or three speaking, and again only if an interpreter was present (vv. 27–28). In this connection, women were not allowed to speak in tongues in public meetings. Paul made clear that while tongues was a genuine gift in the apostolic period and not to be prohibited, other gifts were more important, especially the gift of prophecy (v. 39).

The modern emphasis on tongues is not found in Scripture. Of the Epistles only 1 Corinthians mentions "tongues." The book of Revelation (e.g., 7:9) speaks of languages in their ordinary use. Even in apostolic times there were good reasons for considering tongues as a temporary gift. The exercise of the gift was mentioned only three times in the book of Acts, and there is no record that Christ or the apostles ever publicly participated in tongues. Tongues were intended to be a sign, especially to Israel, in order to win them to Christ and would be appropriate as a fulfillment of Isaiah 28:11 as quoted in 1 Corinthians 14:21: " 'Through men of strange tongues and through the lips of foreigners I will speak to this people, but even then they will not listen to me,' says the Lord." The fact that certain spiritual gifts are temporary is illustrated also in gifts such as apostleship, prophecy, miracles, and healing. First Corinthians 13:8 also states that tongues will cease, though it is not clear when this will occur. Supernatural revelation to individuals which enables them to prophesy ceased once Scriptures were completed, and no one has been able to add one verse to Scripture since the first century.

The major problem with tongues is that in modern use it has been exalted to a position beyond what the Scriptures indicate. Tongues, even in apostolic times, was the least of the spiritual gifts. It is not a test of salvation nor of spirituality, and is not inseparable from the baptism of the Spirit. While every Christian is baptized by the Spirit (1 Cor. 12:13), it should be clear that many Christians who are born again do not speak in tongues. In the early church the exercise of tongues in public depended on an interpreter being present (1 Cor. 12:10; 14:26–28). In view of the fact that no one can demonstrate that he has the gift of interpreting tongues today, the gift, if exercised at all, should be exercised in private. In the early church when special revelation was given, it was also important that ability be given the church to discern what was from God and what was not. Accordingly, the ability to distinguish between the Holy Spirit and the work of demons was important (cf. 1 John 4:1). Taken as a whole, the doctrine of the church as the body of Christ is a central feature of the new program for the present age, which was not anticipated in the Old Testament.

The Church as a Building

As mentioned earlier in connection with Ephesians 2:19–21, the church is often presented as a building built upon Jesus Christ as the cornerstone. In this figure Christ is seen as "the chief cornerstone" (Eph. 2:20). The concept of the church as a building is used in 1 Corinthians 3:11–15, where the foundation is said to be Christ. On this foundation believers erect the building of their lives out of gold, silver, precious stone, wood, hay, or straw. It is said of the building that it will be tested by the fire of judgment (1 Cor. 3:13). The gold, silver, and precious stone represent that which continues after testing by fire, whereas the wood, hay, and stubble are consumed and reduced to ashes. Though not explained, the gold seems to represent the glory of God; silver, redemption or evangelism; and precious stone, the many other facets of the spiritual life that are honoring to God. The building here can also be understood to represent the church and indicates how the church should be living for eternal things. The same concept of a building in which Christ is the cornerstone is found in 1 Peter 2:4–8. Christ, though rejected by the builders, will become "the capstone" (1 Peter 2:7). The church is a "spiritual house" and designed to be a "holy priesthood" (1 Peter 2:5).

The Figure of the Shepherd and the Sheep

In anticipation of the church age, Jesus referred to his disciples as sheep and to himself as the Shepherd. Jesus declared, "I am the gate for the sheep" (John 10:7). Those who enter in will be saved (v. 9). In anticipation of the future age, Jesus added, "I have other sheep that are not of this sheep pen. I must bring them also. They too will listen to my voice, and there shall be one flock and one shepherd" (v. 16). Though Jesus was speaking to the Jews as his flock, he anticipated the future church in which Jews and Gentiles would form one flock under one Shepherd. The important truth indicated in the shepherd and the sheep is the utter dependence of the sheep on the shepherd for guidance, nourishment, strength, and protection. The challenge to the sheep is to hear the shepherd's voice and follow him.

The Last Adam and the New Creation

Jesus was referred to as the "last Adam" in 1 Corinthians 15:45. As such, he is the Head of the new race composed of himself and the church, just as Adam was head of the natural race as the one first created. Accordingly, Jesus is the Head of the new creation (2 Cor. 5:17; cf. Gal. 6:15). Just as the old creation consisted of Adam and his descendants, so the new creation consists of Christ and those who are found in him. As Adam was formed of the dust of the earth and was given physical life in creation, so Jesus in the tomb needed to be resurrected to fulfill his role as the last Adam. He now is able to bestow eternal life and salvation on those who trust him (John 1:4; 6:54; 10:28; 17:2). The emphasis in the doctrine of the last Adam and the new creation is that this is a work of God for human beings, not a work of human beings for God.

The High Priest and the Kingdom of Priests

Christ is the High Priest, and believers in Christ are priests. As is revealed in Hebrews, Jesus had all the necessary qualities of being a high priest, having been appointed by God himself (5:1–10). In his priesthood he fulfilled that which was anticipated in type in Melchizedek, the priest to whom Abraham gave tithes. Like Melchizedek, his priesthood was based on appointment by God, not lineage, and, like Melchizedek, he had no successors. His ministry and position as High Priest continue forever as indicated in Psalm 110:4:

> The LORD has sworn
>   and will not change his mind:
> "You are a priest forever,
>   in the order of Melchizedek."

This makes it possible for Jesus to become "the source of eternal salvation for all who obey him" (Heb. 5:9). Though attempts have been made to date the beginning of Christ's priesthood, it is probably best to consider his priesthood as being eternal even though the functions of priesthood were not assumed until after he became incarnate.

As High Priest, Jesus served his priesthood in heaven (Heb. 8:2). He served realities in the heavenly sanctuary rather than the "shadow of what is in heaven" (v. 5). As Mediator he administered the covenant that is superior to the old covenant of Moses (v. 6). As High Priest he offered his own body as a final and complete sacrifice for the sin of the world in contrast to the daily offerings offered under the Mosaic Law (7:27). In his sacrifice he became our redeemer, our propitiation, and our reconciliation.

On the basis of being our High Priest, Jesus not only offers sacrifice, but he offers intercession for us, as stated in Hebrews 7:25: "Therefore he is able to save completely those who come to God through him, because he always lives to intercede for them."

Individual believers, because they are related to Jesus Christ who is the royal High Priest, also belong to a royal priesthood and have the important function of sharing with Christ in his priestly intercession. In connection with this, believers can offer sacrifices, such as the sacrifice of their bodies (Rom. 12:1), of praise, of doing good, and of sharing, as stated in Hebrews 13:15–16: "Through Jesus, therefore, let us continually offer to God a sacrifice of praise—the fruit of lips that confess his name. And do not forget to do good and to share with others, for with such sacrifices God is pleased." It is important for believers to be fully yielded to the Lord as is embodied in the concept of offering our bodies. It is also vital that we offer praise and thankfulness to God as part of our spiritual experience. Christians should also share with others. The Bible has a great deal to say about giving of our substance. It should be systematic (1 Cor. 16:2), regular, proportionate to God's blessings, sacrificial (2 Cor. 8:2), liberal (9:6), and done cheerfully (v. 7). And in the nature of giving, we must trust God to supply all our needs (v. 8).

As believer priests, those who trust in Christ should engage in the work of intercession, in which Christ is in heaven as our prayer partner. When Christians intercede, they join a prayer meeting already in session and are therefore qualified to pray in the name of Christ (John 14:13–14). In their prayer life believers can function as priests under Christ and can expect God to hear and answer prayer.

The Figure of Christ As the Bridegroom and the Church As the Bride

The figure of Christ as the Bridegroom and the church as the bride is a doctrine not taught in the Old Testament. Though the Bible uses marriage as an illustration of spiritual relationships, nothing like this is found in the Old Testament. Israel was considered the wife of Yahweh, already joined in marriage but proving to be unfaithful to her husband by violating the marriage vows (Isa. 54:1–17; Jer. 3:1, 14, 20; Hos. 2:1–23).

The church in the New Testament is not pictured as a wife but as a bride awaiting the coming of her husband (2 Cor. 11:2; Eph. 5:25–27; Rev. 19:6–8). The present age is viewed as a time of preparation for the bride. In John 14:2 Jesus said that he was going to heaven to prepare a place for his own. Most of the work in the present age, however, has to do with the bride herself, as anticipated in Ephesians 5:25–33. In Ephesians 5:25 Paul exhorted, "Husbands, love your wives, just as Christ loved the church and gave himself up for her." This refers, of course, to Christ's going to the cross and dying on behalf of those who had formed the church, the body of Christ. This is something already accomplished.

In the present age, however, Christ is working with the church "to make her holy, cleansing her by the washing with water through the word" (Eph. 5:26). The reference here is not to some formula, such as that of baptism, but rather to the cleansing and sanctifying power of the water of the Word of God. The church is undergoing progressive sanctification, and eventually this will lead to her presentation as a bride to Christ.

In the future the purpose of Christ is "to present her to himself as a radiant church, without stain or wrinkle or any other blemish, but holy and blameless" (Eph. 5:27). This refers to the ultimate perfection of the church when she meets Christ; and when she sees him, she will be like him (1 John 3:2). The church at that time will be "radiant" and will reflect the glory and perfections of Christ. There will be no "stain" or defilement of sin, no "wrinkle" or sign of old age, and no "blemish" or disfiguration. In every respect, by the grace of God, the church will be presented perfect. Accordingly, the church in the present age has the prospect of the coming of Christ, which will occur at the rapture of the church. The church, instantly perfected, will meet the Lord in the air and go to heaven.

Taking all seven of the figures that relate the church to Christ, one is provided with a panoramic view of the central features of God's present program in the world and his goals for the church. It is clear that the church does not fulfill God's purpose for Israel and does not inherit either her promises or her judgments. Rather, the church is a special purpose of God, hidden from the Old Testament prophets but now revealed in the New Testament. Once the rapture of the church occurs, the program of God will return to the dual lines of treatment for Israel and the Gentiles as separate entities.

22

Signs of the Lord's Return

Background of the Olivet Discourse

Jesus' Olivet Discourse, so named because he delivered it on the Mount of Olives just to the east of Jerusalem, is recorded in three of the four Gospels (Matt. 24–25; Mark 13:1–27; Luke 21:5–36). Jesus gave the discourse in response to questions from four of the disciples, Peter, James, John, and Andrew (Mark 13:3) only two days before the Passover and three days before his crucifixion (Matt. 26:2). The discourse takes into consideration the disciples' anxiety concerning the trend of Christ's public ministry.

The growing opposition and unbelief of the Jewish leaders. Jesus had given his disciples numerous reasons for anxiety. In Matthew 21:33–46 Jesus had given the parable of the landholder whose son was killed by his vineyard tenants. Jesus implied that the son was representative of himself. On several occasions Jesus had told them clearly that he would die (Matt. 16:21; 17:23; 20:18–19). The disciples had followed Christ, anticipating that he would bring in the prophesied glorious kingdom and that they would sit on thrones judging the twelve tribes of Israel (Matt. 19:28–29). Events were not going in the direction that they had hoped, as there was growing opposition from the Jewish leaders. In fact, the disciples knew that the Jews wanted to take his life.

To make things worse, Jesus had pronounced a blistering denunciation of the Jewish leaders (Matt. 23:1–36). In it he had called them hypocrites (vv. 13–14 [NASB], 15, 23, 25, 27–29). He had accused them of making their converts "twice as much a son of hell as you are" (v. 15). They were "blind guides" (vv. 16, 24) and "blind fools" (v. 17). Jesus accused them of having "neglected the more important things of the law—justice, mercy and faithfulness" (v. 23). They were like a dish that is clean on the outside but "inside they are full of greed and self-indulgence" (v. 25). They were "blind Pharisee[s]" (v. 26). They were "whitewashed tombs" (v. 27), "full of hypocrisy and wickedness" (v. 28), guilty of "shedding the blood of the prophets" like their forefathers (vv. 30–31). They were "snakes" (v. 33) and a "brood of vipers" (v. 33). They were "condemned to hell" (v. 33). As a conclusion to this denunciation, Jesus delivered his lament over Jerusalem: "O Jerusalem, Jerusalem, you who kill the prophets and stone those sent to you, how often I have longed to gather your children together, as a hen gathers her chicks under her wings, but you were not willing. Look, your house is left to you desolate. For I tell you, you will not see me again until you say, "Blessed is he who comes in the name of the Lord'" (vv. 37–39).

In searching for comfort from Christ and reassurance of the goals of his glorious kingdom, the disciples were given little to encourage them. As they left the temple and proceeded over the Brook Kidron to the Mount of Olives, the disciples thought they should show Jesus that, after all, things were not quite as bad as he mentioned, for the magnificent temple was being built and was already in advanced stages of construction (Matt. 24:1).

Christ abruptly pointed out the deception of looking at the outside of the buildings: "'Do you see all these things?' he asked. 'I tell you the truth, not one stone here will be left on another; every one will be thrown down'" (v. 2).

The disciples reasoned correctly that if the magnificent temple was going to be torn down, with not one stone left on another, there seemed to be little prospect of a glorious kingdom ahead which they would share with Christ. The construction of the temple had begun in 20 B.C. before Christ was born and was now well along toward completion, though another thirty years would be required to finish the various buildings that were constructed out of stone hewed in the quarries underneath the city of Jerusalem. Secular sources indicate that the stones were often ten, twenty, or even thirty tons, cut precisely to size, put on rollers, rolled from the quarry to the temple site up dirt ramps, and then eased into place. No mortar was required because of the precise fit. For such huge stones to be dislodged implied deliberate destruction.

The three questions of the disciples. When the disciples had reached the Mount of Olives and Christ was sitting with them, four of the disciples—Peter, Andrew, James, and John—came privately to Christ and asked him about the meaning of his pronouncement (Mark 13:3). They said, "Tell us, when will these things happen And what will be the sign that they are all about to be fulfilled?" (v. 4). Their question was threefold: (1) They asked when the destruction of the temple would take place. (2) They asked what the sign of his coming would be— that is, when the glorious kingdom would be fulfilled. (3) And they asked what the end of the age would be—that is, the age leading up to his coming. Questions 2 and 3 are answered together as Christ's coming and the end of the age leading up to his coming both refer to his second coming to the earth.

Each of the three Gospels that recorded this discourse presented additional details not supplied by the others. The first question was not answered in Matthew but was answered in the Luke passage (21:5–36). Matthew and Mark answered questions two and three, with Matthew adding the many illustrations and applications found in Matthew 24:32–25:46.

The Coming Destruction of Jerusalem

Signs of the coming destruction of Jerusalem. Jesus told his disciples, "When you see Jerusalem being surrounded by armies, you will know that its desolation is near. Then let those who are Judea flee to the mountains, let those in the city get out, and let those in the country not enter the city" (Luke 21:20–21). In A.D. 70 the Roman armies surrounded Jerusalem at the time of the feasts and did precisely what this passage predicts. Those who were able to flee from the city were in some cases saved.

Others who remained in the city were slaughtered as the Roman armies breached the walls and destroyed the temple as well as the city. This was in sad fulfillment of what Jesus had predicted concerning the destruction of the temple (Matt. 24:2). At the end of the age preceding the second coming of Christ, Jerusalem will be in a similar situation (Zech. 14:1–2).

Jesus went on to predict, "How dreadful it will be in those days for pregnant woman and nursing mothers! There will be great distress in the land and wrath against this people. They will fall by the sword and will be taken as prisoners to all the nations. Jerusalem will be trampled on by the Gentiles until the times of the Gentiles are fulfilled" (Luke 21:23–24). The precision of this prophecy is evident. This is exactly what happened in A.D. 70. Beginning with the destruction of Jerusalem, Jesus declared that the "times of the Gentiles" would continue until the end of the age—that is, until the second coming of Christ. This is supported by Daniel's prophecies concerning the fourth empire, that of Rome, which in the end time will be revived and not destroyed until the second coming of Christ.

Ever since 605 B.C., when Nebuchadnezzar conquered Jerusalem, to the present time, Jerusalem has been under the control of Gentiles. Though for brief times they seemed to have had temporary freedom, it was short-lived, and the times of the Gentiles have continued to the present time. Even today Israel is in power and in control of their territory largely because of the support of the United States, a Gentile power. Without this support Israel would not be able to survive. The ultimate in the control of the Gentiles will occur in the Great Tribulation just before the Second Coming when the Jews once again will be driven out of Jerusalem.

The Second Coming of Christ in Luke

Having answered the question concerning the time of the destruction of the temple, Jesus then went to the far view, as indicated in Luke 21:27, and described the events leading up to the second coming of Christ, which in many respects parallel those in connection with the destruction of Jerusalem. Here, however, the signs are much greater than a siege of Jerusalem. He declared:

There will be signs in the sun, moon and stars. On the earth, nations will be in anguish and perplexity at the roaring and tossing of the sea. Men will faint from terror, apprehensive of what is coming on the world, for the heavenly bodies will be shaken. At that time they will see the Son of Man coming in a cloud with power and great glory. When these things begin to take place, stand up and lift up your heads, because your redemption is drawing near (Luke 21:25–28).

What Luke summarizes here is described more at length in Matthew 24.

Various Approaches to Interpretation

Though all agree that Luke 21:20–24 was fulfilled in A.D. 70 with the destruction of Jerusalem, a wide difference of opinion exists concerning the fulfillment of other prophecies in Matthew 24, Mark 13, and Luke 21. The theological perspective of the interpreter to some extent determines the interpretation.

Amillenarians tend to avoid detailed exegesis of these passages in favor of a more general approach that many of these prophecies were fulfilled in A.D. 70. Careful attention to the text, however, would reveal that this is an impossibility as the things that were predicted did not come to pass. Though the temple was destroyed, it was not desecrated in the manner indicated, and in A.D. 70 the Great Tribulation, the predicted three-and-a-half years leading up to the second coming of Christ, did not occur.

Finally, and most conclusive, the second coming of Christ, which is closely linked to the prophecies of all three Gospels, did not occur. Though there are similarities between the time of the destruction of Jerusalem and the time preceding the second coming of Christ, the outcome is entirely different, and the prophecies Matthew recorded have not been specifically fulfilled as they relate to the end of the age. In brief, amillenarians attempt to interpret the passage in keeping with their concept that the Millennium is being fulfilled now rather than after the second coming of Christ.

Postmillenarians, though not a viable force in current theology, have a different problem in that they believe that the Gospel is going to bring a gradual improvement spiritually in the world, climaxing in the second coming of Christ. Christ's description of the end of the age does not portray gradual improvement but rather increasing problems, opposition, and even martyrdom.

Still a third approach, that of liberal theology, which, generally speaking, denies the literal fulfillment of prophecy, likewise glosses over this passage and accepts only its general concept that there will be victory in the end.

Only the premillenarian attempts to find a literal fulfillment in specific events related in these prophecies. Even here there is some difference of opinion.

Some premillenarians say that the predictions of Matthew are entirely future, relating them to the Great Tribulation preceding the Second Coming. Others view the opening section of Matthew 24:4–8 as prophecies being fulfilled in the present age, but they say that the specific prophecy of the Great Tribulation starts in verse 9. Still others believe that the break comes at the end of verse 14 and that Matthew 24:4–14 gives general signs to be found throughout the entire age. They say that the prophecies of Matthew 24:15–31 are to be fulfilled in the Great Tribulation.

It is undoubtedly true that Matthew 24:4–14 pictures what will be fulfilled in the Great Tribulation, but these verses also find some fulfillment in the present age and are probably best considered as general signs, observable now but to be fulfilled with more graphic detail in the Great Tribulation. Beginning with verse 15, however, a specific event is described that will begin the Great Tribulation. The verses that follow deal with that final, awful period climaxing in the second coming of Christ.

General Signs of the End of the Age

For one approaching the description that Jesus gave of signs of the end of the age, the task of describing a period, then almost two thousand years in advance, is in itself a tremendous undertaking. In keeping with the accuracy of Scripture, however, the signs predicted have been fulfilled in many respects throughout the present age.

False christs. Because prophecy is difficult to interpret, Jesus warned his disciples against being deceived, especially by false christs (Matt. 24:4–5). Throughout the Christian era there have been many impostors who have claimed unusual powers and have attracted followers. The counterfeits have in due time been unmasked, but new ones appear frequently. Accordingly, false christs are the first of the nine signs Jesus mentioned.

Wars and rumors of wars. War is always a catastrophe, especially for the people who are caught in the midst of the contest. Jesus said, "You will hear of wars and rumors of wars, but see to it that you are not alarmed. Such things must happen, but the end is still to come. Nation will rise against nation, and kingdom against kingdom" (Matt. 24:6–7). The centuries since Jesus have recorded many wars. The twentieth century itself has had two world wars and almost continual warfare in one part of the world or another. Though World War I and World War II were fought to end wars, the end is not yet. Even worldwide wars are not specifically a sign of the end; they are a sign of progress, because the end of the age will fulfill still another prediction of a world war that will be underway just before Christ's second coming (Rev. 16:13–16).

Famines. Famines have plagued the world since the beginning of the Christian era, and in the world today famine is wiping out millions of people every year. Though portions of the earth have plenty, lack of distribution and lack of money have kept much of the world in a situation of undernourishment and famine.

Pestilence. Though not included in the text of the New International Version, pestilence as a characteristic of the age is found in the King James Version. Whether in the text of Scripture or not, pestilence has continued to be a major factor in the world today. Modern medicine has prevented some epidemics that formerly took a large toll of life, but new forms of disease require much medical research before being brought under control, and in many parts of the world medication is not available.

Earthquakes. Scripture has a large place for earthquakes in the sequence of events, and throughout the present age there have been a great number of earthquakes. With the rapid increase in population, earthquakes become more serious as they affect more people. Scripture predicts a final great earthquake just before the Second Coming (Rev. 16:18–20), an earthquake so great that it will devastate "the cities of the nations" (v. 19). Apparently Israel will be exempt, but the cities of nations, or the Gentiles, will be leveled, and there will be tremendous loss of life and property just before the Second

Coming. Earthquakes today are signs of progress but not of the end.

Martyrdom and persecution. Persecution of Christians and even martyrdom are characteristic of our age. The twentieth century has probably witnessed more martyrs than any preceding century as millions have died because of their faith in Christ. Increasing anti-Semitism and increasing anti-Christianity are features of our current world and are predicted by Jesus (Matt. 24:9–10).

False prophets. The twentieth century in particular has featured the rise of more false prophets and counterfeit religions than probably any century in the Christian era. This is in preparation for the ultimate false religion that will sweep the world in the Great Tribulation preceding the second coming of Christ. The twentieth century has witnessed denial of essentials of the faith, such as the Virgin Birth, the deity of Christ, Christ's death on the cross for the sins of the world, Christ's bodily resurrection, and Christ's literal second coming. Though these issues were more clear-cut at the beginning of the twentieth century, they have become increasingly complex with the rise of neoorthodoxy (the use of orthodox terms in an unorthodox meaning) and widespread confusion.

Increased wickedness and loss of fervent love. Jesus said that "because of the increase of wickedness, the love of many will grow cold" (Matt. 24:12). This will occur in the aftermath of false doctrine. It is all too evident that many who profess the name of Christ are worldly and have little zeal for the Lord. Like the Laodician church in Revelation 3, many have left their first love and have lapsed into a state of lukewarmness.

The gospel of the kingdom. The final characteristic of the present age, particularly as it moves on to its close, will be the increased preaching of the gospel of the kingdom, the good news that Jesus Christ will return and bring his kingdom of righteousness and peace on earth. The gospel of the kingdom should not be confused with the Gospel of salvation, which relates to the first coming of Christ, his death on the cross, and his provision of salvation and eternal life for all who put their trust in him. The gospel of the kingdom, however, is God's answer to the wickedness of our modern civilization. It is the bright hope that when Jesus comes the wickedness will be judged and righteousness will characterize the world.

In connection with the prospect of the gospel of the kingdom,

Jesus declared, "He who stands firm to the end will be saved" (Matt. 24:13). This has confused many because it implies that salvation is not a work of God but something that is attained at the end of life. The answer, however, is found in the fact that this is not referring to spiritual salvation but to deliverance from persecution such as will characterize the end of the age. Many in the Great Tribulation will live until the end of the age but others will die because of their faith and therefore will not be on earth when Christ returns. The passage is referring to the godly remnant who will last through the Great Tribulation in spite of everything and who will be awaiting Jesus when he returns. This remnant will be composed of both Jews and Gentiles who are saved and have put their trust in Christ even during that awful period. They will be delivered by the second coming of Christ.

The general signs conclude with a prediction: "And this gospel of the kingdom will be preached in the whole world as a testimony to all the nations, and then the end will come" (Matt. 24:14). The Gospel, whether it is the Gospel of salvation or the gospel of the future kingdom, was intended to be preached to the entire world. Though it is impossible for every individual to be reached in any age, worldwide preaching of the Gospel has characterized the twentieth century. Though the world's population has mushroomed, more people have heard about Jesus Christ than ever before, and, geographically, the Gospel is preached by radio or other means in every portion of the world. The end of the age here, however, is not the Rapture, and it is entirely reasonable to assume that when the Rapture occurs there will be some who have not yet been reached who will be reached in the continued preaching of the Gospel after the Rapture. Scriptures are clear that the Lord "is patient with you, not wanting anyone to perish, but everyone to come to repentance" (2 Peter 3:9). From the human standpoint, the delay in the return of Christ, whether the Rapture or the Second Coming, is occasioned by God's mercy, as he desires more people to hear the Gospel and more to be saved. As in the time of Noah, however, the time of Christ's coming has been fixed by God himself, and Christ will come in keeping with the prophecies of Scripture. Having given general signs that will be increasingly fulfilled as the age moves on to its climax, Jesus then revealed the specific signs that would assure believers that the coming of Christ was near.

Specific Signs of the End of the Age

Problems in interpretation. The interpretation of this portion of the Olivet Discourse is beset by problems that always surface in interpretation of prophecy. Those who do not accept the idea that prophecy can be specific have to gloss over the very specific statements of this passage and, accordingly, do not arrive at a proper meaning. Some have also fallen into the false premise that this prophecy deals with the destruction of Jerusalem in A.D. 70. Though it is true that there are similarities between events leading up to the destruction of Jerusalem and events leading up to the Second Coming, they differ in most details. In A.D. 70 the temple was destroyed. In the events leading up to Christ's second coming, the temple that will then be in existence will not be destroyed, though it will be desecrated. In A.D. 70 the second coming of Christ did not follow the destruction of Jerusalem. Christ's second coming will be a climax to the events of the Great Tribulation. In every important detail the account differs from A.D. 70.

Specific signs are revealed. Careful attention to the details will make it clear that the signs mentioned in Matthew 24 are very specific inasmuch as they will be sufficiently clear to prompt an immediate evacuation of Jerusalem. The key to understanding the sign is what is referred to as "the abomination that causes desolation," spoken of through the prophet Daniel (v. 15). Jesus gave instructions for what the people should do when they saw this taking place: "Then let those who are in Judea flee to the mountains" (v. 16).

The abomination that causes desolation. A similar term is found three times in Daniel (9:27; 11:31; 12:11). As the prophecy of Daniel 11:31 has already been fulfilled, it provides an accurate understanding of what is meant by the abomination. Antiochus Epiphanes fulfilled the prophecy that states, "His armed forces will rise up to desecrate the temple fortress and will abolish the daily sacrifice. Then they will set up the abomination that causes desolation" (11:31). What actually took place is described in the apocryphal books of 1 and 2 Maccabees. As explained in our preceding study of Daniel, Antiochus hated the Jewish people and attempted to destroy their religion. In the process many thousands of Jews—men, women, and children—were killed, the temple was desecrated, and the sacrificial system was stopped. The result was the Maccabean

Revolt which he was unable to stifle successfully. Antiochus, in his desire to desecrate the temple, offered a sow on the altar, which, according to the Law of Moses, was an unclean animal and made the temple unclean, or abominable, for the Jewish people (1 Macc. 1:48). In addition to offering the wrong sacrifice, Antiochus set up a statue of a Greek god in the temple (v. 57). From this historic fulfillment of the prophecy of Daniel 11, it can be understood that there will be a future desecration of the Jewish temple along the same lines. This event will occur three and a half years before the second coming of Christ.

Daniel 9:26–27 says that " 'the ruler who will come . . . will confirm a covenant with many for one "seven." In the middle of the "seven" he will put an end to sacrifice and offering. And he will set up an abomination that causes desolation on, a wing of the temple, until the end that is decreed is poured out on him.' " The time period involved is the seven years preceding the second coming of Christ, and the abomination predicted will take place in the middle of the seven-year period, three and a half years before the end of the period. The future ruler who has made a covenant with Israel will break his covenant at that point and persecute the people of Israel instead of protecting them.

In Daniel 12:11–12 further information is given about this event. " 'From the time that the daily sacrifice is abolished and the abomination that causes desolation is set up, there will be 1,290 days. Blessed is the one who waits for and reaches the end of the 1,335 days.' " The period of 1,290 days is slightly more than three and a half years and speaks of the time when after Christ's return the desecration will be reversed. As in the time of Antiochus, the sacrificial system will be abolished during the three and a half years, and the temple will be desecrated.

Since there is no temple in Jerusalem at the present time and none has been in existence since A.D. 70, these predictions have raised the question as to when the temple will be built. Scripture does not make this clear, but it does indicate that in the seven years preceding the second coming of Christ orthodox Jews will renew their sacrificial system in a temple that has been built at that time. Either this temple will be built before the rapture of the church, or there will be ample time after the rapture of the church to build it. In any event, the daily sacrifices will be offered by orthodox Jews until the three-and-a-half-year period before the second coming of Christ. Then the sacrificial system will be stopped, and the temple will be

desecrated on a specific day. This will constitute a sign so
definite that the Jews will know that the time of the Great
Tribulation has begun.

Second Thessalonians 2:3–4 adds a postscript to this description of the abomination. "The man of lawlessness" who,
according to the Scripture, will be "doomed to destruction" at
the second coming of Christ, and who will "oppose and will
exalt himself over everything that is called God or is worshiped,
so that he sets himself up in God's temple, proclaiming himself
to be God." The Jewish temple will have its sacrifices stopped
as stated in Daniel 12, and the world ruler will set himself up as
an object of worship and will claim to be God. Revelation
13:11–15 describes the activities of the False Prophet who will
perform miracles in support of the world ruler, who is the beast
out of the sea. According to Scripture, "He ordered them to set
up an image in honor of the beast who was wounded by the
sword and yet lived. He was given power to give breath to the
image of the first beast, so that it could speak and cause all who
refused to worship the image to be killed" (vv. 14–15).

The event beginning the Great Tribulation, described as the
desecration of the temple, will be such a reversal of the
preceding time of peace that it will come on a specific day and it
will be widely known that it has taken place. Under these
circumstances it is a signal for those in Judea to flee to the
mountains.

The command to flee to the mountains. Jesus said in connection with the abomination, "Let the reader understand—then
let those who are in Judea flee to the mountains. Let no one on
the roof of his house go down to take anything out of the house.
Let no one in the field go back to get his cloak. How dreadful it
will be in those days for pregnant women and nursing mothers!
Pray that your flight will not take place in winter or on the
Sabbath" (Matt. 24:15–20). According to Jesus' warning, it will
be necessary for those in Judea to flee because there will begin
an immediate persecution of the Jewish people in an attempt to
exterminate them once again as in previous instances in history.
Under these circumstances, they should flee to the mountains to
escape their persecutors and hold fast to the hope that Christ
will come three and a half years later to rescue them. One who is
on the flat roof of his house should take the outside stairway and
not go down through his house lest it delay him in escaping.
Likewise, the one in the field should not return to get more

clothes but rather flee at once. It will be a time of special difficulty for pregnant women and for nursing mothers. The Jews are instructed to pray that their escape will not have to take place on the Sabbath, because on that day orthodox Jews do not travel, and their escape would be very noticeable. The sad fact is, however, that many will not escape. According to Zechariah 13:8, " 'In the whole land,' declares the LORD, 'two-thirds will be struck down and perish; yet one-third will be left in it.' " A similar statement is made in Ezekiel 5:12: "A third of your people will die of the plague or perish by famine inside you; a third will fall by the sword outside your walls." God will, nevertheless, continue to protect a third of those in the Great Tribulation in order to form the nucleus for the nation Israel in the millennial kingdom.

The Great Tribulation. In addition to the initial signs of the end time, Jesus described the Great Tribulation that will follow and will characterize the period for three and a half years, climaxing in the second coming of Christ. Jesus said, "For then there will be great distress, unequaled from the beginning of the world until now—and never to be equaled again. If those days had not been cut short, no one would survive, but for the sake of the elect those days will be shortened" (Matt. 24:21–22).

The human race has experienced trouble ever since Adam and Eve sinned, but the Great Tribulation will be a period of "great distress." It is referred to in Revelation 7:14 as "the great tribulation." Jesus affirmed the general fact of tribulation in John 16:33: "In this world you will have trouble." The Great Tribulation, however, will be in contrast to the general trouble the human race has experienced throughout its history. The term refers to a specific period of unprecedented trouble, as Christ himself referred to it in Matthew 21:21. In Daniel it is referred to as "a time of distress such as has not happened from the beginning of nations until then" (12:1).

As will be brought out in later discussion, the Great Tribulation will be a time when a world dictator, who is a blasphemer and opposed to Christianity, emerges. He will head up a world government and will require all to worship him as God or pay the penalty of death. In addition to the persecution of Christians and Jews this will occasion, the world will experience terrible disasters as described in Revelation 6–18. Most of the world and most of the people living in the world will be destroyed. Because it will be a time so different from any preceding time of trouble, it will constitute in itself a sign that the Lord's coming is near.

Specific Signs of the Second Coming

Because the signs of the Lord's return can be misunderstood, Jesus warned his disciples against any false hope that Christ will come secretly. According to Jesus, there will be many false reports: "At that time if anyone says to you, 'Look, here is the Christ!' or, 'There he is!' do not believe it. For false christs and false prophets will appear and perform great signs and miracles to deceive even the elect—if that were possible. See, I have told you ahead of time" (Matt. 24:23–25).

The Scriptures do not enlarge upon the false christs and the false prophets except as they are anticipated in the coming world ruler who claims to be God and the False Prophet associated with him. Apparently there will be a program of satanic deceit to confuse even those who believe in Christ, if this were possible.

Jesus' second warning concerns premature reports of his return. He said: "So if anyone tells you, 'There he is, out in the desert,' do not go out; or, 'Here he is, in the inner rooms,' do not believe it. For as lightning that comes from the east is visible even in the west, so will be the coming of the Son of Man" (Matt. 24:26–27). Contrary to the first coming of Christ, which created little stir even in Bethlehem, and the rapture of the church, which will probably not be seen by the world, the second coming of Christ will be seen by the entire world. Accordingly, anyone who reports a secret coming of Christ is spreading a false rumor. When the second coming of Christ occurs, everyone will know it, both believers and nonbelievers, because the sky will be ablaze with the glory of God, much as lightning shines from the east to the west.

Along with this display of the glory of God, there will be disturbances in the heavens. Jesus said: "Immediately after the distress of those days the sun will be darkened, and the moon will not give its light; the stars will fall from the sky, and the heavenly bodies will be shaken" (Matt. 24:29). This scene is described in greater detail in the book of Revelation, which pictures disturbances in the heavens occurring throughout the years leading up to the second coming of Christ but especially just before he comes.

Jesus then revealed the specific sign of the Second Coming. "At that time the sign of the Son of Man will appear in the sky, and all the nations of the earth will mourn. They will see the Son of Man coming on the clouds of the sky, with power and great glory" (Matt. 24:30). The sign mentioned here is the glory of God that will spread across the heavens and will be unmistakable evidence that Christ is coming. The nations will mourn because they are not ready. In their unbelief they will have worshiped and served the world dictator instead of Jesus Christ. The coming of the Son of Man, therefore, is a time of judgment, and it is a display of the glory of God.

The Gathering of the Elect

Jesus said that upon his return he will call together his elect: "And he will send his angels with a loud trumpet call, and they will gather his elect from the four winds, from one end of the heavens to the other" (Matt. 24:31). In contrast to the mourning of the nations, believers will recognize it as the time of their deliverance from persecution (cf. Luke 21:28). Mark indicated that the gathering of the elect will not simply be from earth but also from heaven, "from the ends of the earth to the ends of the heavens" (Mark 13:27). Because the Gospels are addressed primarily to the Jewish disciples, some have held that the elect here are only the elect of Israel, but there is no reason for limiting it, because at the time of the Second Coming all the elect, regardless of dispensation and race, will be gathered to participate in the millennial kingdom. At that time Old Testament saints will be resurrected and believers from the tribulation will be raised from the dead. Living Christians will also be gathered. The millennial kingdom will extend to all believers, and at its beginning all the saved will be resurrected.

Following the discussion of signs, Jesus turned to the practical import of the second coming of Christ and the judgments that will follow, which are discussed in Matthew 24:32–25:30; Mark 13:28–32; and Luke 21:29–39. These practical exhortations will be discussed in connection with further study of the second coming of Christ in the book of Revelation.

From these specific signs it can be easily determined that the second coming of Christ to the earth to set up his kingdom is not imminent but will be preceded by very specific prophetic events described in detail here and elsewhere in Scripture. In contrast, the rapture of the church is always presented as an imminent event. No specific prophecies have been given that need to be fulfilled before the Rapture occurs. This confirms that the Rapture differs from the second coming of Christ in the event itself, in the events that precede, and in the events that follow.

23

The Rapture of the Church

The rapture of the church refers to the event prophesied in 1 Thessalonians 4:16–17: "For the Lord himself will come down from heaven, with a loud command, with the voice of the archangel and with the trumpet call of God, and the dead in Christ will rise first. After that, we who are still alive and are left will be caught up together with them in the clouds to meet the Lord in the air. And so we will be with the Lord forever." This Scripture reveals that living Christians at the time of the Rapture "will be caught up," or raptured, with those resurrected to meet the Lord in the air. This event obviously has not yet occurred, but it will be fulfilled in the future.

Various Views on the Rapture

Though there is relative unanimity in the orthodox churches that Christ will return in a formal second coming to the earth, the Rapture has been variously interpreted, with four leading views emerging. In these views the question of when the

Rapture will occur in end-time events is the matter of dispute. (For a more complete discussion of the Rapture, see my book *The Rapture Question* [Grand Rapids: Zondervan, 1979]).

Posttribulationism. Posttribulationism is probably the leading view of the Rapture as it is held not only by some premillenarians but also by all amillenarians and all postmillenarians. It holds that the Rapture will occur as a phase of the second coming of Christ. According to this point of view, when Christ reaches the air above the earth, the church will be raptured and will meet him in the air and will then return immediately with him to the earth. It is called posttribulationism because it holds that the Rapture will occur after the Great Tribulation at the time of the Second Coming.

Midtribulationism. Another far less popular view is midtribulationism. Its adherents hold that the Rapture will take place in the middle of the last seven years before the second coming of Christ. As the last seven years are regarded in general as a time of tribulation, these people hold that the Rapture will occur before the Great Tribulation but not before the entire seven years.

Partial rapturism. Another view held by only a few is the partial rapture theory, which says that only those specially qualified will be raptured at the beginning of the last seven years and that there will be subsequent raptures as others qualify.

Pretribulationism. The pretribulation rapture view, widely held by premillenarians, holds that the Rapture will occur more than seven years before the second coming of Christ, and it is referred to as pretribulational because it is predicted to occur before the end-time trouble.

Only one of these four views is correct, and Bible scholars have argued for years over this difference of opinion.

In view of the fact that there are evangelicals of relatively orthodox faith who hold these positions, the student of prophecy is soon faced with a decision as to which view is correct. A proper approach to the Rapture is to determine what the Scriptures actually reveal about the Rapture and then consider the arguments for and against each of these major positions. There are also certain theological issues in relation to them that need to be considered.

The Rapture in John

The concept of a rapture is not found in Old Testament prophecy and was first announced by Christ in John 14:2–3.

As previously discussed, the disciples had gathered in the Upper Room to observe the Passover, and they were deeply concerned about the trend of recent events. They had anticipated that Christ soon would fulfill the glorious promises of the kingdom on earth because they did not understand the difference between Christ's first and second comings. Accordingly, when there was growing opposition among the Jews and a plot to arrest Christ and kill him, they were deeply concerned about their own future. To make things worse, Jesus in the Upper Room had informed them that one of them would betray him (John 13:18–19, 21). He had also told them that he was going to leave them and that they could not follow him (v. 33). This prompted Peter to affirm that he would be willing to die for Christ. In reply, Jesus informed him that before the rooster crowed in the morning, he would disown Christ three times (v. 38).

In this context of growing anxiety and alarm, Jesus devoted the entire fourteenth chapter of John to comforting the apostles and providing them with further information about their future. He told them not to be troubled. They were to keep on trusting in God and in him. He then gave the reason for this: "In my Father's house are many rooms; if it were not so, I would have told you. I am going there to prepare a place for you. And if I go and prepare a place for you, I will come back and take you to be with me that you also may be where I am" (John 14:2–3).

This was a strange prophecy to the disciples, and Jesus did not attempt to explain it. After all, the disciples did not understand the difference between the first and second coming of Christ. How could they distinguish the Second Coming from the rapture of the church? Just a few days before (see Matt. 24) Jesus had predicted his glorious return to the earth, indicating that he would be victorious over his enemies. At the same time, however, he had warned them of a long period of time leading up to it in which there would be much opposition and even martyrdom. The disciples were still trying to sort this out and were not prepared to understand this new revelation.

For the first time it was revealed in John 14 that prior to the Second Coming there would be a removal of believers in Christ from the earth. They would meet the Lord and go to the place he was going to prepare for them, an obvious reference to heaven. The purpose of this event would be to remove believers from earth and take them to the Father's house. This is an important point in understanding the doctrine, because it makes clear that the purpose of the Rapture is entirely different from that of the Second Coming. At his second coming, Jesus will come back to judge and reign over the earth. In the Rapture he will come to take his own out of the world and take them to his Father's house. The two events have nothing in common except that both are referred to as a "coming." Posttribulationists are hard pressed to explain this passage with any relevance to what the passage actually says.

The Rapture in the Epistles

The Rapture in 1 Thessalonians 4–5. Many years later after the conversion of the apostle Paul, revelation was given to Paul concerning the doctrine of the Rapture. During his three-week visit to Thessalonica in Greece, he had led many to Christ. He was then forced to leave because of persecution. He later sent Timothy back to see how they were getting along, and Timothy then reported to Paul that they were standing true in spite of persecution at the hands of unbelievers. He added that they had some theological questions, and one question related to the order of events at the Rapture. Specifically, they wanted to know if the Rapture took the living Christians from the earth, what would happen to those who had died? In the few weeks since Paul had left, some of that early band of Christians had died, apparently from natural causes. Their survivors wanted to know when they would see their loved ones again.

In providing the necessary information, Paul was building upon the fact that he had previously taught the Thessalonians the truth of the Rapture. It is of interest that, in the three weeks he was in Thessalonica, he already had introduced this great subject. But, like many believers today, they did not understand all the details. Now Paul was in a position where he could tell them, in order, the events that relate to the Rapture and about the Rapture itself.

First, in 1 Thessalonians 4:13 Paul pointed out the practical value of the Rapture in that those expecting the Lord's return do not grieve like others who have no hope. He wrote, "Brothers, we do not want you to be ignorant about those who fall asleep, or to grieve like the rest of men." Christians not only have the hope of ultimate resurrection and renewal of fellowship with believers who have preceded them in death, but they also have the bright prospect of an imminent return of Christ, which any day might cut short their separation from loved ones who have died.

The certainty of the Rapture is brought out in 1 Thessalonians 4:14. Paul wrote, "We believe that Jesus died and rose again and so we believe that God will bring with Jesus those who have fallen asleep in him." The fact that Jesus Christ would die and rise again was the subject of much Old Testament prophecy. That he would die was the constant implication of the sacrifices offered as well as of the specific prophecies such as are found in Psalm 22 and Isaiah 53. In Acts 2:25–28 Peter quoted the prophecy from Psalm 16:9–11 that Christ would rise again:

> "I saw the Lord always before me.
>   Because he is at my right hand,
>   I will not be shaken.
> Therefore my heart is glad and my tongue rejoices;
>   my body also will live in hope,
> because you will not abandon me to the grave,
>   nor will you let your Holy One see decay.
> You have made known to me the paths of life;
>   you will fill me with joy in your presence."

What was once prophecy has now been historically and literally fulfilled. Accordingly, when Paul asserted that the Thessalonians' belief in the Rapture was just as certain as their belief in the death and resurrection of Christ, he was elevating the Rapture to a very important doctrinal position.

Paul also informed the Thessalonians of what would happen to their loved ones who had died. He said, "God will bring with Jesus those who have fallen asleep in him" (1 Thess. 4:14). What did Paul mean by this? When a believer dies, his or her soul goes immediately into the presence of the Lord. According to 2 Corinthians 5:8, "to be away from the body" means to be "at home with the Lord." The reason that Christ is bringing the souls of believers who have died from heaven to the sphere of earth is that he is about to resurrect their bodies, and their souls will enter their resurrected bodies.

Paul then revealed that they need not worry about a time of waiting for reunion with their loved ones who had died. It is not clear exactly when they had expected their loved ones to be reunited with them, but it is evident from 1 and 2 Thessalonians that Paul had taught them about the time of trouble, the Great Tribulation, which would follow the Rapture. It may be that they were concerned that they would have to wait until the climax of the Great Tribulation and the second coming of Christ before they would be reunited. As Paul stated here, they should not have this concern because, as a matter of fact, the dead in Christ will be raised a moment before living Christians are caught up to be with the Lord. Paul said: "According to the Lord's own word, we tell you that we who are still alive, who are left till the coming of the Lord, will certainly not precede those who have fallen asleep. For the Lord himself will come down from heaven, with a loud command, with the voice of the archangel and with the trumpet call of God, and the dead in Christ will rise first" (1 Thess. 4:15–16).

It should be noted that Paul does not quote the Old Testament, because the Rapture was not revealed in the Old Testament but was given by a direct revelation from God to Paul.

Clouds are associated with both the Rapture and the second coming of Christ (Matt. 24:30; Rev. 1:7). The reason for this is that both events involve the atmospheric heavens in which there are clouds. Some have suggested that the clouds mentioned in 1 Thessalonians 4:17 are rather the numerous people involved in the Rapture. They would look like a cloud in the sense of the "great cloud of witnesses" mentioned in Hebrews 12:1. In any case, both the living and the resurrected saints will be caught up, or raptured, to meet the Lord in the air with the promise, "And so we will be with the Lord forever" (1 Thess. 4:17). If the purpose of Christ is to take them to the Father's house, as indicated in John 14, they will then proceed to heaven to fulfill prophecies that relate to their arrival there, including the judgment seat of Christ and other Scriptures. The Rapture was revealed to the grieving Thessalonians with the words, "Therefore encourage each other with these words" (1 Thess. 4:18). Paul held before them the bright prospect of seeing their loved ones, possibly soon, for the Rapture here, as elsewhere, is presented as an imminent event without any prophetic events taking place first.

In 1 Thessalonians 5 the question is raised concerning the timing of the Rapture in relationship to the Day of the Lord. Paul reminded the Thessalonians, first of all, that no specific date for the Rapture has been revealed, but rather it will come "like a thief in the night" and will coincide with the beginning of the "day of the Lord" (v. 2).

The Day of the Lord is a familiar reference in Scripture to a coming time of judgment, including some periods of Old Testament judgment already past but anticipating the final Day of the Lord when Christ returns. It refers to any period of time, however long or short, that involves God's direct judgment on the world. What Paul revealed here is that the Rapture, which closes the dispensation of the church, will open the period known as the Day of the Lord, which includes all the end-time events as well as the thousand-year reign of Christ itself. In this entire period God will immediately judge the sin in the earth and will fulfill many other Scriptures that involve direct intervention in the world. This is in contrast to the period when the church is on earth, for then God generally does not interfere, does not judge the wicked on earth, and does not bring judgment upon that which is contrary to his will.

A common mistake in understanding the Day of the Lord is to date it beginning with the Second Coming. Rather, it begins at the Rapture and includes end-time events following the Rapture.

The references to the Day of the Lord are so plentiful that they justify books written on this subject alone. Some of the references deal with periods of judgment in the past, particularly in the Old Testament, but many of them refer to a future time of specific judgment of God related in a general way to the second coming of Christ. The Day of the Lord is a period not only of judgment, however, but also of the millennial blessings as indicated in the Old Testament prophecies (Zeph. 3:9–20).

The fact that this period is introduced as a "day" implies that it follows a previous day, which, in the nature of the church, was the day of grace ending in the Rapture. The Day of the Lord will begin in a period of darkness, the end-time events leading up to the Second Coming. Just as a twenty-four-hour day proceeds out of darkness into light, so the Day of the Lord will proceed into a time of blessing as well as being preceded by judgment. Like a twenty-four-hour day, it will also end in darkness, or judgment, as the millennial kingdom ends in judgment. In the Old

Testament there are extensive references to the Day of the Lord (Isa. 2:12–21; 13:9–16; 34:1–8; Joel 1:15–2:11, 28–32; 3:9–12; Amos 5:18–20; Obad. 15–17; Zeph. 1:7–18).

The reference to judgment and the Day of the Lord in Isaiah 2 can be construed as referring to past judgments but also anticipating the future judgment related to the second coming of Christ. According to Isaiah 13:9–16, the Day of the Lord includes the past historic destruction of Babylon by the Medes and the Persians, but also seems to describe a future destruction of Babylon, such as is revealed in Revelation 18. The description of the Day of the Lord in Isaiah 13 corresponds to the Great Tribulation of the New Testament, including disturbances in the sky, the stars, and the sun and also desolation on earth and destruction of human life. God says of the Day of the Lord:

> I will punish the world for its evil,
>   the wicked for their sins.
> I will put an end to the arrogance of the haughty
>   and will humble the pride of the ruthless. (Isa. 13:11)

In Isaiah 34:1–8 prophecy is revealed concerning judgments that will fall on the world at the time of Jesus' second coming. The book of Joel, in particular, is devoted to revealing the Day of the Lord (cf. Acts 2:17–21). The events of Joel 2:30–31, including the disaster in the heavens affecting the light of the sun and the moon, coincide with the time of tribulation.

A brighter side, referring to the millennial kingdom itself, is found in Zephaniah 3:14–17, where God is pictured as a forgiving God who will renew Israel and give her peace and joy. From these passages it is clear that the Day of the Lord precedes the Second Coming by a considerable period of time.

Like an ordinary twenty-four-hour day, however, even though the Day of the Lord begins at the Rapture, the specific events of the day do not immediately follow, just as the major events of an ordinary twenty-four-hour day do not occur until daylight or later.

One indication that the Day of the Lord will have begun is that people will be saying, "Peace and safety" (1 Thess. 5:3). This may proceed from the peace treaty imposed on Israel seven years before the second coming of Christ. This, as will be explained in later discussions, will give the entire world a sense of relief from the danger of war, and people will have an increased hope and peace and safety. This will be suddenly interrupted, however, by the beginning of the Great Tribulation with persecution from humans and judgments from God. The world will be overcome by its troubles at that time like a pregnant woman who is overcome by labor pains (v. 3).

Though the Day of the Lord will be very real and will have these characteristics, Paul told the Thessalonians that this day would not overtake them because they belonged to a different time period: "But you, brothers, are not in darkness so that this day should surprise you like a thief. You are all sons of the light and sons of the day. We do not belong to the night or to darkness" (1 Thess. 5:4–5). Though the time of the Rapture itself is unknown and will come like a thief, it will not overtake them with the disaster that is related to a thief, because they belong to a different day. Because the Rapture will occur first, they will be kept from the Day of the Lord, for as was indicated in this context, the Rapture will begin the Day of the Lord, and when the Day of the Lord begins they will be in heaven.

As in other passages on the Rapture, there are certain practical applications. In this section the Thessalonians are exhorted to "be self-controlled, putting on faith and love as a breastplate, and the hope of salvation as a helmet" (1 Thess. 5:8).

The blanket statement was then made, "For God did not appoint us to suffer wrath but to receive salvation through our Lord Jesus Christ" (1 Thess. 5:9). The Great Tribulation preceding the Second Coming is specifically a time of wrath. "Then the kings of the earth, the princes, the generals, the rich, the mighty, and every slave and every free man hid in caves and among the rocks of the mountains. They called to the mountains and the rocks, 'Fall on us and hide us from the face of him who sits on the throne from the wrath of the Lamb! For the great day of their wrath has come, and who can stand?' " (Rev. 6:15–16). Here, clearly, the wrath refers to the events that precede the Second Coming rather than to the Second Coming itself, though it also will be a time of judgment and wrath for unbelievers.

The important point to observe in 1 Thessalonians 5 is that the Rapture begins the Day of the Lord and is not a part of events leading up to the second coming of Christ. Accordingly, Christians do not have to fear the events of the Day of the Lord or the events of the Great Tribulation, because this is not their appointment. Their appointment is rather to meet the Lord in heaven.

The Rapture in 2 Thessalonians 2. In the period between the writing of 1 and 2 Thessalonians certain teachers had arrived in Thessalonica who taught the people that they were already in the Day of the Lord. This expressly contradicted what Paul had taught them in 1 Thessalonians 5 and aroused the apostle to rebut this doctrine. In a word, it was an early appearance of what later was known as posttribulationism—namely, that the church would have to go through the opening phase of the Day of the Lord and the time of trial that is mentioned. Paul, informed of this situation by Timothy, revealed in 2 Thessalonians the judgment of God that would be on these false teachers (1:6–10). He stated the general principle that God will judge the wicked, some at the second coming of Christ and some later in the final judgment revealed in Revelation 20:11–15.

More in keeping with the issue, however, is Paul's statement about this false teaching: "Concerning the coming of our Lord Jesus Christ and our being gathered to him, we ask you, brothers, not to be easily unsettled or alarmed by some prophecy, report or letter supposed to have come from us, saying that the Day of the Lord has already come" (2 Thess. 2:1–2). Apparently false teachers had not only taught that the Thessalonians were already in the Day of the Lord in an attempt to explain their persecutions, but they also had indicated that this was prophesied by Paul and contained in an oral report or a written letter saying that they were already in the Day of the Lord.

In rebuttal Paul said, "Don't let anyone deceive you in any way, for that day will not come until the rebellion occurs and the man of lawlessness is revealed, the man doomed to destruction" (2 Thess. 2:3). What Paul was saying is that the Day of the Lord has not come because the first major feature of the Day of the Lord is the revelation of the man who ultimately will become the world ruler. He will first be revealed as the conqueror of three of the ten countries that had previously been banded together politically. This will occur more than seven years before the second coming of Christ. Inasmuch as this man had not been revealed and the situation described in Daniel 7 and Revelation 13 had not come about, the Thessalonians were not in the Day of the Lord.

Paul identified the man of destiny as one who will "oppose and will exalt himself over everything that is called God or is worshiped, so that he sets himself up in God's temple, proclaiming himself to be God" (2 Thess. 2:4). This man had not been revealed, and he had not begun his blasphemous opposition to God. As this will occur early in the Day of the Lord and will be the springboard from which later events take place, Paul assured the Thessalonians, on the basis of a lack of evidence, that they were not in the Day of the Lord.

Paul further reminded the Thessalonians, "Don't you remember that when I was with you I used to tell you these things?" (2 Thess. 2:5). In other words, Paul was referring to the fact that he taught them that they would not be in the Day of the Lord. Paul appealed to knowledge that they already had concerning the time of the revelation:

> And now you know what is holding him back, so that he may be revealed at the proper time. For the secret power of lawlessness is already at work; but the one who now holds it back will continue to do so till he is taken out of the way. And then the lawless one will be revealed, whom the Lord Jesus will overthrow with the breath of his mouth and destroy by the splendor of his coming (2 Thess. 2:6–8)

Paul apparently had taught the Thessalonians that during the age of grace, in which the church is called out to be the body of Christ, there will be a restraint on sinfulness in the world similar to the restraint exercised in the protection of Job in the early chapters of the book of Job. The best explanation as to who restrains sin is God himself. A common idea that human government restrains sin is refuted by the fact that the final absolute rulership is anything but a restraint of sin, and, in fact, restrains and opposes the work of God and promotes wickedness. Though it is true that laws and police forces tend to hold down crime, it is not the same as the universal restraint God exercises in keeping lawlessness and sinfulness in line with his will.

The day will come, however, when that restraint will be lifted. Paul wrote, "And then the lawless one will be revealed, whom the Lord Jesus will overthrow with the breath of his mouth and destroy by the splendor of his coming" (2 Thess. 2:8). The same one who will be destroyed at the second coming of Christ is here pictured earlier in his lawless career exercising his power in opposition to God and being permitted to do so as God in the power of the Holy Spirit will cease to restrain people from displaying this form of wickedness. Supernatural means will be used by Satan to convince people. "The coming of the lawless one will be in accordance with the work of Satan displayed in all kinds of counterfeit miracles, signs and wonders, and in every sort of evil that deceives those who are perishing. They perished because they refused to love the truth and so be saved" (2:9–10).

If the Holy Spirit and God's power in the world are the ultimate restrainers of sin as is indicated in Scripture, it should be evident that this restraint could not be lifted as long as the Holy Spirit indwells the church. This would require the removal of the church before this man could be revealed. In a word, the Rapture has to occur before this man is revealed, which will be more than seven years prior to the second coming of Christ. This passage therefore supports the pretribulational view and refutes the posttribulational view.

The question is sometimes raised as to the antiquity of pretribulationism versus posttribulationism. It should be clear here that both existed in the early church but that Paul refuted posttribulationism in this passage, and the pretribulational view was what was taught as the orthodox view.

The Rapture in 1 Corinthians 15:51–58. Some time after the revelation to the Thessalonian church, the apostle Paul had occasion to write to the Corinthians and correct many errors that had arisen in this body of believers. At the conclusion of Paul's discussion he introduced the subject of what would happen at the Rapture.

In 1 Corinthians 15 Paul began by pointing out the central and fundamental facts of the death and resurrection of Christ. He noted how important the resurrection of Christ is, because if Christ were not raised, it would prove that his sacrifice was in vain and that he was not the prophesied Son of God. The fact that Christ was raised from the dead, however, gives believers grounds to hold that if one dies he or she will be raised in God's time.

As Paul pointed out, God's normal order is to allow saints to live and die and then be resurrected at some future time. Paul here, however, introduced the grand exception to that rule. He said that in the future fulfillment of prophecy the church will be taken out of the world. Christians who have died will be resurrected, and living Christians will be translated, or changed.

They will receive immortal bodies and take on qualities of life necessary for heaven. Paul wrote:

> I declare to you, brothers, that flesh and blood cannot inherit the kingdom of God, nor does the perishable inherit the imperishable. Listen, I tell you a mystery: We will not all sleep, but we will all be changed—in a flash, in the twinkling of an eye, at the last trumpet. For the trumpet will sound, the dead will be raised imperishable, and we will be changed. For the perishable must clothe itself with the imperishable, and the mortal with immortality. (1 Cor. 15:50–53)

As Paul pointed out, Christians living in their mortal and sinful bodies need to receive bodies that are without sin, imperishable, and immortal. This will be accomplished in a flash, or in a split second, the time it takes an eye to twinkle. The dead will be resurrected, and the living will receive bodies similar to those raised from the dead. They will have bodies, therefore, that can stand in the presence of God unashamed because they are without sin, without decay, and without death.

There is no reference to any preceding events such as will precede the Second Coming. Rather the Rapture is an imminent event. The practical application is stated in 1 Corinthians 15:58: "Therefore, my dear brothers, stand firm. Let nothing move you. Always give yourselves fully to the work of the Lord, because you know that your labor in the Lord is not in vain."

If Christians believe that the Lord could be coming at any time, it is a stimulus to their faith to stand firm in time of trouble. It also encourages them not to be moved or to succumb in any way to the pressures of life. Rather, they will give themselves "fully," or wholeheartedly, to the work of the Lord because they know that following the Rapture they will face the judgment seat of Christ, and their service on earth will be judged and rewarded. As Paul stated, "You know that your labor in the Lord is not in vain" (1 Cor. 15:58).

In all these major passages on the Rapture, the implication is that the time of trouble follows the Rapture rather than precedes it and that it is totally different from Christ's second coming.

The Rapture in the Book of Revelation

The last book in the inspired Scripture is the book of Revelation, which has as its central theme the second coming of Christ. It is called "Revelation" because at the time of the Second Coming the whole world will see Christ in his glory. The emphasis, accordingly, is on his triumphal return and the judgments on the world that are related to it; the millennial kingdom; and ultimately the new heaven, new earth, and New Jerusalem.

Revelation 2:25. Though the primary purpose of the book of Revelation is to deal with the Second Coming, there are occasional mentions of the Rapture. The church at Thyatira, in the midst of trials, was exhorted, "Only hold on to what you have until I come" (2:25). No details concerning the Rapture are given in this passage.

Revelation 3:10–11. One of the passages that clearly supports the pretribulation Rapture is found in Revelation 3:10–11: "Since you have kept my command to endure patiently, I will also keep you from the hour of trial that is going to come upon the whole world to test those who live on the earth. I am coming soon. Hold on to what you have, so that no one will take your crown." This passage is a clear prophecy to the church at Philadelphia that they will not go through "the hour of trial"— that is, the Great Tribulation that is going to overcome the earth. In effect, it is a reminder to them of the pretribulation Rapture. If the intent of the passage had been to keep them "through" this period of trouble, this could have been easily expressed by use of the Greek preposition *dia,* which means "through." Instead, the preposition *ek* is used, which means "from." Coupled as it is with the word *tereo,* it means "to keep from" rather than "to keep through." Though posttribulationists do their best to work around this passage, its clear intent is to promise deliverance from the hour, not simply from the trial. If the Philadelphia church can be taken as a type, or illustration, of a true church, then this is an implication that the true church also will not go through this hour of trial. If the Rapture had occurred in the lifetime of the Philadelphia church, they would have been kept from the Great Tribulation by the Rapture. However, they died before this event took place.

Revelation 5:9–10. In John's vision of heaven in Revelation

4–5, he saw the twenty-four elders and heard them sing a new song. As translated in the NIV, their song is quoted:

"You are worthy to take the scroll
*   and to open its seals,*
because you were slain,
*   and with your blood you purchased men for God*
*   from every tribe and language and people and nation.*
You have made them to be a kingdom and priests to
*   serve our God,*
*   and they will reign on the earth." (5:9–10)*

As stated in this translation, the elders are praising God for his redemption, which made it possible for men to be saved.

In the text used for the KJV, the Textus Receptus, the verses translate, "And they sung a new song, saying, Thou art worthy to take the book, and to open the seals thereof: for thou wast slain, and hast redeemed us to God by thy blood out of every kindred, and tongue, and people, and nation; And hast made us unto our God kings and priests: and we shall reign on the earth" (5:9–10 KJV).

If the KJV is correct, then the twenty-four elders, the "us" who are redeemed, represent those who have already been saved and rewarded. As this is a scene that precedes the Second Coming, it would imply that the church has already been raptured, judged at the judgment seat of Christ, and is now in heaven.

Though either version would lend itself to the pretribulation Rapture, the text of the NIV does permit other interpretations. Though, in most cases, the text used by the NIV is superior to the Textus Receptus, in my opinion, in this particular case, the evidence is strongly in favor of the KJV. Though the matter cannot be resolved completely, the evidence here is in favor of the pretribulation Rapture rather than against it.

Revelation 4–18. In the entirety of Revelation 4–18, no mention of the church on earth is found. Instead, believers are referred to as believing Gentiles or believing Jews but never as the church. The total absence of any reference to the church is difficult to explain unless the pretribulationists are correct that the church is in heaven and not on earth during this period.

The pretribulationist view is also supported by the sealing of the 144,000 in Revelation 7:1–8 and in 14:1–5, where the twelve tribes of Israel are said to be protected in a special way through the Great Tribulation. The fact that they are referred to as Jewish people and not as the church is another indication that God has completed his work for the church, composed of both Jews and Gentiles, and now is following his separate programs for Israel and the Gentiles even though salvation is the same for both. Most posttribulationists, for obvious reasons, spiritualize the passage and deny that it should be interpreted literally.

Revelation 19:1–10. In the revelation of the marriage of the Lamb preceding his formal second coming (Rev. 19:11–16), the bride of Christ is introduced as being already clad in fine linen, bright and clean. This seems to anticipate the Second Coming, which is yet future. If the church is the bride, it implies that the church is already in heaven in keeping with a pretribulation rapture.

The announcement is made not of the wedding itself but of the wedding feast. The angel said to John, "Write: 'Blessed are those who are invited to the wedding supper of the Lamb!'" And he added, "These are the true words of God" (Rev. 19:9). Weddings in the time and culture of Christ had three stages. The first was the formal contract between the parents of the bride and the bridegroom which constituted the actual legal wedding. The second was the claiming of the bride by the bridegroom, usually a year after the agreement was reached. This is illustrated in the parable of the ten virgins in Matthew 25:1–13. The last stage of the wedding was the wedding feast. The fact that the feast was announced here rather than the preceding steps would indicate that the union of Christ and the church had already taken place, another indication of a pretribulation rapture. A bride clad in fine linen that is bright and clean (19:8), would presume the church's resurrection and sanctification and presentation to Christ as his bride.

Revelation 19:11–20:6. In the great description of Christ's second coming in Revelation 19:11–20:6 there is no mention of a rapture, though it is apparent that after his second coming the Old Testament saints will be raised (Dan. 12:1–3; Rev. 20:3–6). In this passage there is no resurrection while Christ is in the process of coming from heaven to earth as required in Thessalonians 4 for the Rapture. The omission of a rapture here, as well as in any other passage on the Second Coming in either the Old or New Testament, is another argument in favor of the fact that the rapture is not included in the Second Coming. As the development of the arguments for the various views of the Tribulation will illustrate, the evidence is weighted in favor of the pretribulation Rapture position.

Pretribulationism: The Rapture Before End-Time Events

In order to examine carefully the arguments for and against the various views on the Rapture, it is necessary, first of all, to clearly state the presuppositions underlying each view. Too often books upholding one view or the other settle the matter by presuppositions rather than by exegesis of the Scriptures involved. This leads to confusion, and often the surviving theory is wrong.

Presuppositions of pretribulationism. The view that the Rapture is pretribulational—that is, more than seven years before the second coming of Christ—involves certain prior assumptions. Pretribulationism can be supported only by a premillennial interpretation of the second coming of Christ. Amillennialism, which is probably the predominant view of the church because of its principle of interpreting prophecy nonliterally, cannot support the concept of a pretribulation rapture and is always posttribulational. Some who hold the midtribulation rapture theory can be premillennial, but their form of interpretation mortgages the clarity of their prophetic interpretation. This is also true of the partial rapture view. Only a clear acceptance of premillennialism provides an adequate base for examining whether the Rapture is before or at the end of end-time events.

Coupled with premillennialism is the assumption that the Bible is inerrant—that is, its prophetic pronouncements are true. Prophecy must be assumed to be just as accurate and true as history, and usually those who deny the inerrancy of the Bible do not support pretribulationism.

Principles of interpretation are also important, as pretribulationism, like premillennialism, depends on interpreting prophecy in its natural sense rather than spiritualizing it or understanding it in a nonliteral meaning as amillennialism does. The same principles of interpretation that lead to premillennialism also lead to pretribulationism, and the more consistently persons are premillennial, the more apt they are to adopt a pretribulational view of the Rapture.

The context of the Rapture passages. As in all exegetical

decisions, what precedes or follows a given passage is very important in determining the context or meaning of the passage itself. It is significant that every passage on the Rapture presents it as an imminent event and never predicts a preceding event though in the providence of God many things may happen before the Rapture. As far as biblical revelation is concerned, these events are not placed before the Rapture. This is true of such major prophecies as the destruction of Jerusalem in A.D. 70, which, of course, preceded the Rapture. In the revelation of this prophecy, however, there is no indication that it would precede the Rapture, and it could very well have followed it as far as Scripture revelation is concerned.

Just as the Rapture will not be preceded by other prophetic events but is presented as an imminent event, so also the millennial kingdom, which immediately follows the Second Coming in the premillennial interpretation, is never presented as an event that immediately follows the Rapture. Rather, the implication is that there will be a preceding time of trouble as implied in 2 Thessalonians 2, where the events of the Day of the Lord follow instead of precede the Rapture. By contrast, every extensive passage on the Second Coming describes graphically the time of trouble which precedes, as in Matthew 24 and Revelation 4–18.

The definition of the church. If the question be asked: Will the church be raptured before end-time events? it becomes very important to define the church as an entity that is distinct from Israel or saints in general. In prophetic passages concerning the Tribulation, both Israelites and Gentiles are described, and some of them have faith in Christ and form a godly remnant. If they are part of the church, then the church is in the Tribulation, and the whole question as to whether the church goes through the Tribulation becomes moot. Many posttribulationists, in an attempt to establish their own point of view, beg the question at the very beginning by assuming that the church includes saints of all ages. The concept that the church is distinct from Israel is a part of dispensational truth that distinguishes the work of God in the Old Testament under the Mosaic Law, the work of God in the present age as he calls out both Jews and Gentiles to form the church as the body of Christ, and the millennial kingdom in which the saints of all ages participate in various ways but maintain their individual and corporate identity. Hence, the church will be raptured or resurrected, and will reign with

Christ in the millennial kingdom, but the saved of Israel as well as the saved of the Gentiles who are not part of the church will also be part of the millennial kingdom. Distinguishing the church from saints of other periods that precede or follow the present age is essential to a correct answer on the pretribulational issue. It is not too much to say that the doctrine of the church, or ecclesiology, determines this aspect of eschatology.

The literal interpretation of the Tribulation. In the refinement of end-time prophecy, it is often pointed out that the period between the Rapture and the Second Coming is more than seven years in duration. There is, first of all, a period of preparation in which the ten-nation group prophesied in Daniel 7 and Revelation 13 is formed. This is followed by a seven-year period designated in Daniel 9:27 in which a covenant is made with Israel. The first half, or the first three and a half years of this seven-year period, is characterized by Israel at peace and protected by the Middle East ruler. At the midpoint of the seven years, however, the covenant is broken and Israel becomes the object of persecution simultaneous with the emergence of the Middle East ruler as a world dictator, and for the three and a half years remaining before the Second Coming Israel, as well as the world as a whole, is in great trouble. Though the Bible does not give a specific term covering this period of more than seven years, frequently in eschatological literature it is referred to as the Tribulation, though the Scriptures do not use the term in this sense. The Scriptures do, however, justify the last three and a half years being designated as the Great Tribulation, a time of unprecedented trouble.

If the question is asked whether the church will go through the Tribulation, the Tribulation must be defined according to this framework of interpretation—namely, in terms of the question: Will the church be raptured more than seven years before the Second Coming? If the literalness of this period or its details are denied and the whole Tribulation period is equated with general tribulation such as the world has now, the issue becomes blurred, and it is impossible to come to a satisfactory conclusion. Furthermore, a denial that the Tribulation is a particular time period involves a denial of the literalness of the prophecies, for the Great Tribulation specifically defines a time of trouble greater than anything that precedes or follows (Dan. 12:1–2; Matt. 24:21). The truth of this is underscored by the fact that Daniel, the great prophet of the Old Testament, and Christ affirmed the distinct character of this period, as did other prophets (e.g., Jer. 30:4–11; Dan. 7:7–8, 19–27, 9:27, 11:36–45, 12:1, 11–13). The definition of both the church and the Tribulation is crucial to a proper handling of this theological question.

The Holy Spirit in relation to the Tribulation. In the present age since Pentecost, the Holy Spirit indwells every Christian, constituting his seal unto redemption. The Holy Spirit also regenerates—that is, gives eternal life—and baptizes believers into the body of Christ. Though the new birth of the believer apparently also was true of believers in the Old Testament, the other aspects of the work of the Holy Spirit in salvation are found only after Pentecost.

Essential to the question of determining the time of the Rapture is discerning the changed role of the Holy Spirit after the Rapture and in the period between the Rapture and the Second Coming. This becomes crucial, as in 2 Thessalonians 2:1–12, where Paul refutes the early posttribulationism that invaded the Thessalonian church with the argument that the events of the Day of the Lord were not taking place. Among them was his pointed reference to the revelation of the man of lawlessness, the political leader of the ten-nation group in the end time as well as the final world ruler dominated by Satan. Paul's point is that he cannot be revealed until that which is restraining sin is removed (v. 8). As noted in previous discussion on this passage, this becomes a very important point, because the man of sin will be revealed more than seven years before the second coming of Christ when he will conquer first three and then all ten countries prior to making a seven-year peace treaty with Israel. According to 2 Thessalonians 2, this cannot happen as long as God is restraining sin, hence, the Rapture precedes these events.

The common attempt to avoid this doctrine by assigning restraint of sin to government cannot be sustained in view of the fact that in the end time there will be an absolute government that will be completely wicked. In other words, government will not restrain sin in the end time. The ultimate restraint of sin must be from God himself, and the presence of the Holy Spirit indwelling the church is God's present method of restraining sin in the world. This can be changed only by the rapture of the church. Second Thessalonians 2, in effect, teaches that the Rapture must occur before the man of sin can be revealed, thereby indicating that the Rapture will take place more than seven years before the Second Coming. A proper understanding of the differences in the ministry of the Spirit in the Old Testament, in the present age, and in the Tribulation period is essential to understanding pretribulationism.

Events between the Rapture and the Second Coming. A careful search of the Scriptures indicates that certain events will follow the Rapture and precede the Second Coming. These include the marriage of the Lamb, since in the Rapture Christ will come as the Bridegroom to claim his bride, the church. This period will also include the judgment seat of Christ, which is distinguished from preceding and following judgments. There will be no place for this in the millennial scene, but it will take place in heaven following the church's being caught out of the world and taken to heaven.

It is also clear that certain events will take place on earth between the Rapture and the Second Coming. In premillennialism it is assumed that there will be Jews and Gentiles saved who will enter the millennial kingdom in their natural bodies. These who survive the Tribulation and enter the millennial kingdom will not be raptured; they will still have natural bodies. They will live, and they can sin and die. This is not true of those who will be raptured. If a rapture would take place at the time of Christ's second coming and every saint be given immortality, there would be no one on earth left to populate the millennial earth. If the church is raptured before the end-time events, it will allow for a period of time in which many Jews and Gentiles will be saved, and though some of these will be killed in the Great Tribulation, those who survive will constitute the citizens of the millennial kingdom. Regathered Israel will be placed in their Promised Land, and Gentiles will occupy the rest of the world.

The end-time judgments on Israel (Ezek. 20:34–38) and the judgment of living Gentiles at the Second Coming (Matt. 25:31–46) both indicate that there will be living saints on earth who will enter the millennial kingdom in their natural bodies. The pretribulation Rapture allows for a literal interpretation of these events without discounting the distinctive details of these prophecies.

The Rapture and the Second Coming contrasted. A careful study of passages describing the Rapture and passages describing the Second Coming makes clear that while both are "coming" in the sense that Christ will come from heaven to earth, the character of the coming, the purpose of the coming, the events that precede, and the events that follow are totally different.

According to the Rapture passages, when Christ comes for the church, he will cause them to be translated, or resurrected, and to meet him in the air with no resulting judgment or change on earth at that time. In contrast, at the Second Coming the Mount of Olives will be split in two with a great valley stretching from Jerusalem down to the Jordan River (Zech. 14:4–5).

The purpose of the Rapture is to take the church out of the world and bring them to the Father's house. The purpose of the Second Coming is to establish Christ's millennial kingdom, and no translation is necessary.

At the translation of the church, the saints will go from earth to heaven, whereas in contrast to the Second Coming the saints will remain on earth and populate the millennial earth.

No judgment of sin on earth will occur at the time of the Rapture. However, at the Second Coming the armies of the world will be destroyed, the Beast and the False Prophet will be cast into the lake of fire, and Jews and Gentiles will be judged as to their eligibility to enter the kingdom.

Christians in the present age who are looking forward to the Rapture are assured that they will be delivered from the day of wrath (1 Thess. 5:9). In contrast, in the period preceding the Second Coming the wrath of God will be poured out on the earth and the great disasters that take place will overtake Christians as well as non-Christians (Rev. 6:12–17). The Tribulation is a time of the wrath of Satan (Rev. 12:6), which is vented on believers of that time; whereas the wrath of God is vented on unbelievers, but the resulting judgments affect the entire race.

The Rapture, as described in Scripture, is an imminent event and therefore will precede the Tribulation. In contrast, the Second Coming will be the climax of the Tribulation and a time when Christ will rescue believers who are under persecution. The Rapture as presented in Scripture is always described as an imminent event, whereas the Second Coming is preceded by a tremendous series of detailed events described in Revelation 6–18 as well as in Matthew 24 and other passages.

The Rapture is a doctrine that is not revealed in the Old Testament and was not mentioned by Christ until John 14. In contrast, the Second Coming is a doctrine of the Old Testament as well as of the New.

The Rapture concerns only the saved, whereas the Second Coming constitutes a judgment on the unsaved as well as a rescue of the saved.

At the Rapture Satan will not be affected; at the Second Coming Satan will be bound for a thousand years before his final judgment, and wicked people will be judged with him.

Though both the Rapture and the Second Coming are described as comings because Christ leaves heaven and comes to the sphere of earth in both cases, the two comings are entirely different. The Rapture and the Second Coming are different from the events described as his first coming. In the Old Testament both the first and second comings of Christ are described, but no one understood that they were two separate comings. In the New Testament the Rapture and the Second Coming are distinguished, and because of the differences of the two comings, many interpreters of the Bible distinguish the Rapture from the Second Coming. The many arguments in favor of pretribulationism should be contrasted with the arguments in favor of posttribulationism.

Posttribulationism: The Rapture at the Second Coming

Problems of definition. Theological discussion concerning whether pretribulationism or posttribulationism is correct has prompted the writing of many books. As previously mentioned, I wrote a 300-page book called *The Rapture Question,* which is a detailed consideration of the problem. I also wrote a book on posttribulationism entitled *The Blessed Hope and the Tribulation,* which is 160 pages long. Condensing the arguments for and against posttribulationism is a difficult task since the subject is quite confusing.

The theological issue is sometimes expressed in the question: Will the church go through the Tribulation? The question itself, however, has been subject to a great deal of controversy, because there is no agreement as to the definition of the church, and there is no agreement as to what constitutes the Tribulation. Accordingly, in order to grasp the problem, it is necessary to examine the various points of view that are involved. For a student attempting for the first time to arrive at a satisfactory conclusion, the theological discussion may seem very difficult.

The nature of the church. Crucial to understanding the issue as to whether the church will go through the Tribulation is the definition of who is included in the church. A common teaching is that the expression "the church" includes all the saved—from Adam to the last person saved. If this is a correct definition, it is obvious that the church will go through the Tribulation, because saints, both Jews and Gentiles, are specifically mentioned in the Bible as being in the period. Accordingly, it is not unusual to find a book advocating posttribulationism taking this as settling the argument.

Premillenarians, however, tend to distinguish the church, which began on the Day of Pentecost, from saints in the Old Testament or saints who will come to Christ after the Rapture. Accordingly, while people will be saved after the Rapture, they are never identified as members of the body of Christ, are never referred to as being baptized by the Spirit into the body of Christ, and in other ways are distinguished as saved Jews or saved Gentiles. If the church is limited to the saints of the present age, the question as to whether the church will go through the Tribulation is a debatable question. All pretribulationists and a few posttribulationists make this distinction of the church of the present age as opposed to saints of other periods. The question then is whether the church, the body of Christ, or the saints of the present age, will go through the Tribulation before the Second Coming.

The nature of the Tribulation. Equally important to a consideration of the subject is the definition of the Tribulation. In other words, what is the Tribulation through which the church will pass before the Second Coming?

Here we have a well-defined difference of opinion on the part of posttribulationists. Generally speaking, advocates of posttribulationism spend most of their time refuting pretribulationism rather than establishing the biblical basis for their own doctrine. Though they agree on posttribulationism, they do not agree as to how this doctrine is supported. In general, there are four varieties of posttribulationism.

Classic posttribulationism. This term has been used to refer to those who have followed the historic position of posttribulationism, which tends to spiritualize or to interpret in a nonliteral way the nature of the Tribulation. It is customary in this point of view to equate our present troubles as much the same as the period of tribulation preceding the Second Coming. Accordingly, these posttribulationists argue that tribulation has already begun. How then can we question whether the church is going through the Tribulation? Some begin this tribulation with the time of Christ; others take it all the way back to Adam. Ignored in this point of view is what the Bible refers to as the Great Tribulation, a period expressly distinguished from all preceding trouble. Daniel 12:1 describes the period: "There will be a time of distress such as has not happened from the beginning of the nations until then." Jeremiah said, "How awful that day will be! None will be like it. It will be a time of trouble for Jacob, but he will be saved out of it" (30:7). Jesus also referred to this period: "For then there will be great distress, unequaled from the beginning of the world until now—and never to be equaled again. If those days had not been cut short, no one would survive, but for the sake of the elect those days will be shortened" (Matt. 24:21–22). He promised the church in Philadelphia that they would be kept from a future time of trouble that was yet to come upon the world: "I will also keep you from the hour of trial that is going to come upon the whole world to test those who live on the earth" (Rev. 3:10). It should be obvious from these references that the time of trouble preceding the Second Coming is not an ordinary time of trouble but is absolutely unprecedented.

If the description of Revelation 6–18 of the period preceding the Second Coming is taken in any literal sense, it is obvious that it defines such an awful period. In Revelation 6:7–8 a fourth of the world is destroyed. In Revelation 9:15 a third of the world is destroyed. The final blow, the seventh vial, in Revelation 16 is described as an earthquake that is greater than anything that has ever occurred. The cities of the Gentiles are totally destroyed, with islands and mountains disappearing and a supernatural hailstorm with hail stones weighing one hundred pounds each falling on the debris (vv. 18–21). Classic posttribulationism, however, says that all of this is purely figurative and that actually the troubles are no different than what we have had throughout the history of the race. Accordingly, some classic posttribulationists can take the position that Christ could come any day, based on the principle that the Tribulation is already past.

Semiclassic posttribulationism. This view also spiritualizes or takes in a nonliteral sense many of the judgments of the Tribulation but does envision that there are still future events to take place, including the emergence of a world ruler and some of the other things that are implied in the book of Revelation. Accordingly, while they do not hold to imminency—that is, that Christ could come at any time, they feel that the period is not a literal period of seven years or three and a half years. The time element is not to be taken in a literal sense at all.

Futuristic posttribulationism. In the light of atomic bombs and post-World War II events, there has been a major shift in posttribulationism away from spiritualizing the Tribulation to taking it in a much more literal sense. Some recognize that there is an awful period ahead, but, nevertheless, they insist that the Rapture will occur after this time period and not before. As posttribulationists concede a much more literal and awful tribulation period than do classic postribulationists, it becomes more difficult for them to hold that a rapture at the end of this period is a blessed hope, for in the Tribulation they describe many will perish.

Dispensational posttribulationism. A recent development in posttribulationism is an attempt by at least one author to hold to a dispensational view—that is, that the church is distinct from other saints but that the church as such is found in the Great Tribulation which is still ahead. Though this view is much more literal in treating the prophecies about the future Tribulation, when it comes to crucial issues, it tends to minimize the awfulness of the Tribulation.

The four types of posttribulationism illustrate the problems that posttribulationists have in sustaining their point of view, and demonstrates that they are not all agreed as to how to support and prove a posttribulational rapture. New books on posttribulationism constantly appear, indicating that posttribulationists do not believe that previous discussions of the subject have proved posttribulationism.

Arguments supporting posttribulationism. Posttribulationists generally agree that if there is a tribulation ahead, the church must go through it in order to be raptured. Accordingly, they hold that the Rapture is a phase of the second coming of Christ; and though they seldom detail the events relating to it, in keeping with 1 Thessalonians 4, they hold that the church will rise from earth to meet the Lord in his descent from heaven to the earth and then will make a U-turn and continue with Christ as he comes to the earth. The events relating to the second coming of Christ will follow, but the Rapture will be accomplished just a short time before, during the descent of Christ. Arguments in support of posttribulationism can be divided under a number of separate topics.

Attacks on pretribulationism. Though many posttribulationists handle the arguments in favor of their position with courtesy and tact, some of the older volumes begin by attacking pretribulationists themselves. They malign the scholarship and integrity of pretribulationists and call them fanatics and their arguments rubbish. This approach does not yield any help in determining the truth of Scripture on the subject.

The historical argument. One of the main arguments of posttribulationism is that their view is the viewpoint of the church at large from the first century until now. Adherents of this view quote church fathers to the effect that the second coming of Christ could occur at any moment, and, of course, this would include the Rapture. A careful examination, however, of the early church fathers reveals that they were confused. On the one hand, they saw that the Scriptures predicted an imminent rapture and, on the other hand, predicted future events such as the world church, world government, and an antichrist. Accordingly, the same author on one page would say that the Second Coming was imminent and then on the next page say that certain events had to happen first. His problem was that he had not distinguished the Rapture from the Second Coming. While the church fathers were in one sense posttribulationists because they held that the Second Coming was imminent, they were trying to be faithful to the Scriptures that teach that the Rapture could occur at any time.

In the history of doctrine there is progression over many centuries, with the Protestant Reformation looming large as a time when many doctrines were reclaimed, such as the doctrine of justification by faith, the priesthood of the believer, and that every Christian is his own interpreter of the Bible. Obviously, further study of eschatology was necessary. Unfortunately, in the Protestant Reformation problems of eschatology were not addressed, even though the Roman Catholic doctrine of purgatory was refuted. The Reformers began with Augustine, who was amillennial and accordingly also posttribulational. It was not until later in the Bible study movements of the last few centuries and in the intensive eschatological research of the twentieth century that pretribulationism has been expounded in a comprehensive way.

The conflict between passages on the Rapture that teach an imminent return of Christ and the passages that imply that there are great events that will precede the Second Coming has been resolved by separating the two events—the Rapture before the Tribulation and the Second Coming after the Tribulation. As pointed out before, this is similar to the contemporary separation of the first and second coming of Christ, which in the Old Testament was obscure and was not really understood until after Christ's ascension. Now no one questions the difference between the first and second comings of Christ because the differences are so clear. The same thing can be learned by comparing the pretribulation Rapture to the posttribulational second coming of Christ.

J. N. Darby is often credited with first making the distinction between Israel and the church in the prophetic program of God. However, this was already latent in the early church fathers. The attempt to trace the pretribulation Rapture to two erratic individuals by the names of Edward Irving and Margaret MacDonald, though advocated by some posttribulationists, has no real bearing on the issue, because neither of these were pretribulationists. Accordingly, this attempt to trace pretribulationism to individuals who had little theological insight is not a sound approach.

The final answer to the question as to whether pretribulationism is correct as opposed to posttribulationism must be settled on biblical grounds alone. Doctrine cannot be settled on the basis of majority opinion.

Posttribulational doctrine of the Tribulation. As has been pointed out, posttribulationists are at odds among themselves as to what constitutes the so-called Tribulation period. The Bible itself never refers to the period of seven years leading up to the second coming of Christ as the Tribulation, though the last three and a half years are called the Great Tribulation.

As has been pointed out previously, posttribulationism fifty years ago largely consisted of spiritualizing the Tribulation and removing it from future expectation as a series of events to be fulfilled. With the atomic bomb, the increasing capacity to destroy human life, and the possibility of great catastrophes, posttribulationism today has moved back into a position where the Tribulation period is considered seriously and where major events must take place before the second coming of Christ. Of course, posttribulationists have a problem declaring that a rapture at the end of this tribulation is a "blessed hope" (Titus 2:13). Posttribulationists also face the problem of what to do about the coming time of trouble if it is going to be as severe as the Scriptures indicate.

According to pretribulational interpretation, there will be an interval including at least three periods between the Rapture and Christ's second coming. First, there will be a time of preparation in which a group of ten nations constituting a revival of the ancient Roman Empire will emerge. Out of this empire will come a political leader who will dominate the scene, gaining control first of three and then of all ten countries. A second period will follow when this political leader will make a seven-year peace treaty with Israel (Dan. 9:27). This peace treaty will be observed for three and a half years and then be broken, beginning a third period in which the political leader will become Israel's persecutor and a world dictator, assuming the role of God himself. The last three and a half years, culminating at the second coming of Christ, will be a period of great tribulation, which according to pretribulationists, will decimate the world and destroy most of the world's population. Christ himself declared that unless it was stopped by his second coming no human being would be left alive on the earth (Matt. 24:22).

Posttribulationists respond to this outline of events between the Rapture and the Second Coming in some cases by spiritualizing and ignoring it and in other cases by denying that it contains specific events as outlined in prophecy. The definition of the Tribulation therefore becomes an important aspect of the question as to whether the church will go through the Tribulation. Though some will go through it unscathed, as illustrated in the 144,000 of Revelation 7 and 14, many others will be killed, as illustrated in the martyrs who are seen in heaven in Revelation 7:9–17. These are people who will have died in the Great Tribulation. The more literally one takes the Tribulation, the less attractive is the concept of a rapture occurring after the Tribulation. A possibility of living through the Tribulation is so slight, —most of the world's population will perish—that it does not seem to measure up to the expectation that the Rapture is a matter of eager and happy expectation.

Posttribulational argument concerning the church. As previously pointed out, most posttribulationists include all saints in the church, and in that case there is no basis for argument. Some posttribulationists, however, concede that the church is a special body of believers, beginning at Pentecost and continuing until the Rapture. The question then becomes whether the church is ever seen in the Tribulation. From Revelation 4:1 until the mention of the bride in 19:7, no mention is made of the church. Tribulation passages, referring to those who are saved, mention them as saved Gentiles or saved Jews, but the term *church* is not used.

Posttribulational view of the imminency of Christ's return. It is essential to posttribulationism as is currently being taught, which includes in most cases a series of events preceding the Second Coming, to explain imminency as a time factor that allows for preceding events. By contrast, pretribulationists believe that the imminency of the Rapture does not allow for any events preceding as far as prophecy is concerned. Posttribulationists tend to deny imminency or redefine it, for they cannot accommodate a series of great events preceding the Second Coming and at the same time say that the Rapture, which follows these events, is imminent.

Scriptures imply that it would be an extended period of time before the Rapture occurred, but prophecy such as described the future of Peter (John 21:18–19), and parables that seemed to imply a lengthy period, have long since been fulfilled. Whether or not imminency could be completely upheld in the apostolic period, at the present time there are no prophesied events that are to precede the Rapture of the church unless one takes the posttribulational viewpoint. If the Lord's coming is blessed, a comforting hope, a purifying hope, and a matter of eager expectation, it is difficult to harmonize this with the posttribulational position that tragic events must precede the Second Coming.

Posttribulational explanation of the resurrection of the saints. In Revelation 20:4–6 a clear prophecy is given concerning the resurrection of saints who die in the Great Tribulation preceding the Second Coming. They will be raised from the dead at the Second Coming and will reign with Christ for a thousand years.

> And I saw the souls of those who had been beheaded because of their testimony for Jesus and because of the word of God. They had not worshiped the beast or his image and had not received his mark on their foreheads or their hands.

> They came to life and reigned with Christ a thousand years.
> (The rest of the dead did not come to life until the thousand
> years were ended.) This is the first resurrection. Blessed
> and holy are those who have part in the first resurrection.
> The second death has no power over them, but they will be
> priests of God and of Christ and will reign with him for a
> thousand years.

It is important to note that this resurrection will not take place in
fulfillment of 1 Thessalonians 4—that is, these believers will
not be raised while Christ is on his way from heaven to earth,
and they will not meet him in the air. This resurrection will take
place after Christ's throne is established on the earth.

The saints pictured in this passage are those saved during the
Great Tribulation. According to the pretribulational position,
the Rapture of the church will have taken place earlier, and for
this reason there is no mention of the church here. The fact that
it is called "the first resurrection" (Rev. 20:5–6) does not mean
that no resurrections will have occurred before but rather that it
will be first in the sense of being before the final resurrection of
the wicked at the end of the millennial kingdom. The resurrection of Christ is already a matter of history, and the resurrection
of Matthew 27:52–53 and the resurrection of the two witnesses
in Revelation 11 will have already occurred. If the pretribulationists are correct, the Rapture and the resurrection in connection with it will also have taken place.

It is important to note that posttribulationists have no specific
text supporting a posttribulational rapture of living saints.
Damaging to the posttribulational argument is the fact that not a
single passage in the New Testament describing the second
coming of Christ includes the aspect of the Rapture—that is, the
translation of living saints and the resurrection of saints who
have died. Rather, in keeping with premillennialism, at the
second coming of Christ, though the wicked dead will have
been purged out, the godly remnant of Israel and the Gentiles
who have accepted Christ will be ushered into their future
estate still in their natural bodies and living on earth in natural
situations. They will not be raptured but will still retain the
same body. Though not dealt with in Scripture, ultimately they
will either die and be resurrected or be raptured at the end of
the Millennium.

Some posttribulationists use Matthew 24:40–41, where one is

taken and another left, as the rapture of the church. However, the context indicates that the one who is taken is taken in judgment, much like the people who perished outside the ark, as illustrated in the previous context (Matt. 24:39). Also, according to Luke 17:37, those who are taken are killed, and vultures eat their bodies. This is exactly the opposite of the Rapture. Whereas at the Rapture the one taken, according to pretribulationists, is the child of God and the one left is the one who is not saved, at the Second Coming the reverse will take place. The one who is taken will be the unsaved, and the one who is left will be the saved who then enters into the millennial kingdom.

Posttribulational arguments on terminology. In the New Testament several words are used to describe the return of the Lord—namely, *parousia*, usually translated "coming"; *apokalupsis*, which refers to unveiling or a "revelation"; and *epiphaneia*, which is translated "appearing." Properly understood, these words are not technical words and could be applied to more than one coming, revelation or appearing. It is often argued that all three are used of both the Rapture and of Christ's coming at the end of the Tribulation. This does not deter pretribulationists, however, from recognizing the distinction between the two comings, since the words are not technical words.

The Day of the Lord. Posttribulationists usually argue that the prophesied period of the Day of the Lord does not begin until the Second Coming. Because the Day of the Lord begins at the Rapture, it is therefore argued that the Rapture must be at the Second Coming also.

As brought out before, the Day of the Lord is a descriptive term for any period in which God judges the world directly. There were days of the Lord in the Old Testament, but the future great Day of the Lord is the one describing the period leading up to the second coming of Christ.

Rather than beginning at the Second Coming, the Day of the Lord will include the time of tribulation preceding the Second Coming. This is supported by many Scripture passages (Isa. 2:12–21; 13:9–16; 34:1–8; Joel 1:15–2:11; 2:28–32; 3:9–21; Amos 5:18–20; Obad. 15–17; Zeph. 1:7–18). According to 1 Thessalonians 5, the Day of the Lord will begin at the Rapture. But if the Day of the Lord, according to the Old Testament, includes the period of time before the Second Coming, as the Old Testament describes it, then the Rapture will have to occur before the second coming of Christ. Accordingly, the posttribulational view, assuming that the Day of the Lord begins at the Second Coming, lacks scriptural support.

Posttribulational argument from 2 Thessalonians 2. According to 2 Thessalonians 2, false teachers had come into the Thessalonian church, teaching them that they were already in the Day of the Lord. Paul refuted this by pointing out that the major events of the Day of the Lord had not yet begun. One of these events is that the man of sin, or the man of lawlessness, has not been revealed. There is evidence that he will be revealed early in the period leading up to the second coming of Christ. Further, in 2:6 Paul told the Thessalonians that something was holding sin back and that the man of sin would not be revealed until that restraint was removed. Though there has been argument concerning this restraint of sin in the world, ultimately, it is a work of the Holy Spirit. In view of the fact that the Holy Spirit has indwelt the church since Pentecost, the presence of the church is a major restraint of sin in the world and a testimony for God. It would be impossible, therefore, for the restraint to be removed without removing the church. In a word, this demonstrates that the Rapture has to occur before the man of sin will be revealed.

As other Scriptures are studied in relation to 2 Thessalonians 2, it seems evident that the man of sin is the same person as the ruler of Daniel 7:8 who will conquer first three and then ten countries that form the reconstituted Roman Empire. Since this will occur more than seven years before the second coming of Christ, because the seven-year treaty follows (Dan. 9:27), a timetable is set up that makes a posttribulational rapture impossible. Posttribulationists try to get around this passage by one means or another, but they have yet to resolve it.

Posttribulational arguments concerning other terminology. In the New Testament the end time is referred to as "the end." The problem, of course, is to determine what is in view in "the end." Because the term is not a technical term, it implies the end of something that precedes. The context of Scripture determines what end is in view. Only one of five texts on "the end" in the New Testament refers to the coming of Christ (1 Cor. 1:7–8), and this, of course, could refer to the Rapture. The other references are not clear as to what end is in view.

Posttribulational treatment of the Rapture itself. Strangely, most posttribulational books do not spend much time analyzing

passages such as John 14:3, 1 Thessalonians 4:13–18, or 1 Corinthians 15:51–52. These are the major passages on the
doctrine of the Rapture, and the problem for a posttributionist
is that they do not offer any support for a posttribulational
rapture. They uniformly imply that the Rapture is imminent
with no prophesied preceding events. This stands in contrast to
the consistent presentation in the New Testament of the second
coming of Christ being preceded by tremendous events.

Though posttribulationists often challenge pretribulationists
to cite a single passage that clearly provides for a pretribulation
Rapture, they do this to cover up their own problem that they
cannot find a single passage that teaches a posttribulation
rapture. This is all the more significant because the Second
Coming is described in great detail in a number of New
Testament passages, yet there is no mention of the rapture of
living Christians. Even the doctrine of resurrection does not
occur at the time of Christ's coming but in subsequent actions.

Disagreements among posttribulationists. Part of the confusion in the arguments between pre- and posttribulationism is
that posttribulationism does not have a consistent approach.
Postmillenarians disagree among themselves on a number of
issues such as the nature of the Tribulation, the doctrine of
imminency, the suffering of saints in the Great Tribulation, the
relation of the prophecies of the book of Revelation to the end
time, the nature of the church, the question of whether
unbelievers have a second chance at the Second Coming, the
specific order of events leading up to the Second Coming, the
judgments at the Second Coming, and the question of what
follows the Second Coming. Their confusion in these major
areas illustrates their confusion of the whole doctrine. Their
problem is that the Scriptures are silent on the salient points of
their position, leaving them vulnerable to question and allowing
the pretribulationists to establish their own position.

Midtribulationism

Variety of Definitions. A major problem that exists in attempting to understand midtribulationism is that no two adherents
follow exactly the same line of arguments. One of the most
common positions is that the Rapture occurs at the seventh
trumpet of Revelation (Rev. 11:15). This is based on the concept
that this is the last of the seven trumpets, and in 1 Corinthians

15:52 the Rapture is said to occur at the last trumpet. It is obvious that a list is always relative to what it is talking about, and in Revelation the trumpets are trumpets sounded by angels to announce judgments on the world. In contrast, 1 Corinthians 15 is the trumpet of the Lord, and it has nothing to do with judgment but rather with the rapture of the church. Further, the argument that the seventh trumpet is the last trump and therefore coincides with 1 Corinthians 15:52 overlooks the fact that there is still a future trumpet in Matthew 24:31 which signals the gathering of the saints at the beginning of the Millennium. Posttribulationists try to solve this problem by saying that this is also the Rapture.

Other midtribulationists place the Rapture after the fourth seal in Revelation 6:7–8. However, to start the Great Tribulation after the fourth seal ignores the terrible judgment of the fourth seal, the wiping out of one-fourth of the world's population: "I looked, and there before me was a pale horse! Its rider was named Death, and Hades was following close behind him. They were given power over a fourth of the earth to kill by sword, famine and plague, and by the wild beasts of the earth" (Rev. 6:8). Seals two and three also speak of war, famine, and great loss of life, certainly signaling a Great Tribulation. Midtribulationists do not face the problem of their interpretation in connection with these Scriptures. Some midtribulationists attempt to find the Rapture in Matthew 24, where the Rapture does not occur. Matthew 24 is anticipating the second coming of Christ and predicts the coming Great Tribulation (vv. 15–22). As pointed out previously, there is no rapture in Matthew 24, and the taking of one and leaving of another (vv. 40–41) refers to the ones who will be taken in judgment at the Second Coming, not to the Rapture that will remove the saints. The variety of midtribulationist explanations points to the confusion they have among themselves and their unwillingness to accept either a pretribulation nor posttribulation rapture. Strangely, both posttribulationsts and midtribulationists land on the seventh seal as the time of the Rapture even though they do not adequately explain the passages that precede or follow in keeping with their view.

Confusion of Israel and the church. One of the important principles to be kept in view in the study of prophecy is distinguishing the prophecies that relate to Israel and her program from the prophecies that relate to the church and her program. Pretribulationists generally regard the first sixty-nine "sevens" of Daniel 9:24–27 as being fulfilled before the death of Christ and view the last seven years of Daniel 9:27 as preceding the second coming of Christ. Between the sixty-ninth "seven" and the seventieth "seven" is the present age, in which the church begins and is completed at the Rapture. To require the church to be on earth during the first half of Daniel's seventieth "seven," as midtribulationists do, would blend the conclusion of the church with the beginning of Israel's restoration, which the Scriptures never do in other contexts.

Midtribulational denial of imminency. By postulating that the first half of the last seven years must take place before the church is raptured, midtribulationists deny the imminency of the Rapture. The doctrine of imminency is implied or stated in every Rapture passage, and never in a Rapture passage is any event described as preceding the Rapture. However, if it is necessary to place the Rapture in the middle of the last seven years, then we should be looking for the coming of the anti-Christ and the coming of the seven-year covenant rather than for the coming of the Lord, and this the Scriptures never do.

Midtribulational misunderstanding of the Day of the Lord. Though all areas of theology tend to mishandle the subject of the Day of the Lord, it becomes clear in the study of 2 Thessalonians 2, as well as in Old Testament descriptions of the Day of the Lord, that the Day of the Lord begins at the Rapture. In 2 Thessalonians 2 the timing of this is identified as the time when the restraining force of the Holy Spirit in the world is taken away by the Rapture itself. As explained previously, 2 Thessalonians 2 says that the man of sin cannot be identified as long as the Restrainer is still present. The man of sin, however, will be clearly identified when he makes a seven-year covenant with Israel, if not before, and this requires the Rapture to occur at least seven years before the Second Coming rather than three and a half years before, as the midtribulationists hold.

Summary of major problems with midtribulationism. Though the midtribulational interpretation of the Bible is by no means standardized, and different interpreters of Scripture explain it in different ways, its major problem is that it denies imminency and robs the church of expectancy as far as the Rapture is concerned. A second factor is that it confuses God's program for the church and his program for Israel. A third area is the mishandling of the book of Revelation in an attempt to find the

Rapture somewhere in the structure of the seven seals. The supporting evidence of this is lacking, as has already been pointed out, and the pretribulational view is preferable as an interpretation of the entire text of the New Testament.

The Partial Rapture View

Definition of the partial rapture teaching. Though held by very few Bible students, the partial rapture theory holds that when the Rapture occur, only those who are spiritually ready and who are looking for the Lord's return will be removed. They often do allow, however, for subsequent raptures to occur in the years that follow whenever an individual becomes ready for the Rapture.

Scriptural basis for the partial rapture theory. Those who hold to the partial rapture theory point to verses that require believers to be looking for the Lord's return. In doing this, they link passages that deal with the Rapture as well as the Second Coming (i.e., Matt. 24:40-51; 25:13; Mark 13:33–37; Luke 20:34–36; 21:36; Phil. 3:10–12; 1 Thess. 5:6; 2 Tim. 4:8; Titus 2:13; Heb. 9:24–28; Rev. 3:3; 12:1–6). An examination of these passages reveals that they are all appeals to look for the Lord's return. The partial rapture adherents take the position that failure to look for his return disqualifies the person for the Rapture.

Like posttribulationists, partial rapturists attempt to use Matthew 24:41 as an illustration of one who is ready and one who is not. A careful study of this passage, however, reveals that it is not talking about the Rapture but about the judgment at the Second Coming when one taken is taken in judgment and put to death and the other is left to enter the millennial kingdom. One of their favorite texts is Luke 21:36: " 'Be always on the watch, and pray that you may be able to escape all that is about to happen, and that you may be able to stand before the Son of Man.' "

The problem with this verse, as well as with many others, is that it puts salvation and qualifying for the Rapture on a works basis instead of recognizing that, according to Scripture, salvation is entirely by grace and not by works. Obviously one who believes in the Lord would be more likely to look for the Lord's return than an unbeliever, but this does not justify introducing a works principle into salvation.

Partial rapturists also tend to overlook the fact that at the Rapture the entire church will be raptured. First Thessalonians 4:16–17 says: ". . . the dead in Christ will rise first. After that, we who are still alive and are left will be caught up together with them in the clouds to meet the Lord in the air." Partial rapturists also ignore the word "all" as in 1 Corinthians 15:51, "Listen, I tell you a mystery: We will not all sleep, but we will all be changed—in a flash, in the twinkling of an eye, at the last trumpet." Like 1 Thessalonians 4, the dead are declared to be raised and the living are declared to be changed, with no distinction as to their works. Though Scripture frequently appeals to works as a demonstration of the fact that one is saved, this is not the ground on which God determines who will be raptured. The partial rapture theory has not appealed to the great majority of Bible expositors. Those who hold to the partial rapture theory imply that they themselves are ready for the rapture but that other Christians are not, which implies that there are two classes of Christians.

Summary of problems of the partial rapture theory. Those who hold to the partial rapture theory base their doctrine on a works principle for salvation, which is not what the Scriptures reveal. Salvation is always by grace, and there is no merit that justifies a person to be raptured. To assume a partial rapture implies the division of the body of Christ into two classes— those who are worthy and those who are not, which is not a scriptural point of view. The partial rapture theory also ignores the "all" as found in 1 Corinthians 15:51 and the clear indication that all the dead in Christ will be raised (1 Cor. 15:52; 1 Thess. 4:16). Both the partial rapture theory and the midtribulation theory have attracted only a few followers, and the main difference of opinion is between pretribulationists and posttribulationists.

The rapture of the church as presented in Scripture is not intended to be the basis of a theological argument but rather an expression of the wonderful hope that Christians have that the Lord may come at any time and that they will suddenly leave this world and go into the presence of the Savior without dying. It is also the grand expectation of Christians that, if they die, their day of resurrection will come and that meanwhile they will be in the presence of God in heaven.

Theological Issues Relating to the Rapture

The truth of the rapture of the church is not only the embodiment of a wonderful revelation giving a Christian hope, it is also important in determining a total theological system. Some of the major theological issues relating to it can be summarized.

Principles of interpretation. A literal, grammatical, and historical hermeneutic, or principle, of interpretation is important, for a true doctrine of the Rapture will not be achieved without paying strict attention to what the Scriptures precisely predict concerning the Rapture. When this is done, the facts point to the pretribulational Rapture.

The place of the church in relation to the Rapture. As pointed out in previous discussion, in order to establish a true doctrine of the rapture of the church, it is important to determine that the church is a special body of saints founded on the Day of Pentecost and culminating at the Rapture. Failure to recognize this is one of the principal causes for the posttribulational interpretation.

The importance of a proper definition of the Tribulation. The term "the Tribulation" is not an accurate term in relation to the entire period between the Rapture and the Second Coming. The Tribulation in general or trouble in general should be contrasted with the unprecedented trouble of what Scripture calls "the Great Tribulation." A proper understanding of what happens in the Great Tribulation and a documentation of the terrible judgments that will fall in that period make any thought of the church's going through this period unthinkable.

The doctrine of the imminency of the Rapture. Only the pretribulational position maintains a proper interpretation of the fact that the Rapture could occur at any moment. As portrayed in every Rapture passage, no preceding events are described, and the events that follow, whether on earth or in heaven, are entirely different from the events that follow the Second Coming. Even though the doctrine of the Rapture is not found in many Scripture verses, it is one of the most important practical concepts of Christian hope, since apart from the Rapture we would not have the hope of the imminent return of Christ.

Order of events relating to the Rapture. In interpreting prophecy and its literal fulfillment, it is important to itemize the events that occur between the Rapture and the Second Coming, both in heaven and on earth. Once this is clearly understood and done, the fact that the Rapture is before these events becomes very clear. Failure to do this and confusion in regard to the events that precede the Second Coming are major causes for expositors failing to arrive at a pretribulational position.

The Rapture and the Second Coming are different events. As already pointed out in detail, the Rapture is an event in which Christ takes the church from earth to heaven; whereas the Second Coming is an event in which he brings the church from heaven to earth. The purposes of the two events are totally different. In arriving at the distinction, careful attention must be paid to the details that are revealed in prophecy concerning the Rapture itself and concerning the Second Coming.

Summary of the Doctrine of the Rapture. Though confusion exists in the church today concerning the doctrine of the Rapture, and many biblical scholars bypass entirely the exposition of its truth, it is, nevertheless, one of the precious legacies that Christ gave to his disciples. In John 14 Christ told his disciples that he would return to take them to the Father's house. Paul wrote that the day will come when Christ will descend from heaven to the air above the earth, command those who have died in him to be raised from the dead, and command Christians who are living to be translated—that is, to receive instant transformation of their bodies. Both the living and the resurrected dead will rise from the earth, meet the Lord in the air, and proceed in triumph to heaven. There the Scriptures relating to the judgment seat of Christ and the marriage of the Lamb will be fulfilled. Meanwhile on earth the detailed program revealed in Scripture which will carry the world to its final climax at the Second Coming will be fulfilled. The blessed hope of Christ's return for his church is one of the precious legacies left by Christ to his own and continues to be a beacon light to Christians beset by the problems of modern life. Christ is coming, and he may be coming soon.

24

The Judgment Seat of Christ

All Judgment Committed to Christ

All people will be judged by God. Hebrews 9:27–28 says, "Just as man is destined to die once, and after that to face judgment, so Christ was sacrificed once to take away the sins of many people; and he will appear a second time, not to bear sin, but to bring salvation to those who are waiting for him." In the history of doctrine attempts have been made to merge all final judgments into one great judgment, but this does violence to what Scripture reveals. The Bible makes clear that all will be judged, but not at the same time, in the same place, or on the same basis. The judgment seat of Christ will be the final judgment for all Christians.

2 Corinthians 5:9–10

According to 2 Corinthians 5:9–10, all Christians will be judged at the judgment seat of Christ: "So we make it our goal to please him, whether we are at home in the body or away from it. For we must all appear before the judgment seat of Christ, that each one may receive what is due him for the things done while in the body, whether good or bad." Several unusual facts relate to this judgment. First, it is a judgment of Christians only. Old Testament saints, Tribulation saints, and millennial saints will be judged at a different time and in a different way, but the judgment seat of Christ will take place in heaven following the rapture of the church, and it will be limited to Christians. In other words, everyone there will be saved and will be rightly in heaven.

A Judgment of Reward

When the matter of judgment is considered, the question immediately arises as to whether a judgment relates to sin. The peculiar fact of the judgment seat of Christ is that it is not concerned with sin but with reward for what has been done well. Everyone there will be justified, or declared completely righteous by God, not because they have attained it by their works, but because God sees each believer in the perfection of the person and work of his Son. Accordingly, the only remaining issue is whether what persons have done is worthwhile from God's point of view. This is indicated in the expression "good or bad" (2 Cor. 5:10). These words relate to value, not to morality. The question is whether a work is good, or worthwhile, in the sight of God, or whether it is bad, or worthless.

The Question of Confession of Sin

If a Christian is not being judged for sin, why is it necessary to confess sin? First John 1:9 says, "If we confess our sins, he is faithful and just and will forgive us our sins and purify us from all unrighteousness." In Roman Catholic doctrine, sins are forgiven that are confessed on earth, but other sins need to be purged away in purgatory because they have not been forgiven. The Protestant church rejects purgatory, but this passage raises the question as to why confession of sin is necessary.

The context of 1 John is that of fellowship with God. It is not talking about ultimate reward, but rather the daily experience of Christians who walk with God. As sin comes into their lives and some disobedience or departure from God becomes evident, they will lose the experience of fellowship with God even though their salvation is still intact. In order to restore this fellowship, it is necessary for Christians to confess their sins to God. They are assured that they have already been forgiven because Christ died for them in the judicial sense, but now it is a question of a relationship between children and their Father. The one who comes to God in confession is assured that God is faithful to forgive and is also just, because Christ has already paid the price. Christians living on earth, accordingly, have to deal with sin, confession of sin, and the fact that if they do not confess they may be subject to the chastisement of God. On passing from this life, however, this is no longer necessary. A further sanctifying work in the hearts of believers is not needed in heaven because they have already been completely sanctified by the very act of resurrection, or translation. Accordingly, the judgment seat of Christ does not deal with sin but rather with the matter of works that merit reward.

Life As a Stewardship

One of the three illustrations that Paul used to explain the judgment seat of Christ is the figure of a steward, one entrusted with something that belongs to his master. In Romans 14:10–12 Paul wrote, "You, then, why do you judge your brother? Or why do you look down on your brother? For we will all stand before God's judgment seat. It is written: 'As surely as I live,' says the Lord, 'every knee will bow before me; every tongue will confess to God.' So then, each of us will give an account of himself to God." The judgment seat of Christ is introduced in this passage as one of the reasons why Christians should not judge other Christians in an attempt to make themselves look better than others. Accordingly, Paul asked why they judged or looked down on their brothers. The point is that one is not in a good position to analyze or evaluate what another Christian is doing. A pastor or preacher necessarily has to rebuke and exhort and, to some extent, recognize sin and judge it, but the issue here is not so much morality as it is evaluation of another person's life. Here God's judgment seat is the final answer, and Christians should recognize that each will be judged by God, and for this reason they should desist from judging or evaluating another person's ministry. As this Scripture indicates, the day will come when every knee will bow and every tongue will confess to

God. But for unbelievers, this will be too late, and they will go on to their eternal punishment. Just as all humans and all creation will have to submit to God, so Christians in a much more pleasant situation will give an account of their stewardship of that with which God has entrusted them.

This truth is a great equalizer in evaluating Christian work, because all Christians are judged not on the basis of what their fellow Christians are doing but on the basis of what they themselves have received from God.

In 1 Corinthians 4:7 Paul raised the question, "What do you have that you did not receive?" No Christian has exactly the same talents, abilities, or opportunities as another Christian. The point is that at the judgment seat of Christ Christians will be judged entirely on how faithful they have been, not on how successful, but rather on what they have done with what God has entrusted to them. The one with few talents has just as much of an opportunity as one who has many. In fact, the more one has, the greater is the difficulty of acting faithfully and using what God has committed to that individual. At the judgment seat of Christ everyone will, in a sense, report on how they used what God put into their hands. This is a very solemn thought as we recognize that everything we have, material and immaterial, comes from God and is entrusted to us for his use and for his glory. Scripture assures us, however, that every Christian will have something which God can praise. As 1 Corinthians 4:5 states, "At that time, each will receive his praise from God."

Life As a Building

Paul uses a second illustration to explain judgment in 1 Corinthians 3, where he compares life to building upon the foundation supplied in Christ. This passage can apply to the local church as well as to an individual. Paul said:

> By the grace God has given me, I laid a foundation as an excellent builder, and someone else is building on it. But each one should be careful how he builds. For no one can lay any foundation other than the one already laid, which is Jesus Christ. If any man builds on this foundation using gold, silver, costly stones, wood, hay or straw, his work will be shown for what it is, because the Day will bring it to light. It will be revealed with fire, and the fire will test the quality of each man's work. If what he has built survives, he

will receive his reward. If it is burned up, he will suffer
loss; he himself will be saved, but only as one escaping
through the flames. (1 Cor. 3:10–15)

In facing the challenges of life, every Christian has the same
foundation of salvation in Christ. This is God's work and is not
something we can do. Paul pictured our life as building on this
foundation with various materials. Six materials are mentioned,
the first three being fireproof and the last three subject to being
reduced to ashes. Though the significance of the materials is not
given here, gold in Scripture obviously is used to reflect the
glory of God, as in the temple and in the tabernacle. Anything a
Christian may do that will glorify God will survive as gold.
Silver is the metal of redemption. The Law required that every
firstborn son had to be redeemed with five shekels of silver
(Num. 18:15–16). Silver, accordingly, speaks of salvation and of
winning souls for Christ. The costly stones are not identified
because they reflect every other act which, from God's point of
view, has eternal value. In contrast, wood, hay, and stubble
represent varying degrees of material worth in this world, but
each is equally reducible to ashes in the fire of judgment. Straw
is of less worth than hay, and hay is of less worth than wood, but
all burn equally. The lesson is clear that at the judgment seat of
Christ our lives will be evaluated according to what counts for
eternity. Worthy works, however, may include many ordinary
tasks, such as a mother caring for her child or a father for his
family, as anything that is pleasing to God will be considered
"gold, silver, and precious stone."

Life As a Race

Paul's third illustration of judgment is found in 1 Corinthians
9:24–27, where he compares life to running a race:

> Do you not know that in a race all the runners run, but
> only one gets the prize? Run in such a way as to get the
> prize. Everyone who competes in the games goes into strict
> training. They do it to get a crown that will not last; but we
> do it to get a crown that will last forever. Therefore I do not
> run like a man running aimlessly; I do not fight like a man
> beating the air. No, I beat my body and make it my slave so
> that after I have preached to others, I myself will not be
> disqualified for the prize.

To win a race, a runner must be disciplined and be in proper physical condition. Likewise, the Christian life requires discipline. A runner also has to put aside any weight or anything that would hinder him or her from running as swiftly as possible. In the Christian life, often the good is the enemy of the best, and it is easy to be encumbered with things that hinder instead of help us win the race.

In Corinth, racing was a common public sport, and winners were given a crown of laurel leaves that would fade away in a few days. Paul pointed out that the crown the Lord will give will not fade away but will last forever. In keeping with this illustration, Paul declared that he himself did not run without aim, for to do so would mean failure to win the race. He had to keep the rules, that is, run to win the prize. In the process, he had to beat his body or bring it into control lest while he urged others to serve the Lord, he himself should be disqualified (1 Cor. 9:27).

The illustration of running a race fits our current generation in which everything moves swiftly. But Christians should remember that the final test as to what is won in the race will be at the judgment seat of Christ. The crown of the victor is compared in 2 Timothy 4:8 to a crown of righteousness: "Now there is in store for me the crown of righteousness, which the Lord, the righteous Judge, will award to me on that day—and not only to me, but also to all who have longed for his appearing." The crown of righteousness is not justification but rather the extent to which the Christian's life has measured up to the righteousness of God. Though not perfect, this will be enhanced by the declaration in heaven of a Christian's perfect righteousness.

James also speaks of the crown of life: "Blessed is the man who perseveres under trial, because when he has stood the test, he will receive the crown of life that God has promised to those who love him" (1:12). This refers not only to eternal life, which every believer possesses, but to life at its fullest, which will be realized in the presence of God.

In 1 Peter 5:4 a crown of glory is mentioned: "And when the Chief Shepherd appears, you will receive the crown of glory that will never fade away." One of the great wonders of our salvation will be that in heaven we will reflect the glory of God—that is, the infinite perfections of his work of redemption for us. Those who have served God well apparently will glorify him even more than others.

John warned against the possibility of losing rewards by failing to live for Christ: "Watch out that you do not lose what you have worked for, but that you may be rewarded fully" (2 John 8).

The crowns believers receive, however, will be cast at the feet of the Savior as seen in the actions of the twenty-four elders of Revelation 4:10: "They lay their crowns before the throne." Though Christians have served God well, all they have done has been made possible only by the grace of God, and to God goes the ultimate glory.

Scripture does not go beyond these descriptions of the crown to describe the rewards for Christians. Undoubtedly, however, the greatest reward will be the privilege of serving Christ. The Scriptures put it simply: "His servants will serve him" (Rev. 22:3). As a Christian has served God in this life, he will be entrusted with a privileged place of service in glory that will give him opportunity to show his love for Christ and his desire to magnify him with his life. Though the ultimate motive for a Christian to serve God should be the constraining love of Christ and the realization of how much Christ loves him, it is a sobering thought that it is possible for a Christian to stand before God saved but with little evidence of service for God in his life. When Paul spoke of the fear of God (2 Cor. 5:11), he dreaded the possibility of standing before God with a wasted life that did not reflect gratitude of heart and love for Christ and that should have been manifested in daily service.

25

The Ten-Nation Confederacy: Rise of the Antichrist

The Middle East in History and Prophecy

The Middle East, which was the cradle of human creation, was also the stage on which the great empires of the past and the great empires of prophecy fulfilled their destiny. Egypt, the first of the great nations, was the cradle of Israel, which grew from a family of seventy to a nation of two to three million before the Exodus. Assyria, the next great empire, with Nineveh as its capital, followed Egypt and was the nation that led the ten tribes of Israel into captivity in 722 B.C.

Nineveh, the capital of Assyria, fell in 612 B.C., and in 605 B.C. Babylon conquered Jerusalem. This began the captivity of Judah and Benjamin, who were led off to Babylon, and eventually Jerusalem was destroyed in 586 B.C.

Babylon, in turn, fell in 539 B.C. and was succeeded by the empire of the Medes and the Persians for approximately two hundred years. During this period some of the pilgrims of Israel went back to the Promised Land and rebuilt the temple by 515

B.C. Later, under Nehemiah, the wall of Jerusalem was built in 444 B.C., and subsequently Jerusalem was rebuilt.

The power of the Medo-Persian Empire, however, was broken by the conquest of Alexander in 334–331 B.C. as Alexander swept through western Asia all the way to India.

Less than a century later the power of Rome began to rise with the conquest of Sicily in 242 B.C., and the rest of the Mediterranean world soon followed. Jerusalem fell in 63 B.C., and by the time Christ was born, all of western Asia, northern Africa, and southern Europe, including a portion of Great Britain, had succumbed to Rome as well.

The course of history, as described in these six great empires, was recorded faithfully in both history and prophecy. History fulfilled predictions concerning Egypt, Assyria, Babylon, Medo-Persia, Greece, and the conquests of the Roman Empire.

The Predicted Revival of the Roman Empire

In contrast to the complete fulfillment of prophecy relating to the first five empires, the Roman Empire has never had the ending predicted in Scripture. That end was connected with the second coming of Christ predicted in Daniel 7:13–14. Daniel recorded:

> "In my vision at night I looked, and there before me was one like a son of man, coming with the clouds of heaven. He approached the Ancient of Days and was led into his presence. He was given authority, glory and sovereign power; all peoples, nations and men of every language worshiped him. His dominion is an everlasting dominion that will not pass away, and his kingdom is one that will never be destroyed."

The fulfillment of the prophecy concerning the Roman Empire is complicated by the fact that the Old Testament, in its prophetic vision, frequently skipped over the whole period between the first and second comings of Christ. Often even the first and second comings of Christ were mentioned in the same sentence, as in Isaiah 61:2, where the expression "to proclaim the year of the LORD's favor" occurs and is immediately followed by "and the day of vengeance of our God." The "year of the LORD's favor" refers to the first coming of Christ, and "the day of vengeance" to his second. When quoting this verse in the synagogue at Nazareth (Luke 4:16–21), Christ stopped in the middle of the verse at the end of the description of his first coming.

Accordingly, prophecy of the Roman Empire, which is fulfilled in part up to the time of Christ, then spans the centuries between and picks up again in the days just before the Second Coming.

In the vision of the Roman Empire in Daniel 7, its terrible destruction is described in verse 7. But the prophecy then goes on to say, " 'It had ten horns.' " While the prophesied destruction of nations by the Roman armies was literally fulfilled, history has never fulfilled what was anticipated by the ten horns. As explained in verse 24, " 'The ten horns are ten kings who will come from this kingdom.' " There has never been a period in the Roman Empire when ten kings have sat simultaneously. Also in 7:8 a ruler is predicted who will uproot three of the ten horns. Verse 24 says, " 'After them another king will arise, different from the earlier ones; he will subdue three kings.' "

According to this prophecy, three of the ten kings will be conquered by this eleventh horn of Daniel 7:8, and subsequently the person represented by this eleventh horn will go on to conquer the entire world (v. 23). The final kingdom is declared to "devour the whole earth, trampling it down and crushing it." The ten-horn stage and the ruler who will conquer three and then all ten of the kingdoms has not yet been fulfilled. Accordingly, along with other passages that indicate that the ultimate form of the Roman Empire will be crushed by the second coming of Christ, these prophecies constitute a prediction of a yet-future rise of the Roman Empire and its ultimate destruction by Christ in his second coming.

The Place of the Ten-Nation Kingdom in the End Time

The prediction that there will be a ten-kingdom stage of the revival of the Roman Empire is one of the important descriptive prophecies of the end time. This prophecy anticipates that there will be ten countries originally related to the Roman Empire that will constitute the Roman Empire in its revived form. The names of these countries are not given, but it can be presumed that Italy, the capital country, would be included, along with major countries in southern Europe and possibly some countries of western Asia and northern Africa which were included in the ancient Roman Empire. Since the names of the countries are not given and there are many more than ten countries in the ancient Roman Empire, it leaves some flexibility in the fulfillment. The prediction, however, requires a political union and then a dictator over the ten countries. With the coming of the Common Market of Europe, now embracing twelve countries, a measure of unity has been achieved in Europe. With the thawing of the Cold War in eastern Europe, the breakdown of Communism, and the unification of East and West Germany, the climate is more favorable now than ever before for the formation of such a ten-nation group. Though the possibility of such a fulfilled prophecy was often scorned in preceding generations, it now becomes a very likely possibility, and even the secular world is predicting some sort of a United States of Europe. From a prophetic standpoint, the importance is that this is a major step in end-time events leading up to the second coming of Christ.

The Predicted Rise of the Antichrist

Though Scripture does not date the formation of this ten-nation political group, and it could conceivably happen even before the rapture of the church, the emergence of the leader who will conquer first three countries and then all ten is an event that necessarily must follow the rapture of the church. Though Scriptures do not give him this title directly, he is commonly known as the Antichrist and as the ultimate fulfillment of antichrist anticipated in the New Testament (1 John 2:18, 22; 4:3; 2 John 7). He is "anti" because he is both against Christ and seeks to replace Christ as he is offered to the world as Satan's substitute for God.

As previously discussed in the doctrine of the Rapture, according to 2 Thessalonians 2, that which is restraining sin, the Holy Spirit indwelling the church, necessarily has to be removed before the man of sin, or the lawless one, other titles of the Antichrist, can appear. As soon as he conquers three of the ten nations and then proceeds to conquer the rest, he can be identified as the predicted one who eventually will become a world ruler. In effect, this places the Rapture first before he can be identified. However, the ten-nation group could be formed prior to his conquering of the three nations without complicating this passage, but their leader would remain unrevealed.

The Importance of the Antichrist

Because the Antichrist will be the principal actor in the end-time events leading up to the second coming of Christ, he will become an important factor in all that is predicted for this period. First, he will bring consolidation to the ten-nation group, which will give him the power to act as the main leader of the Middle East. As will be discussed next, he will then enter into a seven-year covenant with Israel (Dan. 9:27), which will give the time frame for the last seven years leading up to the second coming of Christ. He will also assume power as the world dictator three and a half years before the second coming of Christ, as indicated in Revelation 13:7. As such, he will be the persecutor of both Jews and Christians. He will be conquered by Jesus Christ in his second coming and be cast into the lake of fire (Rev. 19:20).

The Middle East has become prominent in the last few decades because of its dominance in oil, and Israel has emerged as a strong military power. Wars in the Middle East between Israel and her enemies and the war in Iraq have focused world attention on the Middle East. The importance of oil is a major factor in this revival of the Middle East and is in line with prophecies that describe the Middle East as the center of action in the end times. Thus the current world situation is ripe for the fulfillment of precisely what the Bible predicts. The significance of the changing scene in the Middle East and in Europe is that if the Rapture is to precede the formation of a world government under the Antichrist as described above, the Rapture could be very near.

26

Peace in Israel:
The Seven-Year Covenant

In our study of the 490 years of Israel's prophetic future as revealed in Daniel 9:24–27, it was pointed out that the last seven years, when a covenant between the Antichrist and Israel would be entered into, were never fulfilled. As this period immediately precedes the second coming of Christ, it becomes a very important aspect of the prophetic future.

The Last Seven Years before the Second Coming

According to Daniel 9:27, the seven years preceding the second coming of Christ will begin when a covenant is made with Israel by the Antichrist. The details of this covenant are not given, but it presumably will bring to rest the conflict between Israel and her neighbors, a factor that is so prominent in our current world scene. The covenant will be observed for three and a half years and then be broken. Daniel described this future seven years: " 'He will confirm a covenant with many for one "seven." In the middle of the "seven" he will put an end to

317

sacrifice and offering. And he will set up an abomination that causes desolation, on a wing of the temple, until the end that is decreed is poured out on him.'"

As noted in previous study, the reference to the one who makes the covenant goes back to the antecedent "the ruler who will come" (Dan. 9:26). The seven-year period will be divided into two halves. The covenant will be fulfilled during the first half and then will be broken at the beginning of the second half. "The end" described is that of the second coming of Christ.

The Emergence of the Ten-Nation Confederacy

As brought out in chapter 25, prior to this seven-year covenant ten nations will band together in a political union which, from a scriptural point of view, will constitute a revival of the Roman Empire. The ten nations are presented visually in the ten horns of Daniel 7:7 and Revelation 13:1. The ten horns represent ten kings or kingdoms (Dan. 7:24). The emergence of this ten-nation group will necessarily precede the final seven years.

The Emergence of the Man of Sin

As previously pointed out, the man of sin, sometimes referred to as the Antichrist, is described in Scripture as the "little horn" of Daniel 7:8 or as one of the heads of the beast in Revelation 13:3. According to Daniel 7, he will conquer three of the ten kingdoms and eventually rule over the whole world. He is pictured in Revelation 13:7 as ruling over every nation.

When this ruler gains control over ten countries in the revived Roman Empire, he will then be in a position of political power that will enable him to fulfill the prophecy of Daniel 9:26–27 of "the ruler who will come" and will make a seven-year covenant with Israel.

As anticipated in this prophecy, several steps in the fulfillment are indicated: (1) the formation of the ten-nation group; (2) the emergence of the "little horn," or ruler, who will gain control of three of the ten countries; (3) the take-over of all ten countries by the ruler; and (4) the ruler's making a seven-year covenant with Israel.

The Covenant of Peace for Israel

Since Israel was formed as a political entity in 1948 by action of the United Nations, the nation Israel has longed for peace. With military and financial help from the United States, Israel has achieved an unusual independence and military strength and has greatly enlarged the original territories assigned to her. The occupation of these territories, however, has been one of continual turmoil as the Arab world, both in and outside of Israel, is in constant conflict with Israel over her presence in the Middle East. As any observer will soon learn, Israel's ultimate desire is not territory but peace, and Israel has made no attempt to regain the territory promised to Abraham in Genesis 15:18–21. When a Gentile ruler over the ten nations imposes a peace treaty on Israel, it will be from superior strength and will not be a negotiated peace treaty, but it apparently will include the necessary elements for such a contract. It will include the fixing of Israel's borders, the establishment of trade relations with her neighbors—something she does not enjoy at the present time, and, most of all, it will provide protection from outside attacks, which will allow Israel to relax her military preparedness. It can also be anticipated that some attempts will be made to open the holy areas of Jerusalem to all faiths related to it.

Though the particulars of the covenant are not revealed in Scripture, it apparently will bring great relief to Israel as well as to the whole world. The time of peace is anticipated in the prophecies of Ezekiel, which describe Israel as "a peaceful and unsuspecting people" at that time (38:11). In 1 Thessalonians 5:3 the people are quoted as saying, "Peace and safety," before the Great Tribulation overtakes them.

The Covenant Broken

From Daniel 9:27 as well as other passages, we know that the time of peace will come abruptly to an end. The cause of this may very well be the defeat of the Soviet Union as described in Ezekiel 38–39 (see chap. 28 below). It will also coincide with the leader of the ten-nation confederacy proclaiming himself dictator over the whole world and apparently establishing a world empire without achieving it by war. Desecration of the Jewish temple and the stopping of sacrifices will signal the breaking of the covenant. Daniel 9:27 refers to this leader's putting "an end to sacrifice and offering." The same concept is found in Daniel 12:11 where "the daily sacrifice is abolished and the abomination that causes desolation is set up." This follows the historical precedent of Antiochus Epiphanes stopping the sacrifices of Israel, fulfilling the statement that he "will abolish the daily sacrifice" (Dan. 11:31). This, of course, is in keeping with the description of the desecration of the temple described in Revelation 13:14. Christ referred to this event as " 'the abomination that causes desolation,' spoken of through Daniel the prophet' " (Matt. 24:15). Christ said that it would be the signal of the beginning of the Great Tribulation, or the time of unequaled distress for Israel (vv. 21–22). The peace that Israel enjoyed for three and a half years will tragically turn out to be a false peace and the prelude to her unprecedented time of trouble when two out of three Israelites will perish in the land (Zech. 13:8).

Though Israel has a deep longing for peace, it will not be fulfilled until the return of the Messiah, the Prince of Peace who will usher in the millennial kingdom and bring peace to troubled Israel.

27

The World Church:
Babylon Ecclesiastical

Babylon in History

As brought out in the survey of Babylon in the Old Testament
(chap. 12 above), Babylon as a political empire ended in October
539 B.C. when the city of Babylon was overrun by the Medes and
the Persians. However, Babylon as a city and Babylon as a
religion continued. The Medes and the Persians did not look
with favor on Babylonian religion, and the leaders of Babylonian
religion first transferred to Pergamum. Reference was made to
this in Revelation 2:13, where in Pergamum it was declared to
be "where Satan has his throne." Eventually the Babylonian
religion found its way to Rome. There it had influence on the
Christian religion, and traces of Babylonianism can be found in
some of the rituals of the Roman Catholic Church.

Babylon as a political empire was absorbed first by the Medes
and the Persians, then by Greece, and finally by Rome, but it
maintained its corrupting influence throughout history.

The Old Testament abounds with prophecies about Babylon

that have not been fulfilled. These include its ultimate destruction as a religion and as a city. While the final world empire is a Roman empire, in many respects it continues the evil character of the Babylonian Empire.

Revelation 17 and 18 present a prophetic picture of Babylon in the future. Scholars have debated the significance of these two chapters. Probably the simplest and most effective approach is to regard chapter 17 as a prophecy of the ultimate end of Babylon as a religion and chapter 18 as the end of Babylon as a city. However, the woman (religion) and the city are intertwined in their significance in these two chapters.

The Woman and the Beast

John was invited to consider in vision "the punishment of the great prostitute, who sits on many waters" (Rev. 17:1). The woman is described as committing adultery with the kings of the earth (v. 2). John saw her seated "on a scarlet beast that was covered with blasphemous names and had seven heads and ten horns" (v. 3). Though seen symbolically here, the beast obviously is the same entity as was described in Revelation 13:1 and represents the political power of the ten-nation kingdom that will be in power in the first half of the seven years preceding the Second Coming. Revelation 17 is not in chronological order of the events in the book of Revelation but is presented here in the order of its revelation to John. Chronologically, it probably can be placed between Revelation 5 and 6. The fact that the woman is seated on the beast connotes first that the beast is supporting the woman and, second, that the woman is cooperating with the beast to gain control of the world.

The woman is further described as "dressed in purple and scarlet, and . . . glittering with gold, precious stones and pearls" (Rev. 17:4). Purple and scarlet, gold, precious stones, and pearls are familiar symbols of ritual religion. It is for this reason, then, and because of other facts given about the woman in this passage, that the Protestant Reformers identified the woman with the Roman Catholic Church, which they considered apostate.

The Woman and the World Church Movement

In the twentieth century further light has been cast on Revelation 17 by the rise of the world church movement. Prior to the twentieth century the professing church was divided into three major divisions, the Roman Catholic Church, the Greek Orthodox Church, and Protestant churches. Division rather than unification seemed to be characteristic, particularly of the Protestant churches, as hundreds of denominations were formed as well as thousands of independent churches.

In the twentieth century, however, a movement arose to unite churches into one great organization. The leaders of this movement contemplated that the time would come when the Greek Orthodox, Roman Catholic, and Protestant churches would all unite in a great world church with the governing power in a hierarchy controlling the entire church.

The world church movement began with a series of preliminary meetings in 1925 and 1927. In 1938 a temporary ecumenical world church was formed. Further progress was interrupted by World War II, but in 1948 the World Council of Churches was formally organized in a meeting in Amsterdam. The goal of this world church was to unite all Christendom into one great church.

Because of the lack of interest and opposition of evangelical churches, the world church movement has not continued to expand. To some extent it has cooperated with liberal elements both in the church and in the political world, but the existence of this organization may well be the foundation for what is described in Revelation 17.

The world church movement is ill-conceived, as the Bible does not require a world church organization apart from the body of Christ. Undoubtedly some Christians have embraced its approach to church government. When the rapture of the church occurs, however, every true Christian will be instantly removed, and those who are left will be professing Christians without the reality of saving faith. In this circumstance it is easy to see how the world church movement can become completely apostate, as described in Revelation 17. The fulfillment, accordingly, will not be specifically by the Roman Catholic Church but rather by the union of the three major branches of the church that exist in the world today, but without the sanctifying presence of genuine Christians. As such, the world church movement will be not only apostate in its theology but abominable in its religious practices.

The Wickedness of the World Church

Scripture does not hide the awfulness of the departure from the faith that characterizes this world church movement. The woman is described by John:

> "She held a golden cup in her hand, filled with abominable things and the filth of her adulteries. This title was written on her forehead:
>
> MYSTERY
> BABYLON THE GREAT
> THE MOTHER OF PROSTITUTES
> AND OF THE ABOMINATIONS OF THE EARTH.
>
> I saw that the woman was drunk with the blood of the saints, the blood of those who bore testimony to Jesus." (Rev. 17:4–6)

Prostitution was often a part of pagan worship, but the adultery mentioned here refers to spiritual adultery rather than physical adultery. The woman is guilty of compromise and association with apostate religions. She is the ultimate expression of the Babylonian false religions that were often rejected, even by the pagan world. Further, she is declared to be guilty of killing those who do come to Christ in that time, and she is described as "drunk with the blood of the saints" (Rev. 17:6).

The Beast With Ten Horns and Seven Heads

Attention is now drawn to the beast that supports the woman: " 'The beast, which you saw, once was, now is not, and will come up out of the Abyss and go to his destruction' " (Rev. 17:8).

In the book of Revelation several different "beasts" can be identified. Satan is described as a dragon, a powerful beast that ascends out of the abyss which is the home of the demon world (Rev. 12:7–17; 13:1–4, 11; 16:13; 20:2). Another beast is mentioned in Revelation 13:3, the beast that has a fatal wound but is healed. This beast is the world ruler, a man whom Satan dominates and who is actually a man, not a demon. Because both the world ruler and his world empire are dominated by Satan, the world government also is referred to as a beast. Accordingly, the beast is Satan, the world ruler, and the world government. The reference to the beast as that which once was and then did not exist, and then comes up again, as in verses 8 and 11, seems to refer to the world empire, the Roman Empire, which existed in the time of the apostles, seems to have gone out of existence, but is going to rise again and fulfill its role as a beast, or as a world government. "Then I saw another beast, coming out of the earth" (13:11), is the False Prophet (16:13; 19:20; 20:10), an associate of the world ruler.

Attention is then drawn to the seven heads of the beast (Rev. 17:9–11). The understanding of this is declared to be "for a mind with wisdom" (v. 9). The seven heads are declared to be "seven hills on which the woman sits" (v. 9). Because the city of Rome was often considered a city of seven hills, many have considered this as evidence that the woman is basically the Roman Catholic Church and the religion, of course, will be that of the period of the Roman Empire revived. Seven hills are often identified as the city of Rome situated on the Tiber River. The hills are named as Palatine, Aventine, Caelian, Esquiline, Viminal, Quirnal, and Capitoline. Actually, as the city of Rome spread, other hills were added, including a hill known as the Janicylum and the hill Pincian. Because of the reference to the seven hills, the ecclesiastical power here has often been identified with Rome geographically rather than with Babylon.

The passage continues, however, to state that there are seven kings. The angel said to John, "They are also seven kings" (Rev. 17:10). These are indicated as referring to five kings who have already fallen, one who is currently in power, and one who is yet to come. Some scholars believe the seven hills, the seven kings, and the seven heads all refer to the same thing. These seven kings, however, will be followed by an eighth king (v. 11), which, as has been explained, refers to the world government.

If the seven hills are actually seven kings, then the identification with Rome is no longer a proper explanation, and it opens the question as to where the ecclesiastical capital of the world will be in the end time.

The identification of the seven kings is not given, and several suggestions have been put forward as explaining their identity. Some believe that they are seven kings who relate to the Roman Empire—that is, some of the more prominent rulers. When John wrote the book of Revelation, the sixth of the kings was on the throne, but the final one, the seventh, had not yet come because this refers to the ruler of the world empire in the end time.

Another suggestion has been that these seven kings refer to the seven world empires of biblical revelation. These include

Egypt, Assyria, Babylon, Medo-Persia, Greece, and Rome. The revived Roman Empire, then, is regarded as the seventh of these kingdoms. Regardless of how the kings are interpreted, it is evident that God is revealing the identity of the world ruler, described in Revelation 13 and here identified as the seventh king.

If the city of Rome is not intended by the reference to the seven hills, the question remains as to where the world empire of the end time will have its capital. Here the suggestion has been offered that Babylon will be rebuilt and will constitute the world capital city during the Great Tribulation. Because Babylon is clearly identified with the Roman Empire of the last days and is specifically described as a city in Revelation 18, there are some scriptural grounds for this. Inasmuch as the city of Babylon has not been destroyed historically in keeping with the prophecies of its sudden and catastrophic destruction, if the future world empire were to have Babylon as its capital, its destruction prior to the second coming of Christ would then provide a literal fulfillment of the many prophecies in the Old and New Testament relative to the destruction of Babylon.

In addition to attention to the seven heads of the beast, John is reminded again that the beast has ten horns. These are said in Revelation 17:12 to be ten kings who will be associated with the world ruler and will be supportive of his power. The angel said to John, "They have one purpose and will give their power and authority to the beast" (v. 13). Because these ten kings will form the nucleus of political power behind the world ruler, they are declared to be the force that opposes the army from heaven in Revelation 19. As stated in 17:14, " 'They will make war against the Lamb, but the Lamb will overcome them because he is Lord of lords and King of kings—and with him will be his called, chosen and faithful followers.' "

The reference to "many waters" (Rev. 17:1) is now defined as representing the multitude of peoples: " 'The waters you saw, where the prostitute sits, are peoples, multitudes, nations and languages' " (v. 15). The world religion described by the harlot will encompass the entire earth.

The Woman Destroyed

The most amazing aspect of Revelation 17 is the description of the destructionof the woman: " 'The beast and the ten horns you saw will hate the prostitute. They will bring her to ruin and leave her naked; they will eat her flesh and burn her with fire. For God has put it into their hearts to accomplish his purpose by agreeing to give the beast their power to rule, until God's words are fulfilled'" (vv. 16–17).

In the earlier verses of Revelation 17, the woman is described as conniving with the beast to gain world domination. Apparently this will continue throughout the first three and a half years of the seven years preceding Christ's second coming.

At the midpoint of those seven years, however, a dramatic change will take place when the ruler of the ten kingdoms proclaims himself a world dictator and overnight becomes ruler of the entire earth. In this changed situation he no longer needs the woman, and for this reason the ten kings associated with him destroy her, putting her out of commission. Their purpose, as stated in Revelation 17:17, is to relegate all power to the beast. This also opens up the way for the final form of world religion, which is the worship of the world ruler himself and of Satan who is associated with him. He will set himself up as God. Revelation 17 as a whole describes the religious character of the first half of the seven years preceding the Second Coming and is the ultimate fulfillment of the world church movement.

The closing verse of Revelation 17 declares, "'The woman you saw is the great city that rules over the kings of the earth'" (v. 18). Though the woman here is described as a city, it obviously is religious rather than political in its significance. The city of Babylon, however, in its political form, occupies Revelation 18. With Babylon religiously put out of the way in the destruction of the world church, the stage is now set for the final drama, the last three and a half years when the final form of apostate religion will be atheism and the worship of the world ruler.

28

Russia's Last Bid for World Conquest

Background

In the twentieth century the rise and fall of Russia, the largest and most significant state in the Soviet Union, has been a major factor in world history. Though some of the Soviet states may secede over a period of time, the dominant Russian state will survive and occupy the center of the stage. For the purpose of prophecy, Russia will be the designation for the great Soviet power to the north of Israel.

The dramatic prophetic picture of Russia's last bid for world conquest, as recorded in Ezekiel 38:1–39:24, is set in a context of prophecies that relate to Israel's restoration. In Ezekiel 37:1–28 Israel's restoration as a nation and her resurrection from the dead at the time of the Second Coming are described in the symbolism of the valley of dry bones being brought back to life. After the description of Russia's war in Ezekiel 38:1–39:24, a further prophecy is made concerning Israel's regathering to her land as a phase of her restoration. Accordingly, the conflict with Russia is seen in this end-time situation.

Politically the rapid events of the end time form a background to this war. In the end time ten nations will band together under a Roman ruler to form a revived Roman Empire. This ruler will enter into a seven-year peace covenant with Israel as described in Daniel 9:27. Sometime during these seven years that precede the Second Coming, Russia will attack Israel.

The last seven years will be divided into two halves—the first half a time of peace and the second half a time of great tribulation culminating in Armageddon. As prophesied in Ezekiel 38 Russia will attack Israel in a time of peace in an attempt to conquer Israel and establish a dominant position in the Middle East.

Although Israel has military superiority over the countries immediately surrounding her, the possibility of a Russian attack has long been her fear. Russia may be fading as a world power, but it is still a formidable force that could overrun a small nation such as Israel if it engaged in a surprise attack such as Ezekiel describes. A careful study of this chapter will reveal much concerning the end-time events that lead up to the second coming of Christ.

The Invaders

Ezekiel recorded that the main force of the military invasion of Israel will come from the land of Magog:

> The word of the LORD came to me: "Son of man, set your face against Gog, of the land of Magog, the chief prince of Meshech and Tubal; prophesy against him and say: 'This is what the Sovereign LORD says: I am against you, O Gog, chief prince of Meshech and Tubal. I will turn you around, put hooks in your jaws and bring you out with your whole army—your horses, your horsemen fully armed, and a great horde with large and small shields, all of them brandishing their swords.'" (38:1–4)

The names Russia and Soviet Union do not ever appear in Scripture, but this description of the invader clearly fits Russia. The military invasion is described as led by "Gog," referring to the leader and "the land of Magog," referring to the territory from which he will come. Magog is referred to as one of the sons of Japheth in Genesis 10:2 and in 1 Chronicles 1:5. Two references occur in Ezekiel 38:2, 6, and a final reference is made in Revelation 20:8. Gog as the ruler is described as "the chief prince of Meshech and Tubal" (Ezek. 38:2). The expression "chief prince" is translated in the NASB as "prince of Rosh." As *Rosh* is the root of the modern word *Russia,* there seems to be some connection to this land north of Israel. Gog is also related to "Meshech" and "Tubal" (v. 2), but some have found this to be a variation in the spelling of Moscow. Tubal is similar to Tobolsk, an area in the Ural section of Russia. Though the identification is not entirely certain, Tubal seems to relate to the ancient Scythians who immigrated to the north out of the Middle East and ended in the area described as Russia today.

The invading force from Russia is aided by armies from five other countries. Persia (Ezek. 38:5) is rather easily identified as modern Iran, which, though located to the east of Israel, could very easily join with Russia in the attack from the north. The identification of Cush (v. 5) is not entirely clear but is normally related to people who lived in an area between Egypt and the Red Sea. Though located geographically to the south of Israel, it would not be too difficult for such an army to be transported by water to join Russia in this attack. Put (v. 5) is usually identified with the people south of Cush but is another force that could be brought around to join Russia's attack from the north. Gomer (v. 6) is often identified with the ancient Cimmerians who at one time lived in Asia Minor and eastern Europe. Beth Togarmah (v. 6) was a nation located immediately to the north of Israel and would be in a position to join in the invasion.

Any invasion of Israel shows disregard for the God of Israel and fits the atheistic background of Russia in the twentieth century. The geographic background of the army, the theological point of view of the invaders, and the terms that are used to describe them provide evidence that the army is from Russia and will actually invade the land of Israel from the north. Confirming this is the information that the invader will come from the "far north" of Israel (Ezek. 38:6, 15; 39:2). As Israel is only a few hundred miles from Russia, the description of a nation to the far north of Israel could not possibly refer to any other nation than Russia. When one considers that Russia is some six thousand miles wide from east to west, any reference to a nation to the north of Israel would have to be Russia. It is also interesting that Moscow is directly north of Jerusalem.

The Ancient Weapons of Warfare

Though the description of the invader is relatively easy to understand and identify, the problem in interpreting this passage lies in the fact that the writer describes the use of ancient weapons. This is brought out in the introductory statement:

> " 'I will turn you around, put hooks in your jaws and bring you out with your whole army—your horses, your horsemen fully armed and a great horde with large and small shields, all of them brandishing their swords. Persia, Cush and Put will be with them, all with shields and helmets, also Gomer with all its troops, and Beth Togarmah from the far north with all its troops—the many nations with you.' " (Ezek. 38:4–6)

The fact that the army would be equipped with these ancient weapons of warfare instead of modern weapons has moved many to consider the description here in a nonliteral sense. Instead of tanks, they come on horses, which, in the case of Russia, is not too difficult, as Russia still uses mounted troops as a part of their military operation. The shields, swords, and helmets, however, do not fit a modern army.

Some have attempted to explain this terminology by saying that Ezekiel described the war in terms he understood and that we have to substitute modern arms. As the account unfolds, additional weapons of bows and arrows, war clubs, and spears are also mentioned (Ezek. 39:9). The fact that later on these weapons are regarded as providing fuel for fire (v. 9) makes it difficult to imagine them as merely figures of speech that could not be used for fuel, and most modern weapons are made of metal rather than wood. The final answer may not lie in trying to explain this portion of the narrative, but it does indicate that preceding this war there will be a genuine disarmament of the world. Under such circumstances, if Russia wanted to attack Israel and lacked modern weapons, she would be able to manufacture quickly and in great quantity weapons that would equip the army in this way. The main force of the passage, however, is not changed by resolving the nature of the weapons.

Israel Described as a Peaceful and Unsuspecting Nation

In the attempt to determine the time of this war in the prophetic sequence, it is important to note the emphasis upon Israel living in peace at the time of the invasion. Apparently the attack is not expected, and Israel is not prepared militarily to oppose the invaders. There is no mention anywhere of an army standing up against the invaders.

Instead, Israel is described as a nation at peace:

> " 'Get ready; be prepared, you and all the hordes gathered about you, and take command of them. After many days you will be called to arms. In future years you will invade a land that has recovered from war, whose people were gathered from many nations to the mountains of Israel, which had long been desolate. They had been brought out from the nations, and now all of them live in safety. You and all your troops and the many nations with you will go up, advancing like a storm; you will be like a cloud covering the land.' " (Ezek. 38:7–9)

The invaders are urged to attack Israel, but the land of Israel is described as a territory "recovered from war," and the people of Israel are described as those who "were gathered from many nations to the mountains of Israel, which had long been desolate." Israel is further described as a people who have been "brought out from the nations, and now all of them live in safety" (Ezek. 38:8). As pointed out previously, this would fit naturally into the prophetic picture of the first half of the last seven years leading up to the second coming of Christ, which will be a period of peace when Israel is in covenant relationship with the ruler of the ten nations.

The concept that Israel is at peace is further described as entering into the scheming of the invaders.

> " 'This is what the Sovereign LORD says: On that day thoughts will come into your mind and you will devise an evil scheme. You will say, "I will invade a land of unwalled villages; I will attack a peaceful and unsuspecting people— all of them living without walls and without gates and bars. I will plunder and loot and turn my hand against the resettled ruins and the people gathered from the nations, rich in livestock and goods, living at the center of the land.' " (Ezek. 38:10–12)

The cities of Israel are described as unwalled, which corresponds to the modern situation when walls no longer keep out invaders (v. 11). They are also described as "a peaceful and unsuspecting people—all of them living without walls and without gates and bars" (v. 11). Their settling in the land of Israel is described as "the resettled ruins" and the people are said to have been "gathered from the nations" (v. 12). All of this fits naturally into the situation where Israel is in supposed security under the peace treaty with the ruler of the ten nations. It becomes clear as this is compared to the political situation of the time that the attack is not only on Israel but on the whole ten-nation group that controls the Middle East at this time, supporting the concept that this is Russia's last desperate attempt to conquer the world. In subsequent description of Israel, they are described as "[God's] people Israel . . . living in safety" (v. 14).

The Purpose of the Invaders

The passage describing this future war makes it clear that the invaders are seeking material gain. They are said to have decided, "I will plunder and loot and turn my hand against the resettled ruins and the people gathered from the nations, rich in livestock and goods, living at the center of the land" (Ezek. 38:12). In verse 13 they are described as carrying off loot, silver and gold, livestock, and goods. The overwhelming numerical superiority of the invading army is described as "advancing like a storm; you will be like a cloud covering the land" (v. 9). The army is described as coming from "many nations." It will be "a great horde, a mighty army" (v. 15). In contrast to the purpose of the invaders for material gain, God is drawing them into this war: " 'You will advance against my people Israel like a cloud that covers the land. In days to come, O Gog, I will bring you against my land, so that the nations may know me when I show myself holy through you before their eyes' " (v. 16).

The Invasion Described

The prophet describes graphically what will happen when this mighty army invades the land of Israel:

> " 'This is what will happen in that day: When Gog attacks the land of Israel, my hot anger will be aroused, declares the

Sovereign LORD. In my zeal and fiery wrath I declare that at that time there shall be a great earthquake in the land of Israel. The fish of the sea, the birds of the air, the beasts of the field, every creature that moves along the ground, and all the people on the face of the earth will tremble at my presence. The mountains will be overturned, the cliffs will crumble and every wall will fall to the ground. I will summon a sword against Gog on all my mountains, declares the Sovereign LORD. Every man's sword will be against his brother. I will execute judgment upon him with plague and bloodshed; I will pour down torrents of rain, hailstones and burning sulfur on him and on his troops and on the many nations with him.' " (Ezek. 38:18–22)

As this prophecy makes clear, the invasion will arouse "[the] hot anger" of God (Ezek. 38:18), and a series of disasters will take place.

First, there will be a great earthquake in the land (Ezek. 38:19). This earthquake will affect fish, birds, beasts, and all creatures on the ground. Mountains will be overturned, and walls of buildings will fall (v. 20).

The next great judgment of God will introduce confusion in the multinational army so that they will begin fighting each other: "Every man's sword will be against his brother" (Ezek. 38:21). In the confusion brought on by the earthquake, it is easy to understand how the troops could begin fighting each other.

A third judgment is brought on the army in the form of plague and bloodshed. God will use a plague to attack the enemies of Israel, an approach that has also been used in other situations (cf. Isa. 37:36). On top of these problems will come the outpoured judgment of God in the form of floods, hailstones, and burning sulfur (Ezek. 38:22). Though viewed as natural deterrents to the army, there is a supernatural work of God in causing them to occur at this time. As illustrated in Revelation 16:21, the hailstones, unusually large, can be fatal to human life. The reference to burning sulfur is a reminder of the fall of Sodom and Gomorrah (Gen. 19:24). Some have interpreted the burning sulfur as being caused by the earthquake loosing dormant volcanoes to spew out their hot rock. Regardless of how it is explained, the result is obvious. The invading army will be destroyed. God will use this as a means of demonstrating his power to the nations, "And so I will show my greatness and my holiness, and I will make myself known in the sight of many nations. Then they will know that I am the LORD" (Ezek. 38:23).

The Destruction of the Invaders

The prophecy continues, describing the complete destruction of the invading armies: " 'Then I will strike your bow from your left hand and make your arrows drop from your right hand. On the mountains of Israel you will fall, you and all your troops and the nations with you. I will give you as food to all kinds of carrion birds and to the wild animals. You will fall in the open field, for I have spoken, declares the Sovereign LORD" (Ezek. 39:3–5). In the afflictions that God will pour out on the invading army, they will drop their bows and arrows, and their dead bodies will be food for the vultures and wild animals. Though in the King James Version Ezekiel 39:2 is translated, "And I will turn thee back, and leave but the sixth part of thee," it is clear from the context that this is not an accurate translation of a difficult expression in the Hebrew. The New International Version reads, " 'I will turn you around and drag you along.' " In verse 4 it is clear that the entire army will be wiped out and none will survive: " 'On the mountains of Israel you will fall, you and all your troops and the nations with you.' "

The Aftermath of the Battle

After restating that God's purpose is to declare the power of his holy name (Ezek. 39:7–8), the debris of the battle is declared to be fuel sufficient for seven years of burning:

> " 'Then those who live in the towns of Israel will go out and use the weapons for fuel and burn them up—the small and large shields, the bows and arrows, the war clubs and spears. For seven years they will use them for fuel. They will not need to gather wood from the fields or cut it from the forests, because they will use the weapons for fuel. And they will plunder those who plundered them and loot those who looted them, declares the Sovereign LORD.' " (vv. 9–10)

The information that the fuel will last for seven years raises questions as to how this will relate to the second coming of Christ as there seems to be some evidence that this attack will occur toward the end of the first three and a half years of the seven years preceding the Second Coming. This would not leave sufficient time for the fuel to be consumed before the Second Coming. However, the burning of fuel does not in itself constitute a prophetic time table, and even after the second coming of Christ, life will go on and fuel will be necessary. Accordingly, this does not interfere with placing the invasion toward the end of the first three and a half years.

Prophecy describes graphically how the dead will be buried (Ezek. 39:11–16). It will take seven months to bury the dead, and after that, additional dead bodies will be found that will require burying. The scene is similar to that which occurs at the second coming of Christ when the vultures are invited to feed on the dead bodies (vv. 17–20). The scene is different from that described in Revelation 20:7–9 when the earth is destroyed immediately after the war described.

The Purpose of God in the Destruction of the Invaders

Ezekiel quoted God as illustrating in the destruction of the invading army his opposition to wickedness and his purpose to restore Israel:

> I will display my glory among the nations, and all the nations will see the punishment I inflict and the hand I lay upon them. From that day forward the house of Israel will know that I am the LORD their God. And the nations will know that the people of Israel went into exile for their sin, because they were unfaithful to me. So I hid my face from them and handed them over to their enemies, and they all fell by the sword. I dealt with them according to their uncleanness and their offenses, and I hid my face from them. (39:21–24)

The Regathering of Israel

Ezekiel went on to describe how God would restore Israel:

> Therefore this is what the Sovereign LORD says: I will now bring Jacob back from captivity and will have compassion on all the people of Israel, and I will be zealous for my holy name. They will forget their shame and all the unfaithfulness they showed toward me when they lived in safety in their land with no one to make them afraid. When I have brought them back from the nations and have gathered them

from the countries of their enemies, I will show myself holy through them in the sight of many nations. Then they will know that I am the LORD their God, for though I sent them into exile among the nations, I will gather them to their own land, not leaving any behind. I will no longer hide my face from them, for I will pour out my Spirit on the house of Israel, declares the Sovereign LORD. (39:25–29)

This apparently will be fulfilled at the Second Coming.

Though some details of this prophetic account are necessarily not entirely clear, the result of the battle is clear enough. Russia's last bid for world domination will fail completely, her armies will be destroyed, and even her homeland will experience fire sent upon it from heaven (Ezek. 39:6). The final form of Gentile power will follow as the ten-nation group becomes a world government. The destruction of Russia as an obstacle to this and undoubtedly an enemy of the ten-nation group may explain how overnight the dictator of the ten-nation group can proclaim himself ruler of the entire world without opposition. This war may very well be the springboard on which the Middle East ruler is vaulted to power to fulfill the last three and a half tragic years preceding the second coming of Christ when Israel will go through a terrible time of trouble, and the world as a whole will be largely destroyed. Inasmuch as this prophecy has never had any fulfillment in the past, its fulfillment in the future is a grim reminder that God is still on the throne and that the enemies of God will be dealt with in God's time and in God's way.

29

The Coming World Government: Final World Religions

Satan's Imitation of the Millennial Kingdom

In the revelation concerning Satan's fall from his original holiness in eternity past as discussed earlier in Isa. 14:13–16, we find that his ambition was to be exalted like God. It is Satan's purpose not only to take the place of God in worship and obedience but also to establish a worldwide kingdom in competition to the prophetic program of the millennial kingdom in which Christ will reign supreme. Accordingly, in the end time prior to the second coming of Christ, Satan will achieve his purpose of having a world government that will be empowered by him and will produce almost universal worship of himself. As such, the final world government preceding the Second Coming will be Satan's final attempt to supplant Christ and replace him with the worship and service of Satan himself.

The Coming World Government As Revealed to Daniel

As previously pointed out, in Daniel's vision of the four great world empires, beginning with Babylon and following with Medo-Persia, Greece, and Rome, the Roman Empire is described as being destroyed by the second coming of Christ (7:11).

In explanation of the meaning of the image, and particularly of the fourth beast that represents Rome, the angel told Daniel, "The fourth beast is a fourth kingdom that will appear on earth. It will be different from all the other kingdoms and will devour the whole earth, trampling it down and crushing it" (7:23). The Roman Empire conquered much of the world surrounding the Mediterranean, including Northern Africa, Western Asia, and Northern Europe, but it never encompassed the entire globe. Here the prediction is that the Roman Empire in its revived form prior to the second coming of Christ "will devour the whole earth" (v. 23). This will fulfill Satan's ambition to have a kingdom that is comparable to the world government of Christ. The possibility of such a world government has intrigued contemporary historians, especially as they have taken into consideration Germany's two attempts to conquer the world in World War I and World War II.

The Identity of the World Ruler

Much speculation has arisen concerning the identity of the world ruler described in Daniel 7:8 as the "little horn." From Daniel's vision it is clear that this man will gain control first of three and then of all ten countries that form the nucleus of the revived Roman Empire. Additional clues are given concerning this ruler in 9:26, where he is identified as belonging to the people who will destroy Jerusalem. As the Roman armies destroyed Jerusalem in A.D. 70, the future ruler is identified as a Roman ruler though his race and political background are not indicated. This is one of the reasons why Bible scholars believe that the Roman Empire will be revived in ten-nation form and will eventually become a world government.

Daniel 11 gives further information about this ruler who will dominate the end time:

> "The king will do as he pleases. He will exalt and magnify himself above every god and will say unheard-of things

against the God of gods. He will be successful until the time of wrath is completed, for what has been determined must take place. He will show no regard for the gods of his fathers or for the one desired by women, nor will he regard any god, but will exalt himself above them all. Instead of them, he will honor a god of fortresses; a god unknown to his fathers he will honor with gold and silver, with precious stones and costly gifts." (vv. 36–38)

Though biblical scholars have not all agreed as to the identity of this king, inasmuch as he is described as one who is above all, including every god, it seems clear that this passage refers to the future world ruler, for no one else could be said to exalt himself above everything.

Further, this ruler will take the position of being above God— that is, he will be an atheist. This is brought out in Daniel 11:37, where he disregards the gods of his fathers. Though this has sometimes been taken as a reference to the God of Israel, the word *gods* is *Elohim*, which is the common name for God, not the particular name *Yahweh*, which is the God of Israel. Accordingly, it seems clear that he will be a Gentile, but whatever deities his forefathers worshiped he will push aside as unworthy of worship and belief. He will also declare that he disregards "the one desired by women" (v. 37). This has been subject to various explanations, but it probably refers to the hope of women to be the mother of the Messiah. In other words, he will not only disregard all the pagan gods of his fathers but also the biblical hope of the Messiah, Jesus Christ. In place of his worship of deity and his recognition of the Messiah, he will honor "a god of fortresses" (v. 38), that is, a personification of the power to make war. His wealth will therefore be spent on military power.

This ruler is pictured as engaging in the final great world war in Daniel 11:40–44, which includes the war at Armageddon in Revelation 16:14–16. As described by Daniel, there will be a surging battle in the Holy Land with armies from the north and south and a great army from the east. The war will be underway right up to the point of the second coming of Christ. In fact, there will be house-to-house fighting in Jerusalem on the very day of the Lord's return (Zech. 14:1–2).

This same individual is described in 2 Thessalonians 2:3 as "the man of lawlessness," and verse 4 declares that "He will oppose and will exalt himself over everything that is called God or is worshiped, so that he sets himself up in God's temple, proclaiming himself to be God." Orthodox Jews will renew their ancient sacrificial worship in the rebuilt temple during the first three and a half years of the seven years preceding the Second Coming. After this period the ruler will desecrate their temple and establish himself and Satan as the objects of worship.

Christ, in his Olivet Discourse, described the desecration of the temple as the beginning of the Great Tribulation, a time of unprecedented trouble leading up to the second coming of Christ: "So when you see standing in the holy place 'the abomination that causes desolation,' spoken of through the prophet Daniel—let the reader understand—then let those who are in Judea flee to the mountains" (Matt. 24:15–16). The desecration of the temple and the assumption of the position of God by the future world ruler will signal the last three and a half years of Great Tribulation leading up to the second coming of Christ. The worship of the world ruler will, of course, be a part of the worship of Satan that will characterize the end time as brought out clearly in the book of Revelation.

The Coming World Ruler in the Book of Revelation

The future world ruler is introduced in Revelation 6:2 in these words: "I looked, and there before me was a white horse! Its rider held a bow, and he was given a crown, and he rode out as a conqueror bent on conquest." Probably as a result of the outcome of the defeat of Russia in Ezekiel 38 and 39, the ruler of the ten-nation confederacy will find himself in a position where he can proclaim himself dictator over the whole world, and apparently no one will be strong enough to contend against him. Without a fight on his part, he will therefore rule the world as Satan's tool.

In the twentieth century, for the first time in history a world empire became a possibility. A world government would require immediate communication such as radio, telephone, and television. This is now an accomplished fact. A world government would also require rapid transportation, which today is provided by planes. Control of business and finance contemplated in the world government (Rev. 13:16–17) would be provided by giant computers, already a feature of everyday life. The world ruler would also have missile warfare as a means of controlling the world. Modern inventions have reduced the size of our world to where a world government is now mechanically possible.

In one of the parenthetic passages in the book of Revelation, chapter 13, attention is directed to this world government. In his vision John saw a dragon coming up out of the sea (v. 1), and he described the world government in these words: "And I saw a beast coming out of the sea. He had ten horns and seven heads, with ten crowns on his horns, and on each head a blasphemous name" (v. 1). This beast represents the world government as well as its leader. The fact that it comes out of the sea is usually interpreted as coming out of the sea of humanity, or the world as a whole. The harlot of Revelation 17, representing apostate Christendom in the first half of the last seven years, is also pictured as seated on waters that are defined as peoples, multitudes, nations, and languages (v. 15). The sea from which the beast comes is in contrast to the land where the second beast of Revelation 13:11 originates. The existence of ten horns and seven heads corresponds to the ten-horned beast of Daniel 7:7, which describes the revived Roman Empire over which the world ruler will preside. As has been brought out in previous discussion of this world empire, the seven heads are taken by many to represent prominent leaders of the Roman Empire in history, with the seventh head representing the final world ruler. The seven heads in Revelation 17:9 refer to five in the past, the sixth being present when John wrote the book of Revelation. The seventh is the ruler of the ten nations, and the eighth king represents the final form of world government in which the seventh head becomes the head of the empire that is the eighth sphere of rule.

Another explanation describes the seven heads, referring back to the seven major world empires of the Bible—Egypt, Assyria, Babylon, Medo-Persia, Greece, Rome, and the millennial kingdom from heaven (Dan. 7:13–16)—with the eighth king representing the final form of the revived Roman Empire. This view has some obvious problems of interpretation. Regardless of how the heads are described, the picture here is of the ultimate world government.

The world government is said to embrace the characteristics of the Babylonian, Medo-Persian, and Grecian Empires, symbolized by the lion representing Babylon, the bear representing Medo-Persia, and the leopard representing Greece. John said in

Revelation 13:2, "The beast I saw resembled a leopard, but had feet like those of a bear and a mouth like that of a lion."

The power behind the world government is that of the dragon, or Satan. Revelation 13:2 says, "The dragon gave the beast his power and his throne and great authority." The identification of the dragon was also given in Revelation 12:9 where the dragon was identified as the devil, or Satan.

One of his heads will seem to be fatally wounded, a reference to a wound of the seventh head, or ruler of the ten kingdoms. While there are several explanations, probably the best is that he will receive a wound that would normally be fatal but will be supernaturally healed by Satan. The passage does not require nor does it state that he will actually die and be resurrected by Satan, for it is not in the power of Satan to resurrect.

The point is that the ruler of the final world empire will come on the scene with supernatural power, and for this reason the statement is made, "Men worshiped the dragon because he had given authority to the beast, and they also worshiped the beast and asked, 'Who is like the beast? Who can make war against him?'" (Rev. 13:4).

The duration of the rule of the Beast is declared to be forty-two months in Revelation 13:5, which is in keeping with the three and a half years indicated in Daniel 9:27 and the 1,260 days mentioned in Revelation 11:3. Because he will be an atheist and will be under the power of Satan, he will blaspheme God (Rev. 13:6). He will be able to persecute the saints and to martyr countless numbers of them (v. 7). His world rule is described in unmistakable language: "And he was given authority over every tribe, people, language and nation" (v. 7). In addition to his absolute political power, he will be worshiped as God: "All inhabitants of the earth will worship the beast—all whose names have not been written in the book of life belonging to the Lamb that was slain from the creation of the world" (v. 8). The world ruler will have an associate who is described as the "beast coming out of the earth" (v. 11). This associate will be able to do miraculous things, including causing fire to come down from heaven (v. 13), and he will set up an image of the Beast that will have breath (v. 15). It is not clear whether this will be supernatural or natural. In any case, the image is not actually alive.

The world ruler will require all to worship him in order to buy or sell (Rev. 13:16). The so-called mark of the Beast, which will mark his worshipers, will be a token of the immense power and worldwide authority of the Beast. The number of the Beast is declared to be "666" (v. 18) and has been subject to numerous explanations, but probably the best is that it refers to him as a man because the number 6 is less than the perfect number 7. In spite of his satanic power and supernatural ability, he will be only a man and will be subject to God's judgment (Rev. 19).

Throughout the history of interpretation, attempts have been made to identify the 666 with some ruler of the past. Building on the idea of the "fatal wound" described as "healed" (Rev. 13:3), some attempt to make a case for the final world ruler being a person resurrected from the past. To identify him, interpreters have resorted to the numerical equivalents of the names involved. As letters represent numbers in some languages, searches have been made to find a name in which the numbers add up to 666. Jewish scholars in the Old Testament attempted to find numerical significance to Scripture. Most familiar today are Latin numbers. In Latin, for instance, a C is 100, X is 10, V is 5, etc. Some schemes also build on an arbitrary number evaluation, such as A equaling 6, B, 12, etc. On this basis, some tried to identify Henry Kissinger as the Antichrist. Though a number of historical characters have been suggested, including Nero, Judas Iscariot, and more modern names such as Mussolini, Stalin, and Kennedy, the whole system of interpretation involves too much uncertainty to be considered valid. A major flaw is that a resurrection of an ungodly man of the past would not be a work of God, and Satan does not have the power of resurrection which belongs to Christ alone. Accordingly, while the future fulfillment may cast more light on the interpretation, the best approach is to understand 666 as the number of humanity, short of the perfect number 7.

From these Scriptures and others, it is clear that the Bible predicts a world government that will be an attempt on the part of Satan to imitate Christ's universal rule. Instead of being a time of peace and tranquillity, however, it will be a time of terrible destruction and blasphemy and martyrdom—a time of trouble such as the world has never known before, both from the standpoint of political oppression and from the standpoint of the judgments that are inflicted on the earth because of divine wrath. God's judgments are described in the breaking of the seals, sounding of the trumpets, and the pouring out of the bowls of God's wrath in Revelation.

This world government will begin to break up in the end time, as indicated in Revelation 16, in connection with the armies converging on Armageddon. Apparently this will be an attempt on the part of the nations to break away from the world ruler because of the terrible tragedies and troubles that the world has encountered under his rule. All of this sets the stage for the coming of the Lord and is embraced in the preceding period known as the Great Tribulation.

30

The Great Tribulation

Tribulation Versus Great Tribulation

The future time of great tribulation and distress in the world is often confused with the stress that has characterized the human race from its beginning. Jesus had told his disciples the night before his crucifixion, "In this world you will have trouble. But take heart! I have overcome the world" (John 16:33). In the controversy between posttribulationism and pretribulationism, those who believe the church will be raptured at the end of the Tribulation belittle the time of trouble described in Scripture. They claim that the trouble we have now is the trouble predicted. A careful examination of the many Scripture passages that deal with this period, however, discloses that while the world has always had trouble—and it is true as Job expressed it, "Yet man is born to trouble as surely as sparks fly upward" (5:7)—the final time of trouble is set apart as unprecedented. It will differ from all other preceding times of trouble in character, events, and extent. Some recent posttribulationists have aban-

346

doned the idea that the trouble we are in now is the time of tribulation predicted in the Bible, but they still tend to minimize the extent of the trouble.

First Prophecy of the Coming Time of Distress

In connection with Israel's scattering among the peoples of the world because of their sin, as described in Deuteronomy 4:26–28, the promise is given that if they seek the Lord they will be brought back to the Lord:

> But if from there you seek the LORD your God, you will find him if you look for him with all your heart and with all your soul. When you are in distress and all these things have happened to you, then in later days you will return to the LORD your God and obey him. For the LORD your God is a merciful God; he will not abandon or destroy you or forget the covenant with your forefathers, which he confirmed to them by oath." (vv. 29–31)

Though Moses and later prophets clearly prophesied that Israel would be driven out of the land (i.e., in the Assyrian and Babylonian captivities) and later be scattered to the entire world, Scriptures plainly declare that God in grace will bring them back and that the godly remnant who will repent will be brought back to their ancient land. Prior to this, however, they will experience the great time of distress described in verse 30.

The Time of Jacob's Trouble

Jeremiah, who lived in the time of the Babylonian captivity, prophesied this future time of trouble:

> "This is what the LORD says:
>
> " 'Cries of fear are heard—
>   terror, not peace.
> Ask and see:
>   Can a man bear children?
> Then why do I see every strong man
>   with his hand on his stomach like a woman in labor,
>   every face turned deathly pale?
> How awful that day will be!

None will be like it.
It will be a time of trouble for Jacob,
    but he will be saved out of it.'" (30:5–7)

Jeremiah's prediction of this coming time of trouble is similar to what the later predictions of this event describe. It will be particularly a time of Jacob's trouble although it will extend to the entire world. It will be greater than any trouble Israel has experienced in the past, which is saying a great deal, because Israel has suffered greatly in previous periods of apostasy. Like the other predictions of trouble, Israel is promised that they will be saved out of it. In verse 9 Jeremiah promises that they will serve the Lord and that David their king will be raised from the dead. This prophecy, coming as it does from Jeremiah in a time of Israel's apostasy and suffering, describes a future time of even greater trouble yet assures Israel's ultimate deliverance. It is characteristic of the promises regarding this future time of trouble.

The Time of the Saints' Oppression

The awful oppression of the Roman Empire is described in Daniel 7:7–8. To some extent this has been fulfilled historically, but it will be greatly exceeded by the persecutions that will come in the revived form of the empire. The beast described in Revelation 7–8 is the revived form of the Roman Empire with its ten horns. It is ruled by a dictator, the "little horn" of Daniel 7:8. Daniel talked about the fearful destruction by Roman power in the end time: "Then I wanted to know the true meaning of the fourth beast, which was different from all others and most terrifying with its iron teeth and bronze claws—the beast that crushed and devoured its victims and trampled underfoot whatever was left" (Dan. 7:19). Further description is given in verses 23–25:

> " 'The fourth beast is a fourth kingdom that will appear on earth. It will be different from all the other kingdoms and will devour the whole earth, trampling it down and crushing it. The ten horns are ten kings who will come from this kingdom. After them another king will arise, different from the earlier ones; he will subdue three kings. He will speak against the Most High and oppress his saints and try to change the set times and the laws.' "

As is clear from other predictions, though Israel will be the center of Satan's hatred and of the wrath of the Roman rulers, the entire world will suffer, as indicated in verse 23, where the whole earth is declared to be devoured.

In verse 25 the duration of the period of trouble is "time, times and half a time." This is normally interpreted to be three and a half years—that is, time equals one unit, times equals two units, and half a time equals half a unit, for a total of three and a half. This same expression is found in Daniel 12:7 and Revelation 12:14. The idea that the period is three and a half years is confirmed by the forty-two months mentioned in Revelation 11:2 and 13:5 and by the 1,260 days of Revelation 12:6. This three-and-a-half-year period will be the last half of the seven-year period leading up to the second coming of Christ.

A number of important things happen in this period. In Daniel 9:27 the last seven years is divided in half, and in the second half sacrifice and offering are stopped. In Daniel 11:36–45 the period is predicted to close with a great world war with armies from the east, north, and south. This same period is described in Revelation 16:13–16.

In Daniel 12:1, referring back to the closing verses of the preceding chapter, the period is summarized as "a time of distress such as has not happened from the beginning of nations until then. But at that time your people—everyone whose name is found written in the book—will be delivered." This familiar prediction stresses the main idea of the Tribulation, that it is an unprecedented time of trouble and that at its end the people of Israel will be delivered by the second coming of Christ.

The closing verses of Daniel 12:11–12 describe the period: "From the time that the daily sacrifice is abolished and the abomination that causes desolation is set up, there will be 1,290 days. Blessed is the one who waits for and reaches the end of the 1,335 days." The 1,290 days correspond roughly to the three and a half years with some days added relating to the early events of the Millennium after the second coming of Christ. The fact that blessing is pronounced on those that reach the end of 1,335 days means that by that time all the judgments relating to the second coming of Christ will have been accomplished and those still living will be qualified to enter the millennial kingdom.

Unprecedented Worldwide Distress

When Jesus' disciples questioned him about the end time, he provided general prophecies of the troubles that have characterized the world since his first coming and then predicted an event that would begin the Great Tribulation—the abomination of desolation, which is the desecration of the temple (Matt. 24:15). Those who witness this event or hear about it are instructed to flee to the mountains of Judea. The reason for this is summarized in Christ's description of the period: "For then there will be great distress, unequaled from the beginning of the world until now—and never to be equaled again. If those days had not been cut short, no one would survive, but for the sake of the elect those days will be shortened" (vv. 21–22). This confirming word from Christ relative to the awfulness and distinctiveness of the Great Tribulation is taken even further when in verse 29 he talks about the climax of the "distress of those days." He refers to disorder in the heavens. The sun will be darkened and the moon will not give its light. Stars will fall, and the heavenly bodies will be shaken. This is described more in detail in the book of Revelation.

These same truths regarding the end time can be found in Mark 13:14–24. The period will be shortened in the sense that it will be cut off abruptly, not in that it will be made less than three and a half years.

The Coming Day of the Lord

Another descriptive title referring to this period is the Day of the Lord. In general this refers to any time of distress or trouble when God's judgments are poured out on the earth. Accordingly, some Old Testament periods are designated as a Day of the Lord. Scripture bears witness to a future Day of the Lord that will begin at the time of the Rapture, continue through the Great Tribulation, and include the thousand-year reign of Christ. The reason for this designation is that in this period God will deal directly with sin in the world, judging it in a way that is different from his work in the present age of grace.

The Day of the Lord was introduced in 1 Thessalonians 5:1 because it will begin at the time of the Rapture. Like the Rapture, the Day of the Lord is not dated but will come like a thief in the night: "Now, brothers, about times and dates we do not need to write to you, for you know very well that the day of the Lord will come like a thief in the night" (vv. 1–2). The apostle then refers to the fact that the Day of the Lord will begin with what seems to be a time of peace. The three and a half years preceding the Great Tribulation will be a time of relative peace as compared to a time of war. When the Great Tribulation begins, however, this time of peace will abruptly close because the world ruler will break his covenant with Israel and become their persecutor instead of their protector. Accordingly, Paul wrote, "While people are saying, 'Peace and safety,' destruction will come on them suddenly, as labor pains on a pregnant woman, and they will not escape" (v. 3).

Much confusion has been introduced on the subject of the Day of the Lord by the theory that it begins at the time of the Second Coming instead of earlier at the time of the pretribulation Rapture. Many Scriptures in both the Old and New Testaments make clear that the Day of the Lord includes the Great Tribulation and also the period of time leading up to it, though the major events will occur in the Great Tribulation. As mentioned before passages referring to this are found throughout the Old Testament (Isa. 2:12–21; 13:9–16; 34:1–8; Joel 1:15–2:11; 2:28–32; 3:9–21; Amos 5:18–20; Obad. 15–17; Zeph. 1:7–18). These passages picture the time of distress leading up to the coming of the kingdom when Jesus Christ will return.

Some Old Testament passages speak very specifically of events that relate to the climax of the Day of the Lord. Zechariah 13:8–9, for instance, refers to the fact that two out of three in Israel will perish before the Great Tribulation comes to its end. Zechariah 14 describes the climax of the period as Jerusalem's being attacked and ransacked on the very day of the Lord's return.

In 2 Thessalonians the apostle Paul corrected the false teaching of those who taught that the Thessalonians were already in the Day of the Lord because of their trials and tribulations. It is important to observe here that the Day of the Lord as a time period begins with the Rapture. As far as events are concerned, they do not really find detailed fulfillment until the Great Tribulation comes and the man of sin is revealed. Though he is revealed when the seven-year covenant is made with Israel, it may not be clear that he is the one described in Scripture as the coming world ruler until he breaks his covenant with Israel and begins the Great Tribulation (2 Thess. 2:3–4). The major events of the Day of the Lord will occur after the time period has begun much as a twenty-four-hour-day begins at midnight but becomes eventful after the dawn.

The Great Tribulation in the Book of Revelation

In Jesus' messages to the seven churches, he promises the church at Philadelphia that she will be kept from the future hour of trial (Rev. 3:10). This is a reference to the Great Tribulation. What is true of the Philadelphia church is also true of every Christian who is saved before the Rapture, as, obviously, the Rapture will remove them from the earth before the day of trial comes.

Interpreters of the book of Revelation differ as to whether the Great Tribulation begins at Revelation 6:1 or at some later point in the book of Revelation. This depends somewhat on the interpretation of the first seal as to who becomes a world conqueror with a bow without an arrow. This seems to refer to the world empire of the man of sin, and inasmuch as this begins in the last three and a half years of the Great Tribulation, it implies that what follows is the Great Tribulation.

After the fourth seal is broken a fourth of the world is killed (Rev. 6:7–8), certainly a fitting description of the Great Tribulation but hardly a description of the time of peace that precedes. This is also true of the martyrs of the fifth seal (vv. 9–11) and of the disturbances in the skies described in the sixth seal (vv. 12–17).

The sealing of the 144,000 is in preparation for the Great Tribulation and is chronologically before chapter 6. Also, in Revelation 7:9–17 the many martyrs described certainly come from the Great Tribulation, which is the last three and a half years before the second coming of Christ.

The seven trumpets, likewise, seem to qualify for the Great Tribulation, with judgments falling on a third of the earth and on a third of the sea and on a third of the waters of the earth, as in the first three trumpets (Rev. 8:1–13). The fifth trumpet (Rev. 9:1–12) certainly describes a great tribulation, as those who have the mark of the beast are tortured for five months. The sixth trumpet (vv. 13–21) describes the destruction of a third of the world's population. This too would certainly also qualify for the Great Tribulation and describe something of its horror. Revelation 16, in addition to the prophecy concerning details of the world government and some of the problems that relate to it, describes the last series of seven judgments on the earth. The various bowls represent judgments that afflict the entire world and include the final world war described after the sixth bowl (vv. 12–16) and the final bowl (vv. 17–21). When the seventh bowl is poured out a great earthquake occurs, causing mountains and islands to disappear and the great city of Babylon to collapse and be destroyed. In addition, one-hundred-pound hailstones fall on the earth and destroy what is left. It is hard to describe a period of greater horror and destruction of human life and property than is described in Revelation 16:17–21. This is the final blow before the second coming of Christ recorded in 19:11–16. In Revelation 17 and 18 the judgment of God upon Babylon ecclesiastical, which probably occurred before Revelation 6, is described, and the destruction of Babylon as a city in Revelation 18 probably coincides with the prediction of Revelation 16:19 just preceding the Second Coming.

From these many Scriptures it should be abundantly clear that the events of the Great Tribulation are not to be identified with preceding times of trouble. They are unprecedented in scope, in meaning, and in significance. They are especially designed to lead up to the judgment of the second coming of Christ and the establishment of God's kingdom in the world.

Though often interpreted symbolically, these events obviously signal tremendous literal events that will climax the times of the Gentiles as well as God's prophesied 490 years of Israel. They will lead up to and form a platform for the second coming of Christ. Inasmuch as judgments in the past have been literal, this awful period will also be subject to literal fulfillment. It makes all the more real the church's hope of being raptured before these end-time events take place.

31

Armageddon: The Final Destruction of Babylon

Background of Armageddon

The so-called Battle of Armageddon will occur during the final days of the Great Tribulation. As revealed in Revelation 16, God will pour out a series of devastating judgments on the earth. The figure of a full bowl that is turned upside down is used here. The judgments will include painful sores that break out on people who have the mark of the Beast (v. 2). At the second trumpet (8:8–9) a third of the sea will have been turned into blood. Now a further extensive judgment will take place in the second bowl of wrath: all the sea will be turned into blood, with the result that every living thing in the sea will die (16:3). Like the third trumpet, which will have turned a third of the rivers and springs of water bitter (8:10–11), the third bowl of the wrath of God will be poured out on the rivers and springs so that they become blood (16:4–7). This judgment is declared to be especially just, because of the blood of the martyrs that will be shed in the Great Tribulation.

A fourth bowl of wrath will be poured out on the earth in the form of a change of climate, with the sun being given power to scorch people with fire. The fifth bowl of wrath will plunge the earth into darkness, a situation worse than that of the sixth seal (6:12–14), where the sun was turned to blackness and the moon was turned to blood. At the sixth seal the Euphrates River will dry up to prepare the way for the great army from the East to participate in the final world war. These six bowls of the wrath of God will serve as an introduction to what the Bible refers to as Armageddon.

The Final World War

As John contemplated this end-time scene, he recorded, "Then I saw three evil spirits that looked like frogs; they came out of the mouth of the dragon, out of the mouth of the beast and out of the mouth of the false prophet" (Rev. 16:13). An interpretation is immediately given: "They are spirits of demons performing miraculous signs, and they go out to the kings of the whole world, to gather them for the battle on the great day of God Almighty" (v. 14). This introduces an amazing paradox.

At the beginning of the Great Tribulation, through satanic deception and power, a world government was formed, with the ruler of the ten nations of the revived Roman Empire becoming a dictator over the whole world including all the countries of the globe including those of the Western hemisphere. Daniel 7:23 speaks of the entire globe (cf. Rev. 13:7). Now from the same source of power that put this world government together comes the influence to gather the armies of the world to challenge this world government. It is significant that this deception comes from three sources: the dragon, Satan; the Beast, the final world ruler; and the False Prophet, the beast out of the land (Rev. 13:11). The armies of the world are led to converge upon the Holy Land to fight for superiority.

Revelation 16:16 declares, "Then they gathered the kings together to the place that in Hebrew is called Armageddon." Armageddon is a geographic location in northern Palestine, and the term *Armageddon* seems to refer to the Mount of Megiddo. This hill of Megiddo is located near the Mediterranean Sea, but stretching out to the east of it is a broad valley in which numerous battles have been fought in the past. Today it is a rich valley, with crops being planted several times a year. Though it is a broad valley some fifteen miles wide and twenty miles long and leading into several other valleys, it is much too small for all the millions of people that will be gathered for this final world war. It will, however, be the central marshaling place, with armies roving to the south and to the north of this location and from the Mediterranean Sea to the Euphrates River to the east. Armies will be fighting in Jerusalem on the very day of the second coming of Christ (Zech. 14:1–3). The world government that was put together without a fight at the beginning of the Great Tribulation will now be the object of a desperate attack by major armies gathered to fight for superiority. Because of the tremendous judgments of God that will have decimated the earth and destroyed much property and human life, there will be discontent with the world ruler, and others apparently will contend for power. The amazing fact, however, is that the same people who put together the world government at the beginning of the Great Tribulation will now be plotting its destruction.

The answer to this paradox is found in Revelation 19, which describes the second coming of Christ with his heavenly armies. It is apparent that the satanic purpose is to gather all the military might of the world to contend against the armies from heaven. It turns out, of course, to be totally futile, but as in other efforts of Satan, he is compelled by his very nature to do his best to oppose God and in every possible way to stand in the way of God's conquest. This war will be underway for several months before the second coming of Christ. But before he returns, the seventh bowl will bring its terrible judgment upon the world (Rev. 16:17–21).

The Seventh Bowl of Revelation

This final judgment of God is described as a tremendous earthquake, greater than any earthquake the earth has ever experienced. John wrote, "Then there came flashes of lightning, rumblings, peals of thunder and a severe earthquake. No earthquake like it has ever occurred since man has been on earth, so tremendous was the quake" (Rev. 16:18).

As a result of the earthquake, John declared, "The great city split into three parts, and the cities of the nations collapsed. God remembered Babylon the Great and gave her the cup filled with the wine of the fury of his wrath" (Rev. 16:19). Though the identification of the city has been debated, it seems evident, due to the reference to Babylon, that it will be Babylon herself, and this is brought out particularly in Revelation 18. The city here is declared to be split into three parts by the gigantic earthquake, but the judgment of God on Babylon will be carried out throughout the entire earth. The cities of the nations—that is, the Gentile cities—will be shaken to pieces and their buildings will collapse with great loss of property as well as life. It would be hard to imagine a scene of greater worldwide disaster than is described here. Because Scripture specifies that this will be a judgment on the cities of the Gentiles, it is apparent that Israel herself is not involved. Jerusalem will still be intact after this earthquake, as illustrated in the fact that on the day of the Second Coming there will be house-to-house fighting in Jerusalem (Zech. 14:2–3). Though some believe the city destroyed is Jerusalem, this would not be possible if Jerusalem were ruined by an earthquake.

The extent of the destruction will go beyond that of the cities. John declared, "Every island fled away and the mountains could not be found" (Rev. 16:20). The whole topography of the earth will seem to be in convulsions, with islands and mountains disappearing, resulting in loss of life and property that is beyond description.

On top of all these catastrophes, the final plague will be a hailstorm with hailstones weighing a hundred pounds each. "From the sky huge hailstones of about a hundred pounds each fell upon men. And they cursed God on account of the plague of hail, because the plague was so terrible" (Rev. 16:21).

The Destruction of Babylon Political

Having introduced the destruction of Babylon in Revelation 16:19, Revelation 17–18 reveals the details.

As previously brought out, Revelation 17 describes the earlier destruction of Babylon ecclesiastical, the world church movement that will have dominated the first half of the last seven years. Revelation 18, however, describes more in detail the destruction of the city that was divided into three parts (Rev. 16:19). It consists of a lament by the people of the earth that mighty Babylon has fallen. John introduced this by writing:

After this I saw another angel coming down from heaven.
He had great authority, and the earth was illuminated by his
splendor. With a mighty voice he shouted:

"Fallen! Fallen is Babylon the Great!
She has become a home for demons
and a haunt for every evil spirit,
a haunt for every unclean and detestable bird.
For all the nations have drunk
the maddening wine of her adulteries.
The kings of the earth committed adultery with her,
and the merchants of the earth grew rich from her
excessive luxuries." (Rev. 18:1–3)

Scholars differ on the interpretation of this chapter, some
taking it as a reference to Rome being destroyed, some taking it
in a nonliteral sense, and others referring to it as a literal
Babylon that had been made the capital city of the world
government during the Great Tribulation. There is much to
support and commend the interpretation that this is a literal
prophecy referring to a literal city even though it is given the
symbolic name of Babylon, which ties it in to both the political
and religious qualities that have characterized Babylon in
history. Because the world ruler claims to be God, allegiance to
him and commerce with him are described as spiritual adultery.
If Babylon is the world capital, the description of the merchants
in Revelation 18:11–13 makes a great deal of sense. These same
merchants view the city's destruction as a terrible disaster.

The reference to sea captains in Revelation 18:17 has raised
the question as to how Babylon could be a seaport. The answer
is not immediately given, though some would refer this to the
city of Rome. It is possible that the Euphrates River will be
made navigable for barges in this period which would bring
vessels to Babylon. The important emphasis throughout the
passage is that Babylon will be destroyed in one day or one
hour, as is stated frequently throughout this passage (Rev. 18:8,
10, 17, 19).

As brought out in previous studies, because the destruction of
Babylon was never consummated in history, though frequently
prophesied in the Old Testament (Isa. 13–14; 21:9; 47; Jer. 50–
51), a rebuilding of the city and its final destruction here would
serve symbolically as well as practically for the majestic coming

of Christ and as the end of the times of the Gentiles. The final world empire will be Roman as far as its political character is concerned, but spiritually it will correspond to Babylon with its false religion and its worship of Satan.

32

The Second Coming of Christ

The Second Coming: A Major Subject of the Bible

Though the precise phrase "the Second Coming" does not occur in either the Old or New Testament, many passages bear witness to the fact that Christ who came once to provide salvation is coming a second time to rule. Hebrews 9:28 says, "So Christ was sacrificed once to take away the sins of many people; and he will appear a second time, not to bear sin, but to bring salvation to those who are waiting for him." Just as the first coming of Christ accomplished the major purpose of God to provide salvation, so the second coming of Christ will accomplish the major purpose of God to place everything in subjection to Jesus Christ as King of Kings and Lord of Lords. This is a prominent element of references to his second coming in both the Old and New Testaments.

Relation of the Second Coming to the Kingdom of God

Just as the first coming of Christ related to salvation, so the second coming of Christ relates to God's rule in the world. This involves understanding the varied usages and meanings of the expression "the kingdom of God."

The universal kingdom of God. Because God is the omnipotent Creator, he is in control and rules over the entire world. This is brought out again and again in Scripture. In connection with David's praise to the Lord for the Israel's generosity in giving materials to the temple, he said:

Yours, O LORD, is the kingdom;
  you are exalted as head over all.
Wealth and honor come from you;
  you are the ruler of all things. (1 Chron. 29:11–12)

God is frequently described as reigning over the nations (Ps. 47:8; 93:1–2; 97:1; 99:1; 146:10). Psalm 103:19 says, "The LORD has established his throne in heaven, / and his kingdom rules over all." In Daniel's interpretation of the great tree image, he declared that the purpose of Nebuchadnezzar's experience was "that the living may know that the Most High is sovereign over the kingdoms of men and gives them to anyone he wishes and sets over them the lowliest of men'" (4:17). In a similar way, Daniel, indicating that Nebuchadnezzar would experience insanity, stated the same truth in 4:25: ". . . the Most High is sovereign over the kingdoms of men and gives them to anyone he wishes" (cf. v. 32). In Nebuchadnezzar's own evaluation of his experience, he declared that the God of Daniel had eternal dominion over all the peoples of the earth (vv. 34–35).

The spiritual kingdom of God. The kingdom of God is sometimes viewed as a rule of God over those who willingly submit to him as King. This would include all the holy angels and all the elect of humanity. Though God's power extends to his rule over the entire world, the spiritual kingdom is a sphere of voluntary submission to God and includes God's rule over saved Jews and Gentiles in the Old Testament, his rule over the saved of the present age in the body of Christ, and his rule over all individuals who in the future will put their trust in him as Savior. The expression "the kingdom of God" in the New

Testament is used to refer only to those who are saved or to the holy angels.

The Davidic kingdom. The Davidic kingdom is a subdivision of the universal kingdom of God. As experienced in David's time, it began with David's being appointed king. It involved the people of the kingdom of Israel, some of whom were saved and some who were unsaved but came under David's control as king. The Davidic kingdom was theocratic—that is, David was God's appointed representative and ruled in God's name.

The second coming of Christ will be related to all three of these aspects of the kingdom. It will serve to establish God's political rule on the earth over all creatures. It will be a spiritual kingdom, because at the beginning, at least, the kingdom Christ will bring at his second coming will be limited to those who are saved, since all the unsaved will be purged out in the judgments preceding the millennial kingdom. The kingdom Christ will bring will be Davidic in that it will fulfill the promise of a king to reign on the throne of David. While the rule of Christ as David's son will extend only to the children of Israel, he will also be King of Kings and Lord of Lords over the entire world. His kingdom rule will have the dual qualities of extending over Israel in fulfillment of Old Testament prophecies and over the entire world in keeping with God's purpose that he be established as the ruler of the world. Accordingly, references to the second coming of Christ, as found in both the Old and New Testaments, relate to this overall purpose of his second coming in relation to Israel, in relation to the world, and in relation to those who are saved.

Old Testament Predictions of the Coming of Christ

Early predictions of Christ's coming. The Old Testament frequently refers to the ultimate victory of God over the power of evil, beginning in the Garden of Eden in the judgment on Satan. The downfall of Satan and his ultimate judgment is implied in Genesis 3:15 in the statement, "He will crush your head." Throughout the Old Testament God is revealed as the Sovereign One who, though he permits evil, will ultimately judge it and be triumphant over it.

One of the early specific prophecies concerning the Second Coming is found in Deuteronomy 30:3, "Then the LORD your God will restore your fortunes and have compassion on you and

gather you again from all the nations where he scattered you."
The regathering of Israel is one of the purposes of Christ in
returning to the earth. As predicted here, the Lord's regathering
of Israel will result in their being brought back to their land
(v. 5); their spiritual revival (v. 6); the cursing of their enemies
(v. 7); and their prosperity (v. 9). In the light of this, Moses
appealed to the children of Israel to obey the Lord and merit his
blessing.

Christ's coming in the psalms. Psalm 2 is a comprehensive
prediction of the ultimate exaltation of Jesus Christ as the King
of Kings. The psalm opens with the nations being ridiculed for
their foolish thought that they can cast off God's rule:

> *The one enthroned in heaven laughs;*
> *the Lord scoffs at them.*
> *Then he rebukes them in his anger*
> *and terrifies them in his wrath, saying,*
> *"I have installed my King*
> *on Zion, my holy hill." (vv. 4–6)*

Psalm 2 continues with the declaration of the eternal decree of
God in which Jesus is recognized as the Son. The Father says:

> *"Ask of me,*
> *and I will make the nations your inheritance,*
> *the ends of the earth your possession.*
> *You will rule them with an iron scepter;*
> *you will dash them to pieces like pottery." (vv. 8–9)*

This has not yet been accomplished in history but will be
fulfilled subsequent to the second coming of Christ. In view of
this coming judgment of God, the kings of the earth are
exhorted:

> *Serve the LORD with fear*
> *and rejoice with trembling.*
> *Kiss the Son, lest he be angry*
> *and you be destroyed in your way,*
> *for his wrath can flare up in a moment.*
> *Blessed are all who take refuge in him. (vv. 11–12)*

In Psalm 24 God is viewed as the King over the whole earth. The opening verse says:

> The earth is the LORD's, and everything in it,
>   the world, and all who live in it;
> for he founded it upon the seas
>   and established it upon the waters. (vv. 1–2)

As the Psalm closes, it exhorts the gates of Jerusalem to welcome the King of Glory:

> Lift up your heads, O you gates;
>   lift them up, you ancient doors,
>   that the King of glory may come in.
> Who is he, this King of glory?
>   The LORD Almighty—
>   he is the King of glory. (vv. 9–10)

Referring as it does to the city of Jerusalem, it anticipates the glory of Christ's rule in Jerusalem during the Millennium.

In Psalm 50:2–3 the reign of the Lord out of Zion is predicted:

> From Zion, perfect in beauty,
>   God shines forth.
> Our God comes and will not be silent;
>   a fire devours before him,
>   and around him a tempest rages.

Psalm 72 is one of the comprehensive pictures of the millennial kingdom. The "royal son" in verse 1 is introduced as the Judge of the people (v. 2). His just rule and the length of his reign is mentioned in verses 4–5. The coming King

> will rule from sea to sea
>   and from the River to the ends of the earth.
> The desert tribes will bow before him
>   and his enemies will lick the dust.
> The kings of Tarshish and of distant shores
>   will bring tribute to him;
> the kings of Sheba and Seba
>   will present him gifts.

All kings will bow down to him
and all nations will serve him. (vv. 8–11)

His beneficent rule is mentioned in verses 12–14. The abundance of crops and fruit are described in verses 15–16. The psalm closes with "Praise be to his glorious name forever; / may the whole earth be filled with his glory" (v. 19). The description of this psalm does not fit any of the current situations or any point in history but clearly is to be identified with the kingdom Christ will bring at his second coming. It also does not fit the new heaven and new earth, which is an entirely different situation.

Numerous other references to the Second Coming are found in Scripture. Christ's coming to judge the world in righteousness is described in Psalm 96. In Psalm 110 the coming King is pictured as sitting at the right hand of God until the time comes for his enemies to be subdued under him:

The LORD says to my Lord:
"Sit at my right hand
until I make your enemies
a footstool for your feet."
The LORD will extend your mighty scepter from Zion;
you will rule in the midst of your enemies. (vv. 1–2).

The crushing judgment on those who oppose Christ is described in verses 5 and 6. The contrast is between Christ's present position in heaven, where he is waiting for the time when judgment will fall on his enemies, and the judgment that will take place at his second coming. In Peter's Pentecostal sermon he called attention to the fact that the resurrection of Christ was necessary for Christ to fulfill these prophecies (Acts 2:34–36). Christ in his resurrection is pictured as ascending into heaven and sitting on the throne of God, waiting until his enemies be made his footstool. The implication of this passage is that the Davidic kingdom has not yet begun but awaits the time of Christ's second coming when judgment will fall upon his enemies and he will assume actual rule over the children of Israel.

Christ's coming in Isaiah. Isaiah provided a major prediction concerning the coming of Christ:

For to us a child is born,
to us a son is given,
and the government will be on his shoulders.
And he will be called
Wonderful Counselor, Mighty God,
Everlasting Father, Prince of Peace.
Of the increase of his government and peace
there will be no end.
He will reign on David's throne
and over his kingdom,
establishing and upholding it
with justice and righteousness
from that time on and forever.
The zeal of the LORD Almighty
will accomplish this. (9:6–7)

Though Christ is identified as the Son of David and the future King, he is awaiting this future kingdom while on the throne in heaven. Upon his return, his government will be applied to the earth, and he will fulfill the promise of sitting on the throne of David, establishing this kingdom as well as ruling over the entire earth.

Another comprehensive passage relating to the millennial kingdom is found in Isaiah 11:1–12:6. Here Christ's faithful and righteous rule is described (11:2–5). The tranquillity of the millennial kingdom, which will extend to removing the ferocity of beasts, is also described (vv. 6–8). The conclusion is:

They will neither harm nor destroy
on all my holy mountain,
for the earth will be full of the knowledge of the LORD
as the waters cover the sea. (v. 9)

His victory over the enemies of Israel is described in verses 10–16. The praise of the Lord and recognition of his victory is provided in Isaiah 12:1–6.

The fact that the coming of Christ will be a day of judgment upon the wicked is brought out in an eloquent passage by Isaiah (63:1–6).

Isaiah closed with two chapters (65–66) that describe the millennial kingdom in detail as following the second coming of Christ. It will be a time when Jerusalem will be a delight and a joy (65:18–19). Life will be lengthened, and one who dies at a hundred years of age will be a mere youth (v. 20).

The normal activities of life will continue in the millennial kingdom.

> "They will build houses and dwell in them;
>   they will plant vineyards and eat their fruit.
> No longer will they build houses and others live in them,
>   or plant and others eat.
> For as the days of a tree,
>   so will be the days of my people;
> my chosen ones will long enjoy
>   the works of their hands.
> They will not toil in vain
>   or bear children doomed to misfortune;
> for they will be a people blessed by the LORD,
>   they and their descendants with them.
> Before they call I will answer;
>   while they are still speaking I will hear.
> The wolf and the lamb will feed together,
>   and the lion will eat straw like the ox,
>   but dust will be the serpent's food.
> They will neither harm nor destroy
>   on all my holy mountain," says the LORD.
>   (Isa. 65:21–25)

This passage is not being fulfilled today and has never been fulfilled in history. Neither does it conform to the conditions of life in the New Jerusalem and the new heaven and the new earth. It clearly requires a kingdom on earth subsequent to the second coming of Christ in which people will live and die and in which they will have normal lives, though under unusual blessing from God. Nature itself will be blessed with tranquillity among beasts that normally have animosity toward each other.

Isaiah 66 continues the prediction of Israel's blessing in this future kingdom, of the joy that will be in Jerusalem, and of God's eternal presence with his people.

Christ's coming in Zechariah. Among the many other passages that could be related to the Second Coming are the predictions of Zechariah.

"Shout and be glad, O daughter of Zion. For I am coming, and I will live among you," declares the LORD. "Many nations will be joined with the LORD in that day and will become my people. I will live among you and you will know that the LORD Almighty has sent me to you. The LORD will inherit Judah as his portion in the holy land and will again choose Jerusalem." (Zech. 2:10–12)

A dramatic note is sounded in Zechariah 14, where the conquering of Jerusalem by the enemies of God is pictured as occurring on the very day of the second coming of Christ. The Lord said: "I will gather all the nations to Jerusalem to fight against it; the city will be captured, the houses ransacked, and the women raped. Half of the city will go into exile, but the rest of the people will not be taken from the city. Then the LORD will go out and fight against those nations, as he fights in the day of battle" (vv. 2–3).

The verses that follow describe the division of the Mount of Olives into two mountains with a valley between them running from east to west. This will be the unmistakable signal that the second coming of Christ has occurred, and this and other topographical changes will prepare the Holy Land for the millennial period. The outcome of these events is described in Zechariah 14:9: "The LORD will be king over the whole earth. On that day there will be one LORD, and his name the only name." Topographical changes are described in verse 10. Jerusalem will be declared secure and never to be destroyed again. The worship and service of God in the Millennium occupies the rest of the chapter.

It should be obvious from these many Old Testament passages that the second coming of Christ is a major event that will dramatically change the course of earthly events and bring in the promised kingdom in which Christ will reign supreme.

The Second Coming of Christ in the New Testament

The second coming of Christ is not only a dominant theme of the Old Testament but is also pervasive throughout the New Testament. It has been estimated that one out of every twenty-five verses in the New Testament is a reference either to the rapture of the church or to the second coming of Christ and his reign over the earth.

The second coming of Christ in the Gospels. The disciples

were very slow to understand that Christ was going to leave them and then come back again. Accordingly, little was said about the Second Coming until Christ's ministry was well advanced and it became clear that he would be rejected.

One of the early references to Christ's second coming is found in his statement that the disciples would judge the twelve tribes of Israel: "Jesus said to them, 'I tell you the truth, at the renewal of all things, when the Son of Man sits on his glorious throne, you who have followed me will also sit on twelve thrones, judging the twelve tribes of Israel'" (Matt. 19:28). Christ went on to say that they would be rewarded at that time for what they had done for him (vv. 29–30).

In Christ's lament over Jerusalem and his indictment of the Pharisees for their hypocrisy, he referred to the time when he would return and the godly remnant of Israel would recognize that the one coming in the name of the Lord would be blessed (Matt. 23:39).

Many references to the Second Coming exhorted the disciples to preparation in anticipation of the event, as in the Olivet Discourse (Matt. 24:3–25:46). Parallel passages are found in Mark 13:24–37; Luke 12:35–48; 17:22–37; 18:8; and 21:25–28. Prior to the death of Christ, the disciples could not understand the passages on his second coming, and they only gradually understood that there was a time period between the first and second coming after Christ ascended.

The second coming of Christ in Acts. At Christ's ascension the angels told the disciples, "This same Jesus, who has been taken from you into heaven, will come back in the same way you have seen him go into heaven" (Acts 1:11).

In Acts 15:16–18 in the council at Jerusalem, the revelation was clarified that the present age is predominantly a time of Gentile blessing, and that after the present age, in connection with the second coming of Christ, the Davidic kingdom will be restored. James quoted from Amos 9:11–12 how the Davidic tent would be rebuilt and Israel would be restored at the return of Christ.

The second coming of Christ in the Epistles. The apostle Paul, after stating emphatically that God had not cast off his people Israel, said that Israel would be restored to the Lord when a deliverer came out of Zion. Paul used the figure of an olive tree, with the Gentiles being grafted in now for spiritual blessing but Israel being grafted in at that future time. The olive tree represents the place of blessing, especially related to the promises given to Abraham concerning his posterity. Paul wrote: "And so all Israel will be saved, as it is written: 'The deliverer will come from Zion; he will turn godlessness away from Jacob. And this is my covenant with them when I take away their sins'" (Rom. 11:26–27). This is one of many passages that predicts a future restoration of Israel in relation to the Second Coming.

In 1 Corinthians 11:26 the Lord's Supper is declared to be a present memorial to Christ to be observed "until he comes." Again we see a contrast between the present age and what will occur at the Second Coming.

The judgment on the enemies of God that will occur at the Second Coming is revealed in 2 Thessalonians 1:7–10:

> This will happen when the Lord Jesus is revealed from heaven in blazing fire with his powerful angels. He will punish those who do not know God and do not obey the gospel of our Lord Jesus. They will be punished with everlasting destruction and shut out from the presence of the Lord and from the majesty of his power on the day he comes to be glorified in his holy people and to be marveled at among all those who have believed.

The apostle Peter called attention to the fact that apostate Christian leaders will deny the second coming of Christ and scoff at it (2 Peter 3:3–4). As Peter pointed out, they will deliberately turn away from the truth of the Lord's return.

A final dramatic statement of the Second Coming is found in Jude 14–15 where Jude quoted Enoch: "Enoch, the seventh from Adam, prophesied about these men: 'See, the Lord is coming with thousands upon thousands of his holy ones to judge everyone, and to convict all the ungodly of all the ungodly acts they have done in the ungodly way, and of all the harsh words ungodly sinners have spoken against him.'"

The Second Coming in the book of Revelation. The theme of the book of Revelation is the second coming of Christ. The book speaks of the revelation that will come to the entire world when Christ returns. This is stated early in the book, where John wrote, "Look, he is coming with the clouds, and every eye will see him, even those who pierced him; and all the peoples of the earth will mourn because of him. So shall it be! Amen" (1:7).

Jesus described himself as the one "who is, and who was, and who is to come, the Almighty" (v. 8).

The church at Thyatira was instructed, " 'Only hold on to what you have until I come' " (Rev. 2:25). The passage goes on to speak of Christ's ruling with an iron scepter and dashing his enemies to pieces (vv. 26–28). In 16:15 Jesus said, "Behold, I come like a thief! Blessed is he who stays awake and keeps his clothes with him, so that he may not go naked and be shamefully exposed."

The classic passage on the Second Coming, of course, is found in Revelation 19:11–21, where the majestic Christ comes back to earth, judges the world, destroys the armies against God, and casts the Beast and False Prophet into the lake of fire.

Jesus' concluding words in the book of Revelation are "Yes, I am coming soon" (22:20). It is not clear whether this passage is referring to the Rapture or to the Second Coming, but in either case it describes the certainty of the return of Christ.

The Relation of the Second Coming to the Great Tribulation

As most expositors agree, the second coming of Christ is clearly the climax of the Great Tribulation described in Revelation 6–18. Except for those who completely spiritualize the Tribulation, it is clear that the second coming of Christ is an answer to the rebellion of the nations that have chosen to follow a world ruler who is controlled by Satan rather than by Christ. This conclusion makes the suggestion of some that the second coming of Christ was fulfilled in A.D. 70 in connection with the destruction of Jerusalem totally unacceptable. Passages in the New Testament written after the destruction of Jerusalem, including the book of Revelation, clearly predict the Second Coming as a future event.

In Christ's own description of his second coming, he indicates that is will be preceded by the Great Tribulation (Matt. 24:21–29). This period will be a time of great stress when many false christs will appear. The second coming of Christ is described as a climax to these events:

"Immediately after the distress of those days

" 'the sun will be darkened,
    and the moon will not give its light;
the stars will fall from the sky,
    and the heavenly bodies will be shaken.'

> "At that time the sign of the Son of Man will appear in the sky, and all the nations of the earth will mourn. They will see the Son of Man coming on the clouds of the sky, with power and great glory." (vv. 29–30)

The Second Coming of Christ, a Bodily Return

Though it is true that Christ is present everywhere and indwells every Christian, bodily he has remained in heaven. At the Second Coming he will return bodily to the earth. Just as the Ascension was a bodily ascension into heaven, so the Second Coming will be a bodily return to the earth. The angels who met the disciples after the ascension of Christ told them, "This same Jesus, who has been taken from you into heaven, will come back in the same way you have seen him go into heaven" (Acts 1:11). Jesus went into heaven bodily and visibly in the clouds. His second coming will have all these same characteristics.

Though there is a question as to whether the rapture of the church will be visible to the earth as a whole, the Scriptures are clear that the second coming of Christ will be visible to all, both believers and unbelievers. Matthew 24:27 describes it as lightning shining from the east to the west: "For as lightning that comes from the east is visible even in the west, so will be the coming of the Son of Man." Christ further said, "At that time the sign of the Son of Man will appear in the sky, and all the nations of the earth will mourn. They will see the Son of Man coming on the clouds of the sky, with power and great glory" (v. 30). John wrote in Revelation 1:7:

Look, he is coming with the clouds,
    and every eye will see him,
even those who pierced him,
    and all the peoples of the earth
    will mourn because of him.
                        So shall it be! Amen.

The Second Coming of Christ to be Glorious and Visible

The main theme of the book of Revelation is the disclosure of the glory of Christ at his second coming. The high point of the book is chapter 19. All preceding chapters lead up to it; all following chapters indicate the events that will follow his revelation. Accordingly, the display of his glory, as revealed in Revelation 19, is in keeping with all the other information we have concerning the second coming of Christ.

The Second Coming of Christ in Relation to Zion

The announcement of the angels that the second coming of Christ will be like the Ascension (Acts 1:11) will be confirmed when Christ returns to Mount Zion, the same area from which he ascended. As previously noted, when Christ returns, the Mount of Olives will be divided into two hills with a valley running east and west. This will change the area from which Christ ascended. Though Mount Zion is a short distance away, for all practical purposes, Jesus will return to the place from which he ascended (cf. Zech. 14:4).

A number of Scriptures dwell on the fact that Christ is either coming to or coming from Mount Zion in his deliverance of the people of God at his second coming. He obviously will come to Mount Zion first and from this point proceed to go forth and achieve deliverance of those who will have been persecuted in the Great Tribulation. A number of Old Testament Scriptures bear witness to this (Ps. 14:7; 20:2; 53:6; 110:2; Isa. 2:3; Joel 3:16; Amos 1:2). The Lord grants deliverance from Zion, but Scripture is not always clear whether this refers to history or prophecy. He is also said to be the Deliverer who will come out of Zion in Romans 11:26. Scriptures testify that Christ's government will be headquartered in Jerusalem in the millennial kingdom, and it is in keeping with this that his return will be to this point geographically.

The Second Coming of Christ to Feature a Procession of Holy Angels and Saints from Heaven to Earth

In contrast to the rapture of the church, which is a movement of the church from earth to heaven, the second coming of Christ will be a procession from heaven to the earth, including both saints and angels. This is anticipated in Matthew 25:31, which says that angels will come with Christ when he comes in his glory. Jude quoted Enoch as prophesying, "'See, the Lord is coming with thousands upon thousands of his holy ones to judge everyone, and to convict all the ungodly of all the ungodly acts they have done in the ungodly way, and of all the harsh words ungodly sinners have spoken against him'" (Jude 14–15).

The second coming of Christ is given graphic description in Revelation 19:11–16:

> I saw heaven standing open and there before me was a white horse, whose rider is called Faithful and True. With justice he judges and makes war. His eyes are like blazing fire, and on his head are many crowns. He has a name written on him that no one knows but he himself. He is dressed in a robe dipped in blood, and his name is the Word of God. The armies of heaven were following him, riding on white horses and dressed in fine linen, white and clean. Out of his mouth comes a sharp sword with which to strike down the nations. "He will rule them with an iron scepter." He treads the winepress of the fury of the wrath of God Almighty. On his robe and on his thigh he has this name written:
>
> KING OF KINGS AND LORD OF LORDS.

The description of the second coming of Christ is awe-inspiring, in keeping with the glory and majesty of Christ. He is described as "Faithful and True" (v. 11). He judges and makes war with justice (v. 11). His appearance is that of a conqueror with many crowns (v. 12). He is given the name "Word of God" (v. 13). Accompanying him, according to Scripture, are the armies of heaven: "The armies of heaven were following him, riding on white horses and dressed in fine linen, white and clean" (v. 14). Undoubtedly all the saints and the angels are represented in this army from heaven though the primary reference may be to the holy angels.

The description of Christ's second coming is in sharp contrast to his first coming as well as to the rapture of the church. It is clear that his purpose in coming is to judge the world and to extend the rule of God over the earth in the millennial kingdom.

The Purpose of Christ's Second Coming Is to Judge the Earth

According to Revelation 19:15, Christ's purpose is to judge the world: "Out of his mouth comes a sharp sword with which to strike down the nations. 'He will rule them with an iron scepter.' He treads the winepress of the fury of the wrath of God Almighty." On his robe and on his thigh he has this name written: KING OF KINGS AND LORD OF LORDS (v. 16). The events that follow first portray the judgment on the enemies of God, then on the Beast and the False Prophet, and finally on Satan. Other Scriptures indicate that judgment will extend to the entire living population on the earth. In his second coming Christ will terminate his time of waiting on the throne of God for the future subjugation of his enemies. He will then judge the world and bring everything under his authority and power. Noteworthy is the fact that there is no mention of the rapture of living saints in this sequence. This will have occurred years before.

33

The First Resurrection

The Origin of the First Resurrection

The term "the first resurrection" is found in Revelation 20:5–6: "(The rest of the dead did not come to life until the thousand years were ended.) This is the first resurrection. Blessed and holy are those who have part in the first resurrection. The second death has no power over them, but they will be priests of God and of Christ and will reign with him for a thousand years."

Theologians who attempt to put all the resurrections together into one grand resurrection at the end of the present age find in the expression "the first resurrection" sufficient proof that there is no previous resurrection. It does not take much investigation of Scripture, however, to find that this is a false deduction. Several resurrections precede that which is called "the first resurrection." This becomes evident when the order of the various resurrections is laid out.

The Order of Resurrections

Though there are numerous restorations to life in both the Old and New Testaments, resurrection in the sense of being given a resurrection body that will last forever did not occur until Jesus Christ was raised from the dead. His resurrection is the first resurrection (Matt. 28:1–7; Mark 16:1–11; Luke 24:1–12; John 20:1–18).

The second resurrection is recorded in Matthew 27:50–53. The Scriptures declare that when the earthquake occurred at the time of Christ's resurrection, tombs were broken open and bodies of holy people who had died were raised to life. Later, after Christ was raised from the dead, a number of these individuals were seen in Jerusalem. "At that moment the curtain of the temple was torn in two from top to bottom. The earth shook and the rocks split. The tombs broke open and the bodies of many holy people who had died were raised to life. They came out of the tombs, and after Jesus' resurrection they went into the holy city and appeared to many people" (vv. 51–53). The sequence of events seems to be that at the time of the earthquake when Christ died the tombs were broken open— that is, unsealed. The resurrection and the appearance of the people who were raised from the tombs, however, did not occur until after Jesus' resurrection.

The third resurrection will occur in connection with the rapture of the church (1 Thess. 4:13–18; cf. 1 Cor. 15:50–53). At the Rapture "the dead in Christ will rise first. After that, we who are still alive and are left will be caught up together with them in the clouds to meet the Lord in the air" (1 Thess. 4:16–17). This resurrection apparently refers to everyone who is baptized into the body of Christ from the Day of Pentecost until the Rapture. Old Testament saints seem to be resurrected at a later time.

The fourth resurrection is prophesied in Revelation 11. Two witnesses who will be killed for their testimony will be left lying in the streets of Jerusalem and will be raised from the dead on the third day (v. 8). "After the three and a half days a breath of life from God entered them, and they stood on their feet, and terror struck those who saw them. Then they heard a loud voice from heaven saying to them, 'Come up here.' And they went up to heaven in a cloud, while their enemies looked on" (vv. 11–12).

The fifth resurrection is described in Revelation 20:4–6. As the context indicates, this resurrection has to do with the martyred dead of the Great Tribulation. John wrote, "And I saw the souls of those who had been beheaded because of their testimony for Jesus and because of the word of God. They had not worshiped the beast or his image and had not received his mark on their foreheads or their hands. They came to life and reigned with Christ a thousand years" (v. 4). If the resurrection at the Rapture covers all of the saints of the present age since Pentecost, this resurrection relates to the saints who will die in the period between the Rapture and the Second Coming. This will include the martyred dead that are mentioned here specifically. It is amazing how scholars have ignored the plain statement of this passage and tried to make it a general resurrection of all the dead or even make it a reference to the new birth of the believer at the time of his faith in Christ.

The Scriptures here show plainly that this resurrection refers to a particular class of people who will be raised in connection with the second coming of Christ.

The sixth resurrection will be that of the Old Testament saints: "Multitudes who sleep in the dust of the earth will awake: some to everlasting life, others to shame and everlasting contempt" (Dan. 12:2). Though the fact that all people who die will be raised is commonly assumed in the Old Testament, there are relatively few references that speak specifically of their resurrection. This is one of the major passages.

A second major prediction of this resurrection is found in Isaiah 26:19: "But your dead will live; their bodies will rise. You who dwell in the dust, wake up and shout for joy. Your dew is like the dew of the morning; the earth will give birth to her dead."

A third major reference is found in Ezekiel 37 in connection with the restoration of the children of Israel. Though the figure is largely that of the restoration of the nation of Israel, bodily resurrection is also mentioned in verses 13–14: "Then you, my people, will know that I am the LORD, when I open your graves and bring you up from them. I will put my Spirit in you and you will live, and I will settle you in your own land. Then you will know that I the LORD have spoken, and I have done it, declares the LORD."

According to Daniel 12:1, this resurrection will come at the close of the tribulation period described in Daniel 11:36–45:

"There will be a time of distress such as has not happened from the beginning of nations until then. But at that time your people—everyone whose name is found written in the book— will be delivered." The resurrection is mentioned specifically in the verse that follows. Though the chronological arrangement of this passage in relation to the resurrection of the Tribulation dead is not given in Scripture, it is probable that this will follow the resurrection of the Tribulation dead, and the Old Testament saints, accordingly, will be in the sixth and final resurrection of the righteous.

The last resurrection has to do with the judgment of the Great White Throne as recorded in Revelation 20:11–15. In this resurrection all the wicked dead, who up to this time have been in Hades, will be resurrected and cast into the lake of fire.

The order of these seven resurrections should make plain that the resurrection of Revelation 20:5–6 is not first in the sense of being before all previous resurrections. If that is not the meaning, what does the term "the first resurrection" mean?

The Nature of the First Resurrection

As the context indicates, the resurrection of the Tribulation dead will follow the Tribulation but precede the millennial kingdom. In Revelation 20:7–10 the millennial kingdom follows the resurrection of the Tribulation dead. During this time Satan will be bound (vv. 1–3). At the end of the thousand years Satan will be let loose and will cause a rebellion against God. Then he will be judged and cast into the lake of burning sulfur (v. 10). Accordingly, the point of the term "the first resurrection" is that it is first, not in the sense of being number one or prior to all resurrections, but in the sense that it occurs before the final resurrection, the resurrection of the wicked. In other words, the Tribulation dead will be raised before the millennial kingdom and before the resurrection of the wicked at the Great White Throne judgment. To use the term "first resurrection" to refer to the new birth, as amillenarians do in evading the teaching of this passage on the millennial kingdom, or to refer to it as the Rapture, as posttribulationists do, based on the idea that there could not be a resurrection before this, are both inadequate explanations of the expression. The doctrine of resurrection falls into place when one recognizes that that there is a series of resurrections in Scripture, beginning with the resurrection of

Christ and ending with the resurrection of the wicked. In this series the resurrection of the martyred dead of the Great Tribulation is resurrection number five and is probably followed by the resurrection of the Old Testament saints. The resurrection of the wicked is the last resurrection.

34

Judgments at
the Second Coming

Many attempts have been made by Christian scholars to merge all the judgments at the Second Coming into one great judgment. However, careful attention to the details relating to various judgments of Scripture reveal that while everyone will be judged, not everyone will be judged at the same time or in the same way. Prior to the second coming of Christ, there was judgment on Christ when he hung on the cross as a sacrifice for the sin of the whole world. His sacrificial death made it possible for God to extend forgiveness and righteousness to those who trust in Christ as Savior and Lord. As has been brought out previously, after the Rapture believers of the church age will go to the judgment seat of Christ where they will be judged and rewarded according to their works.

At the Second Coming many issues will be brought to a head as Christ establishes his millennial kingdom on earth. At least seven judgments will take place then.

Judgment on the Armies Gathered in the Holy Land

Under satanic temptation and enticement, the armies of the world, according to Revelation 16:13–16, will gather in the Holy Land to fight for superiority. This will signal the breakup of the world government and the rebellion of major nations against the world ruler. Satan will gather the armies of the world to have them present when the second coming of Christ occurs. He will do this with the vain hope that they will be triumphant over the army from heaven. As brought out in Revelation 19, Christ will speak the word and the armies and their horses will all be killed instantly. According to Revelation 19:15, "Out of his mouth comes a sharp sword with which to strike down the nations." The result is that there will be a terrible slaughter of millions of men and their beasts, and vultures will feed on their dead bodies. John recorded, "And I saw an angel standing in the sun, who cried in a loud voice to all the birds flying in midair, 'Come, gather together for the great supper of God, so that you may eat the flesh of kings, generals, and mighty men, of horses and their riders, and the flesh of all people, free and slave, small and great' " (vv. 17–18). Through the centuries people have persisted in the false belief that they can rebel against God and win. Scriptures clearly prove that there is no victory for those who are opposed to God, and judgment is sure.

Judgment on the World Ruler and His Associate

According to Revelation 19:20, the world ruler, designated "the beast," and his associate, designated "the false prophet," will be captured and thrown into the lake of fire: "But the beast was captured, and with him the false prophet who had performed the miraculous signs on his behalf. With these signs he had deluded those who had received the mark of the beast and worshiped his image. The two of them were thrown alive into the fiery lake of burning sulfur."

As will be seen in the study of the Great White Throne, up to this time all the unsaved dead will be in Hades, a place of torment but not a place of permanent punishment. The lake of fire which, according to Matthew 25:41, is "the eternal fire prepared for the devil and his angels," up to this time will have had no one in it. But the Beast and the False Prophet have the distinction of being the first to be thrown into this everlasting punishment. According to Revelation 20:10, at the end of the Millennium they will still be in the lake of fire. The capture and judgment of the Beast and the False Prophet mark the end of the times of the Gentiles (Luke 21:24) which began with the capture of Jerusalem in 605 B.C. by Nebuchadnezzar and the Babylonian armies. From that time until the Second Coming, except for brief periods when Israel asserted her independence, Jerusalem was indeed "trampled on by the Gentiles" (v. 24). The present rebellion against God, which is so characteristic of our generation in which many live as if God does not exist, will come into its judgment at this time, and the earth will be brought into subjection to Jesus Christ as King of Kings and Lord of Lords.

Judgment on Satan

In Revelation 20:1–3 John says that Satan will be rendered inactive for a thousand years after Christ's second coming:

> And I saw an angel coming down out of heaven, having the key to the Abyss and holding in his hand a great chain. He seized the dragon, that ancient serpent, who is the devil, or Satan, and bound him for a thousand years. He threw him into the Abyss, and locked and sealed it over him, to keep him from deceiving the nations anymore until the thousand years were ended. After that, he must be set free for a short time.

To understand this prophecy, it is very important to notice the details. This prediction, like many others, has been tampered with by the amillenarians who have attempted to make the binding of Satan begin with the first coming of Christ. This is not supported by either Scripture or experience. Satan is very much alive and well and still going around tempting, destroying, and murdering, as the Scriptures testify. The context here is clearly the second coming of Christ and the series of judgments that will result from it, as itemized in Revelation 19.

One must distinguish between what John saw and the interpretation that was given to him. What he saw was an angel with a great chain binding Satan and throwing him into the Abyss—that is, the natural home of the demon world—then locking the door and sealing it so that it would be impossible for anyone to enter or leave. God used illustrative language here to make clear to readers that Satan is not going to be loose in the

Millennium to do any tempting. Apparently the entire demon world will also be shackled. In addition to seeing the vision, John was also told the meaning of it—that Satan would be inactive for the thousand years following the Second Coming. John could not see the thousand years but was informed of this fact. Visions must be interpreted, but one is not free to change the factual revelation of the purpose of the binding of Satan. Because this destroys the amillennial point of view, its adherents have strenuously resisted accepting this passage. Nevertheless, it is plain that the second coming of Christ will usher in the millennial kingdom rather than bring it to its conclusion. It is also clear that Satan's binding will begin with the second coming of Christ and continue until the end of the thousand years. As the prophecy itself states, at that time he will be free again for a short period. His final judgment will come at the end of the Millennium when he will be cast into the lake of fire (Rev. 20:10).

Judgment of the Tribulation Martyrs

As previously pointed out, the Tribulation martyrs and apparently all the Tribulation righteous dead will be resurrected at the Second Coming. The purpose for the resurrection is so that they can reign with Christ a thousand years. Scripture clearly reveals the chronological order of the second coming of Christ, the resurrection of the Tribulation saints, and then their reign with Christ a thousand years after his second coming. Here again amillenarians work overtime to try to eliminate this contradiction of their point of view. Common among them is the theory that the resurrection of the martyred dead is simply a symbolic way of expressing their new birth. Accordingly, they reject the concept of a literal resurrection and a literal thousand-year reign of Christ, which Scripture distinctly teaches. Though it is not stated in so many words here in Revelation 20, it is obvious that, having been raised from the dead, the Tribulation saints receive their final reward. Hebrews 9:27 says, "man is destined to die once, and after that to face judgment." As with the church, which was raptured, others will be judged at the time of their resurrection. This is also true of that portion of the church who will be resurrected from the dead. The reward of the martyrs will be that, inasmuch as they have suffered for Christ, they will reign with Christ. This is brought out in

2 Timothy 2:12, "If we endure, we will also reign with him." Suffering relates to this life, reward to the life to come. The Tribulation martyrs will join the church in reigning with Christ on earth.

Judgment at the Resurrection of Old Testament Saints

Old Testament saints will probably be raised at the time of the Second Coming, as stated in Daniel 12:2: "'Multitudes who sleep in the dust of the earth will awake: some to everlasting life, others to shame and everlasting contempt.'" Some say Old Testament saints will be resurrected at the Rapture, but those who are raised at the Rapture are referred to as "the dead in Christ" (1 Thess. 4:16). This phrase seems to relate to those who are baptized into the body of Christ, a work of God that began on the Day of Pentecost and is peculiar to the present age of the church. Accordingly, it seems that the resurrection of the church will be a selective resurrection. This is indicated in Paul's statement in Philippians 3:11 of his desire "to attain to the resurrection from the dead." Obviously Paul believed in a selective rather than a general resurrection of the righteous. A careful search of all the resurrection passages indicates that while every righteous person who has died will be resurrected in time to participate in the millennial kingdom, even the resurrection of the righteous is not accomplished in one resurrection but in a series of resurrections.

As in other instances of the resurrection from the dead, those raised will then be judged. According to Daniel 12:3, "'Those who are wise will shine like the brightness of the heavens, and those who lead many to righteousness, like the stars for ever and ever.'" The principle of resurrection and then judgment must be applied here, as in all cases of resurrection. Accordingly, at the beginning of the Millennium only those who are unsaved will remain in their unresurrected state, and all the righteous will have been raised at one time or another in the proper order of their resurrection.

Judgment on Living Israelites

As brought out in the Olivet Discourse as well as in other passages, there will be left in the world at the time of the Second Coming many living Israelites as well as living Gentiles.

Though many Jews will have been martyred in the Tribulation and then raised at the Second Coming, living Israelites will need to survive the purging judgments relative to their qualifications to enter into the millennial kingdom. Apparently there will also be preliminary rewards for those who have been faithful.

The general theme of Matthew 24:25 is that of preparedness for the coming of the Lord. Those who are wicked will be assigned a place of judgment and death at the time of the Second Coming. Those who are righteous will enter into the kingdom blessing. This is indicated in the parable of the ten virgins. The five virgins who are prepared join the wedding procession of Christ and his church and participate in the wedding feast and the millennial kingdom that follows. Likewise, in the parable of the talents, when the lord comes back, the principle of reward is carried out, and those faithful servants who had the five talents and the two talents will be rewarded with additional responsibilities, as will be true in the millennial kingdom. On the other hand, the man with one talent, depicting one who had the possibility of salvation and reward but lost it through unbelief and wickedness, will be put to death and excluded from the kingdom.

The judgment of Israel revealed in Matthew 24–25 is the climax and clarification of the many predictions of judgment of Israel; sometimes they are judged as a separate people, and sometimes they are included in general judgments (Ps. 9:7; 50:3; 96:13; Eccl. 11:9; 12:14; Ezek. 18:20–28; Dan. 7:9–10; Amos 4:12; Matt. 3:12; 7:22; 8:29; 11:22; 12:36–37, 41–42; 13:30, 40–43, 49–50; 16:27; 22:13; Mark 8:38; Luke 3:17; 10:10–14; 11:31–32; 12:2–5; 13:24–30; 20:45–47; John 5:22; 12:48; Acts 10:42; 17:31; 24:25; Rom. 2:5–16; 14:10–12; 1 Cor. 3:13; 4:5; 2 Cor. 5:10; 2 Thess. 1:5–8; 2 Tim. 4:1, 8; Heb. 6:2; 9:27; 10:27; 1 Peter 4:5, 7; 2 Peter 2:4; 3:7–12; 1 John 4:17; Jude 6, 14–15, 24; Rev. 6:17; 11:18).

The main point in the judgment of living Israelites is whether they are worthy to enter the millennial kingdom. This judgment, like other judgments relating to the Second Coming, makes plain that after the judgments at the beginning of the Millennium the entire remaining adult population will be saved. Obviously this does not apply to children who have not reached the age of responsibility, but all those who are responsible for their salvation who have not trusted Christ will be put to death at the beginning of the Millennium and will have their final judgment at the end of the Millennium at the Great White Throne judgment.

Judgment on Living Gentiles

Many Scriptures confirm that just as the living Israelites will be judged at the second coming of Christ, Gentiles who have survived the Tribulation will be subject to the purging judgment of Christ. This is brought out in particular in Matthew 25:31–46. In this passage the sheep are contrasted with the goats, the sheep representing those who are saved and the goats representing those who are lost. The goats are cast into everlasting fire, which involves their eternal punishment (v. 46). This passage has caused some to stumble because it does not clearly declare the Gospel message and distinguishes the sheep and the goats by their works. In particular, the sheep are distinguished as those who have befriended the brethren—that is, the Jews who are persecuted in the Great Tribulation.

Under the widespread anti-Semitism that will prevail in the Great Tribulation, anyone who befriends a Jew in trouble will be distinguished as a person who has trust in the Bible and trust in Jesus Christ. Accordingly, while their works do not save them, their works are the basis of distinguishing them from the unsaved, represented by the goats. At the beginning of the Millennium both Jews and Gentiles will be judged on their qualifications to enter the millennial kingdom, and only adults who are saved will be allowed to enter. As the millennial kingdom unfolds, as children grow up and face the question of whether they will trust Christ, a sizable portion of the population will go through the motions of outwardly conforming to the rule of the King yet not actually be born again. These will be judged, of course, at the end of the millennial kingdom.

At the second coming of Christ all the righteous will have been judged. Only the wicked will be left in the graves; and the remaining judgments will deal with the wicked at the Great White Throne and with those who are in rebellion against the King throughout the thousand-year reign of Christ. Open rebellion will not be permitted, but apparently the hypocrisy of profession without reality will not be revealed until the end of the Millennium.

This survey of judgments should make clear that the viewpoint of some scholars that all judgments occur at the same time and the same place at the Second Coming is not true. Some judgments will precede the Second Coming, and some will follow.

35

The Millennial Kingdom: Restoration of Israel

A Major Departure From Previous Dispensations

An major event such as the second coming of Christ would obviously bring about a significant change in the earth and its government. If the many prophecies relating to the millennial kingdom are taken in their natural sense, they describe a dispensation that is different from that of the law and also from the present age of grace. The physical presence of Christ will bring about major changes as his rule and authority extend over the entire earth as King of Kings and Lord of Lords and as he assumes the throne of David as the Son of David and reigns over Israel. Amillennialism, which denies such a future millennial kingdom, is beset with many problems as it trys to explain away hundreds of verses that describe this kingdom on earth. Accordingly, the premillennial point of view—that as a result of Christ's coming the millennial kingdom unfolds for one thousand years—is preferable by far, giving to the Scriptures of both the Old and New Testaments the attention and normal interpretation they require.

The millennial kingdom is a major part of the second coming of Christ. It includes the destruction of the armies gathered against God in the Holy Land (Rev. 19:17, 21), the capture of the Beast and the False Prophet and their being cast into the lake of fire (v. 20), the binding of Satan (20:1–3), and the resurrection of the martyred dead of the Tribulation to reign with Christ a thousand years (vv. 4–6). A literal interpretation of Revelation 20:4–6 requires that Christ reign on earth for a thousand years following his second coming.

Such a reign of Christ will bring righteousness to a wicked world, peace to a war-torn world, prosperity to an economically disabled world, new standards of spiritual and social life, and a renovated earth suited for the millennial kingdom.

The Reign of Jesus Christ as the Son of David

In keeping with the announced purpose of God to put a man on David's throne who could rule forever, Jesus Christ will come back to assume this throne. At the present time he is in heaven awaiting this time of triumph over his enemies (Ps. 110:1–2). As the One risen from the dead (Acts 2:29–36), he is qualified to sit on the throne of God forever and without successors. His reign over the house of Israel will be from Jerusalem (Isa. 2:1–4), and from the same location he will also reign as King of Kings and Lord of Lords over the entire earth (Ps. 72:8–11, 17–19). The throne of David is an earthly throne, not a heavenly throne, and is not to be identified with the throne of God in heaven.

The reign of Christ over Israel is a part of his kingdom reign over the entire earth. According to Psalm 2:6–9, it was God's purpose that Jesus Christ would rule over the entire earth. In the revelation given to Daniel in 2:35, the stone, which characterized the kingdom of God, "became a huge mountain and filled the whole earth." This is spelled out in Daniel 7:14, where it is said of Christ: "He was given authority, glory and sovereign power; all peoples, nations and men of every language worshiped him. His dominion is an everlasting dominion that will not pass away, and his kingdom is one that will never be destroyed." The rule of Christ will not only be universal but also completely just (Isa. 2:3–4; 11:2–5).

In its beginning the millennial reign will be over adults who are saved, as both unsaved Gentiles and unsaved Jews will have been purged out and only adult Christians and children will be allowed to enter the millennial kingdom. Their children, however, will be subject to later decision regarding their salvation. Likewise children who are born in the millennial reign will face decision about salvation as they grow up. As the Millennium unfolds, there will come into existence a large number of people who will merely profess salvation without having the reality. This will explain the evil in the Millennium and also the final rebellion at the end.

The place of Israel and their restoration in the millennial kingdom cannot be overemphasized, for Israel is a major part of God's purpose to subdue the whole earth. Accordingly, the return of Israel to the land, their spiritual restoration, and Christ's government over them are essential to God's purpose. As such, the children of Israel will be exalted above the Gentiles and be given a special favored place as God's chosen people (Isa. 14:1–2; 49:22–23; 60:14–17; 61:6–7).

Gentiles will also have a major place in the millennial kingdom but will be second to Israel in their spiritual blessing (Isa. 14:1–2; 49:22–23; 61:5–9).

The Restoration of Israel

The Millennium will be the occasion of the final restoration of Israel. At the beginning of the millennial kingdom Israel will experience her final and permanent regathering (Ezek. 39:25–29; Amos 9:15). Christ's reign over Israel will be glorious and will be a complete and literal fulfillment of all that God promised David (Jer. 23:5–8).

Ezekiel 37 provides a panoramic view of this restoration. Using the symbolism of a valley full of dry bones, God showed the prophet the rejuvenation of these skeletons. The bones rejoined together and tendons covered the bones. Then breath and life entered them.

> The hand of the LORD was upon me, and he brought me out by the Spirit of the LORD and set me in the middle of a valley; it was full of bones. He led me back and forth among them, and I saw a great many bones on the floor of the valley, bones that were very dry. He asked me, "Son of man, can these bones live?"

I said, "O Sovereign LORD, you alone know."

Then he said to me, "Prophesy to these bones and say to them, 'Dry bones, hear the word of the LORD! This is what the Sovereign LORD says to these bones: I will make breath enter you, and you will come to life. I will attach tendons to you and make flesh come upon you and cover you with skin; I will put breath in you, and you will come to life. Then you will know that I am the LORD.'" (vv. 1–6)

The prophecy is described as fulfilled in Ezekiel 37:7–8: "So I prophesied as I was commanded. And as I was prophesying, there was a noise, a rattling sound, and the bones came together, bone to bone. I looked, and tendons and flesh appeared on them and skin covered them, but there was no breath in them." This passage is a symbolic presentation of the restoration of Israel from a situation where there seemed to be no restoration possible to one where they have life and breath and substance. This is explained in Ezekiel 37:11–13:

Then he said to me: "Son of man, these bones are the whole house of Israel. They say, 'Our bones are dried up and our hope is gone; we are cut off.' Therefore prophesy and say to them: 'This is what the Sovereign LORD says: O my people, I am going to open your graves and bring you up from them; I will bring you back to the land of Israel. Then you, my people, will know that I am the LORD, when I open your graves and bring you up from them.'"

Ezekiel was also informed that the kingdoms of Judah and Israel would be reunited, and the two "sticks" would become one (vv. 15–17).

The restoration of Israel is summarized in the word of the Lord to Ezekiel, "'This is what the Sovereign LORD says: I will take the Israelites out of the nations where they have gone. I will gather them from all around and bring them back into their own land. I will make them one nation in the land, on the mountains of Israel. There will be one king over all of them and they will never again be two nations or be divided into two kingdoms'" (37:21–22).

The restoration of Israel will have other characteristics in addition to physical and political renewal. In Ezekiel 37:14 God says to his people, "I will put my Spirit in you and you will live."

An outstanding feature of the restoration of Israel will be the resurrection of David, who will serve as a coregent with Christ. The Lord said through Ezekiel: "'My servant David will be king over them, and they will all have one shepherd. They will follow my laws and be careful to keep my decrees. They will live in the land I gave to my servant Jacob, the land where your fathers lived. They and their children and their children's children will live there forever, and David my servant will be their prince forever'" (37:24–25).

Though many have tried to explain away this passage, it obviously requires the second coming of Christ, the establishment of David's kingdom on earth, the resurrection of David, and David's sharing the throne of Israel as coregent with Christ. The fact that David will share the throne of Christ in the millennial kingdom is brought out in many other passages (Jer. 30:9; 33:15–17; Ezek. 34:23–24; Hos. 3:5). This prophecy cannot be fulfilled today because David has not been resurrected and because there is no Davidic throne on earth. There would be no sufficient reason for questioning what the Scriptures teach here if it were not for the theory that there will be no literal millennial kingdom. Once the reality of the millennial kingdom is accepted, the concept of David's reigning with Christ becomes a very natural outgrowth of the promises God gave to David.

Spiritual Life in the Millennium

General teachings on spiritual life in the Millennium. Because of Christ's physical presence on the earth and the manifestation of his glory, deity, and righteous rule, spiritual life in the Millennium will take on characteristics different from those of any previous dispensation. The fact that all adults will have been saved going into the period will begin an approach to spiritual life that had not been possible in any previous age. According to Isaiah, "The earth will be full of the knowledge of the LORD as the waters cover the sea" (11:9). Jeremiah declared concerning the new covenant:

> "I will put my law in their minds
>   and write it on their hearts.
> I will be their God,
>   and they will be my people.

> *No longer will a man teach his neighbor,*
> *or a man his brother, saying, 'Know the LORD,'*
> *because they will all know me,*
> *from the least of them to the greatest,"*
> *declares the LORD.*
> *For I will forgive their wickedness*
> *and will remember their sins no more."* *(31:33–34)*

The widespread knowledge of scriptural truth as well as truth about the person and work of Christ will be an amazing foundation for spiritual life.

The Holy Spirit will indwell all believers in the millennial kingdom, much as he does in the present age (Ezek. 36:27; 37:14; cf. Jer. 31:33). A summary of the work of the Holy Spirit is provided in Ezekiel 36:24–27:

> "'For I will take you out of the nations; I will gather you from all the countries and bring you back into your own land. I will sprinkle clean water on you, and you will be clean; I will cleanse you from all your impurities and from all your idols. I will give you a new heart and put a new spirit in you; I will remove from you your heart of stone and give you a heart of flesh. And I will put my Spirit in you and move you to follow my decrees and be careful to keep my laws.'"

In addition to the fact that every Christian will be indwelt by the Holy Spirit in the Millennium, there is evidence that there will be many more Christians filled with the Spirit than is common in our present age (Isa. 32:15; 44:3; Ezek. 39:29; Joel 2:28–29).

In contrast to the present age, in the Millennium there will be no opposition from Satan or the demon world, and this will release spiritual life in an unprecedented way. There will be joy and peace and worship characterizing the world in that future day which is found in only relatively small groups of Christians in the present age.

One of the outstanding features of the millennial kingdom will be Christ's reigning in Jerusalem and manifesting his glory visibly. Many prophecies refer to the glory of Christ manifest in the millennial kingdom. The Second Coming itself will be a manifestation of the glory of God (Matt. 25:30). In Psalm 72:19

the whole earth is declared to be filled with his glory. Inasmuch as Christ will manifest all the attributes of God, each of which forms a part of his glory, there will be a revelation of the power and presence of God greater than in any previous dispensation. Christ will be the object of worship and obedience, and those who reject him will have to reject this abundant revelation.

The Place of the Millennial Temple

According to Ezekiel 40:1–46:24, the millennial age will feature a magnificent temple that will serve as the center for the priestly rituals and offerings. Because of the opposition to the premillennial point of view, many attempts have been made to explain away this millennial temple. Amillenarians are obligated to find some other explanation than the literal interpretation, because they do not accept the concept of the Millennium itself. Accordingly, they have made a number of explanations, none of which is supported by the facts. Some have declared that this is a description of Solomon's temple or of the temple that was built by those returning from the Captivity. However, the plans of the temple are totally different, as a comparison of the specifications of Ezekiel's temple (Ezek. 40:5–44:9) and passages referring to the preceding temples (1 Kings 6:2–7:15; 2 Chron. 3:3–4:22; Ezra 6:3–4) show. Failing in their attempt to identify the temple of Ezekiel with previous temples, amillenarians have resorted to spiritualization: the temple is merely a symbol or an ideal and the passages are not intended to convey that an actual temple will be built. Such an interpretation, however, does not fit the revelation given in Ezekiel which goes into great detail about the architecture of the temple and its use, much of which would not have symbolic significance apart from the overall significance of the temple itself.

The most natural interpretation and one that is in keeping with the interpretation of prophecy in general is to accept this prophecy of a future temple as literal—with the anticipation that in the millennial kingdom this temple will be built as specified in Ezekiel. If the premillennial interpretation of Scripture is accepted and the Millennium is recognized in the prophetic program, there remains no reason why such a temple should not be built.

The significance of the temple is that it will provide a suitable vehicle for the worship and service of God in the millennial kingdom, similar and yet different from that provided under the Mosaic Law. The presence of the temple will assure God's dwelling in their midst, not only Jesus Christ on the throne in Jerusalem, but the Father and the Holy Spirit as well. The glory that had left Solomon's temple (Ezek. 8–11) will fill the millennial temple as recorded by Ezekiel 44:4: "Then the man brought me by way of the north gate to the front of the temple. I looked and saw the glory of the LORD filling the temple of the LORD, and I fell facedown." The temple along with the written Word of God and the visible presence of Christ will serve to provide an abundance of revelation to the millennial scene that has not been characteristic of any previous age.

The temple to be built in the Millennium will be much larger than any historic temple of Israel, being a square 875 feet (500 cubits) in width and length. Like previous temples, it will face east and will have an outer wall on the other three sides. The temple will have thirty rooms built on three levels. Except for the western wall, the other three sides will have a large outer court that will surround the temple itself with gates in each of the three walls. One of the outstanding features of the temple, as in the previous temples, will be provision for animal sacrifices.

The provision for animal sacrifices is a subject of controversy. The idea of sacrifices in the millennial kingdom seems to contradict the concept that Christ's one sacrifice was sufficient. As stated in Hebrews:

> Then Christ would have had to suffer many times since the creation of the world. But now he has appeared once for all at the end of the ages to do away with sin by the sacrifice of himself. Just as man is destined to die once, and after that to face judgment, so Christ was sacrificed once to take away the sins of many people; and he will appear a second time, not to bear sin, but to bring salvation to those who are waiting for him. (9:26–28)

In attempting to explain the sacrifices of the millennial temple, the thought is not that the death of Christ is insufficient but rather that the sacrifices are a memorial of Christ's sacrifice on Calvary, much as the Old Testament sacrifices looked forward to fulfillment in Christ's death. The provisions for sacrifice in Ezekiel differ somewhat from those provided under the Mosaic Law. Millennium sacrifices will be required by the ideal circumstances that characterize the millennial kingdom in which sin would lose some of its awful character. The sacrificial system, accordingly, is a reminder of the necessity of blood sacrifice that points back to the death of Christ as the one ground for salvation from sin.

Though the sacrificial system is tied to Ezekiel's temple here, there are other references to sacrifices in the Millennium that support the same conclusion (Isa. 56:7; 66:20-23; Jer. 33:18; Zech. 14:16-21; Mal. 3:3-4). At least five of the Old Testament prophets join in affirming a sacrificial system in the millennial kingdom. The temple and its system of sacrifices will be an important part of life in and around Jerusalem and will serve to emphasize the necessity of life in Christ in the Millennium as well as in other dispensations.

Concerning the worship and service of God in the temple, Ezekiel was informed that the eastern gate should be kept closed. The explanation is, " 'It is to remain shut because the LORD, the God of Israel, has entered through it. The prince himself is the only one who may sit inside the gateway to eat in the presence of the LORD. He is to enter by way of the portico of the gateway and go out the same way' " (44:2-3). The reference to the prince seems to be a reference to David, who is considered a prince under Christ (34:23-24; 37:24-25). The setting, of course, is the time of the millennial kingdom after the second coming of Christ and after the resurrection of David. The ruling that the eastern gate is to be reserved raises the interesting question concerning the eastern wall that is now in the wall of Jerusalem and has been closed for many centuries. The eastern gate of the present wall of Jerusalem is obviously not the same gate as the wall mentioned in Ezekiel 44, though probably both gates will be open when Jesus Christ comes to Jerusalem.

Various regulations were issued by Ezekiel concerning the functions of the priests and Levites in the temple worship. Special sacrifices were to be offered on the first month and the first day (45:18-19). The Passover feast is also mentioned as being observed on the first month of the fourteenth day, an event that followed the seven-day feast of unleavened bread (45:21-25).

Taken as a whole, spiritual life in the Millennium will be on a different level from that of any preceding generation and will form a fitting climax to the experience of the human race throughout the various dispensations.

Social and Economic Life in the Millennium

Salvation of the majority. As brought out in previous study, it is probable that the great majority of the population of the millennial kingdom will experience salvation in Christ. At the beginning all adults will be saved, as others have been purged out. As the Millennium progresses there will be an element of false profession due to the abundance of knowledge of the Lord (Jer. 31:34), but it would be reasonable to assume that more people will be saved than in our present world situation.

Righteousness and justice. In contrast to preceding generations, the millennial kingdom will feature justice and righteousness with Christ reigning on the throne.

> *"He will not judge by what he sees with his eyes,*
> *or decide by what he hears with his ears;*
> *but with righteousness he will judge the needy,*
> *with justice he will give decisions for the poor*
> *of the earth." (Isa. 11:3–4)*

With no need for armaments, all taxes will be used to bring about justice and equity for the people of the earth. Under the righteous judgment of Christ there probably will be a leveling out of wealth and elimination of extreme poverty.

Prosperity. In general, the world will experience unparalleled prosperity, not only in the area of peace and justice, but also in the abundance of material things. Jeremiah described this:

> *"They will come and shout for joy on the heights*
> *of Zion;*
> *they will rejoice in the bounty of the LORD—*
> *the grain, the new wine and the oil,*
> *the young of the flocks and herds.*
> *They will be like a well-watered garden,*
> *and they will sorrow no more.*
> *Then maidens will dance and be glad,*
> *young men and old as well.*
> *I will turn their mourning into gladness;*
> *I will give them comfort and joy instead of sorrow.*

I will satisfy the priests with abundance,
and my people will be filled with my bounty,"
declares the LORD. (31:12–14)

Ezekiel was provided a similar picture:

> " 'I will make a covenant of peace with them and rid the
> land of wild beasts so that they may live in the desert and
> sleep in the forests in safety. I will bless them and the
> places surrounding my hill. I will send down showers in
> season; there will be showers of blessing. The trees of the
> field will yield their fruit and the ground will yield its crops;
> the people will be secure in their land. They will know that
> I am the LORD, when I break the bars of their yoke and
> rescue them from the hands of those who enslaved them.
> They will no longer be plundered by the nations, nor will
> wild animals devour them. They will live in safety, and no
> one will make them afraid. I will provide for them a land
> renowned for its crops, and they will no longer be victims of
> famine in the land or bear the scorn of the nations.' "
> (34:25–29)

A similar picture of millennial bounty occurs in Amos 9:13–14.
There will be just compensation for their labor, and they will
not be robbed of their produce. Isaiah prophesied:

"They will build houses and dwell in them;
they will plant vineyards and eat their fruit.
No longer will they build houses and others live
in them,
or plant and others eat.
For as the days of a tree,
so will be the days of my people;
my chosen ones will long enjoy
the works of their hands.
They will not toil in vain
or bear children doomed to misfortune;
for they will be a people blessed by the LORD,
they and their descendants with them." (65:21–23)

In keeping with this promise of prosperity, the earth will bring
forth abundantly and its Adamic curse will be lifted. As Isaiah
predicted it,

The desert and the parched land will be glad;
    the wilderness will rejoice and blossom.
Like the crocus, it will burst into bloom;
    it will rejoice greatly and shout for joy. (35:1–2)

According to Isaiah, God "will also send you rain for the seed you sow in the ground, and the food that comes from the land will be rich and plentiful. In that day your cattle will graze in broad meadows. The oxen and donkeys that work the soil will eat fodder and mash, spread out with fork and shovel" (30:23–24). Though physical death will continue as a part of the curse pronounced on Adam, apparently the effect of the curse on the ground will be much alleviated, resulting in less physical want and starvation such as characterizes much of our present world.

Health and long life. In his first coming Christ fulfilled the prophecies that when he came he would heal the lame and the sick. Many of the passages, however, go beyond the first coming to the Second Coming and the millennial kingdom. People will live longer in the Millennium, and there will be less illness. Isaiah pictured this millennial situation:

"But be glad and rejoice forever
    in what I will create,
for I will create Jerusalem to be a delight
    and its people a joy.
I will rejoice over Jerusalem
    and take delight in my people;
the sound of weeping and of crying
    will be heard in it no more.

"Never again will there be in it
    an infant who lives but a few days,
    or an old man who does not live out his years;
he who dies at a hundred
    will be thought a mere youth;
he who fails to reach a hundred
    will be considered accursed.
They will build houses and dwell in them;
    they will plant vineyards and eat their fruit.
No longer will they build houses and others live
        in them,
    or plant and others eat.

For as the days of a tree,
* so will be the days of my people,*
my chosen ones will long enjoy
* the works of their hands.*
They will not toil in vain
* or bear children doomed to misfortune;*
for they will be a people blessed by the LORD,
* they and their descendants with them." (65:18–23)*

Isaiah also predicted:

Then will the eyes of the blind be opened
* and the ears of the deaf unstopped.*
Then will the lame leap like a deer,
* and the mute tongue shout for joy.*
Water will gush forth in the wilderness
* and streams in the desert.*
The burning sand will become a pool,
* and the thirsty ground bubbling springs. (35:5–7)*

In the millennial kingdom, in contrast to the decimation of the world's population in the Great Tribulation, there will be prosperity and added numbers. Jeremiah prophesied:

"From them will come songs of thanksgiving
* and the sound of rejoicing.*
I will add to their numbers,
* and they will not be decreased;" (30:19)*

And through Ezekiel, the Lord said: "I will make a covenant of peace with them; it will be an everlasting covenant. I will establish them and increase their numbers" (37:26).

Though the rule of death and sin will still be present in the millennial kingdom, the world's problems will be so alleviated that people will greatly enjoy life, live longer, and prosper in their pleasant circumstances.

Changes in the physical earth. In connection with the temple, Ezekiel predicted that there will be a great river flowing from the temple to the south, having sufficient volume so that one will not be able to wade across (47:3–6). The river banks will be covered with trees (vv. 7–9), and the river will have fish and other living creatures in it. Fresh water will apparently replace the salty Dead Sea, and the river will continue to flow to the south of Israel until it reaches the Gulf of Arabah. Ezekiel described this scene:

> Then he led me back to the bank of the river. When I arrived there, I saw a great number of trees on each side of the river. He said to me, "This water flows toward the eastern region and goes down into the Arabah where it enters the Sea. When it empties into the Sea, the water there becomes fresh. Swarms of living creatures will live wherever the river flows. There will be large numbers of fish, because this water flows there and makes the salt water fresh; so where the river flows everything will live. Fishermen will stand along the shore; from En Gedi to En Eglaim there will be places for spreading nets. The fish will be of many kinds—like the fish of the Great Sea. But the swamps and marshes will not become fresh; they will be left for salt. Fruit trees of all kinds will grow on both banks of the River. Their leaves will not wither, nor will their fruit fail. Every month they will bear, because the water from the sanctuary flows to them. Their fruit will serve for food and their leaves for healing." (47:6–12)

Important topographical changes will take place in the land of Palestine at the second coming of Christ. Zechariah described the cleavage of the Mount of Olives: "On that day his feet will stand on the Mount of Olives, east of Jerusalem, and the Mount of Olives will be split in two from east to west, forming a great valley, with half of the mountain moving north and half moving south" (14:4). Zechariah also commented on the living waters flowing from Jerusalem. In addition to the waters flowing from the temple described in Ezekiel 47, Zechariah revealed that water will flow from Jerusalem both to the east and south to the Dead Sea as well as to the west to the Mediterranean, "On that day living water will flow out from Jerusalem, half to the eastern sea and half to the western sea, in summer and in winter" (v. 8).

Jerusalem and the land around Jerusalem will be elevated: "The whole land, from Geba to Rimmon, south of Jerusalem, will become like the Arabah. But Jerusalem will be raised up and remain in its place, from the Benjamin Gate to the site of the First Gate, to the Corner Gate, and from the Tower of Hananel to the royal winepresses. It will be inhabited; never again will it be destroyed. Jerusalem will be secure" (Zech. 14:10–11).

Scholars who do not accept a future Millennium have difficulty interpreting these prophecies. However, the predictions make so much sense that, taken in their literal meaning, they constitute another support for the doctrine of the millennial kingdom.

Changes in the Holy Land will be in preparation for Israel's possessing the whole area described in Genesis 15:18–21, from the Euphrates River to the River of Egypt. In general, the Holy Land will extend from the north from approximately Damascus, using the Jordan River as the eastern border and the Mediterranean as the western border, and continue south until it reaches the border land of Egypt, the River of Egypt.

Ezekiel outlined how the land will be distributed among the tribes, beginning with Dan at the north, then in order preceding from north to south, Asher, Naphtali, Manasseh, Ephraim, Reuben, and Judah. To the south of this will be the tribes of Benjamin, Simeon, Issachar, Zebulun, and Gad. The possession of the Land, repeated so often in the Old Testament as being Israel's ultimate inheritance, is fulfilled in this millennial picture.

In the center, of course, will be the millennial city, Jerusalem, which is described as having twelve gates. Though much smaller than the new Jerusalem in the new earth, the gates, like the new Jerusalem, will have the names of the twelve tribes of Israel. The northern gates will be named for Reuben, Judah, and Levi; the eastern gates for Joseph, Benjamin, and Dan, the southern gates for Simeon, Issachar, and Zebulun; and the western gates for Gad, Asher, and Naphtali (Ezek. 48:30–34). This prophecy has certainly never been fulfilled in history and requires a millennial kingdom and a millennial situation for its complete fulfillment. One of the important characteristics of Jerusalem in the millennial kingdom is that it will have the visible presence of God, and the glory of God will abide on the temple.

Human history of the present earth will end in this glorious thousand-year period in which Christ will reign supreme in Jerusalem. The Promised Land and its glorious capital city Jerusalem will be eclipsed only by the ultimate new heaven and new earth and New Jerusalem that will exist in eternity.

The Final Rebellion

Satan loosed. As promised in Revelation 20:3, Satan will be loosed at the end of the thousand years, and a rebellion against Christ's millennial rule will immediately follow:

> When the thousand years are over, Satan will be released from his prison and will go out to deceive the nations in the four corners of the earth—Gog and Magog—to gather them for battle. In number they are like the sand on the seashore. They marched across the breadth of the earth and surrounded the camp of God's people, the city he loves. But fire came down from heaven and devoured them. And the devil, who deceived them, was thrown into the lake of burning sulfur, where the beast and the false prophet had been thrown. They will be tormented day and night for ever and ever. (Rev. 20:7–10)

The thousand years of confinement will not change Satan's nature, and he will attempt to take the place of God and receive the worship and obedience that is due God alone. He will find a ready response on the part of those who have made a profession of following Christ in the Millennium but who now show their true colors. They will surround Jerusalem in an attempt to capture the capital city of the kingdom of David as well as of the entire world. The Scriptures report briefly, "But fire came down from heaven and devoured them" (Rev. 20:9).

This brief account brings to conclusion the long history of satanic rebellion against God in which humankind has participated. Now, at long last, evil will be judged, and Satan will be put out of commission.

The army that is raised to attempt to conquer Jerusalem is described in the words "Gog and Magog" (Rev. 20:8), and has confused many expositors. According to Ezekiel 38–39, Israel will be attacked by a coalition of six nations who will attack Israel from the north at a time when Israel is at peace. These are described as "Gog and Magog," Gog referring to the ruler and Magog referring to the people. As Ezekiel records, the battle will be a disaster. The entire invading force will be wiped out, and months are needed to restore order and to bury dead bodies.

The intrusion of the words "Gog and Magog" into 20:8 is not explained, and the sentence is complete if this expression is eliminated. It obviously refers to Satan and rulers and people who are gathered to attempt to conquer Jerusalem. The battle here, however, is totally different from that in Ezekiel 38–39. There the battle takes place in northern Palestine on the mountains of Israel. There the dead are destroyed by a series of catastrophes, of which fire is only one element. There life goes on after the battle, and months are consumed with burying the dead. Here is an entirely different sequence. Here God's enemies are gathered around the city of Jerusalem to capture the capital city. The judgment is immediate as fire comes down from heaven and devours those who are attacking the city. There is no need to bury the dead because they are consumed by fire. The location of the battle is different. The events that precede and the events that follow are different, and in Ezekiel 38 the invasion seems to be a part of the peace period preceding the Great Tribulation. Here it comes at the end of the millennial kingdom. In Ezekiel 38–39 Satan is not mentioned; here he is the main actor. The explanation for the expression "Gog and Magog" seems to be that the people who are gathered to capture Jerusalem here include both leaders and people—that is, Gog, the leader, and Magog, the people, as in Ezekiel 38, but a different people are in mind.

The question may fairly be asked why Satan will be loosed at this time. The Bible does not explain this, but it will be a demonstration of the incurable wickedness of Satan and the fact that even a thousand years' confinement have not changed his rebellion against God. It will support the concept that punishment must be eternal because wicked natures do not change. The judgment on the people who join Satan in rebellion will be a demonstration of the wickedness of human hearts, which will be rebellious in spite of living in an almost perfect environment where there is full knowledge of God and full revelation of the glory of Jesus Christ. Nevertheless, those who in hypocrisy have outwardly conformed to the rule of Christ will now manifest their true colors. It is the final proof that environment alone cannot change human nature, and there must be a new birth, a supernatural act of God in which persons take on a new nature and become children of God and saints. The history of the race has tested humankind under every possible circumstance, and in each of these circumstances it has failed, demonstrating beyond any question that only by the grace of God can anyone be saved in any dispensation, and that only by the grace of God can a race of holy people be brought to heaven. The final judgment on Satan will be evidence that God judges sin, and, apart from grace, there must be divine judgment on sin.

The end of Satan is stated briefly: "And the devil, who deceived them, was thrown into the lake of burning sulfur, where the beast and the false prophet had been thrown. They will be tormented day and night for ever and ever" (Rev. 20:10). The lake of fire has been especially prepared as the final judgment place of Satan and the fallen angels (Matt. 25:41). Here Satan will enter the lake of fire where he will remain forever.

A sad footnote is also indicated in this passage concerning the Beast and the False Prophet who as the world ruler and his associate will have been cast into the lake of fire a thousand years earlier. Here they will still be alive and in torment. "They will be tormented day and night for ever and ever" (Rev. 20:10) refers to Satan and the Beast and the False Prophet. Hard as it is for the human mind to contemplate unending torment, this is what the Bible teaches. Just as heaven goes on forever as a testimony to the grace of God, so the lake of fire will go on forever as a testimony to the righteousness of God.

With the judgment of Satan and of those who joined with him in rebellion against God, the Millennium will come to a sudden close, paving the way for the dramatic scene of the new heaven and the new earth that follows.

36

The Great White Throne Judgment

The Great White Throne Introduced

In John's vision as recorded in Revelation 20 he saw a great white throne: "Then I saw a great white throne and him who was seated on it. Earth and sky fled from his presence, and there was no place for them" (v. 11). The great white throne and him who sat on it were so impressive in majesty that not only creation but the earth and sky also fled before it. Though many thrones are mentioned in the Bible, some on earth and some in heaven, this one stands apart from all others and constitutes the bridge between the past and eternity future, which is described in Revelation 21–22.

The person sitting on the throne is not named, but it is undoubtedly Jesus Christ, the King of Kings and Lord of Lords. As stated in John 5:22, "The Father judges no one, but has entrusted all judgment to the Son," Christ has all judgment committed to him, and it is in keeping with God's purpose that Christ should rule over Israel (Ps. 2:6) as well as over all the nations (vv. 8–9). The concept of Christ's being the Judge is found frequently in Scripture (Matt. 19:28; 25:31; 2 Cor. 5:10). The time of this judgment will be at the end of the Millennium and the beginning of the eternal state, and the judgment is related to both of these factors.

The statement that the earth and sky flee from his presence is indicative of the conclusion that at the beginning of the eternal state our present physical world, such as we know it, will be destroyed and be replaced by an entirely new earth and heaven. We are given further information in Revelation 21:1: "The first heaven and the first earth had passed away, and there was no longer any sea." Though some scholars have resisted the idea that the present earth will be destroyed and, instead, prefer a renovated earth, the description of the present world being destroyed is so graphic in Scripture that there does not seem to be any just grounds for denying this conclusion (Matt. 24:35; Mark 13:31; Luke 16:17; 21:33; 2 Peter 3:10). The fact of the destruction of the earth is especially emphatic in 2 Peter 3:10: "But the day of the Lord will come like a thief. The heavens will disappear with a roar; the elements will be destroyed by fire, and the earth and everything in it will be laid bare." Peter further referred to the present earth as being "destroyed" in verse 11. In any event, it is clear that all present features of the earth, such as the oceans, the Mediterranean, the Holy Land, the Jordan River, and all other earthly boundaries will be absent in the new earth. Inasmuch as our present earth is like a gigantic clock that is running down and has been the scene of sin and rebellion against God, it is fitting that when an eternal situation is set up that will never run down or be destroyed, a new type earth and heaven will be created. Though the Scriptures do not give many details, it may be assumed that the new heaven and new earth will be in keeping with God's purpose to care for the saints in grace throughout all ages to come.

The Resurrection of the Wicked Dead

As Scripture seems to account for the resurrection of all the righteous prior to the second coming of Christ, it may be assumed, on the basis of the description given in this passage, that only the wicked dead will be raised. The Scriptures are silent concerning the lot of saints in the millennial kingdom, some of whom, no doubt, will die in the thousand years and will need resurrection, and some of whom will be living at the end of the Millennium and will need a changed state similar to that of the rapture of the church. Because believers today do not need to have this information, it is not given. The fact that death does not end human existence, however, is clearly brought out in this passage since the wicked dead are resurrected. John said: "And I saw the dead, great and small, standing before the throne, and books were opened. Another book was opened, which is the book of life. The dead were judged according to what they had done as recorded in the books. The sea gave up the dead that were in it, and death and Hades gave up the dead that were in them, and each person was judged according to what he had done" (Rev. 20:12–13). As in other judgments of God, there will be no distinction between small and great in the final judgment. All will be subject to the same standards of divine justice. As is true in other eternal judgments, judgments after death deal with works. For the righteous, it will constitute a time of reward, as illustrated in the judgment seat of Christ. For the wicked, their works are the basis of their judgment. Special mention is made of those who are raised up from the sea, because the bodies of those lost in the sea will have disintegrated and will require an unusual act of resurrection. Whatever the physical or supernatural process, it is obvious that God is equal to this, and they stand before God on the same basis in resurrection as those who have been buried on land.

As verse 13 makes clear, those who are being resurrected are coming from Hades. Here a careful distinction should be made between Hades and the lake of fire.

As Scriptures make plain, the wicked dead who die before this judgment go to Hades, a place of the dead and a place of torment. This is illustrated in the judgment of the rich man and Lazarus (Luke 16:19–31). The rich man goes to Hades and is suffering, in contrast to Lazarus, the beggar, who is at Abraham's side, a place of bliss and rest. The fact that torment goes on in Hades up to the time of the judgment of the Great White Throne is obvious.

The New Testament Hades and its Old Testament equivalent, Sheol, refer to the temporary place of the dead, not of eternal judgment. In some instances they may refer to the grave rather than to the intermediate state of the dead, as illustrated in the translations of Acts 2:27, 31. The NIV also translates hades to mean "depths" in Matthew 11:23 and Luke 10:15. In other instances, as here, it is rendered Hades (Matt. 16:18; Rev. 6:8). It is a matter of judgment as to whether it refers to the intermediate state, or Hades proper, or whether it refers to the place where the body is placed—that is, the grave. In every instance, however, it is clear that this is a temporary situation, not the permanent one, as is brought out here in Revelation 20. The term *Hades* is not the same as *gehenna*. In Scripture gehenna is a synonym for the lake of fire, or the eternal state, in contrast to the temporary state of Hades.

Originally gehenna referred to the "Valley of Hinnom," located south of Jerusalem where the Jews had offered their children to an idol. It was also a place used to dump things that were defiled, and those things were burned there. Accordingly, the fire there seems to have been continuous.

When gehenna is used for eternal punishment, however, it is not simply an adaptation of a local term but one that goes far beyond the Valley of Hinnom and describes the eternal punishment of the wicked.

Christ used gehenna as a term for eternal punishment. He also used the word in his warning concerning the final judgment on sin (Matt. 5:22, 29–30; 10:28; 18:9; 23:15, 33; Mark 9:43, 45, 47; Luke 12:5). The expression occurs also in James 3:6 but does not occur in the book of Revelation. However, it is clearly equivalent to the lake of fire, or the eternal punishment of the wicked.

Christ referred to "the fire of hell," literally the "gehenna of fire" (Matt. 5:22). Gehenna is described as a place "where the fire never goes out" (Mark 9:43) and a place " 'where "their worm does not die, and the fire is not quenched' " (Mark 9:48).

At the Great White Throne Judgment, temporary forms of punishment, such as is described as Hades, give place to the eternal punishment of being cast into the lake of fire. John further described the judgment: "Then death and Hades were thrown into the lake of fire. The lake of fire is the second death. If anyone's name was not found written in the book of life, he was thrown into the lake of fire" (Rev. 20:14–15). Those being resurrected from Hades and the grave will receive a body that can never be destroyed, but unlike the body of the righteous, it is a body that is still wicked, still in rebellion against God, and still deserving God's judgment. Being cast into the lake of fire does not end their existence, as illustrated in the continuance of the Beast and the False Prophet in the lake of fire after a thousand years (v. 10). This is described as the second death.

What is in mind here is that physical death is the first death, in which the soul is separated from the body. The second death, however, is eternal separation from God and is the lot of all those who have not received Christ and have not been resurrected in newness of life.

Those who are judged worthy of the lake of fire fail to meet the requirements of God's judgment in two respects. First, their works are not according to the will of God. Second, they do not have life, as witnessed by the fact that their names are not found in the Book of Life. The term "book of life" relates to the custom of keeping records of one's family tree. In God's dealing with Moses concerning the sin of the people of Israel, Moses said, "Please forgive their sin—but if not, then blot me out of the book you have written" (Ex. 32:32). God refers to the book in the following verse (v. 33). In the New Testament the Book of Life refers to the register of those who have received eternal life (Phil. 4:3; Rev. 3:5; 13:8; 17:8; 21:27).

The Book of Life has been variously construed as originally containing the names of all human beings. But if a person failed to receive salvation, his or her name was blotted out. Accordingly, those who are saved are referred to as having their names not blotted out of the Book of Life. Another concept is that only the names of those who are saved are recorded in the Book of Life. In Revelation 13:8 those who worship the Beast are referred to as "all whose names have not been written in the book of life" (cf. 17:8). This implies that their names never were in the Book of Life and that the Book of Life is restricted to those who are saved. The promise that names will not be blotted out of the Book of Life is tantamount to promising eternal salvation.

Failure to have one's name in the Book of Life is just ground for being cast into the lake of fire, as that person's sins have not been forgiven and he or she has not entered into God's rest.

It is only human to try to find some escape from the rigidity of eternal punishment, but if one dies without salvation, there is no escape. The Bible clearly pictures eternal punishment as continuing forever, just as heaven will continue forever for those who are saved. As heaven will constitute an eternal reminder of the grace of God, so the lake of fire will constitute an eternal reminder of the righteousness of God.

The question has often been raised as to what extent the lake of fire is symbolic rather than literal. Here the Bible does not give us much leeway. The rich man in Luke 16 claimed to be tormented by the flames, and this caused him to be thirsty for water. Whatever may be the character of the eternal punishment, it is obvious that from God's standpoint the nearest way to describe it is that of being tormented in a lake of fire.

Though the doctrine of eternal punishment is repugnant to the unsaved world and troubles even those who are saved, a thorough appreciation of the destiny of the wicked will do much to further zeal for preaching the Gospel and for winning souls for Christ. At the same time it causes Christians to worship and praise God for his grace as manifested in the death and resurrection of Jesus Christ. A confirming note concerning the judgment of the lake of fire is found in Revelation 21:8, which declares that the wicked "will be in the fiery lake of burning sulfur. This is the second death."

Having dealt with the destiny of Satan and the wicked world, John now turns to the bright prospect for the saints in the New Jerusalem.

37

The New Heaven and New Earth

The New Heaven and New Earth Introduced

The character and significance of the new heaven and the new earth and the New Jerusalem occupy the remaining two chapters of Revelation. John recorded his vision of the new heaven and the new earth: "Then I saw a new heaven and a new earth, for the first heaven and the first earth had passed away, and there was no longer any sea" (Rev. 21:1). The old earth and heaven had fled from the presence of Christ (20:11), or had "passed away." As brought out in such passages as 2 Peter 3:10–12, the inference is that a new heaven and a new earth are entirely new creations and are not similar to the old creation.

Though scholars have differed on this point, and some have attempted to support a restored earth and heaven, Scriptures are strong in their statement of the destruction of the old heaven and old earth. They are described as being "destroyed by fire," and "the elements will melt in the heat" (2 Peter 3:10, 12). In view of the tremendous energy locked into every material atom,

413

the same God who locked in this energy can unlock it and destroy it, reducing it to nothing. The atomic structure of matter is possibly referred to in Colossians 1:17, where in connection with Christ it is declared, "He is before all things, and in him all things hold together." Since the power of God that locked in atomic power can also unlock it, it is possible that the destruction of the physical earth and heaven will be a gigantic atomic explosion in which all goes back to nothing. Out of this God could create a new heaven and a new earth as a base for eternity. In any case, the new earth will be totally different from the old earth, and one of these differences is that there will no longer be any seas. All the old landmarks will be gone, and the new earth will look different.

The New Jerusalem Coming Down From Heaven

John in his vision was immediately directed to the New Jerusalem, which is the primary object of the revelation rather than the new heaven and new earth. He wrote, "I saw the Holy City, the new Jerusalem, coming down out of heaven from God, prepared as a bride beautifully dressed for her husband" (Rev. 21:2). The fact that the New Jerusalem is not said to be created at this time but, rather, comes down out of heaven from God implies that it was in existence in the previous period—that is, in the millennial kingdom. As millennial passages make clear, there will be no gigantic city such as the New Jerusalem on earth in the millennial period. If it is in existence at that time, it must be a satellite located in space.

Though the Bible does not comment on this, it is possible that the New Jerusalem will be a satellite city in relation to the millennial earth and that those with resurrected bodies, as well as the holy angels, will occupy the New Jerusalem during the thousand-year reign. They will be able to commute to the earth, much as people go from the country to their city offices and participate in earthly functions without necessarily living in the city. In the descriptions of the millennial kingdom, the saints are described as those who are still in their physical bodies, building houses and planting crops (Isa. 65:21–23), but no picture is ever drawn of the resurrected saints as living beside them. Accordingly, while this provides a possible solution, it should be borne in mind that there is very little direct Scripture to back this up, and it therefore cannot be a dogmatically held doctrine.

More important to John's revelation is the fact that the New Jerusalem is in contrast to the old Jerusalem which, of course, will have been destroyed with the old earth. The New Jerusalem will come down as a city already built. John compared it to a beautiful bride adorned for her husband. The simile of a city as a bride has confused some expositors, but the explanation of verse 2 is probably the best, that it is a literal city, beautiful as a bride.

The New Jerusalem is mentioned in various ways throughout Scripture. It was the eternal city Abraham saw (Heb. 11:8–10). The residents of the city are described in Hebrews 12:22–25:

> But you have come to Mount Zion, to the heavenly Jerusalem, the city of the living God. You have come to thousands upon thousands of angels in joyful assembly, to the church of the firstborn, whose names are written in heaven. You have come to God, the judge of all men, to the spirits of righteous men made perfect, to Jesus the mediator of a new covenant, and to the sprinkled blood that speaks a better word than the blood of Abel.

A study of this passage will reveal that the New Jerusalem, while it is designated as the city for the bride—that is, the church—nevertheless includes in its boundaries the saints of all ages and the holy angels. Accordingly, the church is mentioned specifically, God and Jesus Christ are mentioned specifically, and then the broad category of "the spirits of righteous men made perfect" is mentioned (Heb. 12:23). This final category refers to all who are saved. Everyone from Adam to the last person saved in the millennial kingdom will be an inhabitant of the New Jerusalem. God himself, Jesus Christ, and we assume the Holy Spirit, will also be present in the city, for it is referred to as the temple of God.

The New Jerusalem is mentioned in some millennial passages (e.g., Isa. 65:17; 66:22; 2 Peter 3:13; Rev. 3:12). In some contexts, such as Isaiah 65, the New Jerusalem mentioned in a millennial context has confused expositors. However, in the Old Testament, we frequently find the Millennium and the eternal state considered in the same passage, much as the first and second comings of Christ are considered in passages like Isaiah 61:1–2 (quoted in Luke 4:17–19). The destiny of the righteous and the wicked are often merged, as in Daniel 12:2, though we know from Scripture that there will be a thousand years between. Sometimes the first coming of Christ is mentioned following a reference to the Second Coming, as in Malachi 4:5. In 2 Peter 3:10–13, which refers to the beginning of the Day of the Lord, it goes right on to what happens at its end without reference to the long period of time between. Accordingly, a mention of the New Jerusalem in a millennial passage is no justification for finding the New Jerusalem on earth in the millennial period, nor is it a justification for merging the Millennium with the eternal state, as some amillenarians do. There are many differences between the millennial kingdom and the new earth and new heaven. In the new earth there is no earthly city of Jerusalem and there are no other earthly landmarks that connect with historic sites of the Bible. There is no ocean. In the New Jerusalem there is no death, no sin, and no judgment. All of this stands in contrast to life in the millennial kingdom. Attempts of some scholars to merge the new earth with the Millennium as a way of explaining away a literal Millennium after the death of Christ is not justified by the details of prophetic revelation. Those who hold this position avoid the passages that contradict their conclusions.

Major Features of the New Jerusalem

John recorded not only what he saw but also what he heard: "And I heard a loud voice from the throne saying, 'Now the dwelling of God is with men, and he will live with them. They will be his people, and God himself will be with them and be their God. He will wipe every tear from their eyes. There will be no more death or mourning or crying or pain, for the old order of things has passed away'" (Rev. 21:3–4). One of the great characteristics of the new earth and the New Jerusalem will be that God will dwell with people. In this blessed fellowship, sorrow, death, crying, and pain will be abolished.

Some have attempted to gather from the expression "He will wipe every tear from their eyes" (Rev. 21:4) evidence that Christians will weep for their sins in heaven. The problem with this is that, if Christians are going to weep for their sins, heaven will be filled with tears. What the passage means is that there will be no more tears, just as there will be no death and no crying or pain, "for the old order of things [will have] passed away" (v. 4). The new situation is summarized in verse 5: "He who was seated on the throne said, 'I am making everything new!' Then he said, 'Write this down, for these words are trustworthy and true.'"

In referring to all things being made new, John used the Greek word *poeo*, which has the common meaning of "making or constructing something." As used here, it is a synonym for the word "create" (Gk. *ktizo*). Scripture uses these terms somewhat interchangeably. In Matthew 19:4, for instance, where Christ was speaking of the creation of Adam and Eve, *poeo* and *ktizo* are used in the same passage, referring to the same act. Though the earth and the heavens may be constructed at this time and therefore made new, the saints and angels existed before and were not created at this time. The newness is from the Greek word *kainos*, which can mean "both new in character" and "new in the sense of recency." An illustration of this is Eve being a new creature even though formed from the rib of Adam. Also in the context, though the earth and heavens seem to be altogether new, the New Jerusalem seems to have had a prior existence to this event but forms an important aspect of the new situation (see pp. 415–16).

The Water of Life

The one sitting on the throne said: "It is done. I am the Alpha and the Omega, the Beginning and the End. To him who is thirsty I will give to drink without cost from the spring of the water of life. He who overcomes will inherit all this, and I will be his God and he will be my son" (Rev. 21:6–7). Christ, the speaker here, is able to assure those who come to him that they will receive the Water of Life. This has reference to new life in Christ as mentioned in Isaiah 55:1 and John 4:10, 13–14. The new life in Christ, including all that is involved in our salvation, is a part of our marvelous inheritance as children of God and joint heirs with Jesus Christ (cf. Matt. 5:5; 19:29; 25:34; 1 Cor. 6:9–10; Heb. 1:14; 9:15; 1 Peter 1:4; 3:9).

The Contrast of the Unsaved

Christ continued, however: "But the cowardly, the unbelieving, the vile, the murderers, the sexually immoral, those who practice magic arts, the idolaters and all liars—their place will

be in the fiery lake of burning sulfur. This is the second death"
(Rev. 21:8). What is described here is the characteristic wicked
life of the unbeliever. Those who practiced these things before
coming to Christ in repentance are forgiven and are numbered
among the saints.

Children of God are pictured as overcomers, and their
blessings can be found in Jesus' messages to the seven churches
(Rev. 2–3). Jesus summarizes the reward for overcomers in
Revelation 3:21: "To him who overcomes, I will give the right to
sit with me on my throne, just as I overcame and sat down with
my Father on his throne." Christians, even though their lives
may have imperfections, will receive the eternal blessings of
God. Paul said in 1 Corinthians 3:21–23: "So then, no more
boasting about men! All things are yours, whether Paul or
Apollos or Cephas or the world or life or death or the present or
the future—all are yours, and you are of Christ, and Christ is of
God."

The distinction and destiny of those who are saved and those
who are unsaved are often obscured in this life. In eternity all
these things will come into perspective. Those who have served
the Lord will be rewarded, and those who have failed to trust in
Christ as Savior will bear eternal judgment.

The New Jerusalem As the Bride

In the revelation that follows John was given a particular
description of the New Jerusalem. Expositors have differed as to
whether this passage describes Jerusalem in its eternal situation
or in its millennial situation. Though worthy scholars can be
named on either side of this issue, it is probably better to
consider the whole passage, from Revelation 19:11 through
Revelation 22, as a description of chronological events. Accordingly, while Revelation 21:1–8 describes the eternal situation,
beginning in verse 9 the passage reveals particulars of the
eternal state. It is impossible to describe this scene in its details
as being part of the millennial situation, except as has previously
been suggested as a satellite city. But even then the emphasis
seems to be on the eternal character of the New Jerusalem.

The New Jerusalem was introduced to John by one of the
seven angels who had the bowls of the seven last plagues. John
wrote:

One of the seven angels who had the seven bowls full of the seven last plagues came and said to me, "Come, I will show you the bride, the wife of the Lamb." And he carried me away in the Spirit to a mountain great and high, and showed me the Holy City, Jerusalem, coming down out of heaven from God. It shone with the glory of God, and its brilliance was like that of a very precious jewel, like a jasper, clear as crystal" (Rev 21:9–11).

John was obviously recording what he saw and heard in a literal way. Expositors have differed, however, as to what extent the things he saw were literal—that is, did he see a material city or a vision with typical or nonliteral meaning. Probably the simplest and most consistent approach is to understand the city as a literal city with the literal qualities that are described here, at the same time recognizing that these qualities have spiritual significance and connote something of the abundance of spiritual life that will characterize the millennial kingdom.

The revelation presents Jerusalem as "the bride, the wife of the Lamb" (Rev. 21:9). Obviously, a city is not a bride and a bride is not a city, and it is probably best to interpret this, as in Revelation 21:2, as a city that is like a beautiful bride. In his vision John saw the holy city Jerusalem coming down from God out of heaven, as previously mentioned in verse 2. He described it as being aglow with the glory of God: "like that of a very precious jewel, like a jasper, clear as crystal" (v. 11). The jasper, as we know it, is an opaque jewel, not a clear jewel. Accordingly, the question has been to what extent does the city correspond to the jasper? From its characteristics, it would seem to be more like a diamond than the jasper as we know it today. In connection with other materials of the New Jerusalem, there is a constant contrast between the materials as we know them now and as they will appear in the eternal state. The glory of the New Jerusalem must have been breathtaking as John contemplated it and realized that this was going to be his home throughout eternity.

The Wall and Gates of the New Jerusalem

John described the tremendous dimensions of the New Jerusalem in these words: "It had a great, high wall with twelve gates, and with twelve angels at the gates. On the gates were written the names of the twelve tribes of Israel. There were three gates on the east, three on the north, three on the south and three on the west [possibly named in the order of gates in the millennial Jerusalem (Ezek. 48:30–34)]. The wall of the city had twelve foundations, and on them were the names of the twelve apostles of the Lamb" (Rev. 21:12–14). From this passage, it is clear that the city is square. The directions of north, south, east, and west imply that the earth, as it is today, is round. Gates in the city imply that there is entrance into the city from without.

The wall of the city is described as having twelve foundations containing the names of the twelve apostles (Rev. 21:14). Symbolically the wall indicates exclusion of those who are not worthy to enter the city, and the gates indicate that those who enter can enter by the gates. Obviously the saints of all ages have to dwell somewhere in eternity, and it makes a great deal of sense to see them in a gigantic city that has some of the characteristics of cities in time. The number "twelve" is prominent in the New Jerusalem. It has twelve gates and twelve angels in keeping with the twelve tribes of Israel (v. 12), twelve foundations (v. 14), twelve apostles (v. 14), twelve pearls (v. 21), and twelve crops of fruit (22:2).

The Size of the New Jerusalem

Impressive as the city itself is, with its high wall and other features, the angel then indicated the size of the city: "The angel who talked with me had a measuring rod of gold to measure the city, its gates and its walls. The city was laid out like a square, as long as it was wide. He measured the city with the rod and found it to be 12,000 stadia in length, and as wide and high as it is long. He measured its wall and it was 144 cubits thick, by man's measurement, which the angel was using" (Rev. 21:15–17). The 12,000 furlongs, or stadia, represent about 1,500 miles. The city is gigantic in comparison with any modern city of our present world, and its area is quite adequate to contain the activities of the saints of all ages, especially if its height provides stories or levels. The wall is 144 cubits thick, which indicates a barrier to keep people out who are not worthy. Such a tremendous city, presumably resting on the earth because of its twelve foundations, would occupy a large portion of the new earth, far greater than the area of the Holy Land in history. The fact that the city has gates, implying that people will enter and leave, also connotes that the city is resting on the earth, not in space, at this time.

The Beautiful Structure of the City

John went to great lengths to describe the precise beauty and characteristics of the city.

> The wall was made of jasper, and the city of pure gold, as pure as glass. The foundations of the city walls were decorated with every kind of precious stone. The first foundation was jasper, the second sapphire, the third chalcedony, the fourth emerald, the fifth sardonyx, the sixth carnelian, the seventh chrysolite, the eighth beryl, the ninth topaz, the tenth chrysoprase, the eleventh jacinth, and the twelfth amethyst. The twelve gates were twelve pearls, each gate made of a single pearl. The great street of the city was of pure gold, like transparent glass. (Rev. 21:18–21)

The wall, like the city, was declared to be of jasper, earlier described as "clear as crystal" (v. 11). Apparently this is the overall view of the city.

The city is also described as "of pure gold, as pure as glass" (Rev. 21:18). Here again we have the combination of gold as known in our present world but likened to transparent glass. From a study of the various materials used, it seems that all the materials in the New Jerusalem are translucent and, as such, have no dark shadows. The light of God will penetrate every corner. The twelve foundations are described as being composed of various precious stones, each of which is a study in itself.

The first foundation is of jasper, previously mentioned. The various layers of the foundation are built upon this. The second layer is a sapphire, a jewel that is blue in color and similar to a diamond. The third layer is described as chalcedony, named after Chalcedon in Turkey, and is an agate stone. This is an unusual stone with stripes of various colors but thought to be basically sky blue. The fourth foundation, an emerald, offers a bright green color. The fifth, the sardonyx, is a stone combining red and white colors. The sixth stone is called a carnelian, a stone found either in a reddish tint or a honey color and not considered too valuable. This stone, however, is used with jasper in Revelation 4:3, where it describes the glory of God seated on his heavenly throne. The seventh stone, the chrysolite, according to the ancient writer Pliny, is gold in color and transparent and is therefore somewhat different from the modern pale green chrysolite stone. The eighth foundation, the beryl, is a deep sea green. The ninth foundation, the topaz, is a transparent yellow-green stone. The tenth foundation, chrysoprase, adds another shade of green. The eleventh foundation is violet, and the twelfth, amethyst, is purple.

Though in some cases one cannot be sure concerning the exact color of the stone described, the general picture provided is one of brilliant color with every shade of the rainbow represented and all of it enhanced by the glory of God. The light of the city shining through the translucent foundation must have presented a most impressive picture to John. If people in our present world can create beautiful things, how much more can the infinite God create a beautiful city? This city is an illustration of his infinite perfection as well as his loving grace extended to every child of God.

Earlier the twelve gates, with three on each side, were mentioned. Here we learn that they are made of a single pearl, obviously not a natural pearl but something that looks like a natural pearl. The streets of the city are described as being of pure gold but clear as glass.

The New Jerusalem in the eternal state is square with twelve gates like the millennial Jerusalem but is much greater in size and not the same city at all. That is why it is called the New Jerusalem.

The Temple in the City

John was informed about the temple in the city. "I did not see a temple in the city, because the Lord God Almighty and the Lamb are its temple" (Rev. 21:22). The New Jerusalem is not only characterized by the things that are different from all other places but also by what it does not have. It has no tabernacle or literal physical temple; no sacrificial rituals; no heavenly bodies such as sun, moon, or stars; no darkness; no closed gates; and nothing that brings abomination. All of this, which is in sharp contrast to the millennial situation, makes impossible the fulfillment of the millennial promises in the New Jerusalem. It is significant that the light of the city is God, implying that God is light (John 1:7–9; 3:19; 8:12; 12:35). Inasmuch as believers will be walking in the light of God in eternity, they are exhorted to walk in the light of God's divine revelation in time (1 John 1:5–7).

The Inhabitants of the City

John was given information concerning the general inhabitants of the New Jerusalem. "The nations will walk by its light, and the kings of the earth will bring their splendor into it" (Rev. 21:24). Reference to the nations is in contrast to the reference to Israel and makes clear that the New Jerusalem is not simply the home of Israel or of the church but of the saints of all ages, regardless of race and dispensation (Heb. 12:22–24). Entrance into the city will be provided for those who are saved, because the gates will not be shut (Rev. 21:25). The glory of God shining in the city will make night impossible. Apparently there will be no need for sleep or rest in the New Jerusalem.

On one hand, John was informed, "The glory and honor of the nations will be brought into it" (Rev. 21:26). On the other hand, "Nothing impure will ever enter it, nor will anyone who does what is shameful or deceitful, but only those whose names are written in the Lamb's book of life" (v. 27). Taking John's description as a whole, the city is one of indescribable beauty suitable for the worship and service of God throughout eternity.

The River of the Water of Life

Earlier mention was made of the spring of the water of life (Rev. 21:6). In the New Jerusalem this is embodied in the river of the water of life. John wrote, "Then the angel showed me the river of the water of life, as clear as crystal, flowing from the throne of God and of the Lamb down the middle of the great street of the city" (22:1–2). This corresponds to but is not the same as the river from the millennial sanctuary (Ezek. 47:1, 12) nor that goes east and west out of Jerusalem in Zechariah 14:8. These millennial streams may anticipate but are not the same as the river mentioned here. The presence of this river indicates the abundance of spiritual life that comes from God to those who have put their trust in him.

The Tree of Life

John described the Tree of Life. "On each side of the river stood the tree of life, bearing twelve crops of fruit, yielding its fruit every month" (Rev. 22:2). The description of a street with water running down the center and the Tree of Life on either side of the river is difficult for some expositors to visualize. Some have opted for the idea that the term "tree of life" is a collective term describing the kind of tree, and that there actually will be rows of trees on either side of the river bearing the fruit indicated. This would not be an impossible solution. It is also possible that the Tree of Life is so large that its branches reach over the entire street, and therefore it bears fruit on both sides of the river.

Reference to the Tree of Life goes back, of course, to the Garden of Eden, where there was a similar tree (Gen. 3:22, 24). In Adam's time, if he had eaten of the Tree of Life, he never would have died. Because sin entered the human race, it was far better for humans to live and die and then receive sinless resurrection bodies than it would be for them to continue forever in their sinful bodies. Here in the eternal state, however, the Tree of Life seems to have reference to the continuance of the enjoyment of life throughout eternity. The Tree of Life is said to bear twelve crops of fruit, or one per month, for the benefit of the inhabitants of the city. The reference to "month" indicates corresponding time, which presents a problem when there is no night, no sun, and no moon. Most likely the term "month" should be interpreted as a period of time similar to a month in our present existence.

The passage goes on to say, "And the leaves of the tree are for the healing of the nations" (Rev. 22:2). This has provoked a good deal of scholarly discussion. If in the eternal state there will be no sickness or death, why will there be a need for healing? This reference is one of the reasons why some want to carry this scene back to the Millennium even though it presents many insuperable problems for explaining how the New Jerusalem relates to the earthly scene. The solution to the problem seems to lie in the word *healing*. The word in the Greek is *therapeian*, from which our English word "therapeutic" is derived. It can be understood not simply as for healing but also as health-giving. Though healing is not necessary, the leaves will promote enjoyment of life, just as fruit does in our day. This reference is an insufficient basis for trying to take the whole passage, from Revelation 21:9 on, as a reference to the millennial kingdom. The next statement is perhaps a comment on this, for John recorded, "No longer will there be any curse" (v. 3). Inasmuch as Adam's sin brought a curse upon the human race, including death and sickness, the fact that there is no more curse indicates that there is no more need of healing but only of enjoyment of life in eternity, for which the fruit of the tree is designed.

The Throne of God

Revelation 22:3 goes on to say, "The throne of God and of the Lamb will be in the city, and his servants will serve him." The question is often raised as to what will be the occupation of the saints in eternity. Obviously they would not want to endlessly play a harp or to engage in useless activities. This passage, though not explicit, is beautifully simple: "His servants will serve him." In eternity the overwhelming desire of all children of God will be to show him in some way that they love him and want to serve him. The privilege of service will be paramount and, in fact, may be a reward from God—that is, places of privileged service may be assigned in accordance with one's faithfulness in life. In any case, we will have the joy of doing something for God, however inadequate, to express our eternal thanksgiving for his grace to us.

The Blessedness of the Eternal State

John continued to summarize the glory and blessing of the scene. "They will see his face, and his name will be on their foreheads. There will be no more night. They will not need the light of a lamp or the light of the sun, for the Lord God will give them light. And they will reign for ever and ever" (Rev. 22:4–5). One of the great blessings of eternity will be that we will be able to see God face to face and be identified with him through his name on our foreheads. It will be a time of unparalleled blessing with no night, no need of lamp or of sun or moon. Believers in Christ will be able to reign with him forever and ever.

Assurance of the Certainty of Our Hope

The angel said to John, "These words are trustworthy and true. The Lord, the God of the spirits of the prophets, sent his angel to show his servants the things that must soon take place" (Rev. 22:6). Then Jesus said, "Behold, I am coming soon! Blessed is he who keeps the words of the prophecy in this book" (v. 7). Though the wonder of heaven and the eternal state is difficult to contemplate in our present limitations, it is, nevertheless, absolutely certain that this is our destiny and this is what we have a right to expect as those who are saved by the grace of God. Furthermore, it is not something that is distantly removed. Christ is coming soon, and when he comes, blessing will fall on those who have believed and received the prophecies of this book. The statement that the Lord's coming is *soon* does not necessarily mean following a brief period of time, but that his coming is imminent and will occur suddenly.

John's Response of Worship

Following these tremendous events, John recorded that he fell at the feet of the angel to worship him but that the angel urged him not to do so: "I, John, am the one who heard and saw these things. And when I had heard and seen them, I fell down to worship at the feet of the angel who had been showing them to me. But he said to me, 'Do not do it! I am a fellow servant with you and with your brothers the prophets and of all who keep the words of this book. Worship God!'" (Rev. 22:8–9). The angel, after all, was only God's messenger and was not worthy of worship.

John Commanded to Declare the Prophecy

John was further instructed, "'Do not seal up the words of the prophecy of this book, because the time is near. Let him who does wrong continue to do wrong; let him who is vile continue to be vile; let him who does right continue to do right; and let him who is holy continue to be holy'" (Rev. 22:10–11). The implication of this passage is that the time is too short to change the course of the world's morality and that, although life will go on for both the wicked and the righteous, the Lord is coming soon. The word of prophecy should not be concealed but preached openly.

Blessing Upon Those Who Trust in God

Beginning in verse 12, Christ again is the speaker. He says:

> Behold, I am coming soon! My reward is with me, and I will give to everyone according to what he has done. I am the Alpha and the Omega, the First and the Last, the Beginning and the End.
>
> Blessed are those who wash their robes, that they may have the right to the tree of life and may go through the gates into the city. Outside are the dogs, those who practice magic arts, the sexually immoral, the murderers, the idolaters and everyone who loves and practices falsehood.
>
> I, Jesus, have sent my angel to give you this testimony for the churches. I am the Root and the Offspring of David, and the bright Morning Star. (Rev. 22:12–16).

John was urged to respond because Christ's coming could occur quickly. Jesus is introduced as the eternal one, "the First and the Last" (Rev. 22:13). Those who avail themselves of God's cleansing power through the blood of Christ will be given the right to the Tree of Life and all that that involves. They will also be able to go into the gate of the city (v. 14). Once again a reminder is given that some will be excluded, especially those who practice evil. Christ concluded with the statement that his angel had been sent to give the testimony to the seven churches who were the primary recipients of this book. Christ described himself as "the Root and the Offspring of David, and the bright Morning Star'" (v. 16).

The Final Invitation

In concluding the book of Revelation with its clear picture of the destiny of the saved and the lost, the author gives a final invitation to partake of the water of life: "The Spirit and the bride say, 'Come!' And let him who hears say, 'Come!' Whoever is thirsty, let him come; and whoever wishes, let him take the free gift of the water of life" (Rev. 22:17).

Warning is extended to those who would tamper with the book either by adding or subtracting. To do so would be to tamper with their own destiny. John wrote, "I warn everyone who hears the words of the prophecy of this book: If anyone adds anything to them, God will add to him the plagues described in this book. And if anyone takes words away from this book of prophecy, God will take away from him his share in the tree of life and in the holy city, which are described in this book" (vv. 18–19).

Frequently in the Bible warnings are issued regarding improper use of the Word of God, tampering with it, or changing it (Deut. 4:2; 12:32; Prov. 30:6; Rev. 1:3). The passage assumes that an unbeliever will tamper with the Word of God, but a believer will not. Therefore, the statement "God will take away from him his share in the tree of life and in the holy city, which are described in this book" (Rev. 22:19), does not refer to the child of God but rather to those who could have had their names in the Book of Life if they had trusted in Christ as their Savior.

Concluding Promises

In the conclusion of the book, John recorded, "He who testifies to these things says, 'Yes, I am coming soon.' Amen. Come, Lord Jesus. The grace of the Lord Jesus be with God's people. Amen" (Rev. 22:20–21). Here again is the promise of the coming of the Lord. It is followed by a final brief prayer— "Come, Lord Jesus"—and a final pronouncement of the grace of God upon God's people.

The book of Revelation, as no other book in the Bible, provides a comprehensive picture of the glory of Christ, God's plan for his exaltation and victory over sin, and with it the revelation of the glorious future for the children of God. The closing words of Revelation provide a fitting climax for the Bible. No other portion of Scripture pictures a greater contrast between the lost and the saved and between the blessing of being saved and the awfulness of being lost. Furthermore, the book describes God's ultimate purpose of revealing Jesus Christ, which is its central theme, and characterizes his second coming and his subsequent reign on earth as well as his position in the new heaven and the new earth. In keeping with the promise found early in the book, those who read and take heed of this book will have special blessing (Rev. 1:3).

Subject Index

Abomination that causes desolation, 167, 173–74, 258–60, 317–20, 343, 349–50

Abraham, 10–12; to be a blessing, 42; promises of blessing, 42; delayed birth of an heir, 46–49; name to be great, 42; prophecies to, 10–11. *See also* Abrahamic Covenant. *See also* Land

Abrahamic Covenant, 39–48, 61–63; blessing on all people, 43–44; confirmed to Isaac, 51; confirmed to Jacob, 51–52; fulfillment of, 44–45; provisions of, 40–42; as unconditional, 64–67. *See also* Land

Adam, revelation to, 9, 11; as created, 18; warned, 18–19; sin of, 22–23; cursed, 29–30

Alexander the Great, 149, 151–52; death of, 151

Alexandrian School of Theology, relates to amillennialism, 114

Amillennialism, history of, 114–15; contemporary views, 115–116; difficulty in explaining many passages on kingdom on earth, 389–90; interpretation of 490 years of Israel, 166, 168, 172–73; interpretation of Israel as the church, 67–68; interpretation of Nebuchadnezzar's dream, 132; interpretation of the New Covenant, 184–90; interpretation of Olivet Discourse, 253; kingdom fulfilled in present age, 208; not supported by parable of Matthew 13, 217–18; not supported by parable of the sower, 210; not supported by parable of the weeds, 211–12; objection to future for Israel, 60–61; tends to deny literal interpretation, 60

Antichrist, as the beast, 324–26; rise of, 315–16; as world ruler, 341–42. *See also* man of sin

Antiochus Epiphanes, 153–54, 158–60, 320

Apostles, to judge Israel, 229–30; to be rewarded in heaven, 230; to be servants in the present age, 230–31

Ark, 33–34

Armageddon, 354–59; battle of in final months of Great Tribulation, 354; definition of, 355–56; final world war, 355–56

Assyria, captivity of, 312; empire of, 43

Assyrian Empire, 43

Augustine, on amillennialism, 114–16

Babel, tower of, 37–38

Babylon, 13; ancient history of, 134–36; city of, to be rebuilt in end times, 326; duration of Israel's captivity, 139; ecclesiastical, 322–27; final destruction, 357–59; history of, 321–22; to be overthrown, 143–44; in Old Testament prophecy, 134–42; political, to be destroyed, 357–59; prophecy in Daniel, 140–42; prophecies in Ezekiel, 140; the prophecies of Isaiah, 136–38; the prophecies of Jeremiah, 138–40; as the woman of Revelation 17, 322–24

Babylonian Captivity, 312

Beast, out of the earth, 343; out of the sea, 342; with ten horns and seven heads, 324–26, 342–44

Beth Togarmah, related to future war, 330

Bethsaida, judgment upon, 206

Blessing and cursing motif, 31–32; ends in Genesis 11, 38

Scripture Index